Transport Matters

Addressing the principles of sustainability, spatial planning, integration, governance and accessibility of transport, this book focuses on the key social problems of the twenty-first century: efficient and low energy transport systems which serve the needs of everybody.

The book:

- explores many of the new arguments, ideas and perceptions of mobility and accessibility in city-regions;
- looks at the meaning of the key concepts of sustainable accessibility, the spatial planning model and integrated territorial policies;
- examines the relevance and contribution of these concepts to sustainable transport outcomes in different contexts;
- analyses in more detail the cross-sectoral implementation and governance tools available to cities to secure the European Commission Transport Minister's recent definition of sustainable transport;
- draws together arguments and evidence from Denmark, Sweden, the Netherlands, Germany and the UK in important case studies.

Charting the path towards transport resource efficiency, connectivity and social interaction, this is a book that students, policy makers, practitioners and academics will all find of value.

Angela Hull is Professor of Spatial Planning at Heriot-Watt University and a former local authority town planner.

THE RTPI Library Series

Editors: Robert Upton, *Infrastructure Planning Commission in England*
          and Patsy Healey, *University of Newcastle, UK*

Published by Routledge in conjunction with The Royal Town Planning Institute, this series of leading-edge texts looks at all aspects of spatial planning theory and practice from a comparative and international perspective.

Planning in Postmodern Times
Philip Allmendinger

The Making of the European Spatial Development Perspective
Andreas Faludi and Bas Waterhout

Planning for Crime Prevention
Richard Schneider and Ted Kitchen

The Planning Polity
Mark Tewdwr-Jones

Shadows of Power
An Allegory of Prudence in Land-Use Planning
Jean Hillier

Urban Planning and Cultural Identity
William J.V. Neill

Place Identity, Participation and Planning
Edited by Cliff Hague and Paul Jenkins

Planning for Diversity
Dory Reeves

Planning the Good Community
New Urbanism in Theory and Practice
Jill Grant

Planning, Law and Economics
Barrie Needham

Indicators for Urban and Regional Planning
Cecilia Wong

Planning at the Landscape Scale
Paul Selman

Urban Structure Matters
Petter Naess

Urban Complexity and Spatial Strategies
Towards a Relational Planning for Our Times
Patsy Healey

The Visual Language of Spatial Planning
Exploring Cartographic Representations for Spatial Planning in Europe
Stefanie Dühr

Planning and Transformation
Learning from the Post-Apartheid Experience
Philip Harrison, Alison Todes and Vanessa Watson

Conceptions of Space and Place in Strategic Spatial Planning
Edited by Simin Davoudi and Ian Strange

Regional Planning for Open Space
Edited by Terry van Dijk and Arnold van der Valk

Crossing Borders
International Exchange and Planning Practices
Edited by Patsy Healey and Robert Upton

Effective Practice in Spatial Planning
Janice Morphet

Transport Matters
Angela Hull

TRANSPORT MATTERS

INTEGRATED APPROACHES TO PLANNING CITY-REGIONS

ANGELA HULL

LONDON AND NEW YORK

First published 2011
by Routledge
2 Park Square, Milton Park, Abingdon, Oxon, OX14 4RN

Simultaneously published in the USA and Canada
by Routledge
270 Madison Avenue, New York, NY 10016

Routledge is an imprint of the Taylor & Francis Group, an informa business

© 2011 Angela Hull

Typeset in Akzidenz Grotesk by
GreenGate Publishing Services, Tonbridge, Kent

Printed and bound in Great Britain by
CPI Antony Rowe, Chippenham, Wiltshire

British Library Cataloguing in Publication Data
A catalogue record for this book is available from the British Library

Library of Congress Cataloging-in-Publication Data
Hull, Angela.
Transport matters : integrated approaches to planning city-regions / Angela Hull.
p. cm. -- (The RTPI library series)
Includes bibliographical references and index.
1. Transportation and state--Europe. 2. Sustainable development--Europe. 3. Regional planning--Europe. I. Title.
HE242.A2H85 2010
711'.7094--dc22   2010005287

ISBN: 978-0-415-45422-3 (hbk)
ISBN: 978-0-415-45818-4 (pbk)
ISBN: 978-0-203-93878-2 (ebk)

CONTENTS

Figures and Tables   vi
Preface   viii
Acknowledgements   xii
Abbreviations   xiii

1   Time for change? The rationale for low energy transport provision   1

2   Understanding current patterns of transport behaviour in Europe   18

3   The challenge of putting the environment into transport policy   48

4   Institutional structures for low energy futures: creating integrated
     approaches   79

5   Understanding the institutional barriers to change   108

6   Intervention instruments for sustainable transport futures   136

7   Integrated territorial planning in practice: case studies   176

8   Implementing a sustainable transport package   232

Notes   250
References   251
Index   288

FIGURES AND TABLES

FIGURES

1.1 Cutting emissions in transport   8
2.1 How technology has shrunk the globe   24
2.2 Definitions of sustainable transport   35
3.1 Access to learning opportunities in the county of Devon, England   55
3.2 The comparative accessibility to healthcare facilities by public transport
    for the population at risk to ill health in Merseyside, England   68
4.1 The relationship between settlement size and travel patterns   84
5.1 Inhibitors of organisational coordination   112
6.1 Recent EU legislation on transport   140
7.1 Copenhagen Finger Plan of 1947   181
7.2 Map of the Øresund region   184
7.3 The City Tunnel in Malmö   192
7.4 Survey of mobile users for journey planning   194
7.5 Trends in bus passengers in Malmö 2002–2008   198
7.6 Amsterdam in the national context   205
7.7 New development opportunities and rail infrastructure schemes
    in London   220
7.8 Area covered by the London Congestion Charging Scheme
    in relation to the Greater London area   221

TABLES

1.1 Growth in greenhouse gas emissions from transport in Europe   7
2.1 The concepts of mobility and accessibility compared   20
2.2 Freight transported by transport mode: EU-25, 1995–2005   21
2.3 Passenger transport by transport mode: EU-25, 1995–2004   22
2.4 Typical net residential densities   28
2.5 The impacts of transport policy in Scotland   29
2.6 Benchmarks for a sustainable transport system   37
2.7 Understanding the relationship between urban structure and travel
    behaviour   41
2.8 Social drivers of change   47

3.1 Objectives and solutions for sustainable urban mobility   51
3.2 Measures of accessibility used in local transport planning   54
3.3 Accessibility, mobility and exergy compared   58
3.4 Road traffic impacts on children: the evidence base   64
4.1 Higher order objectives for a sustainable urban transport policy 86
4.2 Structuring rules which underpin transport planning   90
4.3 Effective partnerships for a low energy transport system   101
5.1 Financial barriers in the implementation of sustainable transport policy 109
5.2 Organisational barriers in the implementation of sustainable
     transport policy   112
5.3 The unintended effects of failure to integrate land use and
     transport planning   115
5.4 Cultural barriers in the implementation of sustainable transport policy 116
5.5 Legislative barriers in the implementation of sustainable transport policy 119
5.6 Political barriers in the implementation of sustainable transport policy 120
5.7 Technical barriers in the implementation of sustainable transport policy 123
5.8 How to overcome the barriers to sustainable travel   124
6.1 Public policy instruments to effect change in transport and land use 138
6.2 EU new standards for pollution in grams/km from petrol cars   142
6.3 Overcoming the main implementation issues with respect to the
     promotion of cycling: an example from York, UK   147
6.4 Overcoming the main implementation issues with respect to
     road user charging: an example from central London   154
6.5 Indicators of transport resource efficiency   164
6.6 Sustainability threshold assessment   168
6.7 Policies to reduce carbon from 1) surface passenger transport
     and 2) freight transport   173
7.1 Modal split for land motorised passenger transport in 2004   177
7.2 Growth in greenhouse gas emissions from transport 1990–2006   178
7.3 New 'green' transport initiatives implemented in Malmö   193
7.4 Comparison of case study countries on selected transport indicators 230
8.1 Examples of mobility planning and accessibility planning instruments 237
8.2 Key instruments of a sustainable transport programme   244

PREFACE

This book is concerned with the profligate use of natural resources to serve transport needs in the more 'developed' nations. Since the mid-1950s, transport infrastructure has been expanded to cater for the needs of motorised traffic so that the time to reach distant markets has shrunk and the necessity to walk even short distances reduced. Speed rather than energy efficiency has been the driving force. This concern is underpinned by a normative presumption that the growing emissions of carbon dioxide from transport will hasten the climate change scenarios predicted by the United Nations Intergovernmental Panel on Climate Change (IPCC) models. Since 1995, IPCC reports show growing certainty of the human influence on the climate of the planet, with the Fourth Assessment Report in 2007 (United Nations Intergovernmental Panel on Climate Change 2007a) stating that over 50 per cent of the observed increase in globally averaged temperatures over the last 50 years is attributable to the observed increase in anthropogenic greenhouse gas emissions.

The aspiration of this book is to overturn the instantaneous, egocentric approach to resource consumption and to move to a lifestyle based on more efficient use of globally scarce energy, human, environmental and financial resources. This vision of sustainability was espoused in the Brundtland Report back in 1987 (UN World Commission on Environment and Development 1987) and, despite repeated international agreements (viz. UN Framework Convention on Climate Change 1992; Kyoto Protocol, ratified in 2005) on carbon emissions' restraint, with few exceptions, the basket of greenhouse gas emissions from transport, where measured, is increasing.

Environmental scientists warn that our demands on the planet will soon exceed the system capacity limits and energy experts predict that supplies of conventional oil are insufficient to cope with future demand. With the increasing urbanisation and population growth of the so called 'developing' nations, the 'business as usual' scenario will surely entail more global competition and discord over access to scarce resources such as energy, water and food. Combined, these should be sufficient reasons to reappraise long-term societal aims and aspirations and the sustainability of current practices.

This book is aimed at the graduate and higher undergraduate student, particularly those who have some grounding in or prior knowledge of spatial planning, politics and governance. The approach to answering the question of how nations can shift from high carbon to low carbon and resource efficient outcomes draws on the concepts and theoretical knowledge from many disciplines including regional planning, spatial analysis, urban design, transport planning, ecology, politics, policy analysis and organisational behaviour. The book assumes some knowledge of public policy and implementation, notwithstanding that the consideration of new endeavours will differ from place to place. In this respect, the historical development pathways or trajectories on which nations are travelling influence their hopes for the future and the innovations they can technically and politically support. Later chapters in the book seek to understand how the spatial, political and institutional contexts influence the identification of strategic priorities in specific metropolitan case studies and the mobilisation of public and private resources to respond to these concerns. Urban practitioners will find these accounts of diagnostic value in understanding new policy developments in the integration and synergies between transport planning and spatial/land use planning tools.

In placing transport resource consumption at the heart of global environmental change, this book places transport policy and infrastructure choices as central to the achievement of a more sustainable and energy efficient future. The book first reviews recent material on land use planning, transport planning and public policy implementation to critique the contribution of recent developments in the field of transport and neighbourhood liveability to achieving more sustainable and socially just outcomes. This is a heroic task due to the breadth and depth of the multi-disciplinary material on these subjects.

The aim is not to define in detail what a sustainable transport future might be but to identify how to use the fragmentary multi-disciplinary and practice knowledge to halve the demand and double the efficiency of the way we consume resources for transport. While the focus is on transport it is inextricably linked to the configuration of spatial opportunities or activity locations across the urban and rural fabric. What is missing in current approaches to urban planning is a holistic look at this system interaction, which recognizes that human communities are interdependent and interact with their physical environment. Earlier approaches have served cities poorly because they fragmented the whole into parts, among other reasons. In this respect, the book specifically aims to link the literature on land use and transport planning with ecological principles and public policy implementation. The integration of knowledge and action across these four domains has the capacity to reshape choices, secure new ways of acting and liberate society from waste and resource inefficiency.

Charting this journey through the book are the three central concepts of *mobility*, *accessibility* and *exergy,* which set the boundaries for the discussion on sustainable transport. Mobility characterises the current insatiable demand for movement, accessibility links the need to travel to the configuration of spatial opportunities, and exergy foregrounds the efficient utilisation of resources. These concepts interweave throughout the discussion of other issues and can be likened to tent pegs fixing what is relevant in the discussion, namely competing scenarios or visions and their delivery. The key argument, though, is that the private market and the individual citizen cannot deal with the challenge of adapting to global environmental pressures so it has to be smart-acting big government which must take on the role. Government has to set the opportunity agenda and to use all the tools available to bring about change in a way that levers flows of private capital for low energy projects.

It is not easy to produce a collective action programme to address cross-cutting issues such as climate change and resource minimisation due to the fragmentation of governance arenas and the diffuse pressures for change coming from several different directions. Progress will therefore be dependent on finding the right scale of governance, which can grasp the realities of today's global–local issues as well as link to the lives of all citizens through action programmes that give relevance and meaning to their lives. The metro-scale or the city-region provides the spatial scale of functional interaction between urban and rural areas and the potential to secure horizontal integration between the initiatives of key local stakeholders, while also collaborating vertically, up to higher-tier government and down to local residents, to ensure that actions reinforce each other along the low energy development pathway. The metropolitan region, moreover, is still the locus of most daily experiences for the majority of people: home, work, commuting, school, shopping, community and religious affiliations, recreation and pleasure, and so on.

The contribution of this book is to emphasis that government action has to be undertaken in new ways – to integrate the resources invested in urban areas so as to enhance the capacity and the resilience of communities to respond to global environmental challenges. The book argues that the role for national governments is to set the structuring rules and key outcomes and to dispense public funds so that these are achieved. National governments must then draw back and allow cities and their residents to create sustainable scenarios for integrated policy development and delivery, based on putting into place structures of collaboration that support flexible and continuous change processes, which are transparent and capable of continuously absorbing corrections.

The question this book addresses is, therefore, how to achieve the institutional capacity at the level of city-regions so that ecological systems thinking is used to integrate actions horizontally and vertically across different spatial scales. Discussion on energy efficient futures must enthuse all levels of society and include detailed discussion on future urban form, the integration of planning and transport, ways of achieving zero carbon settlements, and the protection and enhancement of critical environmental capital. Public funding dispensed for infrastructure should steer developers and investors towards more effective integration of public transit within, and between, urban areas, rather than the current disconnection between the planning and regulation of capital investment that characterises the governance of city-region development.

As a chartered town planner, I foresee a strong role for regional planners, land use planners and spatial planners, whatever their nomenclature, in responding to the global challenges posed by urbanisation, poverty, climate change and natural disasters. Intervention to steer investment to specific locations and to set minimum quality standards is central to success across the societal domain, including transportation, economic development, tourism, waste, energy, water, the environment, and resilience to climate change. But the task of setting up a coherent framework and supportive metrics for promoting sustainability amongst the collective consciousness cannot be shouldered by one discipline alone. Nor should it; since sustainability, learning, and governance should penetrate all aspects of governing city-regions. This book will contribute to the extent to which city-regions can 'learn' to govern themselves, to develop sustainably, to distribute equitably and to innovate.

Angela Hull
Edinburgh

ACKNOWLEDGEMENTS

This book has originated from teaching undergraduate and postgraduate planning students at Heriot Watt University about how we can make the UK transport system more accessible to the spatial opportunities around which our lives revolve. Their enthusiasm has been pivotal to this endeavour. On a personal note I would like to thank David Banister for his initial encouragement to publish and my research collaborators over the last ten years, including Reggie Tricker, Sarah Hills, Sotirios Thanos, James Morgan, David Watkins and John Forrester. I thank them all for their support. Special thanks go to Patsy Healey who read the complete draft for the publisher and gave me the inspiration to tightly edit the chapters one more time.

ABBREVIATIONS

ANPR	automatic number plate recognition
AONB	Area of Outstanding Natural Beauty
BRIC	Brazil, Russia, India and China
C	century
CBA	cost benefit analysis
CBD	central business district
CfIT	Commission for Integrated Transport
CHP	combined heat and power
CNG	compressed natural gas
CO_2	carbon dioxide
CO_2 e	carbon dioxide equivalent
CoM	Council of Ministers, also known as the Council of the European Union
DG TREN	Directorate-General for Transport and Energy
EC	European Commission
ECMT	European Conference of Ministers of Transport
EIA	environmental impact assessment
EU	European Union
GCA	Greater Copenhagen Area
GDP	gross domestic product
GHPP	global hectares per person
GLA	Greater London Authority
GIS	geographical information system
g/kWh	grams/kilowatt-hour
$GtCO_2$	gigatonnes of carbon dioxide
GVA	gross value added
HC	halocarbons
HGV	heavy goods vehicle
IC	internal combustion
ICT	information and communications technologies
IT	information technology
ITS	intelligent transport system
LEA	Local Education Authority
LPG	liquid petroleum gas
LUTI	land use and transport integrated

mg/km	milligrams/kilometre
$MtCO_2$	megatonnes of carbon dioxide
MM	mobility management
NAFTA	North American Free Trade Agreement
NGO	non-governmental organisation
NOx	oxides of nitrogen
NPP	net primary productivity
O_3	ozone
OECD	Organisation for Economic and Community Development
OFT	Office of Fair Trading
ORR	Office of Rail Regulation
pkm	person kilometres travelled
pppd	per person per day
$PM_{10/2.5}$	particulate matter
PTA	public transport authority
RTS	regional transport strategy
SEA	strategic environmental assessment
SME	small and medium-sized enterprise
SOx	oxides of sulphur
SSSI	site of special scientific interest
STA	sustainability threshold analysis
STAG	Scottish Transport Appraisal Guidance
SUV	sport utility vehicle
TEN	Trans-European Transport Network
TFL	Transport for London
T5	Terminal 5 at Heathrow Airport
UK	United Kingdom
UN IPCC	United Nations Intergovernmental Panel on Climate Change
US	United States of America
VAT	value added tax

CHAPTER 1

TIME FOR CHANGE?
THE RATIONALE FOR LOW ENERGY TRANSPORT PROVISION

1.1 INTRODUCTION

This book tries to envision what a transport system that meets the needs of the disabled, the weak, the young and the elderly might be like: one that is integral to the urban landscape rather than displacing the lifeblood of the street. It would need to be one that respected the essence of each community and connected rather than created barriers to activity. We are aware in our everyday lives of the dominance of transport infrastructure in our communities: the distant activity and noise from the nearest trunk road or distributor road 20 hours a day; the busy junction in the town or city where impatient drivers and lycra-clad cyclists wait ready to roll; the noisy, polluting buses stopping and starting in our shopping streets; the broad expanses of car parks attached to edge- or out-of-town supermarkets; the bustle of railway stations in the morning and evening rush hours; and the endless waiting and queuing in sterile airports. Moving about our cities is rarely an enjoyable experience for most people.

How has this state of affairs come about when infrastructure is so important in our lives and to the efficiency of the economy? According to O'Sullivan (1980) there is disconnect between the different components of the transport network because of the relentless competition, throughout history, from promoters of new technologies to capture customers from the established transport service providers. Competition and the pursuit of profit would appear, then, to have had a controlling influence on the provision of transport services to different locations in our cities. The palimpsest of layers of private sector provision has been interspersed by public sector investment in transport, welfare and social facilities, particularly since the Second World War. The state has cooperated with, and sought to gain from, private sector endeavour and as investors have looked outwards from the centre of towns and cities the concentration of spatial opportunities has dissipated. Central to understanding the social importance of these processes are the concepts of *inter-linkage*, *connection* and *integration* and, in particular, the *cumulative impact* of the decisions to invest (and not to invest) in transport, housing, health, education, industry, commerce, and leisure facilities. These concepts play an important part in understanding and deciphering the empirical case studies in Chapter 7 and will be explored and developed in later chapters.

One decade into the twenty-first century is timely to reappraise society's aspirations for unfettered mobility and to understand the issues surrounding mobility and accessibility to spatial opportunities given the growing certainty within the scientific community of the anthropogenic causes of climate change. The need for people to travel some distance to the facilities they require can be considered as an impediment to reducing the greenhouse gas emissions from the transport sector. Indeed, the psychological hold of the automobile over movement choices makes it a difficult proposition to control the resource consumption and pollution emissions from transport (Stern 2006). If this is the case, the issue of how to break the current patterns of travel behaviour while achieving other societal goals such as economic growth, social cohesion and environmental protection pose a contemporary societal conundrum. This leads to two key challenges for government organisations if a step change in the entropy or energy utilisation of the transport sector is to be achieved:

*   First, how can society more efficiently connect the spatial distribution of services and facilities with the infrastructure for movement within the city-region? This is a challenge for elected governments and civil servants in collaboration with the main investors in infrastructure and services. This book argues that to meet the challenge requires an integrated policy framework and regulated collaboration between the public and private sectors.
*   Second, how can the institutions of government empower individuals to be more circumspect in their consumption of renewable and non-renewable resources so that their ecological footprint, or impact on the Earth's ecosystems, is reduced while enhancing health and fitness, and neighbourhood sociability? This challenge encompasses the issues of climate change and equitable resource consumption and raises the question of personal responsibility for consumption impacts.

This book is concerned with the part that transport policy can play in stabilising and reducing greenhouse gas emissions and the consumption of scarce global resources. The discussion in later chapters is not so much focused on the images and models of what a truly sustainable transport system might be, though these are lacking in the collective consciousness, but on how society needs to organise to steer available resources towards the creation of energy efficient environments and what kind of intelligence or knowledge is required to promote this collective action capacity.

The book essentially focuses on the process of producing a coherent framework and supportive metrics for promoting sustainability, through proposing a new logic for transport planning that emphasises the accessibility to spatial opportunities and the promotion of active travel opportunities for walking and cycling. Central to the implementation of this new logic is the effective use of the tools of government (viz. legal requirements, fiscal incentives, knowledge dissemination, target setting and monitoring). How elected governments collaborate with key partners is the key here. This includes holistic (ecological) systems thinking to integrate actions hori-zontally and vertically across different spatial scales, with proactive support from higher- and lower-level government and coalitions of interest. The book argues that government intervention has to be undertaken in new ways, with a focus specifically on horizontal integration to achieve capacity at the level of city-regions and to make sure that investments at this spatial scale have positive synergies which produce energy efficient outcomes more effectively. All levels of government need to play their part in creating the new opportunity agenda that encourages this shift in public attitudes and behaviour.

The argumentation for this new logic is built up through each successive chap-ter. The remainder of this chapter outlines the problems posed by transport, through presenting national data on the environmental impacts of transport and the broad palette of policy options that are being discussed by governments within Europe. Current patterns of travel behaviour across Europe are examined in Chapter 2 which is structured according to the categories of data collected. The key concepts of 'accessibility' and 'mobility' are introduced here to illuminate how our knowledge of transport behaviour is structured and how these concepts shape our atten-tion and inform the selection of options for new investment in the built and natural environment. We then move on to examine the dialectical relationship between set-tlement patterns and transport infrastructure. This is the precursor for an in-depth evaluation of the substantial academic research on travel behaviour which is covered in Chapter 3.

In this conceptualisation, transport planning is one component of spatial planning, which influences and interacts with other elements of the built and natu-ral environment. The accessibility and mobility themes are developed further in Chapter 3, which compares their use across the policy sectors of transport, land use planning and public health, and discusses the long-term implications of their use in underpinning ideas for sustainable travel. These two themes are contrasted with the concepts of 'exergy' and 'spatial equity' as principles for securing the delivery of social, economic and environmental objectives through urban planning. Chapter 3 attempts to explain the landscape within which the policy and academic debates on transport and accessibility play out by, grounding the reader in an understanding of how transport infrastructure can both enable and constrain the way we use our towns and cities.

The perspective, in this book, is concerned with moving away from 'isolated' structuring decisions stemming from public and private investment to an approach where the cumulative impacts of previous strategic decisions on the life and health of the city are first appraised and new investment 'directed' to opportunity areas in line with agreed, comprehensively integrated, strategies. The multi-scalar institutional structures for moving towards a more sustainable transport system are the focus of Chapter 4 which provides an in-depth examination of the drivers towards cross-sector collaboration and the strategic tools available to higher tiers of government to structure and shape the attention of economic and social actors.

The key concepts of 'inter-linkage', 'connection', 'integration', 'governance', 'partnership' and 'empowerment' are central to understanding how human and financial resources can be deployed more efficiently and effectively to attain more sustainable accessibility in urban areas. This necessarily involves an evaluation of the efficacy of the decision support tools and techniques available to civil servants and politicians and how they are used in the political process of investment prioriti-sation. Chapter 5 poses the question of whether we have the right tools and political commitment to move towards a low energy future, drawing on European research on the institutional barriers to innovation.

Chapter 6 looks in detail at the types of transport and land use interventions available to reduce carbon emissions and use resources more efficiently. This chap-ter attempts to identify how the positive synergies between interventions can be maximised and the criteria and appraisal tools that can be refined to assess the effectiveness of interventions. Chapter 7 then applies the concepts of 'integration', 'accessibility', 'exergy' and 'governance' to appraise how these interventions have been implemented in several national and city case studies across Europe. Particular attention is given to how strategic steering tools are applied in each country, to understanding the institutional context and culture in each case study, and to draw out the lessons that can be transferred to other contexts.

Chapter 8 reflects back on the empirical case studies of national and city-region interventions to identify the best practice in multi-scalar collaboration, the synergies (positive and antagonistic) between specific interventions, and whether the city-region scale can provide the impetus for a step change towards low energy development pathways.

This chapter, however, has still to set the scene through introducing the main environmental impacts of transport, outlining how these are recorded and charting which European Union (EU) member states appear to be making progress in reduc-ing carbon dioxide (CO_2) emissions from transport. The chapter moves onto discuss the main policy challenges for the planning of people movement and introduces how these are being considered by national and transnational governments.

1.2   THE ENVIRONMENTAL IMPACTS OF TRANSPORT

Transport has several known negative effects on health and the environment. In 2005 the death toll arising from transport accidents in the EU-25 stood above 43,000, with a relatively low level of fatalities in rail, sea and air transport accidents standing in sharp contrast to the 41,300 recorded road fatalities (European Commission 2007a: 126). The expansion of the transport network has had several deleterious environmental effects. First, there is clear evidence of the fragmentation and loss of habitats and species from the barrier transport infrastructure creates to natural migration and the movement of animal populations (European Environment Agency 2004: 14). Second, the expansion of transport infrastructure also increases the extent of surface imperme-ability and thus creates a higher risk of surface water flooding.

However, it is the by-products of the combustion of fuel that have caused the most environmental concern. The products of combustion include benzene, car-bon monoxide (CO), lead, nitrogen dioxide (NO_2), particulates (e.g. PM_{10}, $PM_{2.5}$), and ozone (O_3) which have significant adverse affects on human health and local air quality (Whitelegg 1997). Despite the growth in traffic it is thought that SO_2, NO_2, PM_{10} and hydrocarbons are reducing as a result of European emis-sion standards and improvements to the environmental performance of vehicles following EU directives and voluntary agreements with vehicle manufacturers (European Environment Agency 2004).

More attention is now being given to the interaction of these by-products with global greenhouse gases (carbon dioxide, methane, nitrous oxide, ozone and halo-carbons) that normally occur in the atmosphere in relatively small amounts and have a big impact on climate change. Global level cooperation through the United Nations Convention on Climate Change has instigated action to reduce global greenhouse gas emissions with the first agreed commitment to stabilise emissions made in Rio de Janeiro in 1992. The Kyoto Protocol in 1997 set an overall target for CO_2 equiva-lent (CO_2e) emission reductions of 5.2 per cent by 2010 relative to 1990 levels (European Environment Agency 2008a). The protocol covers four global green-house gases (carbon dioxide, methane, nitrous oxide and sulphur hexafluoride) and two groups of gases (hydrofluorocarbons and perflourocarbons). The Protocol came into force in February 2005 when 141 countries, emitting 61 per cent of global emis-sions, ratified the agreement. These mitigating actions do not yet include the CO_2e emissions from international air and maritime travel.

The United Nations Intergovernmental Panel on Climate Change recently concluded that a reduction of 80 per cent on 1990 CO_2e emission levels by 2050 will be required if the average global temperature rise is to be contained to 2°C (United Nations Intergovernmental Panel on Climate Change 2007a). At the timo, thio wao dofinod ac tho tipping point, at which the most dangerous effects of climate change would occur, to be triggered when global greenhouse gases in the atmosphere reached 550 parts per million (ppm) of CO_2e. The science link-ing 2°C to 550 ppm has moved on, as pollution has increased, so that 450 ppm and even 350 ppm are now considered to equate with a 2°C rise in temperature (Hansen 2007; Meyer 2009).

In 2005, the transport sector consumed more than a third of the final energy consumption and emitted around 20 per cent of all global greenhouse gas emissions in the EU-25 (Bart 2009). Within this total, road transport is clearly the largest energy consumer, accounting for almost 83 per cent of transport's final energy consumption in the EU-25. Road transport was also the largest emitter of greenhouse gases among transport modes, ejecting 93 per cent of transport emissions (excluding international aviation, maritime transport, and electrified railways) (European Commission 2007a: 6).

In addition to these direct pollutants from transport use, transport also has other deleterious environmental effects:

- **Non-CO_2 effects of aviation**. The gases emitted from aircraft at high altitude mean that the warming effect of aviation is greater than its CO_2 emissions alone would suggest. There is no internationally agreed methodology for presenting the warming effect of emissions from aviation (as for CO_2e) and, therefore, they are excluded from emission estimates.
- **Upstream CO_2 emissions**. The refineries that produce transport fuel release CO_2 emissions. In addition, electricity consumed by electric trains and road vehicles is indirectly associated with CO_2 emissions from the power sector (Stern 2006: Annex 7c).

The data in Table 1.1 shows that nearly all the European countries listed have increased global greenhouse gas emissions since 1990. Only Germany, Bulgaria, Lithuania, and Estonia report reductions in emissions between 1990 and 2006. Estonia has reduced emissions from all four modes counted (road, rail, inland water navigation and air), Lithuania from road and rail, and Germany from road, rail and inland water navigation (European Commission 2009: 172). Interestingly, Germany had the highest emissions increase of the countries listed in Table 1.1 from domestic air travel. Since 1990, transport emissions from the EU-27 have increased by 27.4 per cent, averaging a 1.5 per cent increase each year (Table 1.1). The EU Climate Change Action Plan wants to reverse this trend, arguing that there is the potential to reduce energy consumption from transport by 26 per cent by 2020 (European Parliament 2009). Overall, 76 per cent of transport emissions are accounted for from seven EU Member States: Germany, the United Kingdom, France, Italy, Spain, the Netherlands and Poland. Without further action, the 'business as usual' scenario predicts that EU-15 global greenhouse gas emissions from transport will increase from the current 127 per cent of 1990 levels to 135 per cent by 2010 (European Environment Agency 2006a). The recently adopted 120 grams CO_2/km limit on new car emissions is not expected to have much impact on transport emissions before 2010 (European Environment Agency 2006a).

Table 1.1 Growth in greenhouse gas emissions from transport in Europe
(million tonnes CO_2 equivalent)

Country	1990	2006	Annual Average Growth Rate 1990–2006
Ireland	5.2	13.7	6.3 %
Luxembourg	2.8	7.3	6.2 %
Czech Republic	7.5	18.2	5.7 %
Cyprus	1.0	2.1	4.9 %
Portugal	10.1	20.1	4.4 %
Spain	57.5	108.6	4.1 %
Austria	12.7	23.1	3.8 %
Slovenia	2.7	4.8	3.6 %
Greece	14.7	24.1	3.2 %
Rumania	7.7	12.4	3.0 %
Poland	25.4	38.6	2.7 %
Malta	0.3	0.5	2.6 %
Hungary	8.5	12.7	2.6 %
Netherlands	26.4	36.1	2.0 %
Norway	11.3	14.6	1.7 %
Italy	104.0	133.2	1.6 %
EU-27	779.1	992.3	1.5 %
Belgium	20.6	26.1	1.5 %
Denmark	10.7	13.6	1.5 %
Iceland	0.6	0.8	1.4 %
Slovakia	5.0	6.0	1.1 %
France	118.8	138.6	1.0 %
Latvia	2.9	3.5	1.0 %
United Kingdom	118.9	136.7	0.9 %
Lichenstein	0.1	0.1	0.7 %
Finland	12.8	14.4	0.7 %
Sweden	18.4	20.2	0.6 %
Switzerland	14.6	15.7	0.5 %
Germany	164.4	162.0	−0.1 %
Bulgaria	11.0	8.7	−1.4 %
Lithuania	5.8	4.5	−1.5 %
Estonia	3.4	2.4	−2.0 %

Source: Adapted from European Commission (2009: 172), reproduced with permission

In his review of the economic impacts of climate change Sir Nicholas Stern described climate change as the greatest example of market failure ever seen (Stern 2006). Because of the high abatement costs of global greenhouse gas emissions from transport, he considered that transport should be one of the last economic sectors to change (See Figure 1.1). Table 1.1 suggests that this lack of urgency to address the global greenhouse gas emissions from transport is mirrored by most of the national governments across Europe. Stern's comments are quoted at length in the box below because of the political importance they have had on transnational and national strategy documents.

Transport is one of the more expensive sectors to cut emissions from because the low carbon technologies tend to be expensive and the welfare costs of reducing demand for travel are high. Transport is also expected to be one of the fastest growing sectors in the future. For these two reasons, studies tend to find that transport will be among the last sectors to bring its emissions down below current levels.

Cost effective emission savings from transport are initially likely to come from improvements in the fuel efficiency of oil-based transport vehicles, behavioural change, and use of biofuels. There are limits to the role that biofuel could play in transport as land availability and technological constraints could drive up the cost. IEA (2004) analysis suggests that efficiency improvements and biofuels could together contribute to 7 gigatonnes CO_2 savings by 2050 at a cost of \$25/tonne CO_2. Efficiency improvements account for about three quarters of this carbon saving; this could be obtained using measures such as more use of hybrid cars.

If innovation policy is used to bring down the cost of low carbon transport technologies (such as hydrogen or electric powered vehicles), then these will become viable options in the longer term. However the electricity or hydrogen would have to be generated in a low carbon way for these technologies to be truly low carbon. It is very uncertain how quickly the costs of these technologies might come down. A study by the IEA found that hydrogen could fuel up to 30 per cent of road transport vehicles by 2050, but with significant downside potential. Analysis by Anderson (2006) finds that by 2050 at a cost of \$25/tonne CO_2, hydrogen could account for 10–20 per cent of fuel for road transport vehicles globally.

Figure 1.1 Cutting emissions in transport. Source: Stern (2006: Annex 7c), reproduced under licence

While transport is likely to be largely oil-based in 2050, it is important for it to decarbonise in the longer term if stabilisation at 550ppm CO_2 e is to be achieved. For example, in the period beyond 2100, total global greenhouse gas emissions will have to be just 20 per cent of current levels (around 5 gigatonnes CO_2 e, which is roughly the same as today's emissions from agriculture). It is impossible to imagine how this can be achieved without a decarbonised transport sector. Climate change moves transport policy into a much more challenging policy arena, because it either requires expensive technologies or a radical change in travel behaviour to implement a low carbon economy. The Institute of Economic Affairs (2006) predicts that transport emissions will double by 2050, reaching 12 gigatonnes CO_2 under the 'business as usual' scenario. global greenhouse gases can linger in the atmosphere for a hundred years before dispersion (Meyer 2009). If this is the case, it is important to start making significant progress sooner rather than later.

The issue then becomes what actions need to be taken to ensure that as little carbon as possible is released between now and 2020, the date when the most recent UNIPCC projections suggest that significant reductions must be secured? The second question we need to ask is what has been holding us back? Why haven't we been able to produce a transport system that protects the natural capital critical to global functioning, that meets the travel needs of all citizens and supports the economy?

1.3 LOW ENERGY DEBATES

There have been many debates on the energy and resource efficiency of the transport sector from at least the early 1990s. World leaders at the United Nations World Commission on Environment and Development in 1987 resolved to work towards 'sustainable and environmentally sound development pathways' and called for a new approach to economic growth in order to eradicate poverty and enhance the resource base of current and future generations (United Nations World Commission on Environment and Development 1987: 1). Sustainable development, in this definition, focused on the patterns of resource use and the equitable sharing of resources within and across generations. Whitelegg (1997) considered that natural resource protection could be achieved in the transport sector if decision makers adhered to the following set of (first order) sustainable principles:

1   Minimise the dependence on fossil fuels
2   Cut the consumption of raw materials
3   Reduce emissions of CO_2 and other greenhouse gases
4   Cut pollution to groundwater and seas
5   Minimise the land use requirement
6   Reduce the impact on habitats
7   Reduce soil erosion caused by transport infrastructure
8   Stop the use of ozone depleting substances (Whitelegg 1997: 105).

Protecting the stock of natural resources is now accepted as a key principle in transport planning. In 2006, Sir Nicholas Stern reviewed the evidence on the environmental impacts of transport but did not consider there was a need for strong government environmental regulation of transport and urban development. However, the United Nations Intergovernmental Panel on Climate Change in 2007 argued authoritatively that over 50 per cent of the observed increase in average global temperatures since the mid-twentieth century was due to the observed increase in anthropogenic global greenhouse gas emissions (United Nations Intergovernmental Panel on Climate Change 2007). As Table 1.1 shows, the global greenhouse gas emissions across Europe have increased by 27 per cent since 1990. Stern's recommendation in 2006 to governments to resolve the problem of growing global greenhouse gas emissions from the transport sector was to prioritise the following interventions: information policies to promote behaviour change; support to bring forward new clean vehicle technologies; and that polluters should pay the 'full' carbon price for their pollution. The remainder of this introductory chapter explores these options and introduces some of the institutional issues that will be pertinent to the success of the transport sector in contributing to global greenhouse gas/CO_2e emission reductions. The aim of this introductory chapter is to provide the reader with the background policy context before the more substantive transport issues are addressed in later chapters.

The immediate cause of the phenomenal growth of transport emissions is clear: people are travelling more and more, and especially on roads. As Whitelegg (1997) and Dupuy (1999) have noted, it has taken a hundred years of corporate partnership between governments, motorist organisations and enthusiasts to reach the position where the car is the dominant means of transport in our cities. This social movement, intent on a singular purpose and armed with public subsidy, has reoriented space to serve the car efficiently to the detriment of the communities and lifestyles that appeared to brook the car's progress. Reinserting structures that can kindle local interaction and low energy lifestyles, one could argue, will take the same resources of partnership and funding. A new logic in decision making will be required to widen the choice of transport available to all citizens while addressing the diverse travel needs of different generations and ethnic groups.

Technology offers the potential to significantly reduce CO_2 emissions from road transport. Short-term measures such as 'clean' fuels and fuel efficiency improvements are already being implemented, supported by fuel taxes and a renewable road transport fuel obligation in many countries. Biofuelled and hybrid electric vehicles for road travel are already on the market and thus offer a dramatic reduction in CO_2 and other greenhouse gases (Köhler 2007). The railways can be decarbonised using electricity from renewable sources. Compressed natural gas (CNG) and bioethanol are seen as promising medium-term options since they fuel internal combustion (IC) engines similar to current petrol and diesel engines, which limits the development cost (Rietveld and Stough 2005). Second generation biofuels using the wastes from agriculture, forestry and the food industry, and thus avoiding soil deterioration and competition with food crops, are currently being produced and demonstrated for energy content and emissions in countries such as the UK, Germany, Slovakia and Sweden. In the longer term, lignocellulosic bio-fuels could be used to power aviation and hydrogen fuel cells to power road transport and rail but these technologies are unlikely to be mainstream until 2020 and may be much later unless the development of the technology is supported by public subsidy (Köhler 2007). Fuel cell prototypes are currently being tested by the East Japan Railway Company and through the European hydrogen train project (www.hydrogentrain.eu) (Hayat and Atkins 2007).

The technological path to low energy consumption is an expensive and long-term option and is unlikely, on its own, to deliver sufficient reductions to meet the challenging UNIPCC targets. In order to significantly reduce carbon emissions, clean vehicle technologies would need to be combined with other measures such as the pricing of carbon consumption and 'lower-tech' policy measures to influence travel behaviour.

Travel could be charged on the basis of the relative levels of CO_2 emissions emitted. Transport CO_2 charging has not been exploited well so far in Europe but combined with a redesign of fuel taxes to incentivise clean vehicles and fuels it could start to link the external impacts of transport to the actual behaviour of travellers. The general case for road user charging has been thoroughly debated in the literature and the several benefits include raising finance to enhance public transport, reducing congestion, improving the efficient use of the road network, and securing CO_2 reductions and other environmental benefits (Balcombe et al. 2004). Glaister and Graham (2006) and McKinnon (2006), however, consider that the implementation costs of road user charging for vehicles in the UK will restrict its application to all but a few urban locations. But given the recent and projected traffic growth in the Netherlands, the government there passed legislation in 2009 to base all vehicle taxes from 2011 on the distance travelled. The success of the implementation of this scheme will provide an exemplar for other nations to follow.

Behaviour change strategies are generally seen in the policy literature as the most cost-effective measure to reduce CO_2 emissions from transport and seek to significantly change individual travel choices towards lower-carbon modes including active travel. Behaviour change interventions include company travel plans, car pools and car clubs, personalised travel planning, the promotion of public transport, cycling and walking, and training for eco-efficient driving. However, the accelerated implementation of these measures may not be sufficient on its own to make an impact. Anforth et al. (2008) modelled the implementation of land-based low energy transport measures in Yorkshire and Humberside in the UK to assess the contribution to CO_2 reduction by 2020. The package of measures included the introduction or extension of bus rapid transit systems, light rail networks, rail electrification, public transport smartcards, workplace and school travel plans, home working and teleworking, travel awareness and education, personalised journey planning, grocery home shopping, car clubs and car sharing networks, high occupancy vehicle lanes, mileage-based and urban congestion charging systems, car free zones and approaches to car free housing development. They found that the accelerated implementation of these measures would not be sufficient to stabilise CO_2 emission levels in Yorkshire and Humberside back to 2001 levels by 2020.

It would appear that each of these approaches, on its own, is unlikely to be sufficient to close the diverging gap between the current rising levels of carbon emissions from transport and the UNIPCC requirements for carbon emission reductions.

1.4   MOVING TOWARDS LOW ENERGY FUTURES

This book argues that the key to bringing the science of climate change and the impacts of current transport behaviour to politicians and the public is engagement and communication. Because of the ubiquity of the road network, changing the mindset of politicians, civil servants and the public away from a car-dominated culture will be intrinsic to achieving behaviour change. European transport research has found that appointed or elected government at the city or city-region level frequently has no clear vision of the transport development priorities needed to achieve more sustainable transportation (Bertolini 2003; Kennedy *et al*. 2005). In similar vein, Stephen Wheeler (2010) found from his review of regional planning initiatives across Europe and North America a sizable gap between regional visions of sustainability and current practice. This research suggests further dialogue and engagement with all levels of society, to envision what a sustainable 'mobility' future might be like and to help bring to the public consciousness the sustainable scenarios and the action required to get there. Societal debates on the scenarios and solutions for achieving low energy living environments are the prerequisite to changing behaviour and developing the new policies that will 'cultivate' such change.

Research on the organisational barriers to innovation in Europe and the USA points to similar gaps between rhetoric and action, with findings that suggest a lack of synergy between the land use and transport priorities in the investment strategies for infrastructure, an insufficiency of stable funding for the more sustainable modes, and little attention to neighbourhood design in transport intervention (Hull 2005). Unless the priorities of all built environment investment are realigned to achieve health-promotive environments and the localisation of activities, incremental change to the transport system will take too long to impact on lifestyles and culture (Köhler 2007). One can predict that a society dominated by fossil-fuel-powered road transport is likely to continue to squander natural resources and assets and detrimentally affect local accessibility to services and social support networks.

Often the blame for inaction is placed at the feet of politicians. Table 1.1 suggests that the political commitment by EU member states to radical policy change on carbon emission reductions from transport clearly waivers. This can be explained, on the one hand, by supply-side policies in the new EU member states to catch up with the transport network that richer member states have amassed. On the other hand, the slow, incremental approach to energy reduction in other EU states is partly due to politicians' perception of the hostility that large sections of society feel towards the removal of the access advantages their cars currently provide. Urban planners have provided parking spaces outside people's homes, workplaces, shopping centres and recreational areas. Whole cities have been restructured to cater for increasing numbers of cars. It would take radical change to remodel the city so that public transport becomes widely available for all activities. There appears to be little urgency from the car industry or from within government to lead a movement for radical change. This can be explained by the economic might of the car regime in Europe and the government revenue-raising potential from the industry. In 2005, over £20 billion (€22.7 billion) was raised in fuel tax revenue alone in England (Glaister and Graham 2006: 1415). Whitelegg (1997: 60) points to the close links between government agencies and the car regime with the '*high distance intensity*' of the strategic transport network perceived as a driver to achieving economic growth policies. Transport policy is thus inextricably linked with socio-economic goals that compete with environmental targets for societal acceptance and support.

Technological solutions are often favoured by politicians since they disturb the present functioning of the system as little as possible, but even here politicians have been risk averse. There has been insufficient investment in the fuel production, distribution and refuelling facilities for the technologies considered to be the most promising in reducing global greenhouse gas emissions: electric vehicles, fuel cells and hydrogen (H_2) IC engines (Kennedy *et al.* 2005; Hayat and Atkins 2007; Köhler 2007), although large-scale investment in the new refuelling infrastructure for biomass-based fuels is underway in Germany, Slovakia and Sweden, and for electric vehicles in Denmark (see Chapter 7). Designs for a Toyota Prius type electric vehicle, which can be charged directly from the electricity distribution network either alongside the road network or overnight in a garage, are close to commercialisation (Köhler 2007). However, if this technology is to be more widely deployed in the near future, regulations need to be put in place to ensure that all new residential developments have recharging points, and that recharging and/or refuelling points for new technologies can be retro fitted into the built environment alongside main distributor routes and interchanges.

Imagining a future reality without the reliance on the private use of motorised vehicles seems to be off the societal radar at the moment. There are few images and models of what a sustainable city-region might be like and the infrastructure needed to support low energy development pathways (Neuman and Hull 2009). While there are demonstrations of electric-powered buses in all large cities, travel planning and bicycle days, these are often superficial demonstrations and inconsistently applied (Whitelegg 1997; Köhler 2007). Unless successful low energy initiatives are nurtured and replicated in different contexts there will be little understanding of what the realistic alternatives might be. Chapter 7 offers good practice examples of integrated policy making from several European nations; however, the different institutional settings in these comparisons must first be understood. Solutions are context dependent (Rietveld and Stough 2002) so that the opportunities to adapt the transport system in one context, where design and provision are decided by elected government (e.g. Sweden), may not be available in another context, where provision is secured through public and private sector cooperation (e.g. the UK).

Current institutions (viz. organisations, decision networks and routines) were set up to resolve some social problem in the past and therefore relate to previous modes of public regulation or private resource protection. The new approach to governing, involving elected and non-elected participants, often termed governance, relies on a widening consensus amongst public and private sector actors of what the problems are and how to address them. In this new context of public–private partnership, gaining public acceptability on how to resolve 'problems' surrounding sustainable development and climate change is a new challenge, which according to Salet and Thornley (2007), few existing institutional structures are equipped to perform.

Reaching consensus on what actions will cut carbon emissions from transport *and* enhance sustainability *and* quality of life are issues that cut across the levels of government and administrative boundaries, and professional and disciplinary cultures (Banister 2002a). A key hindrance impairing the formation of effective partnerships is when the vision and rhetoric of change is not aligned with policy and practice. This has a tendency to create confusion for both government partners and members of the public (Wheeler 2010). Effective joint action requires partners to be clear about their responsibilities, to understand each other's values and ways of working and how mutual benefit can be achieved. Effective partnership working between public and private sectors, and the relevant professions, would appear to be a prerequisite to achieving an integrated response to resource minimisation through securing multidimensional solutions that can serve several goals at the same time (Bertolini and le Clercq 2003). Several transport researchers have commented on the limited nature of knowledge on partnership approaches to innovation, decision making for different contextual conditions and the reciprocal effects of low energy demonstration projects (Pratt 1996; Geerlings and Stead 2002; Rietveld and Stough 2002; Hull 2005; NICHES 2007).

The challenge for joint working is, therefore, to maximise the synergies between the goals and the resources of developers and regulators. Research in the UK has found that the professional culture of transport officers and politicians can act as a barrier to innovation and risk taking, particularly where there is little knowledge of the likely impacts of new approaches to transport policy (Hull and Tricker 2006). Interviews with transport officers found that risk aversion is related to the departmental mindset or path dependency ('*We've always done it this way*') of the transport profession. One example given, of interdisciplinary failure to communicate effectively, concerned a road resurfacing programme in a UK city, where the transport engineers were seeking to increase road speeds but were unwilling to incorporate the cycle lanes requested by the transport planners (Hull 2008a).

European transport research has found that transport officers generally find the scale, scope and complexity of sustainable transport issues daunting and that they struggle conceptually with understanding the components of a sustainable transport strategy and lack knowledge of the relative merits of the available interventions (Ferrary 2008, May *et al.* 2008). The current models for predicting impacts focus on car travel and therefore provide little indication of the relative merits of other modal solutions (Hull and Tricker 2006; NICHES 2007; Hull 2008a). Transport officers in UK research draw attention to the paucity of decision support tools which can identify the most sustainable transport options and, specifically, the combination of measures appropriate in their city (May *et al.* 2008). Research by Pratt (1996) and Hayat and Atkins (2007) highlight additional gaps in the armoury of tools available to transport officers. These include the 'whole-life' cost assessment of scheme options, and the health and social impact assessment of urban design initiatives, economic measures, access restrictions, land use reallocation, and infrastructure provision.

1.5 SETTING THE AGENDA FOR FUTURE ACTION

The previous section has reviewed the challenges for politicians and professionals, such as transport and land use planners, who will have a key role in providing a territorial or place-based strategy that plans for the introduction of low energy transport infrastructures. To do this effectively, these professions will have to embrace a much wider agenda than hitherto. The capability to integrate climate change and global environmental hazards into city strategies will become a success factor for city-regions in the future, influencing the functionality, the economic performance as well as the quality of life of cities. Climate change may herald a paradigmatic change in urban planning or may be just another missed learning opportunity. This final section in the introductory chapter summarises the discussion so far and sets a marker for the thematic approach in later chapters, through spelling out the general sustainability principles and their translation into key themes for transport planners and city governors.

Adapting to climate change and low energy development is a new field of activity for city-regions, but some specific decision making principles can be identified that are integral to managing ecosystems more effectively than hitherto. Some of these principles, based on ideas of sustainability, have had salience for a considerable time now, based on the stewardship of resources and sustainable yields promoted at the United Nations Conference on Environment and Development in Rio de Janeiro in 1992 and at the Millennium Summit in New York in 2000 (United Nations Statistics Division 2005, European Commission 2007b). Central to these principles are:

*   Maximising human welfare, and minimising resource depletion, energy use, waste production, and vulnerability against natural and environmental hazards
*   Dematerialisation through reducing the material resources needed per unit of gross domestic product (GDP)

- Ensuring activities do not damage important environmental features or exceed the environmental capacity of a resource system
- Building capacity in the ability of people to sustain lifestyles compatible with continued environmental integrity using caution where there are threats of damage and insufficient data (Selman 1996).

These principles foreground the protection of ecological and social resources to promote resource reduction and resilience to future global environmental hazards. Integrating them into the design of products and practices may also have economic competitive benefits over the short to medium term. This book argues that they should be considered as central to decision making on the dispensation of public funds and to promote a governance culture that promotes resource reduction and resilience by building adaptability and diversity into the built and natural environment. This is a task that touches various sectors of urban and regional development.

International and EU policy solutions to climate change have, however, focused attention on carbon accounting and the economic costs of failing to reduce global greenhouse gas emissions. The EU Emissions Trading System is the EU's key tool for cutting CO_2 emissions cost effectively. Carbon allowances under this scheme have been traded since 2005 by the 12,000 companies covered and attempts are being made to incorporate the transport sector within this scheme. There is a danger that in addressing carbon flows in isolation from air pollution, waste production, and urban sprawl we may fail to recognise the wider impact of abatement measures and the potential trade offs (Wood *et al.* 2007). As the media vilifies the petrol-guzzling sport utility vehicles (SUVs) we may fail to see the links between transport infra-structure, settlement structures, building and site design, health and obesity-busting policies, and the refurbishment of the public realm, etc.

The management literature tells us that exhortation and information provision will not spark change. Rather, genuine weight has to be given to assessing the environmental impact of investment options and sustainable ways of living and through putting in place new structures for decision making (viz. new rules, new incentives and sanctions) (Lowndes 2001; Köhler 2007). The new logic of integrated decision making, this book argues, requires leadership at the city-region scale and supportive institutional structures to secure behaviour change to low energy travel choices. The journey to resource minimisation is along a very bumpy road and city governors will need to deal with significant opposition and establish public acceptability for new approaches. This will particularly apply to interventions that entail road user charging, increased parking charges, higher taxation on travel and fuel, and the introduction of personal carbon credits.

The following themes form the agenda of tasks that transport and land use planners, referred to as spatial planners in this book, will need to address to effect change that leads to low energy development pathways. Particular attention is given to:

- How the principles of sustainability and resilience can be incorporated into strategies, plans and project appraisal processes
- The type of policy instruments or measures which might encourage low energy development pathways
- The integration of knowledge, technology and mitigation and prevention policies and the benchmarking of progress
- Engagement and dissemination of trustworthy and easy to understand information through public media and the internet
- Structures that support problem-solving and coordinated approaches that are continuously capable of absorbing corrections
- Collaboration on good practice and avoiding maladaptation.

The themes will be revisited and developed through subsequent chapters.

CHAPTER 2

UNDERSTANDING CURRENT PATTERNS OF TRANSPORT BEHAVIOUR IN EUROPE

2.1 INTRODUCTION

Before we can establish the details of an action plan for city governors and spatial planners to galvanise change towards low energy travel choices, the effects of our current travel behaviour and the concepts that shape this behaviour must first be understood. The following two chapters deal with these two issues in turn.

This chapter summarises the patterns of travel across Europe and offers an account of the trends in travel over the last thirty years. A precursor for producing a more energy efficient transport system is first, to understand the travel choices households and businesses make in response to the perceived options available and, second, to understand the cumulative impacts of these movement patterns on society and its ecosystems. The way the available transport infrastructure is used provides a commentary on not only the convenience and ease of use of that infrastructure in moving around cities but also the way in which infrastructure shapes our selection of where to live and where to shop and how to move between the two.

Before reviewing the evidence on travel behaviour from academic and government commentaries and statistics, the chapter first introduces the two concepts of accessibility and mobility, which are central to the analytical frame used to unpack the data. Introducing these two contrasting heuristic analytical tools at this early stage in the discussion will help the later critique of the supply and use of transport infrastructure, and also lay the groundwork for developing a conceptualisation around what 'sustainable transport' could mean. These concepts will be developed further in Chapter 3, which compares their use across the policy sectors of transport, land use planning and public health, and discusses the long-term implications of the different conceptions for sustainable travel. The chapter then moves onto explain how transport provision (and demand) has been shaped by wider societal economic, social and environmental objectives. This is followed by a summary of how the EU, as a higher tier of government and potential influence on travel behaviour, has responded to the perceived challenges for transport across Europe. We then move on to gain an understanding of the dialectical relationship between the built environment form and the transport services provided. This is the precursor for an in-depth evaluation of the substantial academic research on this topic in Chapter 3., which should be seen as the springboard for reorienting the reader towards a conceptualisation of sustainable transport that derives its focus from the principles of exergy, or resource minimisation, and which promotes the delivery of social, economic and environmental objectives through the transport system.

2.2 CONCEPTUALISING MOVEMENT PATTERNS IN URBAN REGIONS

'Getting around from place to place' is essential to human engagement and endeavour (Thrift 1996; Urry 2000). There are two derivations of how this essential human condition has been conceptualised, which are compared in Table 2.1. The first, which is defined here as a conception of mobility, is derived from classical location theory that presumes all economic actors are essentially profit-maximising individuals and, therefore, hypothesises that there is a direct correlation between changes in the transport system (e.g. transport costs) and journey length (Banister 2002a; Ney 2001; Geurs and van Wee 2006). This conception has held the attention of geographers and transport engineers who have examined and measured the geography of flows and the movement patterns between origins and destinations, noting the average speeds and predicting the direct costs of travel. The connectivity of the transport network has also received sophisticated analysis from the freight sector, where speed across the network infrastructure is central to the 'just-in-time' planning of vehicle movements and supply chains (Rodrigue 2006). Connectivity, or speed of access, is often used as a benchmark synonymous with (expected) economic growth (Ney 2001). The concept of mobility, then, is arguably a concept of growth emphasising increasing flows of vehicles and speeds across the network infrastructure.

A derivation of the concept of mobility is the concept of accessibility. Accessibility can be defined as the 'ease of reaching' a range of activities at different destinations. Accessibility, therefore, includes the spatial distribution and the quality of the services and facilities within reach of an individual or organisation (Social Exclusion Unit 2003). This is a social science conception of movement concerned with people's needs and their financial and time availability. According to Geurs and van Wee (2006: 151) 'activity-based accessibility measures ... the combined effect of land use and transport system changes'. This concept of accessibility has several applications. Social researchers examine the availability of public transport to access employment and other services within a reasonable travel time (Ney 2001; Social Exclusion Unit 2003; Geurs and van Wee 2006). Spatial planners match the accessibility requirements of specific types of economic activity to the accessibility characteristics of sites they reserve for development in their land use plan. Urban designers apply the concept of accessibility when defining sustainable neighbourhoods where the essential services of education, shopping, etc. are within walking distance. Ney (2001: 168) defines accessibility as 'slow, life-sustaining, and environmentally sustainable mobility within small areas'.

Table 2.1   The concepts of mobility and accessibility compared

Concept	Mobility	Accessibility
Definition	A movement concept: 'ability to move'/'ability to travel'; Speed of reaching destination (Jones 1981; Rodrigue 2006).	'Ease of reaching': the ability of social groups to reach destinations where they can carry out a given activity (Bhat et al. 2000; Social Exclusion Unit 2003).
	Free-flowing towns and cities (EU 2007b).	Accessible and connected, intermodal transport services (EU 2007).
	Macro-mobility: a focus on long distance travel (Knoflacher 1981).	Micro-mobility: a neighbourhood concept (Knoflacher 1981); Slow travel (Ney 2001).
	Infrastructure or transportation-based accessibility (Stanilov 2003; Geurs and van Wee 2006).	Activity based accessibility (Stanilov 2003; Geurs and van Wee 2006).
Variables measured	Number of vehicles on the road by type of vehicle; Average car travel speeds; Congestion levels; Transport costs.	Physical barriers to accessibility; The quality of the physical links between locations; Diversity of activities at locations; Accessibility of different social groups and/or geographic zones.
Debates	Mobility is essential to life and economic growth versus mobility is a luxury good, and any negative effects should be paid for in full. Internet technology will reduce the need to travel.	The unemployed and low income groups are disadvantaged in their employment chances by the poor quality of public transport in cities.

2.3   CHANGING TRAVEL PATTERNS ACROSS EUROPE

The concept of mobility has clearly influenced the collection of statistics by national governments on travel behaviour. Collected annual statistics focus on the distance travelled by mode of transport for both freight and passenger transport. These provide an important measure of the trends in travel patterns from which CO_2 e emissions can be calculated. Transport volumes are continuing to grow in nearly all EU member states (European Commission 2009). In 2005, transport emissions accounted for 20 per cent of all global greenhouse gas emissions in the EU-25 (Bart 2009). Across Europe, road transport emitted around 900 million tonnes CO_2 in 2005 with roughly half of these emissions from urban transport (Bart 2009). Road transport predominates for both freight and passenger transport. Of the total freight moved in 2005, road and sea transport dominate the market with 44 per cent and 39 per cent respectively (European Commission 2007a).

Table 2.2 below compares the mode used by freight in 1995 and 2005 and two intervening years. Across the EU, freight movements increased by 31 per cent

Table 2.2 Freight transported by transport mode *EU-25, 1995–2005 (in billion tonne-kilometres)

	Road	Rail	Inland waterways	Oil pipelines	Sea	Air	Total
2005	1,724	392	129	131	1,525	2	3,903
2004	1,683	392	129	129	1,484	3	3,819
2000	1,487	374	130	124	1,345	2	3,462
1995	1,250	358	117	112	1,113	2	2,972
percentage change 1995–2005	37.9	9.2	10.2	17.5	34.6	31.1	31.3
percentage annual change	3.3	0.9	1.0	1.6	3.0	2.7	2.8
percentage change 2004–2005	2.5	−0.2	0.3	1.5	2.8	−0.4	2.2

Source: European Commission (2007a: 69), reproduced with permission
Note* Road includes: national and international haulage by vehicles registered in the EU-25. Air and sea data are derived estimates by the Commission.

between 1995 and 2005, from nearly 3,000 billion to 3,903 billion tonne-kilometres (tonnes carried multiplied by distance travelled). This is equivalent to moving a tonne of goods over 23 kilometres a day per EU inhabitant (European Commission 2007a: 69). The largest growth in transported goods was in road and sea transport, which each grew by more than a third. Close behind is air transport with a growth of 31 per cent. There was a small increase in goods transported by rail, but rail reduced its modal share for freight from 12.1 to 10 per cent. Although the performance is insignificant in the averaged EU data, freight transport by inland waterways is especially important for some countries, such as Belgium and France, which increased their traffic by 50 per cent and 30 per cent respectively.

Road transport (viz. cars, powered two-wheelers, buses and coaches) accounts for 84 per cent of passenger-kilometres travelled in 2004 (European Commission 2007a: 4). Table 2.3 shows that passenger transport (passenger numbers multiplied by distance) increased by nearly 18 per cent between 1995 and 2004. Car travel was the most important means of travel for passengers in 2004 accounting for nearly three-quarters of the kilometres covered (European Commission 2007a: 104). Over this ten year period, air transport (intra-EU and domestic only) nearly increased by half, increasing its modal share for passenger transport to 8 per cent in 2004. Powered two-wheelers, passenger cars, and trams and metros all recorded increases of over 16 per cent, while passenger transport by sea slowly declined during this period (European Commission 2007a: 104).

Table 2.3 Passenger transport by transport mode: EU-25, 1995–2004
(in billion passenger-kilometres)

	Passenger cars	Powered two-wheelers	Bus and Coach	Railway	Tram and metro	Air*	Sea*	Total
2004	4548	143	502	352	75	482	49	6061
2003	4399	140	493	347	73	454	49	5958
2002	4372	136	489	351	72	435	50	5903
2001	4277	135	493	355	72	441	50	5823
2000	4196	132	492	353	71	440	49	5734
1995	3787	120	474	324	65	324	55	5149
percentage change 1995–2005	17.7	19.7	5.8	8.6	16.4	48.8	−11.1	17.7
percentage annual change	1.8	2.0	0.6	0.9	1.7	4.5	−1.3	1.8
percentage change 2003–2004	1.3	2.2	1.8	1.2	2.9	6.3	−0.8	1.8

Source: European Commission (2007a: 102), reproduced with permission
* These figures are for domestic journeys only.

Qualitative surveys of travel patterns in European cities show that the main reason for the increased distance travelled in the EU since 1990 is not an increase in the number of journeys made but in the length of the trips (European Conference of Ministers of Transport (ECMT) and Organisation for Economic and Community Development (OECD) 2002; Crass 2001; ECMT 2001). In Europe, people on average make 3.5 trips each day and the proportion of car trips has increased by nearly 10 per cent since 1990. The new EU member states experienced some of the highest increases with car trips tripling in Poznan to 1.20 per person per day (pppd) and an increase of 170 per cent in Tallinn to 1.92 trips (pppd). The EUROSTAT data shows that EU citizens on average travelled 32 kilometres per day in 2004 by cars, trains, buses and coaches. Of this total, car transport accounted for 27 km, buses and coaches (3 km), railways (2 km) and trams and metros (0.5 km) (European Commission 2007a). Notably missing from this dataset are figures for bicycle travel which in certain flat locations, with supportive local policies, can displace patronage from buses and reduce walking activity.

It is important not only to explain these trends in travel patterns but more importantly to understand the societal issues that lead to reliance on passenger car travel and the increasing use of air travel. Travel figures average out and homogenise behaviour and while they show the absolute trends in mobility and the direction of change they reveal little about the travel needs and requirements of different social groups. In the transport planning literature, the differences and similarities in travel behaviour, within and across countries, are attributed to a number of factors. These factors are discussed under six categories below: 1) technological factors; 2) socioeconomic and demographic factors; 3) spatial development patterns; 4) transport policies; 5) financial or pricing policies; and 6) institutional issues. While these factors are examined separately below for simplicity, later chapters will tease out their interdependent links in order to suggest more effective strategies for sustainable futures.

TECHNOLOGICAL FACTORS

Technological improvements in transport since the early sixteenth century have extended the geographical spread of travel with two distinct spatial impacts. On the one hand, technological advances have led to global shrinkage (Knowles 2006; Lakshaman and Anderson 2005) (see Figure 2.1). The 'enabling and space-shrinking technologies' (Lakshmanan and Anderson 2005: 159) of recent developments in transportation and communication have speeded up both time and space (Pooley and Turnbull 2000; Pooley et al. 2006). Recent developments in satellite technology enable the logistics industry to 'visibly' track jet transport, fast container ships and their cargoes round the world (Lakshmanan and Anderson 2005: 159). The transport of high value goods in the agricultural and manufacturing commodity chains, particularly have a wide geographical range (Rodrigue 2006: 386). For example, salad greens, exotic vegetables, and flowers are ordered daily from the far side of the earth and flown straight to the customer, while the heavier, lower value goods are handled by maritime and rail transport systems across global markets. Across Europe 44 per cent of freight (tonne-kilometre) was transported by road in 2005 (EC 2007: 71) with a heavy proportion of foreign freight vehicles traversing through the central European countries of Germany, Switzerland, and Austria (McKinnon 2006: 207).

At the same time technological advances, such as the internal combustion engine and reinforced concrete, have led to the expansion of urban areas over the last 100 years (O'Sullivan 1980: 45). The mass production of Ford cars and advances in the technological efficiency of the car has produced an affordable product in the developed world. O'Sullivan's historical analysis suggests that the 'provisioning [of] this new-found freedom of movement generated a major expansion of the industrial complement of developed economies in the car industry and its auxiliaries and generated political pressure to expand the public facility for using the product' (O'Sullivan, 1980: 46).

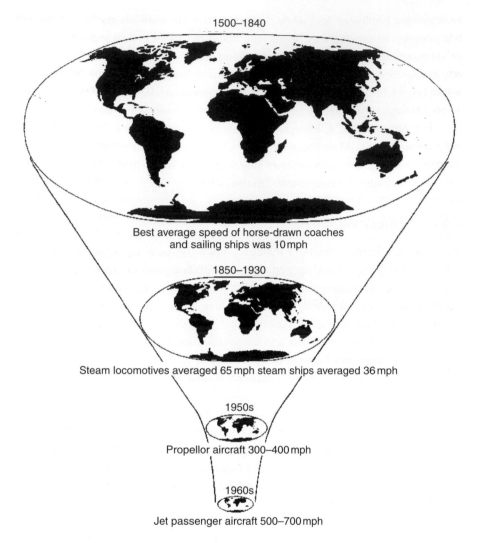

Figure 2.1 How technology has shrunk the globe. Source: Knowles (2006: 417), reproduced with
permission of Sage Publications

The public and private sectors have worked closely to promote new technologies. Advances in technology have been heralded as either solving the congestion
on the roads (e.g. railways in the 1820s) and/or as reducing the transaction costs
in terms of the travel time (O'Sullivan 1980; Hensher and Brewer 2001). Many
give credence to the private sector as the instigator for the development of new

technologies. Köhler (2007) suggests that a 'technological regime' drives the advances in new technology; citing the existence of such a regime in the logistics industry, consisting of airport operators, the aviation industry, purchasers and suppliers, and computer services. While O'Sullivan (1980) argues that new technologies would not be incorporated into the built environment to the same extent as they are without public sector promotion.

Intelligent information systems are already being used to promote safety and ease traffic flows in cities, to facilitate train and airline reservations, car hire and access real-time travel information, as well as analyse the travel behaviour of customers (Priemus 2007a). Future developments through the penetration of information and communications technology (ICT) networks are expected to improve the quality of the service which can be offered to car drivers through automatic vehicle guidance mechanisms, intelligent speed control and dynamic route real-time information (Priemus 2007a). Pooley et al. (2006) suggest caution in theorising the changes that may emerge from the introduction of new technology in the twenty-first century. They find from studying the assimilation of 'new' transport technologies in the UK that the new opportunities for speed and mobility exclude many people and have not significantly changed transport aspirations or behaviour.

Socioeconomic factors

While the technology associated with the car and road infrastructure and related services has expanded dramatically to allow faster and more flexible travel, travel time surveys suggest that the daily travel time budget on regular travel activity has remained constant at between 60–90 minutes (Commission for Integrated Transport 2001; Pooley et al. 2006; European Commission 2007a; Köhler 2007). British workers apparently have the longest journey-to-work times in Europe at 46 minutes per day on average (Pooley and Turnbull 2000; Commission for Integrated Transport 2001). Men and women have different transport mode behaviour with men dominating the more privatised and flexible forms of travel (such as the car and bicycle), while women are credited with dominating bus travel and walking modes.

The most notable economic trends have been the growth in the service and tourism industries, which have responded to the growth of consumerism generally in the twentieth century and the desire for travel as a social activity. This latter trend calls into question previous disciplinary assumptions that travel increases in direct relationship to the quality and expansion of the transport system ('induced demand') (Banister 2002a). There has been growing car ownership across Europe, except in Finland and Sweden, with people generally aspiring to owning one or more cars (ECMT/OECD 2002). Higher disposable incomes and the greater availability of cars in Eastern Europe and the fast-growing developing countries (China, India, Brazil and Mexico) has fuelled car ownership levels in those countries, while the availability of low cost flights has increased the demand for air travel in Europe (Whitelegg 1997; Köhler 2007). Evidence suggests that a person in a car owning household will, on average, make 66 per cent fewer trips by bus and 25 per cent fewer by rail each week than a person in a household with no car (Balcombe *et al.* 2004: 1). Once committed to a certain mode of travel, transport behaviour is usually sustained until the person relocates to another location and has to plan their journey to work again (Balcombe *et al.* 2004). In nearly all European cities increases in car owner-ship are associated with reduced patronage levels for public transport. Exceptions to this trend of lower public transport patronage have been found to exist in Russian cities (ECMT 2001) and Zurich and Singapore (Newman and Kenworthy 1999).

Model simulations suggest that car drivers are rather inelastic in their response to increases in driving costs with only one per cent of drivers using other modes when driving costs increase by 10 per cent (Vuk *et al.* 2007: 17). Certain social groups are sensitive to changes in commuting costs and road user charging (Pratt 1996; London case study Chapter 7). Car drivers appear to be more sensitive on average to changes in travel time than price increases (Vuk *et al.* 2007; de Groot and Steg 2006). The converse seems to apply to public transport users who, on average, are more sensitive to price increases with 4.2 per cent predicted to change mode if the public transport fare increased by 10 per cent (Vuk *et al.* 2007: 17).

Household size has changed dramatically since the 1960s with the traditional family of working father, mother and two children becoming the minority. The increas-ing importance of women's employment to the family income has implications for distance travelled, child rearing rotas and even the type of holiday chosen (Sultana 2006). The travel patterns of dual income families have become much more com-plex with one partner often travelling substantial distances to work or partners living apart. It is often, but not always, the female partner who has the shortest commute distance. Families where both adults are working often have complex trip chaining journeys to work, dropping off a child outside the school gates, picking them up again at the end of the day and transporting them to a social club.

As yet, there has been little research on these changing lifestyles, and demo-graphic factors such as the increasing elderly and global migrants, and their impact on travel behaviour (Urry 2000; Scheiner 2006; Banister and Hickman 2007; NICHES 2007). The travel needs of the growing number of old people in many European countries as a result of improvements to health provision in the last cen-tury will require more customised services to meet their travel aspirations and to ensure their safety. Continuing globalisation, climate change and European integra-tion will encourage more economic migrants to find employment in more successful economies than their own. This may balance out the effects in some countries of an ageing population and low birth rates, but these trends will create new accessibility needs and mobility patterns.

SPATIAL DEVELOPMENT PATTERNS

Changes in urban form are offered as the most important factor in explaining travel mode choice by many commentators (Hall 1995; ECMT/OECD 2002; White 2002; Pooley et al. 2006; Sultana 2006; Bart 2009). The urbanisation of major European cities since 1990 is still continuing with urban areas expanding much more than population growth (European Environment Agency 2006a). There has been a decline in city centre residents in several European cities, as well as in cities in the USA and Korea (ECMT/OECD 2002). New housing and commercial development is almost exclusively suburban, which increases journey lengths and reliance on the car (Hall 1995; European Environment Agency 2004). It is either the absence of land use policies or the failure to implement policies of concentration that have led to the decentralisation of jobs and activities, making journey patterns increasingly complex (Pooley et al. 2006). In these circumstances, where the fixed route public transport network is less convenient, those who can afford a car switch for the greater convenience and flexibility offered to combine work trips with shopping and health trips.

Bart (2009) compared the relationship between trends in transport emissions, population, gross domestic product and artificial land area (i.e. built-up sprawl) across Europe between 1990 and 2000. Multiple regression analysis revealed a strong relationship between the growth in artificial areas and the growth of transport CO_2 emissions. This was particularly noticeable in the data for Spain, Portugal and Ireland. Using the Corinne land use data base, Bart has been able to confirm Newman and Kenworthy's (1989) findings that there is a strong link between the density and form of urban development and the consumption of fuel. Newman and Kenworthy found there was a strong increase in petroleum consumption when population density fell below 29 persons per hectare. Housing and workplace density are key factors in the propensity to rely on passenger car transport and in the provision and frequency of commercial bus services (White 2002; Handy 2005; Knoflacher 2006; Sultana 2006). White (2002) suggests a break-even service, in the UK regulatory context, requires an average of 10–12 passengers in each direction on all bus services. The distances between bus stops, which affect bus speeds, are also a factor in patronage levels. Bus stop spacing of around 550 metres minimises stop time and reduces trip times. Typical residential densities in the UK context are given in Table 2.4 below.

Table 2.4 Typical net residential densities

Housing type	Density (persons per hectare)
High density terrace, multi-occupation	200–350
Inner-city redevelopment, flats	150–250
Public sector subsidised housing estates	70–150
Private, medium density	40–80
Private, low density	> 40

Source: Adapted from White (2002: 81)

We can surmise from this that low density housing below 40 persons per hectare incurs several resource costs:

- Public transport is not profitable and would have to be cross–subsidised or subsidised by a government body as a necessary welfare service
- Basic utilities (e.g. gas, electricity, telephone and water) are more expensive to install and maintain, requiring a longer pipe or cable feed
- Postal deliveries are expensive to run in low density areas, as a result of the growing real labour costs
- As urban areas expand they consume open space and natural habitats disappear (White 2002: 82).

The lifestyle choices of individuals are influenced by their values, preferences and cultural affiliations but are also shaped by the spatial configuration of employment and residential locations in the area where they live and the travel journey between (Pratt 1996; Knoflacher 2006; Sultana 2006). Investment in new infrastructure such as leisure facilities and road improvements can have unexpected social and cultural impacts. For example, Gray (2009) found people were taking a long distance '*whim trip*' to drive 100 miles/161 km to visit a new multiplex cinema in Inverness and drive home the same evening. Understanding how different social groups respond to new opportunities and existing constraints in their work and leisure trips is still an under-researched area in transport planning (Sultana 2006).

TRANSPORT POLICIES

To understand the drivers behind transport planning one must understand the scale and the power of the car industry in each nation and region. The transport sector generated over 10 per cent of the EU GDP in 2000 and employed over 10 million people (European Commission 2001a). The technological regime in the car industry, therefore, has substantial political weight. Politicians are wary of the political discord that can be released by the combined power of vehicle manufacturers and dealers, road builders, the oil industries, the logistics industry and rural dwellers. The technological regime promoting the car industry is credited with creating a '*car culture*' through lobbying for the expansion of the road system and facilities for drivers (Pratt 1996; Dupuy 1999; Ney 2001).

The road network has been extended and improved since the 1950s, resulting in higher car travel speeds, and expectations of the provision for speed (Buehler 2008). The profession of transport engineering has played a central role in this, working up detailed designs for speed and safety enhancement using their problem-solving approach to engineering roads (Himanen *et al.* 2005). These designs for road schemes tend to linger around in the mindset of transport engineers and planners, with land reserved in land use plans for their eventual construction (Bertolini 2003). Government policies for major transport scheme investment further support road schemes rather than investment in bus facilities by applying appraisal criteria that rank proposals on the basis of the travel time saved by car drivers. Travel time savings tend to be an illusion, many argue, since savings to one individual journey mean increases to other journeys. New road investment will also induce demand, which will eventually erode any initial travel time savings (Ney 2001; Cervero 2002). The Scottish Transport Appraisal Guidance (Transport Scotland 2008) includes the potential to increase government funds (e.g. taxes on the consumption of transport fuel) as a scheme appraisal criterion. Table 2.5 considers what some of the impacts of this road dominated focus in Scotland might be.

Table 2.5 The impacts of transport policy in Scotland

Climate change	*Transport accounts for 28 per cent of Scotland's CO_2 emissions*
Energy security and peak oil	Motorised transport is dependent on imported oil
Public health	Obesity prevalence is soaring in Scotland and it is now estimated that 64 per cent of men, 57 per cent of women and 32 per cent of children are either over-weight or obese. Obesity increases the risk of health problems such as diabetes, heart disease, stroke, cancers and osteoporosis. Active travel modes could have a significant impact in preventing and mediating many forms of chronic disease.
Communities and social inclusion	In 2007, 57 per cent of people living in the 15 per cent most deprived areas of Scotland had no access to a car for private use (compared to 25 per cent in the rest of Scotland). Over 930,000 older and disabled people now have concessionary bus passes. Air and ferry services to the Scottish Islands are subsidised. Communities are severed by transport infrastructure (roads, rail). Walking and cycling neighbourhoods enhance social interaction and trust.
Economic growth	External costs from congestion, accidents and pollution. Perception that integrated transport systems are integral to successful economies. Road tolls on bridges were removed in 2008.
Environment protection	New road infrastructure and urban sprawl have obliterated habitats. Greater storm-water problems from additional hard surfaces.

Source: Audit Scotland (2006); Scottish Government (2009b)

The connectivity of roads, the services for refuelling the car and passengers, the ease of parking at the destination all give car drivers a distinct advantage over public transit users:

> Free parking places and subsidised commuting are forms of redistribution of scarce resources and money between groups of commuters (defined in terms of travel mode used and distance travelled), with potentially unattractive effects on sustainability and equity.
>
> (Rietveld and Stough 2002: 9)

Given the substantial resource investment in road space for the car in most cities it has been difficult to implement transport policies that seek to secure significant increases in public transit patronage as a sustainable people mover. To obtain reductions in the environmental load from transport would require enhancements to the spatial integration and interoperability of public transport, combined with policies that make car use less attractive, such as reduced parking availability or substantial increases in parking costs in cities. Some cities have achieved high public transit patronage through limiting motorised access to their central areas. Amsterdam has achieved this by using their land-use, transport and fiscal policies to make the city a more liveable and healthy environment (see Chapter 7). The pathway to a sustainable transport system requires a multi-sectoral approach to addressing the issues raised in Table 2.5.

Public transit modes have lacked sufficient investment for many years. Although the larger urbanised areas have witnessed additional investment in public transport in recent years, which has increased patronage levels, demand and supply are still much lower in small and medium-sized cities and in the EU accession countries (ECMT/ OECD 2002). Partnerships between the public sector and privatised bus and rail operators have brought new investment into public transit in some countries but also created legal barriers to achieving modal integration. In the UK, for example, the fair trading restrictions placed on private transport operators make integrated timetables and ticketing a major problem, and prevent local government services from running in direct competition with bus operators. Commercial objectives also make it difficult to sustain under-used public services outside of the peak commuting times.

Governments have been shy of imposing speed restrictions or charges, and restricting access to residential areas for polluting vehicles (Rietveld and Stough 2002). Buehler's (2008) comparison of the USA and Germany shows how important taxation policy has been in the USA in making car use cheaper, easier and normal.

> In 2006, the combined cost of owning and operating a similar car was about 50 per cent higher in Germany than in the USA [and] operating costs per kilometre were 2.5 times higher in Germany.
>
> (Buehler 2008: 8)

Few countries have followed Germany's example of using the taxation system, land use and transport policies to reduce road space, to enhance safety, encourage active travel and improve local environments (Buehler 2008). As a result, Germany's CO_2 emissions from transport reduced by 1.5 per cent between 1990 and 2006 (European Commission 2009: 172). Carbon and distance-based taxes (see the Netherlands case study in Chapter 7) can be used to make travel by car more expensive and demand-management policies can slow down and restrict access to cars in certain parts of urban areas. The lack of a national policy framework for sustainable urban travel is frequently mentioned (ECMT 2001; Atkins 2003, 2007; Hull and Tricker 2006), which leads to sustainable transport policies (for example, bus and rail strategies) being pursued in isolation from other sector strategies. The range of perverse effects in this situation includes:

> non-complementary policies; direct incentives to travel more; improving system efficiency which creates demand to travel; contradictory outcomes; change without improvement; absence of evidence or negligible impact; non-acceptance or lack of uptake by users [...] Many decisions are taken within one particular sector without any serious attention being given on the impacts across sectors. In some cases, these decisions have major effects on the transport system, not just in the immediate term but also in the longer term.
>
> (Banister 2005a: 66)

FINANCIAL AND PRICING POLICIES

While the expansion of the road network and the upgrading of the strategic transport network have been expensive for the public purse and required high levels of materials intensity, land take, energy consumption and pollution (Whitelegg 1997), there have been productivity gains for the economy. According to Eddington (2006: 1) a five per cent saving in travel time for business travel is equated with £2.5 billion (€2.85 billion) of cost savings which is equivalent to 0.2 per cent of the UK GDP.

Transportation policy has conventionally assumed that the economic benefits of new infrastructure would automatically outweigh the negative impacts (Ney 2001). While technological developments have provided opportunities for faster and more flexible mobility and therefore economic benefits to businesses, market signals do not acknowledge the direct and indirect negative impacts this entails (Pratt 1996; Ney 2001; Rietveld and Stough 2002; European Environment Agency 2004). Economists warn that:

> without [price] signals there are inevitable problems of excess demand. People will just keep consuming oblivious of the implications for the resources that they deplete [....] just supplying something without pricing for its use leads to overuse.
>
> (Button 2005: 43)

Most road infrastructure is a 'public good' provided by the state, with the costs of use principally incurred by someone other than the user. The rapid expansion of road infrastructure and housing in the suburbs after the Second World War was made possible through income tax relief and other subsidies (O'Sullivan 1980). Underwritten by public subsidy, the demand for mobility increased and road infrastructure has become pervasive in rural and urban areas, in many cases, crowding out other modes. This distorts the transport market (Ney 2001; Rodrigue 2006) since road users (viz. passenger cars, freight vehicles and buses) do not directly pay for the provision and maintenance of road infrastructure, nor the public services that provide the safety management and emergency health care when needed. On the other hand, many privatised rail companies have to provide for all their capital costs including the use of railway tracks (Rodrigue 2006: 387). There are also weaknesses in the market 'pricing signals' which externalise the costs of travel, including the direct costs to the environment and to health (see Table 2.5). The relative costs of owning and using a car have reduced in many countries while fares for rail and bus services have increased since the early 1990s (Rietveld and Stough 2002).

INSTITUTIONAL ISSUES

Certain norms and values and routinised decision making practices are institutionalised in all societies (Giddens 2000). These provide the 'macro-structures' within which micro-processes and individual actions take place (Pratt 1996). Pratt (1996: 1361) draws attention to *'the tensions between micro-processes and macro-structures, between agents and structures [...] A key concept in structuration analyses is that of the institution as the active site of mediation between structures and agents.'*

The practices of the real estate market, the labour market and working practices, taxation policy, public sector funding and procurement practices, and professional cultures provide the context, or the macro-structures, within which individual mobility decisions are enacted (Scheiner and Kasper 2005). These help to explain mobility patterns through the 'space–time structures', modal investment, and other *'dynamic and permeable resources'* that they release (ibid.: 46). *'Neither lifestyles nor mobility can be separated from macro-structural frameworks"* (ibid.: 46).

Dramatic changes in the commissioning and the institutional regulation of the transport sector are cited as factors that help to account for the differences and similarities in travel behaviour, within and across countries (Hensher and Brewer 2001; Rietveld and Stough 2002). One of the most dramatic changes has been the privatisation of public sector monopolies and economic deregulation in the transport sector across Europe. The partial withdrawal by the state in service provision has necessitated new forms of economic regulation to ensure that prices do not escalate where there is a natural monopoly (railways, water, energy, etc.) and the promotion of competition in the selection of incumbents to ensure the best level (or minimum level) of services for the contract fee.

Privatisation has an effect on the price and quality of service to users (White 2002) and decreases the power and capacity of the public sector to plan the connectivity of transport infrastructure and the interconnection between public transport services and commercial and residential development. Privatisation has made it much more difficult to cross subsidise services where there is little market demand (Gifford 2005). Measuring the quality of service tendered by different competitors and preventing the creation of private monopoly situations through collusion and the exclusion of new entrants has been difficult to achieve in practice (O'Sullivan 1980; Evans 1990; Hensher and Brewer 2001; House of Commons 2006).

An inadequate national level coordination or regulatory framework is often reflected in inefficient or counterproductive institutional roles and procedures. This can take several different forms. Incomplete decentralisation of responsibility is noted in some Central and Eastern European countries where the power to decide on urban travel has been transferred to regional and local levels of government who have no control over sources of funding (ECMT 2001). This is also the case in the UK, where the fragmentation of the public sector at the local and regional levels, with the emergence of new non-elected bodies has blurred responsibilities and introduced competing priorities (Lowndes and Skelcher 1998; Lowndes 2001; Hull and Tricker 2006). This raises issues of accountability which can easily be exploited, and used as an excuse for failure. One unexpected consequence of lack of autonomy at the local level is that local government in the UK has become fairly dependent on car parking revenue (that they control) and is, therefore, unwilling to discourage on-street car parking in central areas. Because of the increasing propensity of the perverse effects of government policies, Rietveld and Stough (2005: 6) call for new rule structures to '*drive technological change towards sustainability outcomes.*'

2.4   EU TRANSPORT PRIORITIES

The EU has a transport competency and hence, as a higher tier of government, exerts some influence over the transport policies of member states through regulations, directives, funding and policy priorities. EU transport and energy policies have slowly moved from encouragement to increasing use of regulation.

The white paper on transport in 2001 recognised the balance the EU Council of Ministers would have to make between the increasing demand for mobility caused by economic growth and the enlargement of the EU, and:

•   worsening congestion in urban areas and the trans-European network;
•   poor quality services;

- safety on the roads being affected;
- damage to the environment including the emission of greenhouse gases and other pollutants; and
- the low level of accessibility to some regions and those in the periphery of the EU, especially in new member states (European Commission 2001a; Tsamboulas 2005).

Nevertheless, EU transport policy in 2001 focused on securing the efficient functioning and management of the trans-European network (TEN) of highway infrastructure, railway freight corridors and inland waterways, and on safeguarding the economic competitiveness of the European global region (European Commission 2006). The white paper anticipated that processes towards a stockless economy and the specialisation of production in different world regions would continue (Schade *et al.* 2007: 11) and that freight traffic would therefore increase in the Union by 38 per cent overall by 2020, with heavy goods traffic increasing by 50 per cent (European Commission 2001a; European Environment Agency 2007). Transnational rail networks were a specific priority, with the white paper calling for intermodality between modes and between freight and passenger transport, and interoperability to enhance system performance through the harmonisation of technical standards and the deployment of new communication technologies. Extending the transport infrastructure is the most common policy response in Europe to deliver enhanced competitiveness and social cohesion (Ney 2001; European Environment Agency 2004), despite the lack of evidence to support the link between regional economic growth and new transport investment (Banister and Berechman 2001).

While the short-term priority in the white paper was transport growth to support economic growth, the long-term (10–20 years) strategy aimed to internalise the external costs of transport on the environment initially through road user charges and special taxes (Jensen and Richardson 2004; Tsamboulas 2005). This was in line with the agreement struck at the Council of the European Union (2001) meeting in Gothenburg which placed breaking the link between economic growth and transport growth at the heart of the sustainable development strategy.

Shifting the modal balance of transport away from transport reliant on non-renewable sources of fuel (transport is 98 per cent dependent on oil, 70 per cent of which is imported) is at the core of the Organisation for Economic Co-operation and Development (OECD[1]) and the EU Council of Ministers' *Strategy for Integrating Environment and Sustainable Development into the Transport Policy*, which they discussed and supported in April 2001. As Figure 2.2 shows, human and ecosystem health and minimising the use of non-renewable resources are at the heart of these organisations' definitions of sustainable transport.

1   'An environmentally sustainable transport system is one that does not endanger public health or ecosystems and meets needs for access consistent with a) use of renewable resources at below their rates of regeneration, and b) use on non-renewable resources at below the rates of development of renewable substitutes.' (www.oecd.org/env/ccst/est).

2   'A sustainable transport system [is] defined as one that:

i)   Allows the basic access and development needs of individuals, companies and societies to be met safely and in a manner consistent with human and ecosystem health, and promotes equity within and between successive generations;

ii)   Is affordable, operates fairly and efficiently, offers choice of transport mode, and supports a competitive economy, as well as balanced regional development;

iii) Limits emissions and waste within the planet's ability to absorb them, uses renewable resources at or below their rates of generation, and, uses non-renewable resources at or below the rates of development of renewable substitutes while minimising the impact on the use of land and the generation of noise.' (Council of Ministers 2001)

Figure 2.2 Definitions of sustainable transport

The 2001 transport policy acknowledged that the successful management of demand for private transport use would require action at the national and regional government levels due to the powers of subsidiarity which lie with these governments (European Commission 2001a; Bertolini 2003; Jensen and Richardson 2004; Tsamboulas 2005). The white paper called for comprehensive strategies and collaboration between the transportation system and other policy areas to address the emissions from passenger cars. The policy sectors mentioned include economic policy, urban and land-use planning policy, social and education policy, urban transport policy, budgetary and fiscal policy, competition policy, and research policy.

In the mid-term review of the 2001 transport white paper the decoupling of transport growth from economic growth is replaced by an aspiration to disconnect mobility from its negative side effects (European Commission 2006; European Environment Agency 2007). More urgency is given to tackling the global greenhouse gas emissions from road froight, air transport and maritime transport which continue to grow. EU Directives have limited certain pollutants (CO, NOx, hydrocarbons, PM) through regular revisions of the emission standards for new vehicles. Despite the progress made through these European standards and the Directive on biofuels (2003/30/EC) the 21 per cent increase in the numbers of cars sold between 1995 and 2004 more than offsets any emissions reductions due to increased CO_2 efficiency (Bart 2009). Air quality in cities is still a major problem for human health and fails to meet the limit values set by European regulation (European Environment Agency 2007: 4). Some of the more muted statements in the 2001 white paper are emphasised more strongly in the mid-term review. More attention is given to reducing the air pollution related problems, noise pollution and the intrusion on the landscape from motorised transport. National and regional governments in the EU are exhorted to include environmentally friendly modes of travel and demand management policies in their transport strategies.

The mid-term review aims to secure a high level of mobility for businesses and people, to expand job opportunities and to support economic growth in a more energy efficient way. Sixteen areas of action are proposed and 14 of these relate to enhancing supply-side efficiency. The review proposes the development of an infrastructure charging methodology based on the internalisation of external costs. Yet research suggests that even when users pay the full external costs this would only reduce the growth in transport demand by 6 per cent by 2025 (Eddington 2006: 31). Mention is made of the potential of biofuels, but there is no vision of how to develop a low energy transport system or an understanding of the transition time involved in developing the fuelling infrastructure within the existing built environment.

In 2008 and 2009 the EU introduced a common framework for increasing the CO_2 efficiency of freight transport and new passenger cars. The green transport package of July 2008 proposes charging freight operators for the environmental costs of road haulage activities (European Commission 2008). This was followed by the climate-energy package of April 2009 which includes two binding pieces of transport legislation on member states (Council of the European Union 2009). First, they are required to achieve a 10 per cent share of energy from renewable sources in their transport energy consumption by 2020. Second, it is now mandatory, rather than a voluntary action, to reduce CO_2 emissions from new passenger cars to 120 grams CO_2/km by 2015 through a series of phased targets.

The EU's most recent climate-energy package is designed to achieve a 20 per cent reduction of global greenhouse gas emissions by 2020. Trends in the production of pollutants are a key benchmark to measure transport's impact on local health and global climate change but few countries have set carbon reduction targets specifically for the transport sector, despite the growing emissions from passenger transport, aviation and shipping. Since the Stern Review's (2006) recommendation that governments should act urgently to stabilise CO_2 concentration levels at 550 ppm CO_2 e, more recent climate change research suggests these concentration levels need to be lower (i.e. 350 ppm) and that the tipping point may happen in 2020 rather than 2050. Commentators suggest that it will be necessary to make drastic reductions in global greenhouse gas emissions in all sectors including transport (Köhler 2007; Council of the European Union 2009).

Action to achieve more sustainable urban environments will require a much broader agenda than climate change mitigation and vehicle efficiency. The European Commission has been active in supporting demonstration projects on low energy urban transport solutions through the CIVITAS Initiative and research on how to measure progress towards sustainability. There has, however, been relatively little attention expended on the cumulative effects of transport and land use policies at the city level (Hull 2010). Arguably, transport investment has an impact on pollutants, the consumption of natural resources, health and safety, and the distribution of social and economic benefits. All of these need to be measured to understand the synergies between different intervention measures. Table 2.6 suggests a set of performance measures for the '*central attributes*' of a more sustainable transport system taken from the EC's SUMMA (2003) project , European Environment Agency (2005) and Kennedy *et al.* (2005: 394).

Table 2.6 Benchmarks for a sustainable transport system

Criteria	Indicators
Accessibility	Access to public transport Access to basic services Accessibility of origins and destinations
Health and safety	Accident-related fatalities and serious injuries Exposure to transport noise Exposure to air pollution Walking and cycling as transport means for short distances
Cost effectiveness	Energy efficiency Generation of non-recycled waste Public subsidies
Impacts on competitiveness and generation of wealth	Gross value added External transport costs Benefits of transport
Consumption of natural capital	Land take Consumption of solid raw materials Damage to habitats and species
Production of pollutants (local and global)	Emissions of greenhouse gases Emission of air pollutants Runoff pollution from transport infrastructure Discharge of oil and waste at sea

Source: Adapted from SUMMA (2003), European Environment Agency (2005) and Kennedy *et al.* (2005).

The indicators in Table 2.6 can be used to assess the progress towards transport sustainability at national and city-region levels but will be dependent on improvements to the quantity and the robustness of data collected. Many EU member states have incomplete datasets describing the performance and the impacts of their transport infrastructure (Himanen *et al.* 2005). The sample sizes in national quantitative surveys will need to be increased with more consistency in measure definition to enable the long-term trends to be analysed. Quantitative data availability is a concern in project evaluation, which aims to evaluate the direct and indirect impacts of the project on CO_2 emissions, other pollutants and costs. At the city-region level qualitative data on the process of decision making towards sustainable futures by partnerships of stakeholders, as well as by individuals in households, should be monitored to under-stand both the raised awareness of climate change and the behavioural response to the implementation of economic instruments. This people-centred data collection requires a range of research techniques including '*travel diaries, longitudinal data sets, or surveys of individual workers based on household structure, and especially their preference of jobs or housing location choice*' (Sultana 2006: 394).

2.5 THE CO-EVOLUTION OF TRANSPORT AND LAND USE

This section moves on to an examination of the body of knowledge on how urban transport and land use characteristics have evolved in different geographical and historical contexts. Chapter 7 analyses this interaction through several detailed case studies from European states and their main cities. This section aims to identify some of the main trends and to summarise academic research that has attempted to tease out the interactions between transport and land use.

The transportation system has evolved in relation to human endeavour and demand for movement between widening geographical points across regions of the world. Supply-side developments since the 1970s have allowed extensive personal mobility with convenient travel to virtually all global destinations. Travel is seen as necessary for economic growth and a reward for economic success. Connectivity to global markets and to global investors is prioritised in national government poli-cies with intra-national growth areas linked into global communication corridors. The economic regime has driven infrastructure investment in each nation through predic-tions of the growth requirements and forced out the funding to provide the perceived transport system advantages. This process has transformed our lifestyles through regional and global connectivity but also changed many urban environments so that they cater essentially for motorised traffic. Although we assume these develop-ments have changed the lives and provided opportunities for most of the population (Eddington 2006), arguably this hyper-mobility has only touched significantly the lives of little more than half the population (Holmans 1996; Ruston 2002).

Massive public funds have been invested in transportation such that it is seen as an '*effective guidance system tool*' for market growth forecasts (Chapin and Kaiser 1979: 621). The transportation system is perceived to '*shape the comparative advantage of different regions and their attraction for industry. This in turn influences the geography of employment and the market for housing and services.*' (O'Sullivan 1980: 90). Shifting market priorities open up new development areas and products, leaving former sites of market activity to await regeneration or redevelopment when funds become available. This is most notably witnessed in the freight industry: '*Shifting freight transport advantages have been an important historical factor in the growth and decline of cities and can still be a critical factor in determining an urban area's future.*' (Chapin and Kaiser 1979: 621).

At the city scale, transportation investment alters the accessibility of different parts of the city-region and firms locate or (re)locate to take advantage of the benefits released (Holl 2006). This is borne out by the experience of Amsterdam (in Chapter 7) where transportation investment has led to structural changes in land use patterns in terms of the (re)development potential and created a new hierarchy of transport corridors.

The preoccupations of the different disciplines involved in planning city-regions have had considerable influence on how we conceptualise the interlinkages between transport and land use. The socialisation of transport engineers, transport planners, transport economists, architects and land use planners in their academic and research training emphasises different cultural norms and values. For example, the gaze of transport engineers and transport planners over the last century has been focused on the flows between the nodes (viz. links, junctions and terminals) in the network, the attraction or pull of the activity centres, and the safety, travel time and cost of travel. Their effort has been concentrated on the functioning of the transport system, specifically the travel-to-work flows across city-regions and on making efficient use of the existing transport network (Chapin and Kaiser 1979; O'Sullivan 1980; Knoflacher 2006; Sultana 2006). Because of the long-term effects of transport infrastructure on the accessibility of geographic locations (and of social groups), transport economists and geographers have seen the issue as a spatial economic problem of distance decay – of how to overcome the friction of distance between central places and the opportunity cost of the resources involved (O'Sullivan 1980: 23). In order to understand the costs and benefits, and the use, of the transport system this cluster of professionals undertake detailed research using the concepts from network theory, flow theory and location theory (O'Sullivan 1980; Jensen and Richarson 2004).

The interdependencies between the built environment and transport are not at issue in the academic literature, although the direction of influence is still being debated. Strategic or regional land use planners try to predict how the changes in transport investment and land use characteristics will interact with each other, and what the implications will be for urban transport policy. Two key interlinkages are noted in the transport planning literature. The existing transportation infrastructure is thought to have a pervasive effect on the land development pattern, including the spatial concentration and segregation of activities. The type and the intensity of development at locations in the city-region, and the design of access to these activity centres (including parking), significantly affects travel demand and the performance of the transport system (Chapin and Kaiser 1979; O'Sullivan 1980; Priemus *et al*. 2001; Himanen *et al*. 2005; Holl 2006; Sultana 2006; Banister and Hickman 2007; NICHES 2007).

However, these system-wide effects of investment in the transportation infra-structure and the feedback effects on the settlement pattern and travel behaviour are not taken into account by transport planners and engineers (Knoflacher 2006). It has been essentially left to the land use planning authorities at the local level in Europe to intervene in the development of urban transport infrastructure and spatial opportunities in two ways. First, they have sought to substitute proximity of activ-ity for travel through encouraging higher density development and the clustering of activities at defined centres and sub-centres. Second, they have attempted to coordinate, and thereby influence, the development of activities at specific locations according to their accessibility needs and the provision of public transport.

Substantial research effort in the 1990s was spent on understanding the link between transportation and land use both in Europe and North America following the provocative research by Newman and Kenworthy (1989, 1999). Much of this research found only a weak relationship between urban structure and travel behaviour. These studies were mainly quantitative regression analyses using very simplified assumptions – an independent variable and two dependent variables – and measures of travel aggregated to the city level. Many studies also excluded meaningful variables such as the availability of other modes of travel, accessibility to services and pedestrian friendly streets. There were some very detailed studies which compared urban neighbourhoods in terms of density and street layout without factoring in the distance from the neighbourhood to the centre of the urban area (Naess 2006b). Table 2.7 is based on the analysis by Hickman and Banister (2005) of the early research findings and includes some more recent, and more comprehensive, findings.

Table 2.7 Understanding the relationship between urban structure and travel behaviour

---

Resident population size: dispute as to whether population size impacts on modal choice, travel distance and energy consumption

---

- No correlation between urban population size and modal choice in the USA (Gordon *et al.* 1989).

- The largest settlements (> 250,000 population) display lower travel distances and less travel by car (ECOTEC 1993).

- The most energy efficient settlement in terms of transport is one with a resident population of 25–100,000 or > 250,000 (Williams 1998).

Resident population density: dispute as to whether increasing density impacts on modal choice, travel distance and energy consumption. Various views as to optimum urban form in reducing car travel; ranging from compact cities to 'decentralised concentration' and even low density suburban spread.

- Increasing densities reduces energy consumption by transport (Newman and Kenworthy 1989).

- There is no clear relationship between the proportion of car trips for work journeys and population density in the USA (Gordon *et al.* 1989).

- As densities increase, modal split moves towards greater use of rail and bus (Wood *et al.* 1994).

- As densities increase, people are more likely to walk than drive to their local shopping centre in the USA (Boarnet *et al.* 2008).

- Compact cities may not necessarily be the answer to reducing energy consumption, due to effects of congestion; also decentralisation may reduce trip length (Breheny and Rockwood 1993; Gordon and Richardson 1995).

- Travel distances for commuting and shopping by car are much lower in compact urban structures than in lower density or dispersed urban areas (Jenks *et al.* 1996; Schwanen *et al.* 2004).

- Density is the most important physical variable in determining transport energy consumption (Banister 1997).

- Higher densities may provide a necessary, but not sufficient condition for less travel (Owens 1998; Curtis and Headicar 1994).

- As people move from big dense cities to small, less dense, towns they travel more by car, but the distances may be shorter (*Hall in Banister* 1998).

- Higher densities and high income populations correspond to higher energy use for leisure travel by plane (Holden and Norland 2005).

- In the EU-25 the relationship between the growth of artificial areas (urban sprawl) and the growth in transport CO_2 emissions is very strong, and much stronger than population growth and per capita GDP growth (Bart 2009).

Continued

Table 2.7 *Continued*

Provision and mix of services: *dispute as to whether local provision of services and facilities, and a jobs–housing balance, impacts on modal choice, travel distance and energy consumption.*

- A ratio of jobs to housing units (0.75–1.5) has a relatively small influence on commuting time (Giuliano and Small 1993).
- Local provision does not determine modal choice, personal and household characteristics are the determinants (Farthing *et al.* 1997).
- Local provision of facilities in new residential developments reduces average trip distances, but does not significantly affect the proportion of journeys by foot (Farthing *et al.* 1997).
- Land use mix is associated with reduced trip lengths (Frank and Pivo 1995), lower level of per capita auto ownership, increased transit usage for the journey to work (Cervero 1988).
- Diversity of services and facilities in close proximity reduces distance travelled, alters modal split and people are prepared to travel further for higher order service and facilities (Banister 1996).
- There is an inverse relationship between the proportion of car trips for shopping and business establishment density in the USA (Boarnet *et al.* 2008).

Location: *dispute as to impact of location – in terms of distance from urban centre, strategic transport network and influence on green belt – on modal choice, travel distance and energy consumption.*

- Location of new housing development outside existing urban areas, or close to strategic transport network, or as free-standing development increases travel and influences mode split (Calthorpe 1993; Curtis and Headicar 1995).
- Location is an important dimension of energy consumption and car dependency (Banister 1997).
- Distance from the city centre is correlated with higher energy consumption for everyday travel (Naess 1997).
- Travel distance on weekdays is longer the further away the respondents live from downtown, the closest second order urban centre, and the closest urban rail station (Naess 2006a; 2006b).
- Development close to existing urban areas reduces self-containment and access for non-car owners (Headicar 1997).
- The proportion of rail journeys decreases with increasing distance from the railway station (Cervero 1994; Hickman 2005).

Continued

Table 2.7 *Continued*

Socio-economic: *dispute as to impact of personal and household characteristics on modal choice, travel distance and energy consumption. Also as to whether personal and household characteristics are more important determinants of travel than land use characteristics.*

- Trip frequency increases with household size, income and car ownership (Hanson 1982).
- Travel distance, proportion of car journeys and transport energy consumption increase with car ownership (Naess 1993; Naess and Sandberg 1996).
- Socio-economic and attitudinal characteristics are more important determinants of travel than urban form (Stead *et al.* 2000).
- Attitude factors are at least more strongly, and perhaps more directly, associated with travel than land use characteristics (Kitamura *et al.* 1997).
- Neighbourhoods with higher deprivation scores in urban areas are associated with lower average travel-to-work distances (Lloyd and Shuttleworth 2005).
- Commuting distances tend to increase if the respondent is male, has a high income, has moved recently to the present dwelling, has car-oriented transport attitudes, is middle aged and/or has a long technical or economic education (Naess 2006a).
- Neighbourhood design seems to affect the degree to which people drive alone to work and the degree to which they walk or cycle (Cervero and Gorham 1995).
- People living in neighbourhoods with smaller blocks and/or a higher percentage of four-way intersections take fewer daily driving trips (Boarnet *et al.* 2008).

Source: Adapted from Table 6.1 Banister (2005: 104–106)

The studies in Table 2.7 present a snapshot of the broad relationships between the configuration of infrastructure and spatial opportunities, and the propensity and type of travel in different geographical and historical contexts. They attempt to throw light on the interdependency of transport and land use but tend to ignore:

1 The relationships between local travel and activity choices and the wider context
2 The location decisions made by households at different stages of their life-cycle.

The spatial configuration of transport infrastructure and activities across a city-region and connectivity to the spatial opportunities are important contextual factors which influence household choices. Proximity to major road and rail networks provide opportunities to increase travel speeds and extend the commuting distance that can be covered in a fixed time budget. In most cities, inter-urban and intra-urban commuting journeys have become increasingly more complex with the growth of dual-income families, suburbanisation of the population and employment centres. If we wish to understand the co-evolution of transport and land use in different geographical and historical contexts then we need to delve deeper into institutional contexts and decision making processes.

2.6 TRANSPORT SUPPLY AND DEMAND IN THE CONTEXT OF WIDER ECONOMIC, SOCIAL AND ENVIRONMENTAL OBJECTIVES

The system effects of local decisions on transport and land use intervention have implications for both the national efforts to mitigate climate change and the local options to achieve a sustainable urban transport system. Understanding the multi-scalar effects of local choices is addressed more fully in Chapter 4. This chapter concludes by tracing out some of the broad outcomes of the evolution of trans-national transport priorities.

The recent debates on climate change and global greenhouse gas emissions have raised two policy issues for the transport sector. The first concern is the growing pollution levels from the transport sector in most regions of the world. Across Europe only Germany, Bulgaria, Lithuania and Estonia have managed to control and substantially reduce the growth in emissions from the transport sector (Table 1.1). These member states have achieved this by strong fiscal policies on energy efficiency and alternative fuels for road and rail travel, and through control over the location of new development. EU policies have already delivered improved energy efficiency in new cars which is being extended to buses, light vans and heavy lorries. Encouraged by the EC and national governments, car manufacturers have developed a number of hybrid models and electric cars. But the uptake and penetration of alternative fuels and new transport technologies in society depend on the infrastructure support provided by government for clean energy technologies (viz. electric, bio-fuel and hydrogen) to influence public choice for these initially more expensive modes. Hybrid electric vehicles are already on the market, and Toyota has developed an electric vehicle, but few countries are integrating the new technology for the battery charging of electric vehicles into the fabric of the built environment. Chapter 7 examines the policy lessons that can be learnt from the change to low energy development pathways in Sweden and Germany by analysing the decision processes that characterise what appears to be successful strategies for change management in these countries.

The EU and the US government both plan to implement a cap and trade carbon system to control the emissions from transport in their administrative domain. The environmental performance of the transport system is being captured solely through energy use and emission indicators at the current time (Geurs and van Wee 2006). This focus is likely to continue with the international policy emphasis on mitigating climate change. Three transport sectors are increasing the distances travelled: leisure travel by car; freight transport by road, and air transport. Air transport and freight transport, with the notable exception of Sweden, have been subject to less regulation than car travel. Regulations in both these sectors have concerned the harmonisation of practices and standards to remove market barriers to expanding capacity and connectivity to external markets (Holl 2006). Although the public has much greater knowledge of environmental issues and people wish to protect their quality of life, this does not currently appear to extend to reducing their personal travel demands.

The second issue is the role that development planning and management can have in reducing urban sprawl and enhancing the quality of local neighbourhoods. Most city-regions in Europe and beyond have been growing at lower densities and experiencing urban sprawl over the last 20 years, leading to a greater dependency on the car. Bart's (2009) research findings bring further potency to Newman and Kenworthy's findings that increasing fuel consumption is correlated with urban sprawl and density. The research on transport and urban form summarised in Table 2.7 has also demonstrated that density and settlement size interact with travel behaviour and thus energy use. For instance, we know that certain land use characteristics:

> are favourable for reducing energy use per capita: high population density for the city as a whole; high density within each residential area; centralised settlement within cities and towns (i.e. higher density in the inner part than on the fringe); centralised workplace location; low parking capacity at workplaces; decentralised concentration at the regional level; and a high population for each city
>
> (Holden and Norland 2005: 2149).

These findings should provide some renewed parameters for urban planning which promote higher densities, mixed uses, quality designed neighbourhoods with open space and active travel facilities, and the extension of public transit systems (Bertolini 2003: Kennedy et al. 2005). Bart (2009) argues for a strong policy response from the development planning system to implement urban growth boundaries or green belts to contain urban sprawl and offer a realistic choice of using public transit to access work, leisure, shopping and education activities without reliance on the passenger car.

The discussion in this chapter has relied on the interpretation of quantitative data aggregated to the national level to explain current patterns of travel behaviour. The statistics that might help our understanding of the travel needs of different groups in society and how demographic and lifestyle changes in the future will affect travel choice are hard to find.

This section, therefore, concludes by summarising in Table 2.8 some of the key social issues that have been discussed in this chapter and which national governments across Europe will need to address in the future. Demographic and economic change can provide opportunities and constraints on government decision making and an early understanding and incorporation into policies will help to prepare for future uncertainty and complexity (Pratt 1996).

While there is growing awareness in the population of environmental issues and understanding of climate change (Haanpää 2008, National Centre for Social Research 2008; Scottish Government 2009a) there is no evidence that growing awareness translates into travel behaviour change. Equally uncertain is how open or resistant to new technologies (viz. telematics/intelligent transport systems) and work practices individuals in the future will be. Or even what impact on travel behaviour and residential locations the uptake of new technologies may have in the future. The EU project TELDET concluded that one fifth of the European labour force would have the opportunity to telework in the future (Schade *et al.* 2007: 8). While it is thought that teleworking will ease the morning and evening rush hour congestion, it may generate new and extended demands for leisure experiences with family and friends (Banister and Hickman 2007). Certain lifestyle groups have specific forms of mobility profiles. For example, if more people have the opportunity to work from home, accessibility to their 'workplaces' may not be such an issue, leading to opportunities for more rural or isolated living. Holden and Norland (2005) found that single households and higher income households who choose to live in central high density areas in Oslo compensated by travelling long distances for leisure purposes.

There have been critical voices from environmentalists that strategic national and regional transport planning has been too focused on economic priorities that tend to support 'hyper-mobility'. Not only has this led to spatial fragmentation, the dispersal of activities, and the growth of energy intensity, it has also led to the decline of community in our cities according to Whitelegg (1997: 13):

> Thirty years of transforming a society and a space economy to high levels of mobility and energy intensity have failed to notice the decline of community, the loss of people from the streets, and the increasing isolation of children, the elderly and women as the built environment fails them and through them fails the idea of community itself
>
> (Whitelegg 1997: 13).

The argument put forward by Pratt (1996) and Whitelegg (1997) is that the political preoccupation with 'hyper-mobility' and 'space–time compression' has not benefited all equally but rather these perceived benefits have been amassed by some at the expense of others. At the global level, the damage caused by the energy and raw materials consumed and the pollution emitted is principally felt by the poorest nations of the world most vulnerable to the hazards of climate change (sea level rise, fluvial flooding, drought, hurricanes, etc). At the local level, a culture of high distance mobility and high levels of consumption reduces the time available to engage in neighbourhood or community issues about the intrusion of traffic, the priorities for local schooling, healthcare and the environment (Whitelegg 1997: 60).

This raises the question of how individual choices can be moderated to the common good so that there is increased acceptance that we all have a collective responsibility for the impact of our own travel choice decisions (Banister 2005a). We can conclude this chapter with the finding that significant action is now being taken to improve the CO_2 energy efficiency of transport but that further attention should be given to understanding the constraints that configure the choices individuals and households make so that transport and land use planners in the future can enrich their decision making with the knowledge of these affects on transport behaviour.

Table 2.8 Social drivers of change

Drivers of change	Social issues
Demographic and life cycle change	Stagnation of population and an ageing society in most European countries. Changes to child-rearing patterns. Migration of younger population from the EU Accession and other countries to founding member states.
Economic change	Economic growth at lower growth rates & more flexible work models and work times. Ongoing process of European integration and globalisation. Rising global inequalities raising security and safety concerns. Increasing energy prices. Increased importance of e-commerce.
Lifestyle change	Growth of car ownership in EU Accession and BRIC countries. Increasing demand for more flexible and dispersed travel patterns in city-regions. Growth of exotic tourism locations. Hyper-mobility. Increased uptake of ICT and teleworking.
Spatial change	Continued suburbanisation process and growth of agglomerations. Gentrification of central city locations following infrastructure and public realm improvements impeding social inclusion of low income groups.
Social awareness	Increasing awareness of environmental issues such as climate change, resource consumption and noise pollution.
Social acceptability	Issues concerning the acceptability of i) alternative fuels and new technologies; ii) demand management to reduce penetration of car in urban areas; iii) carbon based taxes.

Sources: Urry (2000); Scheiner (2006) ; Schade *et al.* (2007); NICHES (2007)

CHAPTER 3

THE CHALLENGE OF PUTTING THE ENVIRONMENT INTO TRANSPORT POLICY

3.1 INTRODUCTION

Chapter 2 brought together the knowledge on travel patterns across Europe and sought to understand the reasons for increased reliance on car travel, including how urban structure is thought to influence travel behaviour. The chapter ended with a list of the socio-economic factors that will shape the willingness of economic and civil actors to embrace behaviour change in the future. This chapter focuses on government actors and specifically the concepts and tools used by civil servants who, through their decisions and advice, influence the ease of movement around city-regions. The focus is on how transport infrastructure at the local level can enhance individual accessibility and quality of life. Chapter 4, which follows, takes a much broader perspective on the tools available to formal systems of government to initiate innovative practices of resource minimisation in people's daily lives.

The concept of mobility has been highlighted in the earlier chapters of this book as a central co-ordinating device for the discipline of transport planning across the world. Catering for the growth in car use has been the main objective of transport planners and engineers over the last 50 years. With hindsight this was dubbed the 'predict and provide' approach to road investment, and had a singular focus on catering for the predicted travel demand based on projections of traffic flows and car ownership (Goodwin 1996; Vigar 2000). These highly skilled engineers have also expended considerable effort on designing the infrastructure (viz. roads, railways and aircraft) to ensure better safety levels.

Since the 1980s concern for the degradation of the environment (viz. soil, air, water, fauna and flora) has led to the development of various tools of project and strategy/plan appraisal and their application made a legal requirement for EU member states. Major transport schemes since 1988 have required an environmental impact assessment (EIA) and transport strategies and plans have been subject to a strategic environmental assessment (SEA) since July 2004. Major transport and development proposals are now formally assessed to examine the environmental impacts they may have, including the predicted impacts on the transport system with measures identified to ameliorate negative impacts. Since 2004, the cumulative impact on the stock of environmental resources of development proposals in agreed, forward-looking, strategies or plans should be assessed. Environmental protection and nature conservation are, therefore, now accepted objectives for transport planners.

If there were any doubts concerning the importance of conserving natural resources and the negative effects of transport on climate change these should have been dispelled by the Stern Review reporting in 2006 and highlighting the exorbitant economic costs of failing to change behaviour and decision-making criteria. The examination of global greenhouse gas emission data in Chapter 1 found a steady increase in global emissions from transport in nearly all EU-27 member states since 1990 (See Table 1.1). Few member states have taken radical action to reverse these trends. This chapter, therefore, poses the question: Why has it taken so long for politicians and transport planners to acknowledge, and address, the cumulative negative environmental effects of transport use? Several commentators, including Ney (2001: 145), suggest that transport planners are in a *state of confusion*' concerning the centrality of transport to the debates on the long-term health and integrity of the planet. The focus is, therefore, on the concepts embedded in the tools used by transport planners to measure the 'ease of reaching' spatial opportunities. How do the tools in use help, or obscure, knowledge of the way individuals use the transport infrastructure available to them? How has research from the wider social sciences about how individuals choose travel options been incorporated into transport models?

This chapter essentially focuses on institutional mindsets and taken-for-granted assumptions of relevance to transport planning. The concepts of 'mobility', 'accessibility', and 'exergy' are reviewed and contrasted. The first two concepts are 'movement' and 'movement between places' concepts, while the principles of 'exergy' question the need to consume resources, to make that journey. The rationale for this chapter is to assess the potential for concepts and decision support tools to inform decision-takers on several societal concerns simultaneously and, therefore, have the potential to prioritise the objectives of reducing CO_2 emissions from transport, improving health, reducing accidents, and enhancing the quality of life in urban areas in synergistic ways.

This chapter has several objectives:

1   To understand the normative underpinnings of key concepts in transport planning and how these are being adapted to respond to the concerns of climate change and the quality of life in urban areas
2   To examine how research on individual travel behaviour has been incorporated into models of accessibility and transport policies more generally
3   To understand how ecological systems thinking can be incorporated into transport decision making to enhance the spatial integration of facilities and infrastructure
4   To examine the potential of spatial or territorial planning to achieve more sustainable transport futures.

3.2 DEFINING SUSTAINABLE ACCESSIBILITY: ACCESSIBILITY AND CONNECTIVITY

Accessibility and mobility are key concepts in transport planning and have generally been seen as desired characteristics of physical locations and households respectively (Weber 2006: 400). These concepts, particularly mobility, have influenced the modelling of the transportation system through a focus on the 'impedance' or restrictions on the mobility of households (White 2002). This section first examines how these concepts have been defined and applied in planning for transport. Then we counterpose the concepts of mobility and accessibility with the concept of exergy, an approach which aims to minimise the consumption of resources in order to conserve the Earth's vitality and diversity.

CONCEPT OF MOBILITY

Jones (1981: 1) defines mobility as '*the ability of an individual, or type of person, to move about.*' Simply measured, mobility has two components – one is determined by the availability and density of the transport system to that individual, household or firm in their current location; the other by the characteristics of the individual, for example do they have a car available or are they able to use public transport? The recent growth of cheap airline travel has also provided a global dimension to mobility through granting individuals and organisations access to a much wider spatial spread of activities and resources.

In theory, the relationship between the characteristics of the transport network and spatial opportunities can be modelled to show the most convenient routes through the network between two points. The barriers to movement can be identified and the opportunities for availing of public transport to undertake potential trips. Land use and transport integrated (LUTI) models use 'zone to zone', or 'point to point' measurements of accessibility (Stanilov 2003). More sophisticated models can incorporate travel impedance such as dense traffic, road works, bus priority measures, speed humps, speed cameras, etc. LUTI models tend to be insensitive to this level of detail and the trip chaining of journeys (Mitchell 2005; Shepherd *et al.* 2006). LUTI models generally have four stages, beginning with trip generation by origins, trip distribution to destinations, mode choice and route assignment. The models have assumed that trips between an origin–destination pair are simply a function of the cost of travel between that pair only, and computed on the basis of a monetary value for the time spent in transportation and the waiting period (Shepherd *et al.* 2006). The value of time is conferred by the type of trip (viz. work/other). Direct user costs, such as parking charges, are treated as part of the generalised cost assessment. A criticism of the application of these models is that they tend to focus on time savings for middle class, white, male commuters, and that they crudely segment households by car availability (Weber 2006).

Table 3.1 Objectives and solutions for sustainable urban mobility

OBJECTIVES

Free-flowing towns and cities	Greener towns and cities	Smarter urban transport	Accessible urban transport	Safe and secure urban transport

PROBLEMS

Free-flowing towns and cities	Greener towns and cities	Smarter urban transport	Accessible urban transport	Safe and secure urban transport
Increasing traffic in urban areas leads to permanent congestion.	Domination of oil as a transport fuel, which generates CO_2 and air pollutant emissions.	Cities will face a permanent increase of freight and passenger transport fluxes because of lack of space and environmental constraints.	Citizens expect affordable and flexible mobility solutions.	Pedestrians and cyclists are vulnerable to accidents in urban areas and there is perceived low personal security of passengers.

SOLUTIONS

Free-flowing towns and cities	Greener towns and cities	Smarter urban transport	Accessible urban transport	Safe and secure urban transport
• Good connections between modes • Good parking facilities outside city centres • Urban charging schemes • Better traffic management and information • Car pooling and car sharing • Efficient freight transport.	• The development of new and clean technologies (energy efficiency, alternative fuels) supported by green procurement. • Traffic restrictions and green zones (pedestrianisation, restricted access zones, speed limits, urban charging, etc).	• Intelligent transport systems (ITS) and urban traffic management to control urban mobility, including freight distribution. • Smart charging systems, better traveller information and the standardisation of interfaces and interoperability of ITS applications in towns and cities.	• Innovative solutions for high quality collective transport. • Intermodal terminals for collective transport, and good links between suburban and urban transport networks. • An appropriate EU legal framework for public transport is essential.	• Behaviour change/strict enforcement of traffic rules.

Source: Compiled from Directorate General for Energy and Environment (2007)

These models are useful for quantifying the cost to the economy through predicting the time delays experienced as a result of the 'bunching' or congestion of traffic in the morning and evening commuting peak periods. For instance, the Scottish Government calculated in 2003 that the annual cost of congestion on the ex-urban strategic roads in Scotland was £71 million (€83 million) (Scottish Executive 2005). Eight of the 44 routes monitored in 2003 experienced 'serious' or 'severe congestion' for more than one hour per day.

Congestion within urban areas is an issue the EU has raised in a green paper on mobility (Directorate General for Energy and Transport 2007). This consultation paper states that the policy objective is a '*fluid, properly functioning transport system* [which] *allows people and goods to arrive on time*' (ibid.: 2). Five key challenges (*problems*) to sustainable urban mobility are identified that urban administrations are asked to address so that cities can provide 'seamless mobility services' and continue to function as successful engines of the European economy (NICHES 2007). Table 3.1 summarises the challenges and the range of solutions identified in the green paper.

Speed is, therefore, perceived by decision makers as a desired characteristic of the transport network, both between and within urban areas, and is embedded in our social consciousness through the media promotion of new car models and air travel. These aspirations cannot be divorced from the downsides of 'hyper-mobility', which besides global greenhouse gas emissions, include disproportionate distributional impact on children, young people and the elderly (Whitelegg 1997; Grayling *et al.* 2002; Barnardos *et al.* 2004; Schweitzer and Valenzuela 2004) which will be examined later on in this chapter.

CONCEPT OF ACCESSIBILITY

Accessibility can be simply defined as the ease with which people can access services at different locations. As a perceived attribute of a physical location it can be quantitatively measured using topological, cumulative opportunity, population potential, or space–time measures of accessibility, separately or in combination (composite) (Handy and Niemeier 1997; Halden *et al.* 2000; Weber 2006). These measures essentially compute the interconnectivity of locations and services, which people are assumed to need, using the available transport system. In its simplest form (topological accessibility), accessibility is computed as a 'point to point' measurement from home to work or other spatial opportunities. Population potential accessibility is a measure of the population characteristics in a defined radius from a given location served by spatial opportunities. For example, retail planners calculate the characteristics of the catchment area population when assessing locations for new superstores. Cumulative opportunity measures sum all the available spatial opportunities (jobs, facilities) within a defined zone and weight them by a measure of deterrence (average commute time) to show how easily they can be reached by households. Space–time accessibility focuses on individuals and their activities across space and time, acknowledging the spatial temporal constraints faced by individuals accessing facilities and services, and taking into account access by transport modes, opening times, and physical barriers (Zandvliet and Dijst 2006).

Geographical information system (GIS) based models are increasingly being used to compute the ease with which an individual can undertake an activity at a specified location by all transport modes at specific times of the day (Bhat *et al.* 2000). Several factors impact on physical accessibility such as travel time, cost of travel, location of facilities and services, transport mode and timing of service delivery. GIS can be used in service planning to identify areas and social groups with low accessibility to welfare and commercial services (Bhat *et al.* 2000). Specific accessibility thresholds are increasingly being used by health and social services, transport, spatial planning, social inclusion and economic development organisations to benchmark and compare the accessibility of their services to social groups in different parts of their administrative area (see Table 3.2). Accessibility, therefore, has the potential to be an integrative mechanism. For example, the EU's conceptualisation of accessibility has both economic and political inclusiveness dimensions. Measures of accessibility have been used to identify the relationship between the peripheral locations in Europe and the core cities of London, Paris, Brussels and Bonn. The Committee for Spatial Development (1999: 69) gives improvements in accessibility a high priority as a policy target: '*Good accessibility of European regions improves not only their competitive position but also the competitiveness of Europe as a whole*'.

There are also social dimensions to accessibility as hinted at in the following quote:

It is possible, and even desirable, to reduce mobility (which means increasing accessibility), to have stronger local economies (which means producing more things locally and eliminating damaging long-distance travel), and having healthier children (which means reduced healthcare bills)

(Whitelegg 1997: 7).

Accessibility is one of the five national objectives (with safety, economy, efficiency and integration) in the UK Ten Year Transport Plan published in 2000 (Department of Environment, Transport and the Regions 2000a). As applied in the UK, the concept of accessibility has both economic and social dimensions. In response to national government concerns that certain social groups (the unemployed, physically disabled and low-income households) faced constraints in accessing public services by public transport, local transport authorities undertook an accessibility audit for these 'at-risk' groups to inform their local transport plans. Government guidance at the time recommended three quantitative measures of accessibility depending on the technical skills and data resources available (Department for Transport 2004a):

* Simple access measures that measure point to point
* Threshold measures that measure accessibility against minimum/normative travel time or distance threshold levels to the nearest service destination
* Continuous measures that include some measure of the attractiveness of origins to a range of destinations, expressed in terms of generalised time or cost, and therefore reflect the degree of choice available to individuals.

Table 3.2 Measures of accessibility used in local transport planning

Measure	Access	Threshold	Continuous
Purpose	Assess the ease of access to the public transport network, i.e. from the home to the nearest appropriate bus stop or railway station.	Identify the proportion of population in a given area able to access a spatial opportunity within a minimum set travel time or distance.	Provide an indication of the accessibility of a residential location in terms of the spatial opportunities or activities that can be accessed within a certain travel time and cost.
Data input	i) location of public transport stops ii) distance of home to nearest service	i) travel characteristics such as journey time, distance, cost or generalised cost ii) socio-demographic data iii) characteristics of facilities and services	i) total door-to-door travel time, distance, cost or generalised cost ii) total no. of jobs/ shops available at an identified location iii) incorporates a deterrence function based on increasing time, distance and/or cost to opportunities
Indicators in use	*The proportion of the population having access to a bus service with a minimum frequency of at least four services per hour, from a bus stop situated within a 10 minute walk of their home. The proportion of potential service users living within 400 m of the nearest facility.*	*The proportion (or number) of elderly within a 10 minute walk of the nearest doctor. The proportion of households with no access to a car within a specified travel cost of their nearest hospital.*	*The proportion of pupils of compulsory school age in receipt of free school meals able to access their nearest school within 15 minutes, compared to the equivalent value for all pupils of compulsory school age.*

Source: Compiled from Department for Transport (2004a: 8–13) and Reneland (2000: 132)

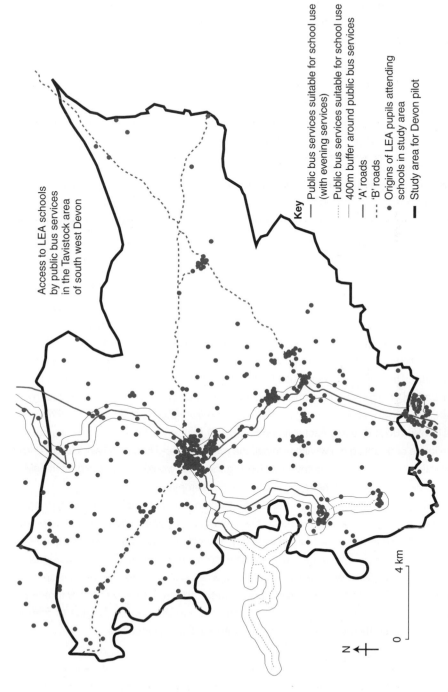

Access to LEA schools
by public bus services
in the Tavistock area
of south west Devon

Key

—— Public bus services suitable for school use
(with evening services)

········ Public bus services suitable for school use

———— 400m buffer around public bus services

———— 'A' roads

·–·–· 'B' roads

● Origins of LEA pupils attending
schools in study area

—— Study area for Devon pilot

N

0   4 km

Figure 3.1 Access to learning opportunities in the County of Devon, England. Source: Department for Transport (2004a: 9), reproduced under licence
Note   LEA: Local Education Authority

These three measures are compared in Table 3.2 according to their purpose, the data requirements and the indicators in use. The 'access' measure is a simple straight-line topological measure. 'Threshold' measures incorporate government standards for accessibility to public services and are used to identify the geographical locations that either meet or fall below the time, distance or cost standards.

Accessibility to schools and hospitals by public transport can be plotted in map form as a distance contour (400 m) from the nearest bus stop or route (Figure 3.1) or a journey time isochrone. Figure 3.1 combines an access measure with a threshold measure to highlight the variations in accessibility across an administrative or service area. Composite measures (access, threshold and continuous) can be used to show the accessibility of potentially excluded groups (households without a car, people under 18 years of age, and people over 65 years of age) to existing or proposed spatial opportunities. GIS enables the analysis and visualisation of different types of data sets in map form portraying space–time accessibility to services and identifying the 'hotspots' of unequal access.

CONCEPT OF EXERGY

The concept of exergy is based on a concept of growth which is not dependent on the increasing use of scarce energy, human, environmental, and financial resources. It focuses on energy efficiency and, therefore, growth in value rather than physical quantities or flows. Exergy is a measure of resource input and how resources are used efficiently. The concept is being used in the design of dwellings through using, for example, natural energy reservoirs (the ambient heat and cold) for air conditioning. Exergy is, therefore, based on '*extract*[ing] *increasing value from the same level of resource use*' (SUMMA 2003: 8) using Factor 4 and Factor 10 principles. Factor 4 principles set the challenge of doubling the wealth with half the resources and Factor 10 aims for a 10-fold reduction in resource consumption. Achieving the latter would require the dematerialisation of the economy and the re-localisation of consumption.

The same principle applied to transportation would question the need to travel and would prioritise renewable resources to transport goods and people where necessary. The potential of 'virtual accessibility' (Gudmundsson 2000) is '*being able to access information and people without moving from a certain place, by using electronic facilities*' (Brodde Makri 2002: 40) such as cell phones, the internet and text messaging. New technology has the potential to reduce the need to travel to access information and experiences but this information, and the social influence of friends, may also create the desire to experience more spatial opportunities.

Low exergy design principles accentuate a lean and mean approach to energy and materials use throughout the life-cycle of product development, production and utilisation (van Timmeren 2005). Spatial components affect the carbon intensity of the built and natural environment. Newman and Kenworthy's (1989) research found that urban form variables such as population density were inversely correlated with transport energy consumption. Similarly, alternative locations for the siting of key facilities within the built fabric, such as shopping centres or hospitals, will affect total energy consumption and emissions of vehicles accessing the facility (Sjöstedt 2005). In the logistics industry, researchers have highlighted the 'duplication' of road freight kilometres where up to a third of all road freight kilometres are completed when either the vehicle is empty or where manufactured or partly manufactured products are transported over distances greater than 100 km, passing the local manufacture of the same product (Whitelegg 1997; McKinnon 2006).

Critical to the implementation of resource minimisation priorities in the lived environment is knowledge dissemination of low exergy solutions, including strong feedback systems between the different physical scales (viz. site, neighbourhood, city-region, EU member state), accelerated learning through mobilisation of stakeholder knowledge, and 'reality checks' with government, market and civil society partners. Carbon accounting is being developed as one tool to measure the sustainability of the production and consumption processes, with a carbon trading market now established across the EU for large companies. Carbon allowances could also be specified for households to enhance understanding of the effects of their personal choices on local and global environments. Recent climate change scenarios provide stronger evidence that resource minimisation in transport should be taken seriously but we are still a long way from measuring transport efficiency in terms of energy efficiency, improvements to the quality of human life and furthering human potential (World Wildlife Fund 1991; Brodde Makrí 2002).

To conclude this section on the examination of the concepts of mobility, accessibility and exergy, Table 3.3 below compares their key features. Mobility is concerned with unconstrained movement and is, in this respect, now a luxury good for which external costs should be internalised. Accessibility focuses on lifestyle requirements to access jobs and services and responds to life-cycle and social group needs. The concept of exergy is borrowed from ecology to highlight the opportunities to reduce societal use of resources, through promoting low engineered solutions to societal needs.

Table 3.3 Accessibility, mobility and exergy compared

Mobility
A movement concept 'Ability to travel' or 'Ability to move' Mobility is not essential to life and in economic terms is a luxury good and should be paid for in full

Accessibility
Physical/vehicular accessibility: 'get-at ability' or 'The ability of people to reach destinations at which they can carry out a given activity' Social group accessibility/need to travel

Exergy
Minimisation of non-renewable resources More efficient use of resources Requires design innovation to use four times less input (Factor 4) and 10 times less input than traditionally used in product development (Factor 10)

3.3   INDIVIDUAL ACCESSIBILITY AND QUALITY OF LIFE

Travel behaviour is a complex phenomenon to understand and is influenced by the contextual supply issues identified in Chapter 2, which include the internal structure of settlements and the convenience of the road network and public transport (Banister and Hickman 2007). This section examines what we know about how individuals use the available transport infrastructure in their daily lives. The previous section has suggested that behavioural factors are rarely captured by quantitative transport models which tend to be based on '*simple bivariate relationships (such as density and travel)*' (Banister and Hickman 2007: 6). Several factors appear central to understanding individual travel behaviour. First, the cultural attitudes of travellers to specific transport modes are a key influence on vehicle (car, van, bicycle, etc.) ownership and, therefore, travel behaviour. Second, traveller's perceptions of the ease of reaching the facilities and services they require on a daily or weekly basis by different modes will also determine modal choice. Finally, there are also other factors associated with gender, age, income and the number of hours spent working that influence travel behaviour (Weber 2006: 399). Our knowledge of the relationship between the factors associated with travel mode choice is still undeveloped, and there may be bi-directional influences (Kitamura *et al.* 1997; Mokhtarian and Saloman 2001; Handy 2005).

Behavioural factors are as important as the spatial configuration of the built environment in understanding individual behaviour. The evolution of settlement patterns and the concentration of spatial opportunities affect leisure and shopping travel behaviour, which now accounts for around 80 per cent of private car use in many western economies (Ruston 2002). For example, the development of large superstores with sales space of 2,500–4,000 sq. metres and ample car parking spaces (500–5,000), selling a range of goods including food, clothing, entertainment media, alcohol, and home goods under one roof has encouraged households to undertake one or two big shops a week rather than several small trips, thus increasing the necessity of using a car. Conversely, high density and a mix of business activity in a neighbourhood is correlated with fewer car journeys (Spiekermann and Wegener 2003; Boarnet *et al.* 2008; Buehler 2008). This has been the focus of residential and retail policy in Amsterdam for many decades (see Chapter 7 case study). Transport economists have shown that non-work trips for household maintenance and social interaction are more responsive to price (price elastic) than work trips and are more likely to be made close to home when appropriate destinations are available (Golob and McNally 1997).

TRAVEL-TO-WORK BEHAVIOUR

Special attention has been given to understanding travel to work behaviour by transport economists and planners for two reasons. First, the cost and convenience of a person's journey to work is a major item in the household budget (Giuliano and Narayan 2004) and, second, because congestion in the morning and evening peak travel periods is a highly sensitive political issue (O' Sullivan 1980). Because of the latter, travel to work has been predominantly conceptualised by transport planners as a trip generation and allocation problem rather than a demand side issue (Pratt 1996). Researchers have examined the journey to work in relation to residential and employment location choice; as a determinant of mode choice; as an indicator of urban spatial structure; and as the anchor of daily activity patterns (Giuliano and Narayan 2005). The cost of housing and the daily commute are linked in large cities as house search entails ever-widening distances from the central area. Some studies have found accessibility to the central area is a key variable valorised in the bundle of qualities that give dwellings their value (O'Sullivan 1980: 260). In other studies, accessibility was found to be just one factor valorised, together with the internal characteristics (surface area, equipment, type of dwelling) and neighbourhood characteristics (environmental quality, school proximity, and the proximity of other valued services) in property values (Boucq 2007: 2).

The political importance of work trips is reflected in government data collection, with the segmentation of trips into 'work' and 'non-work'. The statistics in the UK show that work trips are longer in distance and time and more likely to have a single occupant (71 per cent single occupancy in the morning peak compared to an average of 60 per cent single occupancy (Department for Transport 2004b; Department for Transport 2006a)). In the latter case, car-borne travel for the journey to work often leaves other household members using other modes to access daily travel needs (Giuliano and Narayan 2005: 126). Travel by public transport in UK has become relatively more expensive than by car since 1996 (Department for Transport 2007a). Giuliano and Narayan (2005: 126) suggest that '*long-distance commuting, by car or train, is economically feasible only for the highest income British households*'.

Conventional LUTI models attempt to portray the broad transport network characteristics in a case study region and then make various assumptions about trip generation and mobility based on the aggregated behaviour of large numbers of people and the attractiveness of the spatial opportunities available. Typically the diversity in socio-economic circumstances is reduced to three types, employment to four categories, land use to three types, and trips and transport modes to five types (Speikermann and Wegener 2003). The models produce authoritative numbers of trips made, journey lengths, modes of travel used and the resulting energy consumption and emissions based on the input assumptions concerning decision processes at one point in time (Banister and Hickman 2007). Glaister and Graham's (2006) modelling of the London congestion charge simply dealt with the total vehicle mileage derived from modelling the costs per vehicle kilometre and average traffic flows with all vehicle types standardised to passenger car unit equivalents per hour. These models cannot identify the micro-decisions that take place in terms of the timing of the journey, changes in the intensity of use of cars or choice between alternative modes.

Models tend to focus on cash budgets and characterise the transport system as broken into disjointed modes, rather than the real world of multi-modal travel and trip chaining (Hutton 2007). The space–time budgets of travellers have to incorporate the search for parking and the walk to the destination or interchange, the walk from one bus stop to another at the interchange, and the combination of steps, escalators and luggage in the travel landscape (Hutton 2007). One would expect considerable differences in transport needs and perceptions of ease of travel and expected delay to vary across the population. Qualitative research in the last ten years has revealed the complicated daily travel patterns of high income earners and dual-earning households with caring responsibilities. Using travel diaries it was found that the highest income quintile in the UK made 31 per cent more trips on average than the lowest quintile group and travelled nearly three times further (Giuliano and Narayan 2005; Department for Transport 2006a). It is likely that workers with caring responsibilities will have a more constrained journey time schedule since they may have to combine non-work trips with the work trip (i.e. trip chaining) (Timmermans *et al.* 2002). The co-location of services or the spatial concentration of opportunities becomes more important for complicated modern lifestyles. This also holds true for individuals without access to a car, influencing the ease with which they can travel to and from home or work to a range of services such as shops, medical and child care, and leisure facilities by walking and public transport (Hall 1998: 278).

The causal relationships between travel and choice of residential location, car ownership, socio-economic characteristics, personal attitudes and preferences are still not understood. The evidence that is available comes from small qualitative samples of specific groups (for example, visually impaired, children, young adults, or single person households) and how they use a given area and its facilities (Storey and Brannen 2000; Cole-Hamilton 2002; Thomas and Thompson 2004). This social research gives an insight into how the variables of time, information, financial resources and perceptions of safety and cleanliness in the urban environment vary between social groups. Relatively little is known about what people in particular circumstances regard as an acceptable amount of travel to reach places of work, leisure, shopping, health, education and other facilities that are critical to their quality of life (Department of Environment Transport and the Regions and Transport, Research and Consultancy 2000).

This short review of the factors that might explain individual travel behaviour has identified several dimensions of travel behaviour that are relatively under reported in transport research:

- Few studies take a detailed longitudinal analysis of the decision processes and the wide range of urban form and socio-economic influences on travel such as religion, locality and household composition (Shuttleworth and Lloyd 2005; Banister and Hickman 2007).
- Most assume that travel is a derived demand, i.e. that travel is solely undertaken in order to get to a destination. That we might walk, cycle, use our car or go on a bus journey purely for its own sake (e.g. health, pleasure or relaxation) is not considered.
- Very few studies have focussed on the destinations themselves and the activities undertaken there as topics of relevance to the journey choices made. Most of the studies of non-work travel also tend to aggregate all non-work travel (i.e. social visits, shopping, escorting children, conducting personal business, leisure, holiday travel, etc.) into a single category (Handy 2005).
- Few studies incorporate data on transport network infrastructure in terms of actual waiting periods and public transport reliability and punctuality.
- Few studies are sensitised to the availability of information an individual may have concerning the quality and price of services/goods available in the immediate vicinity; the need to travel to purchase goods (online purchases); and the timing and connectivity of public transport to different locations.
- Few studies recognise individual time constraints which flow from the tasks individuals need to conclude in different time periods (e.g. lunch hour) and whether the desired activity is available (opening times) during these time periods.

- Few studies analyse the intra-household interactions that occur between household members when making travel decisions (Scott 2006). These joint activities may involve complex trip chaining. For example, a potential trip chain might involve dropping off a child at school or childminder on the way to work; collecting the dry cleaning and purchasing food during the lunch hour; followed by collecting the child from school/childminder and visiting the library or the swimming pool before returning home.

- Few land use transport models are directly capable of capturing local sustainability issues such as the exposure of the population to pollutants and noise, land coverage and landscape fragmentation (Speikermann and Wegener 2003: 53). Their zone-based spatial resolution is too coarse to represent environmental phenomena other than total resource use, total energy consumption or total CO_2 emissions.

TRANSPORT AND QUALITY OF LIFE

The role that transport plays in connecting communities and neighbourhoods and the impact of transport infrastructure on those same communities often appears to fall below the transport planners' gaze (Geurs and van Wee 2006). The social and quality of life issues on the transport agenda are wrapped up in concepts of topographical accessibility and travel time savings for road traffic. This rarely engages with the social opportunity and social equity issues of transport provision, including the impact on local pollution and lifestyle choices.

Air pollution adjacent to main roads has been linked to increased rates of respiratory illness amongst vulnerable groups in the local population. Estimates of the annual health costs of man-made particulate air pollution in the UK in 2005 were estimated at £20 billion (€22.7 billion), with particulate pollution reducing the annual average life expectancy by around 8 months (National Audit Office 2008: 15). There is scientific evidence of a clear association between increases in nitrogen dioxide (NO_2) and increased respiratory disease, and the carcinogenic effects of benzene emitted from car exhausts (The Royal Commission on Environmental Pollution 1994; Litman 2002). People in urban areas are especially affected by benzene, particulates and nitrous oxides (Nijkamp et al. 2003; Quinet 2003). Reviewing evidence from the 1990s, Whitelegg (1997: 150) found that air pollution:

- aggravates cardiovascular and respiratory illness;
- adds stress to the cardiovascular system forcing the heart and lungs to work harder;
- reduces the lungs' ability to exhale air and speeds up the loss of lung capacity;
- damages both the cells of the airway's respiratory system and the lungs even after symptoms of minor irritation disappear; and

- may contribute to the development of diseases including bronchitis, emphysema and cancer.

The EU has been the driver behind research into air pollution from industry and transport, setting standards for CO_2, SO_2, NO, PM_{10}, and more recently $PM_{2.5}$. There is evidence that air quality near busy urban roads exceeds EU and national government standards by as much as 25 per cent (Whitelegg (1997). Radical action has been taken in many European cities to deal with the worst cases of air quality, specifically targeting the commuting journey, and restraining car use in large cities using day permits and charges (e.g. Athens, Istanbul, London, Oslo and Stockholm).

In addition to the effects of local air pollution on health, there has also been a gradual deterioration in the tranquillity of urban streets. The EU recognised this in introducing a directive on the mapping of noise in 2002 (2002/49/EC) which encourages the collection of information and the drawing up of noise abatement plans. Non-acceptable noise pollution is defined by the World Health Organisation as noise levels that exceed 55 dB (LAeq) for outdoor living areas and that exceed 45 dB (LAeq) on the outside façade of dwellings at night (World Health Organisation 2000). The LAeq is a measure of the equivalent continuous sound pressure level in decibels and in England and Wales it is estimated that these levels are exceeded for 55–68 per cent of the population (quoted in National Audit Office 2008: 22). In large cities noise pollution at night from emergency service vehicles, and cars speeding and parking, disturb the sleep patterns of those who live in the city centre and along the main roads (Barnardos et al. 2004). Traffic noise from the speed and volume of traffic on main roads may actually deter pedestrians or cyclists from travelling along the road. The air and noise pollution from road and rail vehicles and from tyres can have a cumulative psychological impact on communities and particularly the elderly, the young and those with mental or behavioural problems who have less resilience. There is evidence that the speed and volume of traffic deters children and parents taking physical exercise through active travel often because of feelings of insecurity and fears of being hit by speeding or heavy traffic in urban areas (Barnardos et al. 2004). These perceived barriers suppress more healthy lifestyles.

Transport infrastructure creates a physical barrier which has a social impact on local residential communities. Road infrastructure and vehicular traffic, for example, both sever a residential area allowing for safe crossing places only at designated pedestrian crossing facilities for the elderly, the disabled, and the more vulnerable members of society (Bradbury et al. 2007). What was once considered normal lifestyles: people dominated streets, community surveillance, local streets as play streets and meeting areas, and walking and cycling as a daily routine have all been relinquished for the benefit of the car. The quality of life in urban areas has deteriorated as a result of car dependency which affects both car families, who are less likely to be inculcated into healthy lifestyles when young, and non-car families who may feel socially excluded from certain facilities and mobile lifestyles.

Children's charities and lobby groups have collected an evidence base to show that the UK has one of the worst track records for child pedestrian casualties in Europe (Department of Environment, Transport and the Regions 2000a). Using roads near schools, parks and playgrounds places, children are at high risk of harm, and the risks are the greatest for children living in areas of high deprivation (Barnardos *et al.* 2004: 19). Table 3.4 summarises some of the evidence.

While motorised traffic has undoubted positive effects in terms of journey convenience for car users, it creates disbenefits for others. These are distributed unequally both spatially and across social groups, with the negative externalities often being borne by those who live in locations characterised by the flow and density of motorised traffic. Environmental pollution levels are noticeably higher in central urban areas and residential areas adjacent to the motorway network. In addition, provision for motorised traffic creates disruption to local communities in terms of severance of footpaths and neighbourhoods, and safety risks for pedestrians and cyclists. The discussion of the negative distributional effects of road use has not been a key policy priority, rather the positive effects of new road investment and accessibility have been emphasised as part justification of continued public expenditure. The right to mobility is unevenly shared.

Table 3.4   Road traffic impacts on children: the evidence base

- Road crashes are a leading cause of non-intentional death for children in the UK (Department for Transport 2003).
- About 12 per cent of all deaths in the 5–14 year old age group are caused by road crashes (Child Accident Prevention Trust 2004).
- In 2003, 3224 children aged 0–15 years old were killed or seriously injured on the roads (Department for Transport 2004c).
- The estimated value of preventing road traffic collisions in Great Britain is £12.2 billion (Millward *et al.* 2003).
- More than 25 per cent of child pedestrian injuries take place in the 10 per cent of most deprived wards (Social Exclusion Unit 2003).
- Children living in areas of high deprivation are five times more likely to be killed in a road crash than those in wealthier households (Grayling *et al.* 2002).
- The casualty and fatality rate is declining most slowly for those in lower socio-economic groups (Social Exclusion Unit 2003).
- A total of 88 per cent of child pedestrian casualties and fatalities occur while children are trying to cross roads (Department for Transport 2003).
- Surveys have shown that children are aware of these risks: 70 per cent of children want drivers to slow down near their school, and 50 per cent want more places to cross the road (Brake survey of 11–14 year olds 2003).

Source: Compiled from Barnardos *et al.* (2004: pp.3–4)

3.4 MEASURING SOCIO-SPATIAL EQUITY

The Brundtland report (United Nations World Commission on Environment and Development 1987) emphasised the importance of socio-spatial and socio-temporal equity in their definition of sustainable development. The issue of equity is also currently an important consideration in international discussions of the costs of mitigating and adapting to global environmental hazards (viz. Bali Action Plan 2007; Copenhagen Accord 2010). Public sector intervention at local and national levels has also had the objective of equality of opportunity as an ordering principle in strategies and plans agreed by elected politicians. Section 3.2 has identified the concept of accessibility as having the potential to inform the forward plans and budget allocations of public sector service providers. Using GIS techniques and local data on the diversity of social groups and their access needs, the concept of accessibility can become a coordinating and integrative tool for city-region managers.

This section focuses on people, the impact of investment decisions on their 'ease of reaching' essential activities and how the measurement of the socio-spatial distributional impacts of transport is developing. It first summarises why LUTI models have not provided the answers to help land use and transport planners work together to monitor the land use and transportation interactions and balance travel demand and mode share. It secondly introduces how the measurement of accessibility offers a cross-sectoral approach to acknowledging individual travel needs and the interdependencies between land use, travel behaviour and accessibility.

The evaluation of the socio-spatial distributional impacts of transport interventions has been a relatively underdeveloped area of transport policy despite the frequency of aspirational statements in transport strategies, such as 'To improve the transport choices households have available to reach a range of services' or 'To promote accessibility to everyday facilities for all, especially for those without a car'. As intimated in earlier sections, part of the reason for this is that the monitoring data collected tends to be input- (low floor buses, bus stop information) or output-related (numbers of journeys by mode, journey times by road, number of bus services). Transport monitoring focuses essentially on trips and not the distribution of spatial opportunities that are involved in an individual's daily programme within the time available to them.

Despite recent progress in the development of LUTI models, they tend to be blind to the different characteristics and abilities of individuals and, therefore, the socio-economic impacts of policy (Handy and Niemeier 1997, Kwan 1998; Miller 1991; David Simmonds Consultancy et al. 1998; Brodde Makrí 2002; de Bok and Sanders 2005). GIS has provided a more precise geography to LUTI models through mapping data on traffic counts and accident locations, and network infrastructure features such as the location of bus stops, traffic signals, etc. GIS applications have also advanced transport service planning through modelling the 'point-to-point' accessibility of various destinations using public transport (Hensher *et al.* 2004). The available travel choice sets and route allocations are enhanced through connecting a LUTI model to GIS. However, the large variety of behavioural responses to choice sets, the accessibility needs of actors, and the large variety of land use and infrastructure-related location characteristics are essentially simplified to a limited set for ease of model calibration (de Bok and Sanders 2002). The level of detail is not sufficient to include detailed land use issues of density, liveability, street types, or to capture the heterogeneity of location choices (Walker *et al.* 2007; Hull 2009). It is these site level issues that directly support land use planning analysis and decision making. LUTI models tend to focus on city-regions and to plan for long-term scenarios rather than testing the relative effectiveness of alternative intervention strategies such as increasing densities, mixing land uses, active travel, and improving public transit priority (Moudon *et al.* 2005).

Currently available LUTI models typically use data that are too aggregated to link the short-term changes in travel behaviour with specific land use planning actions at the local level (Moudon *et al.* 2005). They describe location choices using spatially aggregated zones and aggregated accessibility measures (de Bok and Sanders 2002). There are no feedback loops in the models so that the synergistic effects of the co-location of land uses on travel activity and the opportunities to make a series of linked journeys (trip chain) are not evaluated (Moudon *et al.* 2005; Walker *et al.* 2007). As such, LUTI models are not sensitive enough to the different circumstances of people and their propensity to engage in travel and therefore unable to capture the actual or potential social impacts of changes in land use or transportation operations (Moudon *et al.* 2005).

Recent EU research has started to develop an econometric methodology to take account of the quantitative costs of environmental and congestion impacts of road and rail transport to provide the evidence base for infrastructure charging policies (European Commission 2003). These approaches focus on the cost behaviour and the cost structures of these transport modes in order to derive the social marginal costs and benefits of transport. The econometric approaches are generalised methodologies appropriate for administrative areas (local, regional, national administrations) using market prices to evaluate impacts where data is available and using the willingness-to-pay or willingness-to-accept techniques for non-market impacts (e.g. damages to health). These are ground-breaking initial attempts to measure the socio-spatial impacts of travel but again they aggregate individual preferences across broad administrative areas and separate land use from transportation.

In section 3.2, accessibility was shown to be an important concept in several different policy domains (education, health, employment, and welfare services) to identify the ease of access by different social groups to specific categories of spatial opportunity by public transport. The concept, in this sense, is directly related to the qualities of the transport system (viz. service frequency, interoperability, cost; and perceptions of safety) and the qualities of the land use system (viz. concentration of facilities and density). The cost and availability of transport is a key deterrent to people on low incomes in considering post-compulsory education and accessing health services and employment (Office of the Deputy Prime Minister 2003). Younger people (aged 16–24) and the elderly (aged 75 and over) have more difficulty in accessing services than the general population (Ruston 2002: 1). Accessibility to workers, customers and suppliers is a key consideration in business location decisions and a key component in identifying the resource efficient solutions underpinning the concept of exergy. This section now moves on to examine the recent development of accessibility planning to support the integration of land use and transport planning concerns.

Accessibility planning has both strategic level and local level applications. At the strategic level accessibility assessment is applied as a transdisciplinary exercise across a number of policy sectors (e.g. transport, land use, education and health) to produce a strategic map or audit of the main spatial opportunities and the spatial and temporal factors affecting accessibility across the city-region. Two main techniques are used at this broad level: accessibility maps and catchment analysis. Accessibility maps calculate the accessibility by census output area to the key spatial opportunities (e.g. work, education, health care and major services) and other locally important destinations.

In catchment analysis, the catchment population for key destinations is analysed comparing the access to these spatial opportunities for different social groups. For example, in Figure 3.2 below, a composite accessibility measure has been used to show the comparative accessibility of people at risk of ill health in each ward to health services compared to the entire population of the metropolitan area. The analysis excluded health facilities in neighbouring authorities. Figure 3.2 depicts the ratio of these two measures combined: the geographic concentration of the population at risk and data on the accessibility of different wards to health services using public transit. A high value shows that the 'at risk' population experiences worse levels of accessibility than the entire population.

Local accessibility assessments interrogate a more comprehensive database to allow local authorities to set their own local accessibility indicators (Department for Transport 2004a). The database would include the spatial location of vulnerable social groups using indices of multiple deprivation overlaying data on access to services such as food shops, places of worship, community centres, cultural facilities, dentists, leisure/recreational facilities (e.g. cinemas and sports centres), tourist facilities, pharmacies, post offices, banks, retail and libraries. Additional information can be obtained from data fusion, local surveys including travel diaries, community audits and tracker studies, and trade information. Surveys of local people are used to discover local transport issues and concerns (e.g. *'bus timetables don't match reality'*, *'seat at the bus stop is too low'*, *'taxis are expensive'*, *'dial-a-ride won't*

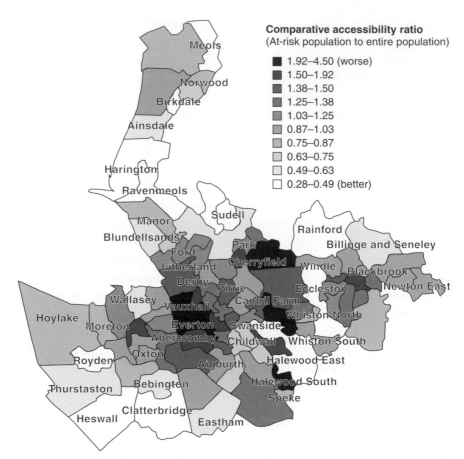

Figure 3.2 The comparative accessibility to healthcare facilities by public transport for the population at risk to ill health in Merseyside, England. Source: Department for Transport
(2004a: 14), reproduced under licence

do hospital trips') and identify which groups of people have accessibility problems,
where these people currently go, where they want to go, why they want to go there
and the best solutions available.

The mapping can be refined to analyse travel cost information, reliability and
other factors. Local mapping audits can be more focused on specific sections at a
resolution using zones of 100 metres. The audits can measure the specific characteristics of the journey, the physical ability and preferences of individuals and identify the
perceived journey barriers to reach essential services. Accessibility audits, therefore,
compare the characteristics that people possess in terms of their physical accessibility
(car ownership, physical mobility, mental health) and access to resources (finances,
information) with the spatial arrangement of facilities or opportunities.

To be of value an accessibility audit must influence the generation of policy options and the appraisal of investment projects. The development of the evidence base on the location of facilities, different population groups and their perceptions of ease of access to facilities, and the accessibility of spatial opportunities is the key factor in prioritising development and expenditure on infrastructure. Rarely is the evidence base available to deepen the analysis to understand how accessibility changes as a result of transport and land use interventions. In most transport research the measurement of the accessibility of 'at risk' groups to key services is simplified to the connection between two points and the timetabled availability of bus services at a desired frequency. In the appraisal of new projects, accessibility is an aggregate measure of the accessibility of the entire population to the transport system (e.g. the number of people who have access to a car or live within 250m of a daytime hourly public transport service) (Department for Transport 2004d). The aspiration to appraise the welfare consequences of a project would take account of the generalised social and environmental impacts alongside the economic impacts measured as travel time savings to car drivers and commuters. These could then be monetised and presented as a benefit:cost ratio. However, the data and methodology is not robust enough to weight and compare the direct and indirect impacts of transport projects on environmental and social criteria (David Simmonds Consultancy 1998; Lyons *et al.* 2001) *'because the evidence base is relatively new, and some of the effects are inherently hard to monetise'* (Eddington 2006: 34).

It is consistency of data that is holding back the effective use of accessibility audits in the appraisal of transport proposals. There are some useful academic applications of accessibility to simulate household and developer responses to transport interventions and to assess the effects of trends in accessibility over time on health, spatial locations, and social groups (Sermons and Seredich 2001; Witten *et al.* 2003; Bertolini *et al.* 2005; de Bok and Sanders 2005; Apparicio and Sequin 2006; Boucq 2007; Du and Mulley 2007; Walker *et al.* 2007). Boucq (2007) measured the added value of accessibility gains induced by a new tram line in Paris using a sophisticated analysis which controlled for dwelling and neighbourhood effects. She concluded from evidence of the increases in residential property values that the infrastructure had noticeably improved accessibility in the target location.

Each of these studies has used a similar research process in terms of the mapping, interpretation, and analysis of accessibility that also can be used by government decision makers. The key steps in the process are as follows:

I   The first step in the process is to establish a cross-sector stakeholder partnership that will own and act on the accessibility audit findings. Their initial task is to agree the overall design of the study and the economic, social and spatial goals the study will address. For example, the partners may wish to use the findings to set appropriate accessibility targets in their service plans, to identify locations well served by public transport for new development; or to improve services for low income populations living in neighbourhoods less well served by spatial opportunities. These decisions will determine whether additional information on geo-demographic data (e.g. households without cars, disabled individuals, unemployed, 16–25 year olds) and public transport data need to be collected.

2   Step two quantifies accessibility levels based on the measurement of time, distance and/or cost of travel between origins and destinations. Measures of accessibility used include access (average distance or minimum distance), threshold or continuous measures such as gravity potential (see Table 3.2; Apparicio and Sequin 2006). The mapping of time, distance or cost for the policy issue decided in step one should be based on measures that are understandable to partners. This may be based on a threshold measure of the availability of public transport services within certain minimum travel times, continuous travel time isochrones or travel cost contours (Bertolini *et al.* 2005).

3   Step three identifies priorities for action and areas/social groups with different levels of accessibility. For the partners, the accessibility assessments provide a quick-scan, visual assessment of problems and opportunities. At the strategic level of decision making they can track how policy agendas for land use, health and employment are incorporating acceptable/maximum thresholds for local walking/cycling and access to public transport services or the relative accessibility of spatial opportunities in the region to non-car modes or transport (Figures 3.1 and 3.2). At the site level, GIS can test the accessibility impact of improving bus journey times and frequencies to proposed residential developments (Department for Transport 2004a: 43).

4   In step 4 the different service partners (public and market actors) can develop collective initiatives and actions based on their joint interpretation and analysis of the accessibility conditions. This may involve investing in locations with low levels of accessibility, or targeting specific social groups for service improvements. Locations with (planned) land use which are hampered by the current accessibility conditions of the location could be addressed through interventions in the transport system.

GIS accessibility modelling, in this way, provides a consistent approach to identifying unequal access to opportunities and to show where improvements are needed to public transport provision. This information can be included in development planning documents but the most effective policy response is investment and action by the transport operators and other service providers to improve the local provision of services and ease of access to them. The process of accessibility planning needs to incorporate a feedback loop so that the impacts of land use and transport interventions on the accessibility of spatial opportunities are more fully understood.

According to Weber (2006) and Whitelegg (1997) transport interventions in the last millennium have tended to prioritise the travel time savings of one social group (car drivers) and penalised other travellers (e.g. non-car owners). Hull and Tricker (2006) found from research undertaken in the UK that there is a disconnect between different public sector service providers right from the early stages of problem identification, the generation of options and the design and approval of interventions (Hull and Tricker 2006). This can lead to a spiral of events whereby transport planners react to the *'fluctuations in demand set off by unanticipated land use changes'* and their solution of increased transportation capacity enhances the attractiveness of adjacent land creating more development activity and additional traffic volumes (Blandford *et al.* 2008: 3). This spiral continues until broken by lack of funding or severe congestion points to alternative solutions. It is at the early stages of option generation that tools for option appraisal, which can guide how land use and transport planners work together, are missing (Dudley 2003; Moudon *et al.* 2005; May *et al.* 2008). What is needed is a broader option generation and appraisal framework *'in which land use, travel behaviour and accessibility impacts are reflected, along with related societal and ecological impacts'* (Geurs and van Wee 2006: 140). The concept of accessibility which has been developed through a 'GIS for transport' software package can provide a heuristic tool to address these broader concerns in a systematic and comprehensive way.

3.5 THE CONTRIBUTION OF SPATIAL PLANNING

The land use regulatory system can be a powerful tool to restrain and influence the travel behaviour of individuals through development location policies that, for example, seek to co-locate residential and commercial property, or ensure that new development is well served by public transport. Both of these policy examples have implications for travel behaviour by enabling individuals without access to a car to access a minimum range of services by foot and bicycle. In this way, location and densification policies can reduce the market effects of segmentation and dispersal of spatial opportunities in countries that have effective land use planning systems. Giuliano and Narayan (2004: 127) contrast these conditions with those they found in the US where *'the price of private vehicle travel is so low that highly segmented and dispersed land-use patterns are easily supported; only the lowest income segment of the US population faces price-related constraints on mobility.'*

Spatial planning acknowledges the interdependencies between land use and transport patterns and other public policy measures. In the US example above, fiscal policy has an antagonistic relationship with the policies the urban design movement is promoting to secure the creation of compact neighbourhood development with all daily services within walkable reach. This New Urbanist movement has been particularly influential in the US from the 1990s onwards campaigning against the separation of activities and the car-dependent environments there (Calthorpe and Fulton 2001). The interaction between social health outcomes, people and the design of places was noticeably highlighted in Jane Jacobs' seminal work back in the 1960s (Jacobs 1961). She drew attention to how human interaction in places is influenced by the diversity and the design of the built environment. More recently the sustainability agenda has brought to the fore the discussion on what makes a city a sustainable or liveable place. The United Nations World Summit on Sustainable Development in Johannesburg in 2002 heralded transport infrastructure as a key component of integrated policy making which, with land use planning, could provide affordable, energy efficient transportation improving energy efficiency, reducing pollution and adverse health effects and limiting urban sprawl.

At the EU level, sustainable development is interpreted in terms of social inclusion and economic growth. At the national level, governments have set out their sustainable development strategies, which aim to enhance economic, environmental and social sustainability while prudently using the nation's natural resources. City vision statements claim to do all of this and enhance community capacity, social interaction and the opportunities for healthy mobility through walking and cycling. These statements tend to be aspirational, offering something for everyone and their components tend to be implemented piecemeal. Many city administrations have tested and introduced a number of measures to influence travel behaviour. These include deterring long-stay parking in the city centre, deterring access by polluting vehicles, encouraging workplace car parking restraint, improving public transport provision in partnership with the private transport operators, including park and ride facilities on the edge of urban areas. Park and ride has had some success removing cars from the city through providing free car parking on the outskirts and efficient bus travel to the centre, particularly where on-street car parking in the centre has been deterred either through pricing or provision.

While many city administrations have used the tools available to them (e.g. legal powers, financial resources, etc.) to systematically implement a key policy for a defined spatial area (e.g. to enhance the distinctive qualities of the city centre) few administrations have expended the same fervour to implement goals that cut across all their deliberations, such as reducing CO_2 emissions. Politicians are reluctant to take risks where outcomes are uncertain. For example, they fear that restraining car parking in the city centre may lead to '*footloose shoppers and tourists* [...] *tak[ing] their custom elsewhere*' (Marshall 1999: 176).

Although plans and strategies seek to integrate the economic, environmental and social dimensions, there is a deficiency of tools to make this happen in an integrated way. Transport policies aim to promote conditions that encourage the use of more environmentally friendly modes of travel (walking, cycling, public transit, low emission vehicles) while providing the transport infrastructure links required for economic growth, and land use policies aim to foster cultural diversity, mixed uses, spatial linkages between activities, and public goods while protecting historical and environmental resources. They have at least one purpose in common of improving accessibility to goods and services, as well as other policies that have synergistic effects. GIS accessibility modelling is one tool that can provide the evidence base to support socio-spatial equity in transport and land use planning.

However, the steps required to maximise the synergy between transport and land use objectives at the multi-scalar levels of decision making are often absent. The formal strategy documents for transport and land use are often prepared to different timescales and for different government department agendas. Both plans and their respective strategic environmental assessments (SEAs) maybe produced by the same organisation and may share a common database. But while they have several processes in common – evidence base, option appraisal, public consultation and monitoring – these are rarely jointly carried out and are often monitored on the attainment of different targets and indicators.

Spatial planning is a potential integrative mechanism across policy sectors. But, like sustainable development, it is often easier to agree the process of who should be involved, and when, in decision making than to agree how conflicting values can be resolved and what principles should inform equitable and fair outcomes. In many ways, the UNIPCC climate change scenarios are helpful in this respect because they provide a clear set of required environmental change outcomes over a defined future timescale linked to emissions reductions to ensure that ecosystem overload is not reached. They add to the certainty in terms of understanding the cause and effect of the production and consumption patterns leading to climate change, and identify clearly those activity patterns that are increasing in their negative impacts. At the strategic level of planning, the carbon emission reduction scenarios provide a clear set of preferred outcomes which should strengthen the SEA of strategic-level decisions.

It is at the city-region, or strategic level, that the cumulative effects of different policy areas become apparent through implementation that is effective or counter-productive. It is at this level, that the forward planning of future development patterns plays a key role in the coordination of the development aspirations of both market and state actors. But it is the development approval process for new development where the design issues of resource minimisation, enhancement of the built environment and the empowerment of local people through opportunities for diversity and exchange can be secured. It is a process that supports and questions the sustainability of development proposals, often through forestalling poorly designed development.

Regulation to manage the use of buildings and land has, however, too often been shoehorned into reacting to well developed investment strategies (discursively and physically) late in the design process rather than specifically setting a clear sustainable agenda for the city-region that addresses the key strategic issues. In civil engineering, this is referred to as an 'end of pipe' intervention since it relies on a technical solution which does not necessarily eradicate the problem at its source. Investment decisions are often driven by the short-term opportunities perceived by developers, and backed by company investment strategies shaped by historical practices. Like sedimentary layers, these actions are injected into the topography of the built and the policy landscape with little concern to the implementation of local government strategies. Land use regulators have been criticised as following societal trends rather than proactively setting agendas. Often the development permit process is the responsibility of a lower tier of government, which may seek to secure alternative or short-term goals. The process of how the alignment of strategic city-region level goals with decisions on detailed development design can be achieved, based on consensus rather than legal requirements is a key multi-scalar government issue. It is sufficient to note at this juncture that the development permit process provides a significant implementation opportunity to achieve sustainability through:

- Promoting the interconnectivity of locations, making it easy to get from one place to another within the city (Taafe 1996: 166; Brodde Makri 2002)
- Requiring densification of new development around public transport corridors and modal interchanges to ensure a critical mass of facilities and customers
- Planning for the most vulnerable in society (e.g. children, elderly, disabled) to ensure that they can use the built environment safely
- Involving all groups in society in planning their neighbourhoods
- Enhancing the attractiveness of streets to secure the volume of pedestrians that will sustain diverse local services, such as retail and frequent public transport, and increase social interaction and child safety and reduce crime (Jacobs 1961; Barnardo's *et al.* 2000, 2004)
- Ensuring that new developments do not sever existing walking and cycle routes and that they, in turn, promote these travel modes
- Promoting the protection of natural resources and low-engineered natural solutions (designing in nature) in developments
- '*Investigating the negative, and perhaps permanent, impacts to people, communities, or ecosystems*' as a result of new developments (Weber 2006: 400)
- Supporting the general maintenance and revitalisation of the street environment.

3.6 REALISING INTEGRATED TERRITORIAL POLICIES

The assessment of the issues and practice reviewed in this chapter so far lead to two questions. First, what are the issues that could engender joint working at the local level between different policy sectors? Second, what mechanisms are available to integrate territorial policies? The concept of sustainable development was hailed as an integrative mechanism in the early 1990s but, without operational delivery tools, has not achieved a step change in practice, although it has demonstrated a capacity to raise awareness of broader issues. The review of practice has shown that the concept of accessibility has secured links between transport and social objectives when assessments have been carried out. Similarly, the SEA Directive requires transport goals to be reconciled with environmental goals. Research in the Netherlands reaches a similar conclusion that 'the combination of the goals of improving sustainability and accessibility appears central to overcoming the current friction among major environmental issues, social aspirations and economic imperatives' (Bertolini et al. 2005: 208).

Accessibility planning can improve the coordination of the targeting of public sector investment across land use, transport, and social service (health, education, social care) policy sectors to improve the socio-spatial equity of service access (Halden et al. 2000). To be effective, this needs to cover the joint consideration of the location of facilities, the scheduling of activities, as well as the availability, suitability and affordability of all modes of transport. Sustainable accessibility (viz. walking, cycling, public transport modes) can be enhanced through land use measures (concentration and diversification of functions, a people-centred design approach of developments and neighbourhoods) and through transport measures (clean fuel, system interoperability) (Dijst et al. 2002; Kwok and Yeh 2004; Bertolini et al. 2005; Banister and Hickman 2007). To be of use to service planners, qualitative studies based on perceptions of the barriers to accessing travel modes and local facilities, for different social groups would need to be carried out on a regular basis. This would extend the current practice of accessibility assessments from a purely quantitative evidence generation exercise to one that integrates resources from public and private sector agencies to deliver a joint plan to improve service accessibility. Joint working across service sectors taps into the tools and opportunities that exist in other policy sectors, but would need to be supported by financial and monitoring criteria to sustain the interaction.

Interviews carried out in England (Hull 2008a) with national experts from five different policy sectors sought their views on how to achieve more sustainable transport outcomes and what the drivers to this would be. The one driver they all agreed on was the need to reduce CO_2 emissions. EU and national climate change reduction targets for CO_2 emissions and other greenhouse gases may provide a new opportunity to support policy objectives across several service sectors by promoting the joint planning and implementation of carbon reduction strategies. This may well lead onto consideration and action on the sustainability principles of resource minimisation and the reduction in use of non-renewable resources.

Building up the knowledge base on the cumulative effects of policy actions on the sustainability of specific city contexts, through collecting evidence on the negative and positive distributional impacts on people, communities, and ecosystems as a result of changes in carbon consumption or accessibility could better integrate transport decisions with the many significant social and environmental issues (Weber 2006: 400). Bertolini and le Clerq (2003: 577) suggest that the synergies can be maximised through:

> Developing conditions for as large as possible a share of the more environmentally friendly modes in urban mobility, while at the same time maintaining, and possibly increasing, the amount and the diversity of activity places that can be reached within an acceptable travel time.

The joint design of strategies and programmes and joint monitoring of policy delivery against sustainability principles has the ability to deliver economic, social, environmental and institutional sustainability objectives (Edén et al. 2000). This approach has been tested in relatively small-scale neighbourhood schemes (Hull 2006), but is much less developed at the higher spatial scales of governance. For policy integration to happen, national and state level government sustainable development strategies need to be consistently applied across all policy sectors to secure the integrative capacity of these tools (accessibility, SEA, indicators). If government sustainable development strategies were applied consistently to monitor all delivery organisations financed through public funds, a more integrative approach to policy delivery could be reinforced and complemented through the use of integrative monitoring tools.

Interactive working across policy sectors at national and state government level is often driven by current social and political issues. Theme teams on issues of obesity or crime are established across government departments to examine how departmental policies can promote solutions to the problem. But quite often sustainable transport objectives are undermined by the policies of other departments or national government policies that generate travel or increase the distances to be travelled to visit a service. For example, while transport planners are trying to improve the accessibility of healthcare centres through improved bus provision (Sustrans 2004), simultaneously local healthcare organisations are closing local health centres and hospitals for cheaper more modern centralised service provision. At the local level, community-wide strategies or visions for the future are often bypassed by the higher-tier government priorities which require certain policies and targets to be implemented, undermining local level achievements.

3.7 CONFLICTING INTERPRETATIONS AND VALUES

This chapter has introduced some longstanding and some newer conceptualisations of transport accessibility and sought to understand how these ideas help to link the practice of transport planning with wider socio-political values of environmental protection and the minimisation of global greenhouse gas emissions. The EIA and SEA Directives have sought to place the environment into transport planning, but have arguably not yet engendered a deep understanding of sustainability in transport practice.

The science of sustainability is well known and the reasons for living by sustainability principles are widely understood. What is lacking is a consistent political response to sustainable development. The broad definition of sustainable development incorporates several different normative dimensions which lead to inconsistency in implementation. This chapter has attempted to chart some of the institutional discourses on sustainable development and accessibility from which these definitions emerge (Ney 2001) and has started to chart the path towards greater sustainability, drawing on the ecological principles of 'exergy' or the minimum input of resources to resolve a systemic problem. Whitelegg (1997: 107) neatly lists the transport agenda which will put transport in the twenty-first century on the path to sustainability:

- Transport must reduce its environmental impacts to within the earth's carrying capacity
- Any calculation of transport's contribution to global unsustainability must include the whole productive cycle (to include the abstraction of raw materials including fuel, vehicle production and maintenance, infrastructure construction and maintenance, and the disposal of wastes
- The necessary changes to mobility patterns must be equitable distributes, both between societies and between individuals within those societies
- Targets should focus not only on reducing environmental impacts but also on meeting second order objectives such as improving health, reducing accidents and providing a better quality of life
- Decisions on how changes are to be made must be taken at the most appropriate level.

In answering the question – Why has it taken so long for politicians and transport planners to acknowledge, and address, the cumulative negative environmental effects of transport use? – this chapter has focused on the way in which the conventional tools used in transport planning help, and obscure, our understanding of the way individuals use the transport infrastructure available to them. The next two chapters focus on the formal institutions of elected government and the strategic-level tools available to politicians and civil servants to initiate innovative practices of resource minimisation in people's daily lives. Chapter 5 continues with this theme to explore the barriers to using these government tools effectively to liberate society from waste and resource inefficiency.

The discussion in the two following chapters draws on political and social theories to help us understand the norms and values we acquire during socialisation, how these differ across social groups, and how social groups or different factions in society use their power to embed their values in social practices. Power is manifested by the control over resources (authority, finance, legal, information, action) (Ostrom 1986). Power can be overt or covert, and is embedded in current authority and decision-making structures (Bachrach and Baratz 1963). How power plays out in each city is different in this respect and in its historical, natural geographical and economic conditions. For example, low density countries tend to have different transport problems to high density countries. High income countries usually put higher emphasis on environmental aspects of transport than low income countries (Rietveld and Stough 2002).

So the values and concerns of powerful groups in society will differ at any one point in time, and as governments try to reconcile these differences they may be reflected in government policies. Civil society organisations can also increasingly wield power and influence through electronic means using lobby group websites and text messaging to organise boycotts of specific company products. The effect of these power plays on government policy and the resulting inconsistencies between government statements tend to reinforce historical trends and resource allocations. This chapter has examined the concepts that constrain institutional mindsets, the next chapter seeks to understand the decision-making mechanisms for government intervention and the tools available for public policy integration.

CHAPTER 4

INSTITUTIONAL STRUCTURES FOR LOW ENERGY FUTURES
CREATING INTEGRATED APPROACHES

4.1 INTRODUCTION

The review of the literature in Chapters 2 and 3 has identified institutional issues as the building blocks to initiating new approaches to resource consumption. These chapters specifically focused on the 'concepts in use' and the political priorities of transport planning and national and transnational tiers of government. However, the quantitative data on national global greenhouse gas emissions from transport presented in Chapter 1 drew attention to the lack of progress in cutting back the consumption from polluting, non-renewable sources of energy in transport. Explanations from the academic literature highlight the lack of political will to initiate change, the presumption given to travel-time savings for car and freight transport, and the insufficiency of tools for civil servants to assess the selection of interventions across policy sectors to reduce consumption efficiently.

A key argument advanced in these early chapters is that neither market actors nor individual citizens can deal with the challenge of adapting to global environmental pressures since the individual 'payoff' benefits from changing their behaviour are not clear. In game theory this is called the 'prisoners' dilemma' – whether to remain silent under questioning or to implicate another suspect (Dawkins 1989; Poundstone 1992). If this is the case, the argument in this chapter is that national and transnational government must exert their agency to set an opportunity agenda of incentives and constraints that will both lever flows of private capital for low energy projects and encourage citizens to reduce resource consumption and waste.

Chapter 3 promoted the use of the principle of exergy, which derives from ecology and underpins the conception of sustainable development. This concept encourages the prudent use of natural and man-made resources, using the design principles of reducing the resource inputs by Factor 4 and Factor 10 in the production process (see Table 3.3). It would focus attention on the net growth in value of products and services through reduction in resource inputs and would help both to protect ecosystems and set society on the path towards the dematerialisation and re-localisation of the economy. This approach, however, is perceived by a large proportion of society as anti-progress and out of kilter with existing production cycles and the culture of modern society. As such, the very essence of sustainability criticises existing value choices and the direction and outcomes of the modern myth of advancement. It brings into question 'what is modern?' and 'what will progress in the future look like?'. The West has grown rich from an economic system based on consumption, sourcing the input resources cheaply and selling final products at the price the market can afford. The principles of sustainability (Section 1.3) as espoused by Whitelegg (1997), therefore, appear to conflict with the values of the capitalist market system and the success of nation states measured through the consumption of resources (i.e. gross domestic product (GDP)).

Until recently, there have been few threats or consequences if we just carried on as normal; wars and famines, droughts and floods, have seemed far removed from our everyday existence in the developed West. Stronger scientific consensus on anthropogenic climate change, coupled with more erratic weather and erratic price increases in petrol suggest that we need urgently to adopt a precautionary approach to the protection of natural ecosystems (United Nations World Commission on Environment and Development 1992). If there are reasonable grounds to suspect that the services these ecosystems provide maybe irreversibly damaged, measures to prevent degradation should be taken before the full scientific evidence is available. But this leaves the question of what are the essential changes that must be made? Scientists call for CO_2 emissions to be reduced by 80 per cent below 1990 levels by 2050 to stabilise climate change at the 2°C 'safe' rise. Other scientists suggest we are on target to reach a 2°C increase in temperature by 2020 (Hansen 2007; Meyer 2009). Sustainability is a deep challenge to the economic players in society who have achieved their dominance through the market philosophy and the accumulation of capital assets. Market values of freedom of choice, overt consumption, and individuality are embedded in societal culture.

Moving away from current production and consumption patterns challenges existing ways of living and challenges embedded power structures and values in society. The market exchange system undervalues or underprices human and natural resources in market decisions (Himanen et al. 2005). Market decision-making criteria are implicated in the more 'developed' nations consuming more of their equitable share of global resources. A 'fair share' of global resources would be just less than 2 global hectares per person. Scotland has an ecological footprint of 5.37 global hectares per person (North Lanarkshire Partnership 2006: 7). To reverse these consumption levels will require behaviour change by all members of society. The issue is how to engage in a meaningful way with the public about these issues and what course of action can we create that will make ordinary individuals part of the process so that they are willing to change their behaviour? Should this be a moral crusade led by the church and the mosque, suggesting that certain types of consumption are 'bad' and that accumulation for show and vanity is 'morally wrong'? There is a role for scientists and educational institutions, including the media, to demonstrate how the global sourcing of our needs and the pollution from consumption is closely linked to the 800 million people (Ray 2008) in the world struggling to find sufficient food and the 'natural' disasters developing countries are faced with. Yet knowledge of climate change impacts does not equate with awareness, and awareness of the appropriate resource reduction measures does not necessarily turn into adaptive action (Haanpää and Peltonen 2007; Haanpää 2008).

This chapter identifies the mechanisms and the tools for engagement that national governments in developed countries have to set a high energy-efficiency opportunity agenda. This will entail a 'root and branch' overhaul of the existing resource allocation criteria which inform decision taking. Governments have been reticent of upsetting the basis of their economic success (Lowndes 2001; Giddens 1990) and have relied, instead, on awareness raising and information provision in the hope of producing more discerning consumers. In addition, governments have used a series of economic instruments (e.g. taxes, charges, etc.) on products and behaviour which perform poorly in terms of depleting global natural resources, and provided dispensation for 'clean' technological innovations that reduce consumption of carbon. There is, however, still a reliance on producing 'input' guidance for lower tiers of government to customise and localise the problem and seek sustainable solutions through their own decision-making processes. The national government in Sweden, however, has set a series of environmental outcomes for lower tiers of government to achieve (see Chapter 7).

Part of the problem of behaviour change is the existing organisation of government. The landscape of government is differentiated by a fragmented array of elected bodies and non-elected agencies covering different spatial scales (neighbourhood, district, metropolitan area, sub-regional, regional, national, etc.) often with boundaries that are not co-terminus. Some of these organisations are formal decision-making bodies, while others are primarily policy/service delivery agencies. The landscape is also populated by private sector and non-governmental organisations (NGOs) which have different values, agendas and concerns (Evans et al. 2002). Public sector decision making is often a mutual partnership between the public and private sectors, denoted by the concept of governance. Private sector organisations are profit-making bodies that pay a dividend to their shareholders. NGOs tend to have a single theme focus and, while covering all their costs, also rely on volunteers. Public sector organisations usually have a remit to provide for the whole of the community within their jurisdiction irrespective of the individual's ability to pay for the service offered. However, public sector organisations are increasingly run on strict value for money criteria in order for the government to keep a tight rein on the public sector borrowing requirement. The different values implicit in these organisations often require some compromise if they are to collaborate successfully on new ventures.

To achieve the resource reduction required to stabilise climate change will require unprecedented levels of social organisation to implement the radical shifts in policy and the new investment focus on low energy solutions. There is substantial evidence that climate change policies have impacted neither on land use planning legislation and decisions (Haanpää and Peltonen 2007) nor on transport strategy and scheme appraisal practices so far (Hull and Tricker 2005). Chapter 5 will explore the reasons for this failure to incorporate climate change mitigation and adaptation strategies into major infrastructure policy and provision. In those countries where the market philosophy prevails, public transit services (bus, tram, rail and air travel) are provided by private sector organisations and run to a commercial agenda. Transport infrastructure is normally funded by the public sector as a public good, and often public resources are made available to secure more frequent, and reliable, public transit services to the CBD and to housing locations where residents are reliant on public transport. Public transport is the more resource-efficient means of travel in a sustainable future and an appropriate service to link residential areas to commercial and employment areas needs to be in place before demand restraint measures for the car can have an effect. The implementation of sustainable transport measures relies on integrated working across different policy domains and the public and private sectors.

To reduce our ecological footprint will necessitate a complete overhaul of our implicit values and accepted ways of working until new resource-efficient practices become embedded in society. This raises several questions concerning how to support each other along this journey:

•   What actions will be most effective in stabilising our global greenhouse gas emissions by 2020?
•   How should we measure the progress made?
•   What structures and mechanisms do we need to put in place to achieve the levels of resource reduction required?
•   Who should lead the behaviour change and what are the respective roles of other stakeholders?

In addressing these questions, this chapter examines one of the key drivers of sustainability which concerns public policy integration. The policy issues spread across transportation, buildings, energy production, agriculture, industrial and waste processes, and the health of the population. There are synergies and overlaps between these domains and how they play out in the urban context. The chapter first examines the concept of 'integration' since the key argument in the discussion of institutional capacity to initiate change is the ability to integrate policy development and delivery across these domains. It then goes on to understand the existing mechanisms for decision making before describing the steering tools available to elected governments.

4.2 THE CONCEPT OF INTEGRATION

An integrated approach to decision making is a prerequisite for sustainability, but the concept of integration has several dimensions. A sustainable approach requires a holistic philosophy identifying the connectivity between the elements, or ecosystems, of our global existence and the effects of our proposed actions. At the first (higher) tier level, 'conceptual integration' concerns the melding of the criteria of sustainability into all decision making to ensure:

1   Social progress that meets the needs of everyone
2   Effective protection of natural ecosystems (water, air, soil, habitats, species)
3   Prudent use of natural resources
4   Maintenance of stable levels of growth and employment (Department of Environment, Transport and the Regions 1998a).

To think sustainably in this way, requires another level of integration ('performance integration') between the actions of decision takers (individuals and organisations). If we assume that the state must take on the burden of addressing climate change through taking the lead on behaviour change, public performance integration concerns the coordination of decision making by public bodies at both the horizontal scales of governance and vertically between the tiers of government. Stead's (2003) review of the literature on integration found that there were several different interpretations of integration. Integration is discussed in terms of the coherence and consistency of policies and strategies (conceptual integration), and in terms of the collaboration, cooperation, and coordination between different public sector agencies (performance integration). In many countries, the organisational integration of the public sector is a specific problem due to the diversity and fragmentation of government institutions and interventions (Hull 2005). Even within the same (public) organisation, departments have different concerns and cultures and diverging agendas (Mittler 1999; Hull et al. 2006).

The contextual factors which are driving policy integration are both organisational and environmental. One driver is the search for partnership approaches to address and solve the cross-cutting social issues facing governments, which include climate change but also complex and intransigent social problems like crime, pollution and obesity that cannot be tackled by one department or agency alone (Lowndes 2001; Stewart et al. 1999). This acknowledges that to understand these issues requires knowledge that crosses disciplinary boundaries and that the search for a more effective public sector requires a jointly focused approach by a number of public, and private, organisations.

The conceptual and performance inter-linkages between transport and land use have been well documented in Chapters 2 (Sections 2.3 and 2.5) and 3 (Sections

3.3 and 3.4). Renewed debates on sustainability of settlement patterns in the 1990s strengthened the conceptual integration of the location of spatial opportunities and the strategic urban infrastructure (see Chapter 7 case studies). These debates influenced the ABC location policy in the Netherlands (See Chapter 7), new urbanism in the USA, the deliberations of the Urban Task Force in the UK, and called for a design led approach to urban intensification to achieve a closer integration between transport, planning and urban design. This 'new' conceptual understanding was based on research into the relationship between settlement form and travel patterns. Hickman and Banister (2005) have summarised the main conclusions from this research, which are presented in Figure 4.1 below. This suggests that a 'sustainable' settlement has a minimum population size of at least 25,000 people with high density and mixed use developments, which are well located to public transport interchanges and corridors to instil more local travel patterns.

1	The location of new development, particularly housing, should be of a substantial size and located near to or within existing settlements so that the total population is at least 25,000 and probably nearer to 50,000. The provision of local facilities and services should be phased so as to encourage the development of local travel patterns.
2	Average journey lengths by car are relatively constant (around 12 km) at densities over 15 persons per hectare, but at lower densities car journey lengths increase by up to 35 per cent. Similarly, as density increases, the number of trips by car decreases from 72 per cent of all journeys to 51 per cent. Car use in the high density locations is half that in the lowest density locations.
3	As settlement size increases, the trips become shorter and the proportion of trips by public transport increases. Diseconomies of size appear for the largest conurbations as trip lengths increase to accommodate the complex structures of these cities.
4	Mixed use developments should reduce trip lengths and car dependence. Although research here is limited and concentrates on the work journey, there is considerable potential for enhancing the proximity of housing to all types of facilities and services.
5	Development should be located near to public transport interchanges and corridors so that high levels of accessibility for all can be provided. But this may also encourage long distance public transport commuting. Free flowing strategic highway networks are likely to encourage the dispersal and sprawl of development and stretch commuting.
6	The availability of parking is a key determinant of whether a car is used or not and further research is required to determine appropriate standards linked to accessibility levels.

Figure 4.1 The relationship between settlement size and travel patterns. Source: Banister and Hickman 2007: 19, reproduced with permission

These integrated concepts on how to reduce the need to travel have been translated into government policy guidance in many countries (e.g. the Netherlands, Sweden and the UK) through policies to increase the density of development in urban areas, particularly on previously developed sites ('brownfield') to reduce the distance travelled for basic necessities and to encourage a greater intensity and diversity of activities in each neighbourhood. Performance measures (e.g. 'sequential test') have also been introduced to ensure site selection for new development which will encourage more compact development and the prioritisation of sites well served by public transport. Chapter 3 also profiled research suggesting that the mechanisms at work between transport and land use interaction are much more complex than previously thought and differ according to the local and regional context of settlements. The research summarised in Figure 4.1 is based on the theoretical relationships between settlement form and mix of uses, and the pollution from travel patterns, rather than on how households actually select spatial opportunities in the built environment.

The location of the facilities we need every day and the accessibility by different transport modes influences our travel patterns. The performance of transport policy delivery while supporting government policies for growth (new settlements, town extensions, economic regeneration) has undermined local design policies for neighbourhood environments including active travel promotion. While investment in public transport is seen as important to reduce the reliance on private car use, long-distance commuting using public transport can undermine the regeneration efforts where the journey originated (Ney 2001; Hickman and Banister 2005).

Conceptually, the causality between transport, energy use and pollution is more straightforward for policy makers to understand and address. The key elements of a strategy to reduce global greenhouse gas emissions from transport are well known and revolve around a reduction in the use of motorised vehicles (powered by the internal combustion engine.) However, while there is general consensus on the type of measures which might be appropriate to consider in a sustainable transport strategy there is disagreement around the importance of the car in the transport hierarchy. Table 4.1 summarises two approaches to identifying what the higher order targets for a sustainable urban transport strategy should be. Bayliss (1998) and Bertolini and le Clerq (2003), propose a hierarchy of objectives at the local level that prioritise the implementation of walking and cycling opportunities and has strong links to the policy objectives in other sectors such as health and social policy. The hierarchy also prioritises innovation in environmental technology through improving the performance of vehicles. It is a hierarchy, therefore, that implicitly serves the objectives of several policy areas. It is clear and simple in its message and supports measures that encourage sustainability and enhance quality of life.

Table 4.1 Higher order objectives for a sustainable urban transport policy

Bayliss (1998: 45); Bertolini and le Clerq (2003: 576)	*EU Working Group on Sustainable Urban Transport (2004b: 31–32)*
1 Increasing as much as possible the opportunities for walking and cycling.	1 Controlling car use, preferably through pricing of road use and/or parking, but with limits on road use and parking restrictions as a second best approach.
2 When walking and cycling are not realistic possibilities, increasing as much as possible the opportunities for transit while at the same time improving the environmental performance of transit (e.g. cleaner and more efficient engines, shorter journey distances).	2 Improvements to public transport operation in the form of changes in fares, service levels, reliability, and quality.
3 Most longer and less frequently made journeys should be capable of being made efficiently by public transport or other multi-occupancy vehicles.	3 Land use policies to support (1) and (2) in the form of increased density, mixed development, and development in association with public transport.
4 (1) (2) and (3) should only be limited by the economic and environmental capacities of the area, while paying the full external costs and respecting wider economic, social and environmental objectives.	4 Improvements to the operation of the road network, including reallocation of road space, traffic calming, selective low cost capacity improvements, and support for less polluting vehicles.
5 When transit is also not a feasible option, improve the environmental performance of the car.	5 Information technology to help users to use the resulting transport and land use system efficiently and, through telecommunications, to travel less.
	6 Improvements to walking and cycling within this context.
	7 The use of 'soft' measures, including the raising of awareness to reinforce the strategy.
	8 Improved management of freight within this context.
	9 Provision of new infrastructure only where it remains fully justified in the context of the measures listed above.

The European Union Working Group on Sustainable Urban Transport is composed of transport planners, engineers, and environmentalists from academia, local authorities, NGOs and European organisations. Despite their claim to have produced an integrated strategy covering transport, health, social issues, education and economic development, it is not clear where the overlapping synergies lie. The focus here is on improving the flow of traffic on the existing transport network through road pricing, information technology and traffic management measures.

Their top priority is a series of economic disincentives to control car use, which may be socially regressive. Land use measures come in at number three, and cycling and walking, as the sixth priority. It is not clear how this agenda will decouple transport growth from economic growth. This hierarchy seeks to deliver the political priorities of the EU Council of Ministers in 2004 rather than challenging the underlying (political) assumptions.

In conclusion, we can summarise this section on conceptual policy integration by pointing out that there is broad consensus that transport issues require support from other policy domains to address the most pressing transport problems, but that the understanding of how transport can help achieve the policy objectives of other domains is still not strong. While the EU and national governments call for sustainability to be integrated into policy decisions or for the integration of the '*environmental perspective into transport policy and the sustainable transport perspective into other policy areas*' (European Environment Agency 2007: 9) the guidance rarely explains how policy integration can be achieved in practice (Rietveld and Stough 2002: 5; Stead 2003; Hull 2004). This gap in performance integration reflects the significant supply-side contextual differences between urban and rural areas and between the EU-15 and the EU-12.

Our understanding of how to achieve a timely reduction in global greenhouse gas emissions using democratic and consensual means is unclear. There is general social awareness of the negative impacts of transport with 60 per cent of respondents in a 2006 survey agreeing that transport has detrimental climate change impacts and 14 per cent suggesting that car users should pay more on busy roads (National Centre for Social Research 2008). This raises the question of what incentives will be effective to achieve behaviour change if public sector policies continue to provide more of the same opportunities for travel by car. Gaining consensus on more radical policy approaches will cut across several policy sectors, requiring joint approaches to pilot and understand the range of unintended outcomes that might result. A transparent process of dialogue with members of the public and the different levels of governance is accepted as a precondition for change (EU Working Group on Sustainable Urban Transport 2004). Transport strategies need not only to consider the decentralisation of population and spatial opportunities (urban–hinterland linkages) but also the diversity of transport needs, attitudes and values of an increasingly ageing population.

The transport sector on its own is not able to achieve significant emission reductions. Often, transport organisations are reacting to the decisions made in other policy sectors. For example, the closure of hospitals and schools and the location of new ones have significant public transport provision and funding implications (Atkins 2003). Sometimes the joint working necessary for effective policy delivery is constrained by the accountability to specific departments of a higher tier of government, which requires certain targets to be met. Service failures at the local level are not entirely a malfunctioning of local government, since higher tiers of government structure what local delivery agencies can achieve through legal rules and standards, policy frameworks, and resource regimes, with little attention to the cumulative effects on other policy sectors.

The concept of governance acknowledges the role that the private sector and NGOs play in public decision making and delivery. Policy integration needs horizontal and vertical integration to happen simultaneously within organisations and across several different agency boundaries. Interactive working across policy sectors in elected governments is often a reaction to directives from higher tiers of government. It is piloted and tried but does not necessarily change organisational working practices. Researchers evaluating the success of organisations designing and delivering innovative approaches to service delivery have found the importance of gaining the support of the dominant actors in the organisation. This is because certain political priorities dominate or structure organisational decision making (Storper 1996; Brenner 1999), which can create a barrier for new approaches to transport policy such as more sustainable mobility solutions (Wixey and Ruiz 2003). Power is manifested by the control an individual or organisation has over resources (authority, finance, legal, information, action) (Ostrom 1986).

How power plays out in each organisation and each city is different in this respect and in its historical, social and economic conditions. Power can be overt or covert, and is embedded in current authority and decision-making structures (Bachrach and Baratz 1963). The power embedded in certain organisations make them difficult to ignore. For instance, because funding for transport infrastructure is provided by federal or national governments, localities tend to compete for this funding which is devolved through a separate bureaucracy built around the funding rules (Blandford *et al.* 2008). The values and decision-making rules of the funding bureaucracy will be institutionalised in all those organisations that depend on this funding source. The practices and rules of decision-making regimes structure, shape and constrain the choices of less powerful organisations. It also means that the mechanisms for reducing energy consumption and integrating policy approaches need to be created within the existing bureaucratic system.

This discussion of the issues surrounding performance integration has raised several questions:

- Who is going to coordinate the behaviour change towards a sustainable transport system based on low energy inputs?
- Are there mechanisms that can be deployed within the existing governance system to ensure the collaboration and the cooperation of organisations and individuals?

•   Should new mechanisms be created from within the existing governance system to coordinate integrated policy approaches?

•   Where are the leaders to be found that can take society through to a low energy future and what level of government or governance should be coordinating the action?

The normative presumption has been made in earlier chapters that the leadership roles for radical change should be the responsibility of national and city-region governments. The remainder of this chapter explores the strategic steering tools available to these levels of government before addressing how the tasks of cooperation and integration could be achieved across the scales of governance, from micro to macro, and through partnerships with businesses, institutions, developers, NGOs, and individuals.

4.3   STRATEGIC TOOLS FOR THE GOVERNANCE OF SPACE

This section examines the resources or tools that can be used by elected governments to change behaviour and how they can be deployed in partnership with other stakeholders. It first deals with the rules that implicitly determine how partnerships are set up and play out based on the types of resources different actors bring to decision making and delivery. Many academics have theorised on the sets of rules which structure interaction between organisations. On a general level these have been categorised as 'formal' and 'informal' rules for action (North 1990; Lowndes 2001; Healey 1997; Ostrom 1986, 1990; Rietveld and Stough 2005). Informal rules, or ways of acting, change very slowly and include *'values, norms, practices, customs, and traditions'* (Rietveld and Stough 2005: 3). Many of the latter rules have become institutionalised in social practices since we unconsciously take them for granted. Formal rules also *'tend to be quite resilient and resistant to change'* and include *'codified statutes, constitutional provisions, laws, regulations, and high level administrative orders. They focus on such things as property rights, judicial, and administrative orders'* (Rietveld and Stough 2005: 3). Rules over time, particularly informal rules, are interpreted, developed and re-expressed (for a fuller discussion of this, see Flyvberg 1998; Lowndes 2001; Silverman 2003).

Institutional theorists have examined how formal and informal rules structure the way organisations carry out their work. For example, interaction between government institutions has historically been set out in legal statutes, which give legal powers to act on specific issues to certain agencies in the government bureaucracy and specify how they should interact or work with other organisations. Institutional theory has examined the 'hard infrastructure' of institutions (organisations and their resources of power, personnel and finance) and their informal codes of conduct for

Table 4.2 Structuring rules which underpin transport planning

Structuring rules	Application to the transport sector
Scope rules: which select possible and appropriate outcomes	Structured around single modes. Operational issues of cost efficiency, cost minimisation and safety predominate. Highway infrastructure is seen as a public good and thus requires a strong government steer. Increasing concern with congestion on the strategic road network. Little attention given to social equity issues and sustainable modes. Few opportunities to debate modal and policy integration.
Boundary rules: which determine the entry and exit of participants	The timing of the interaction between transport operators and government agencies is set in laws. Specific competition laws may also set boundaries for interaction between private operators. Laws and administrative rules give opportunities for the public to participate at various stages in the decision making on transport and urban infrastructure.
Position rules: which assign participants to positions	Transport operating companies are assigned legal rights to offer services on specified routes, and these may be highly regulated in certain circumstances. Public sector bodies regulate and coordinate organisations that operate transport services and maintain transport infrastructure. Legislation assigns specific duties to elected and non-elected public bodies. The key vertical coordination of the transport sector varies between countries, with some where all regulation lies with national agencies, and others where there is a strong coordinating role assigned to 'regional' agencies. Often the horizontal coordination of services is left to local administrations, often with few powers available to them.
Authority rules: that specify the actions actors can take	Powers to act are given through legislation. Transport operators and developers acquire considerable authority through their operational expertise. Public sector authority comes through election, tax-raising powers and land ownership where these are allowed. Local administrations have legal or administrative authority over the development of land and can raise revenue through car parking permits, road tolling charges and local enterprises.
Pay-off rules: that distribute in advance expected benefits and costs	Expected benefits are identified in advance for actors in the transport arena. Commercial operators secure their profit levels and receive public subsidies for operating non-commercial services. Pensioners and disabled individuals can travel by bus at no, or reduced, cost. The public sector gains an effective public transport service with increasing standards of quality.

interaction ('soft infrastructure'), with variants focussing on the economic mecha-nisms (North 1990; Chang 2002) and the social mechanisms for interaction (Young 1995; Vigar *et al.* 2000; Ostrom and Ahn 2003).

Ostrom (1986) has theorised a more dynamic model of how organisations and actors negotiate for position in the '*action arena*' and the ability of actors to mobilise and deploy more effectively their resources within this game play. The model has different layers of interaction and feedback loops, where the rules negotiated at one level open up opportunities for some actors at another level with the effect of constraining other actors. Ostrom (1986: 463) has tested the model in her work on water, waste and international aid in developing countries which highlighted that access to resources is a competitive game and that, without enforceable rules, actors would be tempted to '*free-ride*' at the expense of others.

Central to Ostrom's model of interaction are five variables or '*rules*' that can enhance understanding of the level of control that each participant has over action choices and, hence, the opportunities they have to negotiate and influence the outcomes of any interaction. Table 4.2 applies Ostrom's five structuring rules to the transport sector to understand the roles that different actors are authorised to play in delivering transport infrastructure and the resources or power these actors may have to negotiate for additional resources during the delivery process. Ostrom's five rules cover the possible and appropriate outcomes (*scope*), the entry and exit of participants (*boundary*), the roles assigned to participants (*position*), the range of actions actors can take (*authority*), and rules that distribute the benefits and costs in advance of interaction (*pay-off*). These rules of engagement are negotiated (overtly or tacitly accepted) in advance between participants and influence the extent to which they are able to use the rights and responsibilities they have gained. Table 4.2 summarises the discussion below on how the rules and resources are currently deployed in the transport sector.

SCOPE RULES

In many countries the organisation of the transport system is structured around single modes such as highways, railways and air travel. The management of these modes tends, then, to focus on modal operational issues, giving more attention to issues of cost efficiency or cost minimisation for the transport operators, rather than taking an integrated approach to planning transport across all modes (Whitelegg 1997). The provision of highway infrastructure has been considered as a public good in most countries and, therefore, provided through a planned programme by the public sector. Similarly, public transport has also been considered a public good, under various political regimes, with significant public resources allocated to improving provision. Debates on transport tend, therefore, to be organised according to specific modes, with few appropriate strategic arenas for integrated transport debates and for the relatively new concepts of demand restraint and mobility management (Wixey and Ruiz 2003). Few countries have a national transport policy, which by definition would involve an integrated consideration of the different transport modes. Discussions on funding appear divorced from transport strategies and are rarely clearly linked to national transport policies.

Market ideologies since the 1980s have strongly been translated into public sector decision making accentuating the norms of cost efficiency and value for money in the transport sector and crowding out non-market norms and incentives (e.g. equality of opportunity or access). EU transport policy, on the one hand, has promoted close linkages between economic competitiveness, job creation and transport efficiency (European Commission 2006). On the other hand, the issues of equitable access to facilities and the distribution of the external costs of transport production and consumption have become less prominent.

BOUNDARY RULES

Secondary legislation, administrative orders, regulations, and policy directives select the actors in the transport arena and the timing of their contribution to transport decision making and delivery. These rules identify the participants, amongst a crowded field of stakeholders, who should be involved at what stage in the policy delivery process. In some countries, such as the United Kingdom and the USA, boundaries are set by competition laws which specify how the privatised train and bus companies should compete with each other. Specific government agencies are tasked with enforcing these competition laws. In the UK, this is carried out by the Office of Fair Trading (OFT) and sector specific bodies such as the Office of Rail Regulation (ORR) and the regional area traffic commissioners (for the bus industry).

Public sector bodies are granted specific powers and responsibilities which provide boundary rules beyond which they should not act (*ultra vires*). These limit the actions they can take and therefore the transport arenas they can participate in. There are strong lines of interaction, particularly accountability and dependency, between local transport authorities and the government department responsible for transport. Some local and regional authorities have wider powers of involvement in transport planning and delivery.

Boundary rules often give members of the public a right to participate at specific stages in public sector decision making. In some countries, such as France and New Zealand, 'third party' rights are specified in law which give members of the public a right to appeal to a higher-level administration when an elected local administration significantly departs from their public, statutory land use strategy. In most countries public participation in urban and regional transport projects is very limited despite the entitlement given through legal and administrative rules. A survey of eight European countries in 2002 found that the mechanism to encourage the involvement of the public sometimes only amounted to an announcement that a decision had been made (GUIDEMAPS 2003). Since this survey, the mechanisms for capturing public views and concerns earlier in the decision-making process for major transport infrastructure have been strengthened in many EU countries in order to reduce the overall number of individual objections which might delay these major schemes at the later public inquiry stages (See Chapter 7 case studies).

POSITION RULES

Transport operating companies, public and privately owned, are legally assigned powers to deliver services usually according to a public timetable on specific routes on the network. These positions in a regulated transport market will be assigned after a tendering process which has set some appropriate minimum service standards. For example, in the case of London, the public agency Transport for London has the power to set standards for the bus service to be delivered including the training of drivers. Certain social groups in society may receive a privileged position in respect of the transport system. This may be due to high income, work privileges, or as patrons who can access the service at no, or a low, cost (e.g. the disabled and elderly), or individuals enrolled to represent consumers on service passenger advisory groups.

The regulation and coordination of the transport sector is usually assigned to the public sector. The historic division of responsibility for transport has divided responsibility along modal lines with separate government agencies for highways and railways at the national level. In many government systems the spatial integration of transport modes is devolved to elected 'regional' governments which often have secondary legislative powers. Where this is not the case, or only operates weakly, administrative powers are dispensed to local government administrations, working singly or jointly, to coordinate transport provision through the production of a transport strategy or plan for their area, and to promote and negotiate for improvements to passenger transport with the operators. The institutions that are established to deliver a more coordinated and efficient transport system operate at the metropolitan or travel-to-work area and often have the powers to enter into contracts with both the bus and train operating companies.

In most countries, the management of the local highways, the organisation of local bus services, and the planning for transport and land use are the preserve of local government. These roles are often shaped and constrained by higher tier authorities.

AUTHORITY RULES

Private sector companies gain considerable authority due to the expertise they acquire through the operation of transport services and the investment and development process. Government bodies acquire authoritative resources through election into office by the electorate and, thus, acquire authority through representing members of the public in their jurisdiction. Further authority, and considerable power, comes through the ownership of land and infrastructure, and tax raising powers where these have been devolved from national government. Authority and power are gained by public bodies that effectively control transport services through their own operating companies.

Local government also derives considerable authority through their control over development permits, but their actions tend to be tightly circumscribed by higher tiers of government and although they have discretionary powers these tend to cover areas where there is little public support (road tolling, demand management measures and charges) or for expensive tasks that are not seen as politically important (data collection, monitoring and enforcement). Some countries in Europe have started to link the funding available to local government to their performance on delivering regional and/or national government policies. This provides an additional element of control by higher-tier authorities over lower tiers. Where additional funding is received to encourage certain actions from local government, this may provide an incentive to implement national government policies more effectively (Rietveld and Stough 2005). The funding for major local transport schemes (costing more than £5 million (€5.8 million)) is usually tightly controlled by higher-tier authorities. Surveys have found that the transport portfolio does not have a lot of political authority within local government administrations being crowded out by other statutory services such as education and welfare (Atkins 2003; GUIDEMAPS 2003; Hull and Tricker 2006).

PAY OFF RULES

It is implicit in the structuring rules of operation that commercial operators are expected to make secure profits, underpinned through substantial investment in infrastructure by the public sector. In the UK, 80 per cent of fuel duties can be reclaimed by bus companies registered with the area traffic commissioners. It is expected that social obligations will be delivered or subsidised by the public sector. This includes the provision of public transit services that would not be profitable for the commercial operators to provide. The benefit for society is a reasonable level of provision of public transport services running to the agreed timing and schedule of journeys. For specific sections of society (the elderly and the disabled) there may be benefits in terms of free access to public transport. Implicit in the efforts taken by the public sector to plan transport provision is that the provision will increase in quality and quantity over time and that higher tiers of government will provide the funding required to enable this to happen.

This brief summary of how Ostrom's structuring rules apply to the coordination of the transport system provides an example of how rules, through the resources they bestow, structure the way organisations (public and private) interact and set relationships of dependency between organisations. These structuring rules are introduced to demonstrate that new ideas and approaches need to negotiate this spider's web of inter-relationships. Innovation does take root in different service areas within local government despite the constraints from regulatory requirements and professional practices (Lowndes 2001). The goal of resource minimisation, however, requires project champions who can influence how the public and private sectors and civil society interacts through restructuring the rules and established practices to change behaviour and decision-making criteria. The issue then becomes: Which tier of government (in existence or to be established) should 'take the lead' both organisationally and financially?

The state, civil society and market sector relationships vary from country to country on the basis of historical structuring rules and negotiated alignments. The power of the state may be limited or seem limitless, falling along a continuum of minimum involvement of the state in civil society (ensuring law and order, defence of the realm) to interference in domestic/household decisions (freedom of speech, number of children). The welfare state and the welfare society fall within these two extremes, where the state plays a strong role but one which is heavily circumscribed. Civil society can constrain government action through exercising their rights to vote in government elections, and/or referenda on taxation, and or political lobbying and thus shaping the resources available to the state to carry out their election priorities. Inevitably a partnership approach between the state, the private sector and civil society is the key to change. Partnership working to resolve societal problems can create 'weak ties' of trust to build bridges between actors and the potential for new approaches, but they are difficult to sustain over time without some form of contract specifying procedures, rights and incentives for joint working (Lowndes and Skelcher 1998; Lowndes 2001; Wixey and Ruiz 2003).

STRATEGIC TOOLS

Leaving aside, for the moment, which spatial scale of government or governance should take the lead to effect radical change to reduce global greenhouse gas emissions and to lead society towards a low energy future, this section examines the tools available to the state. There are a number of policy options available to the state that include: 1) the direct provision of more sustainable transport options; 2) regulation to ensure that the decisions of market actors are more sustainable; 3) taxes on carbon and non-renewable energy consumption and public funding for low energy solutions; and 4) information provision and advice.

PUBLIC PROVISION

There are many examples where the state has taken on the responsibility for the direct provision of a service either run on full economic cost, or on a deficit funded basis with any profits being ploughed back into the service. Many city transport services, including airports, and services such as water, waste and energy are run on these lines to ensure that the service is provided at the standard society aspires to and at an affordable cost (e.g. public transport in Vienna and the Portland CBD). Ownership of infrastructure also gives control over standards and, in theory, ease of implementing service changes (see Chapter 7 Malmö case study). However, the maintenance and investment requirements of these systems are often prohibitive for city budgets, and the option of private sector delivery and ownership is often seen as more appropriate. The public sector has to balance out the perceived advantages of private sector finance versus losing control of public assets (Vickerman 2005). The risks of service failure normally remain with the public sector, through the payment of subsidies to ensure appropriate safety standards (and compensation when systems fail) and to cover unexpected losses of profit. Policy change towards low carbon energy is a complex delivery process where the state may have to rely on the private sector to develop the low carbon infrastructure network.

LEGAL TOOLS

Legal regulations provide a powerful tool for supranational and national governments to control the behaviour of organisations and individuals, particularly where there are penalties for non-compliance. Politically, the necessity for regulation and the expected cost of compliance needs to be accepted by society. The EU has successfully set minimum pollution standards through legal regulations for industrial processes and vehicles, where the negative effects of the emission impact are fairly certain. The Directive on Air Pollution (98/69/EC) set an industry standard (Euro 4) for the emissions from motor vehicles and the new standards (Euro 5 and 6), which apply from 1 September 2009, set stricter emission limits for particulates and NOx for new cars and vans sold in the EU market. EU legislation through the Environmental Impact Assessment Directive (EC 85/337, amended by Directive EC 97/11), and the Strategic Environmental Assessment Directive (2001/42/EC) set requirements for the environmental appraisal of major development proposals and for government strategies and plans.

National governments use legal powers to constrain the agency of lower tiers of government by specifying the decision-making practices and rules they must adhere to. These specify the criteria which must be used to assess potential solutions and options being considered (e.g. value for money criteria, delivery of a higher-tier sectoral plan), set time deadlines for decisions, or the type of mitigation process to be used. Some state which organisations should be involved in the decision making and at what stage (i.e. boundary rules). Standards are also set through administrative order and through statutory plans. These, for example, may set requirements for a minimum density for new development and standards for open space, drainage and landscaping either as requirements or in the form of a best practice guide. In the latter case, '*standards are not absolute but more in the nature of guides or criteria to be followed under average circumstances*' (Chapin and Kaiser 1979: 369).

FISCAL MEASURES

Higher tiers of government traditionally raise income through taxes on market transactions (e.g. value added tax, transport fuel duty), and personal and wealth taxes to implement their policies. Fiscal measures are therefore an important tool to control carbon consumption. Major transport funding relies on state funding so this is another budget area which can be diverted to low energy options. Current taxation levels on energy use are insufficient to address the climate change challenges on their own, and the effectiveness of increased taxes would depend on the elasticity of demand and political willingness to impose the appropriate level of taxation. Taxes at the point of purchase can be socially regressive, since they hit the least well off hardest.

Given public unacceptability of increased taxation, there are two options available to governments to address the climate change challenge. The first is to raise a greater proportion of state income from behaviour that is profligate with carbon and reduce taxes on low carbon products and processes so that the total tax burden is not increased, while putting in place some measures to protect the low waged. The Dutch government in 2009 passed legislation to raise revenue from the distance travelled by motorised vehicles rather than a combination of fuel and vehicle ownership taxes. This approach could also include a reduction in corporate taxes when businesses invest their surplus profits in low carbon infrastructure. A second, and related, measure is to divert some of the taxes currently being extracted by the state into developing a low carbon infrastructure. Transport taxes could be used to put in place the biofuel or hydrogen gas infrastructure needed to power low energy vehicles. Similarly, taxes on gas and electricity consumption and taxes on the surplus profits of these companies could be recycled into the low carbon infrastructure which might include enhanced energy conservation measures in buildings, combined heat and power plants, and renewable energy installations.

Increasingly, market mechanisms to control behaviour are being used, instead of legal regulations, as the solution which has the lowest administrative cost to society and the lowest cost to business. The EU Emissions Trading Scheme is the cornerstone of EU efforts to deliver the Kyoto target of 8 per cent CO_2 reductions by 2012. This covers the emissions of the largest 12,000 companies, which have been given a carbon allowance to trade with each other, selling off or buying further carbon allowances as needed. This mechanism is characterised by transparency of cost and with the opportunity to reduce carbon allowances over time. While, the latter reduction of carbon allowances has not yet been realised, the scheme has been trialled and accepted by the market actors involved.

INFORMATION AND AWARENESS RAISING TOOLS

The provision of appropriately detailed information on how to reduce resource consumption and to adapt to climate change is an important role of all levels of government. Information provision tends to be an over-used tool by governments who provide too much information, which is not customised to the needs of recipients. There is often a problem of the lack of coherency and consistency between government departments evidenced when recipients receive information recommending different actions.

Public sector land use and transport strategies and plans are the main tools used to give information to investors and developers about the location of needed investment. The value of these tools is that they are periodically updated and that they provide some certainty concerning the appropriateness of development proposals. Strategies for radical behaviour change over the longer term should, therefore, connect to the available resources and spatial opportunities and local community preferences on how they would like to live their lives, prescribing how society can ameliorate the effects of climate change (Köhler 2007). The preparation of strategic visions of the future worked up with civil society members is a prerequisite both to gain consensus on the preferred actions which are necessary and to give public agencies some defined (and well conceived) sustainability outcomes and targets to work towards. Strategic regional planning was seen as important back in the 1970s: '*If it is to be socially inclusive, it has to provide mobility for all who need it, including those who would be forgotten by the "objective" and "efficient" laws of supply and demand*' (Chapin and Kaiser 1979: 618). Society needs a '*guidance system planning process*' which relates transport to other aspects of economic and social life and '*which coordinates land use planning outputs internally and with other planning activities*' (environmental, ecological, social cohesion) (Chapin and Kaiser 1979: 618).

Government strategies are being informed by futures scenario-building exercises which factor in the possibility of transnational energy, water and food wars by 2050 (http://www.foresight.gov.uk/). Transport modelling is also used to suggest more efficient use of transport and spatial opportunities (Banister 2000a; May *et al.*

2002, 2008; Banister and Hickman 2005, 2007). Although these scenarios factor in a key role for enhanced public transport infrastructure, with new housing locations in areas well-served by public transport, there is usually little idea of how an integrated transport system will be developed to reduce energy consumption and offer accessible walking neighbourhoods. Banister (2005b) backs the planning system to change behaviour through control over development locations and greater attention to the environmental and social aspects of transport. Banister and May et al. (2002) conceive of an integrated modal system being achieved through pricing signals, regulatory controls and enhanced bus provision.

Government strategic frameworks for fundamental change need to be consistent across all policy sectors, using all the resources at the disposal of the public sector, and clear and transparent about how change will be achieved. There are several future scenarios to contemplate. It is unlikely that the private sector will take a lead on climate change, due to the 'prisoner's dilemma' challenge. Future scenario planning for a petroleum crisis envisages a greater role for municipal and regional institutions to manage the sourcing of resources locally, with an increased emphasis on social cooperation (http://www.foresight.gov.uk/). The criteria for the dispensation of government funds will need to factor in the costs and benefits of investment over at least a thirty year period to demonstrate the sustainable benefits of investment. To this end, national governments should adopt equitable and consistent appraisal criteria across all modes, with consistent pricing of transport modes including their external costs.

The case studies in Chapter 7 show how intrinsic the ownership of legal powers to introduce new decision-making criteria and the ability to raise taxes is to the capacity to initiate and sustain new (radical) approaches to public sector intervention. Where elected local government also has substantial land holdings or ownership of public and/or private companies, this, too, gives additional autonomy and authority to that tier of government. While these tools and resources are essential components of an unfettered approach to behaviour change, without close working with local stakeholders, a collective action programme to address the cross-sector issues will not effectively engage horizontally with key actors or vertically up to the support provided by higher tiers of government and down to citizens.

PARTNERSHIP WORKING
Fundamental adaptation to climate change clearly involves winning over the hearts and minds of the business community and the electorate. Partnership is about collaboration and communication, and the government's central role initially is presenting the scientific case on climate change and stimulating dialogue and the exchange of ideas between different organisations and with civil society. Ultimately

the government hierarchy can employ all the tools above to engineer behaviour change through the direct provision of low energy solutions, information on the most effective measures and the steering regulations and financial incentives. Innovation and new approaches flourish on a small scale but seem to clash against other priorities when attempts are made to mainstream them in an organisation. The two main forces enabling or preventing innovation are market factors and national government action and/or inaction. In a study of airport and port regeneration, businessmen interviewed generally considered that EU liberalisation policies, the removal of employment protection, government controls over aviation charges, the abolition of duty-free, and the review of national aviation policy and/or loan write-offs were far more significant for the competitiveness of their operations than local government (Evans *et al.* 2002: 434). Clever deployment of the legal and financial incentives by both national and transnational governments can bring new partners together and introduce and reinforce new patterns of behaviour.

New ways of thinking and doing can be encouraged between organisations engaged in genuine problem-solving if the levers provided by the tools of government are used effectively. This can be achieved by higher tiers of elected government provided they structure the interaction carefully to ensure successful collaboration and the preferred outcomes. Organisations that rely on public funds can be set specific carbon reduction targets, tied to the funding, clearly explaining the reasoning behind policy connections between transport and climate change. A working agreement or contract with service deliverers can also make the outcomes and processes transparent, showing how money will be reimbursed and how underlying conflicts will be identified and addressed.

Effective partnership working with other organisations to achieve climate change adaptation is essential, but so, too, is the existence of product champions within existing organisations to sell the concept of a low energy transport system network (Wixey and Ruiz 2003; GUIDEMAPS 2003). As in all successful project management, the manager with the appropriate organisational knowledge should be well resourced, with clear responsibilities and a skilled support team to produce results. This will overcome some of the conflicts that arise during collaborative working due to the differing goals of participants, lack of trust and unequal resources (technical information, physical and reputation resources) (Hensher and Brewer 2001: 241). Table 4.3 lists a number of key prerequisites for success in partnership working in the different stages of policy delivery: 1) the initial stage of encouraging or piloting new behaviour/ways of acting; followed by 2) successful mainstreaming of the new approaches, within departments of a large organisation and/or between organisations in the local area.

Table 4.3 Effective partnerships for a low energy transport system

Enabling partnerships	Maintaining partnerships
Project champion and project driver	Close physical location
Similar resources/goals	Clearly defined mandatory requirements
Two way needs	Champions at all levels
Financial gain or added value	Political/high level support
Mandatory requirements	Consistency of staff/personnel
Clear links between policies	Informal contacts/exchange of information and
Good historical relations.	resources
	Common commitment.

Source: Adapted from Evans and Hutchins (2002); Hensher and Brewer (2001); GUIDEMAPS (2003: 38); Stead (2003)

Clearly defined mandatory requirements, product champions at all levels within an organisation, and a high level of political support are key reasons for the continued existence of partnerships for innovation. In the case of airport expansion at Manchester, a leading politician's ability to understand the strategic significance, mobilise a coalition of public and private sector partners and quell local political opposition through engagement and innovative environmental mitigation concessions proved a powerful motivation for success (Evans *et al.* 2002: 435). Partnership networks of strategic stakeholders in the local area can drive new approaches to energy efficiency across the whole network:

> Consensus building with interactions among members plays a significant part in developing collective efficiency. Strategic networks provide 'blurred boundaries' for learning to occur. The process of developing collective efficacy in networks is assisted by 'skilled organizers' who span the enterprise boundaries of each member and transfer learning. Innovations by one member need to translate into network-wide innovation. The network needs to be structured in a way that facilitates the emergence and action of these types of liaison role for organizational success.
>
> (Hensher and Brewer 2001: 240–41)

4.4 INTEGRATED PLANNING AT DIFFERENT SPATIAL SCALES

The previous section has introduced some of the key features of partnership working and the governance tools at the disposal of the state. The issues of coherence and consistency of policies within an organisation and horizontally across the public sector in an urban area, raised earlier in this chapter, are also relevant to the evaluation of the effectiveness of the interaction between the different tiers of government. The state can provide a strong steer to the private sector and civil society on resource minimisation, provided the overall message is clear and consistent and is reinforced downwards through the tiers of government. This section, therefore, explores how the interests, and the authority and position resources of the *'vertical intergovern- mental'* (Stead 2003: 1) network of organisations can be combined and integrated to deliver low energy futures. It also seeks to define the level of government that has both the requisite tools of government (direct provision, financial, legislative and information) and the breadth of understanding of spatial interactions to organise the necessary vertical and horizontal collaboration on behaviour change. There are two main strategic tasks. The first is to shape the rules of the game towards low energy development pathways, and the second is to maximise the synergy of effort through the spatial integration of interventions. The core question is how much regulation is required to support innovatory approaches and to then mainstream the new learning within everyday decision-making practices in government, private and civil society? Progress will be dependent on finding the right scale of governance (partnership between government, market actors and NGOs) to grasp the realities of how the global–local interacts, as well as link to the lives of citizens in the area through action programmes that give relevance and meaning to their lives.

As discussed in Chapter 2, a key driver behind the vertical integration of spa- tial policy are the international agreements (such as the Kyoto agreement) and the EU directives on energy efficiency and environmental performance. Global scientific consensus on the agreed 'safe' limits for global greenhouse gas concentration lev- els (550 ppm CO_2 equivalent, quoted in Stern 2006), for example, reinforces these agreements between nation states and provides clarity and transparency to the required actions. There is unlikely to be one template of success for the balance between rules and incentives, as the case studies in Chapter 7 demonstrate. The remainder of this chapter prepares for the later discussion on good practice princi- ples, by concentrating on the responsibilities and interaction between the national and regional levels of government, and then goes onto to examine the city-region and local level interactions.

NATIONAL AND REGIONAL INTERACTIONS

National governments have the responsibility to provide a stable framework for inte- grated, public policy making, ensuring the availability of funding incentives to improve the opportunities for success in implementing low energy and sustainable transport policies (European Conference of Ministers of Transport 2001). Regions and cities look up to national government to assess the urgency of the need for change as translated through the regulatory framework and the criteria for major transportation funding. Legal and administrative guidelines from national government set strong *a priori* assumptions to lower tiers of government about the scope of the policy options local government should choose. Higher tier authorities provide most of the funding for major transportation projects, and both regulatory reform and the criteria for accessing major transport funding can challenge lower levels of government to change existing decision-making practices (Rietveld and Stough 2005).

The EU model of subsidiarity is based on the decentralisation of decision making and coordination of responsibilities at the lowest level of governance appropriate to the task. EU policies have sought to strengthen the institutional and technical joint capacity of decision-making bodies at the regional level, through dialogue to share policy innovation, and to enhance the vertical integration and delivery of EU policies. Strong regional government is seen as a political driver to coordinate horizontally across the public service policy sectors (land use, transport, health and education) and to liaise efficiently with regional agencies and private sector providers. Separate regional transport authorities can play a major role in delivering some of the components of a sustainable transport system, including comprehensive passenger information systems, provision of school transport, coordinated ticketing arrangements (such as multi-operator travelcards), infrastructure investment (notably interchanges) and the planning, construction and financing of light rail systems (White 2002: 4). An elected regional tier of government has the political machinery to resolve the political issues that arise between local government administrations on such issues as parking strategies and can achieve some reconciliation of economic priorities with the sustainable longer-term patterns of development and transport use.

The pattern of subsidiarity varies across Europe, with some nations where the political leadership is centralised (e.g. the UK) and others where local government has the autonomy to implement essentially local priorities (e.g. Sweden and Denmark). Many regional tiers of government (federal structure) are elected, raise taxes, produce transport policies, and fund and provide services. Even where there is this level of devolution to the regions, it is heavily subscribed by the national government using legal tools to set the framework for regional and local government interaction. In Germany, the state uses a range of planning and policy guidelines, legal instruments and funding mechanisms to define the links between municipalities, regions and the state, in the land-use and transport planning arena (GUIDEMAPS 2003). In France, decentralisation to the regional and local levels is characterised by the state preserving a monopoly of technical competence to influence the decisions of lower levels of government.

National and regional tiers of government, depending on the sharing of responsibilities, should provide suitable regulatory structures (legal or administrative) to steer and empower city administrations to require the best available low energy solutions to development needs. Higher tier governments can require that the sustainability of ecosystem management is first demonstrated before new development proposals are accepted, using financial incentives and monitoring for compliance. In addition, the integration of public transit modes could be enhanced through the requirement for a 'sustainable transport audit', to ensure that strategies and proposals encourage public transport, walking and cycling. Mitigation measures can be required for schemes that score poorly on the sustainable transport audit such as public realm improvements, bus and cycling enhancement, reductions in car parking space, workplace parking levies and congestion charging in the development area. This would provide a mechanism to deliver the policies in the sustainable development plan (viz. land use and transport plan, climate change adaptation plan) for mixed use development, active travel, frequent public transport, etc. (see Table 3.1). Public sector agencies can be set a target date to produce and implement their own travel plans to reduce the car dependency of their employees (Akerman 2006). Past experience has shown that getting people to consider different options (how to decide a development application or travel choice), once they have become used to doing it a certain way, is a formidable task.

Unless political consensus can be reached on the location, road tolling and parking restriction issues at the national or regional levels, the city is faced by the prisoner's dilemma of horizontal competition between cities in the same region (Rietveld and Stough 2005: 16). Without the certainty of this strategic direction, city administrations may focus on narrow, and easier to implement, single sector policies raising additional funds through car parking provision and charges, which may undermine the implementation of national and regional policies.

CITY-REGION AND LOCAL LEVEL INTERACTION

Cities are expected to be the growth machines of the future, but will also bear the brunt of market recessions. The top league, global cities of the future are seen by investors as those that have quality residential and leisure facilities, and well ordered public transport connections between business headquarters and international flight connections (Sassen 2001; Scott 2001; Taylor 2004). This requires multi-modal transport interchanges to residential and employment locations in the city-region connecting to a lively and vibrant, mixed-use central business district. Commuting patterns suggest that it is at the city-region that the effective management of transport and the urban dimension can be attained. It is at this spatial level that social and economic linkages can be integrated through the transport system to ensure sustainable and efficient choices for the community (Commission for Integrated Transport 2003; Neuman and Hull 2009). Cities are growing centres for tourism and if the attraction of cities can be increased by the quality of life improvements, this will concentrate activity and might reduce the demand for travel globally. It is also in the urban areas where the development challenge of this millennium will take place: finding homes for new immigrants, education and training provision and sustainable access to jobs and services.

Cities, therefore, hold the key to moving spatial structures to a state where the distances travelled are much less than at present (Whitelegg 1997: 216). City administrations need the tools to increase neighbourhood densities, expand the utilisation of open space and create walkable environments through negotiation or edict with development promoters. New employment should be located close to railway stations and other public transit interchanges, and used as an opportunity to regenerate these areas and promote active travel infrastructures and opportunities (see Malmö case study in Chapter 7). For many city administrations, the most attractive commercial sites tend to be around the edges of existing settlements, building on the trends of the last decade or so. A sequential test for development proposals can be used to prioritise locations that serve the needs of walkers first, followed by cyclists and public transit users. Cities also hold the key to thinking about how to reduce the distances over which freight is moved, by sourcing products locally and through establishing local distribution centres where loads can be stored and repackaged for local delivery.

The city-region or metropolitan region is the level at which urban travel policies are most effectively made and implemented (European Conference of Ministers of Transport 2001), since this is the level at which the challenges to sustainable living become most visible and the spatial scale at which land use and transport policies can be integrated. Some cities and metropolitan regions have tax-raising powers (e.g. Portland Metro, USA and Swedish cities) as do some metropolitan level transport authorities (e.g. US and Swedish transport authorities). Without the authoritative (e.g. legal powers, significant land ownership) or financial resources it is difficult for city-region authorities to coordinate private and public actors around effective low energy solutions. They can collaborate and cooperate on accessibility measures and flagship projects on carbon neutral development, and they can produce integrated land use transport strategies and issue best practice guidelines. But these are, arguably, insufficient to mainstream change towards more sustainable transport systems.

Essential to effective city-region delivery of a low energy development pathway must be spatial strategies that create positive synergies between the resources and priorities of urban and rural areas in the most equitable and resource-efficient way. The spatial strategy should cover the city-region to ensure spatial integration and coordination of policy across all component authorities and to address the cumulative effects of different policy sectors on spatial interaction (Bayliss 1998; Stead 2003; Hull 2008c).

Many city level administrations have localised the global carbon targets and developed their own measures and indicators to raise awareness of climate change and resource minimisation with city stakeholders and citizens. The key issue here is getting away from the traditional delivery of services organised by sectors and thinking more holistically. Looking specifically at how to deliver multi-modal integration, the Transportation Research Board (1996: 6–9) warns that '*unless the selection criteria and programming structure capture the community's priorities as well as enable fair comparison of highway, bus and alternative modes, traditional modal orientation will continue*'. The key to achieving a more holistic approach to sustainable cities is a clear context or road map set by higher tiers of government, and constant communication with elected officials and organisational leaders about the benefits of resource minimisation and how to achieve it through integrated holistic approaches.

NEIGHBOURHOODS

Although the strategic level planning of interconnected infrastructures across the city-region, and outwards, is an important mechanism for exploiting low energy outcomes, it is at the level of the neighbourhood that sustained behaviour change will be instigated. The neighbourhood level is, therefore, the ideal spatial scale for engaging with ordinary members of the public concerning how they can be empowered to achieve improvements to their living environments through low energy solutions. Local people are the experts on how their neighbourhoods work and their needs should be the priority in negotiations with developers to create 'win–win' situations for all in accepting new development. Providing community organisations and groups of residents with small amounts of funding to enable office space and meeting facilities will allow new projects valued by residents to get off the ground (Hull 2006).

Engagement at the very local level tends to be forgotten or poorly resourced by city officials, unless the neighbourhood is a constant source of irritation through high crime levels, high levels of debt, or constant lobbying to protect neighbourhood resources. Even when the state intervenes to regenerate a neighbourhood, the residents are rarely consulted for their opinion of what works and what does not in their neighbourhood. Once effective working relationships are established and community representatives are well resourced, they can be the mechanism not only for collaboration but also for education and advocacy (Hull 2006). Few residents have experienced well designed neighbourhoods to know that connectivity, ease of walking and cycling, open spaces and biomass are also important to quality of life and mental health. Knowledgeable residents are more likely to care for their environment and be open to behaviour change (Macnaughten and Urry 1998; National Centre for Social Research 2008).

In conclusion, this chapter has argued that national and transnational government must exert their agency to set an opportunity agenda of incentives and constraints that will both lever flows of private capital for low energy projects and encourage citizens to reduce resource consumption and waste. This new invest-ment focus on low energy solutions will require a complete overhaul of our implicit values and accepted ways of working until new resource-efficient practices become embedded in society. The chapter has shown how each level of spatial governance can contribute to moving towards more sustainable outcomes. The challenge is to knit these tiers together through a clear and consistent strategy which allows flexibil-ity and learning, and, just like 'Brighton Rock' (candy stick with place name running through the middle), wherever you cut into the tier of governance you will receive the same message on resource minimisation. Chapter 5 moves on to examine the potentials and pitfalls in the new institutional structures which this level of social organisation will require. Chapter 5 finds that the net-like supportive structure is not yet in place in most countries because of weak governance capacity to integrate at the city-region and national spatial levels. These deficiencies of governance capacity lead to gaps in deliberation between strategic or forward thinking, the policy genera-tion stage and local level strategies, and the operational delivery of services. As a result, issues that deserve attention, but are outwith the current policy priorities, fall through the gaps between policy sectors. The next chapter examines these barriers to radical change in more detail.

CHAPTER FIVE

UNDERSTANDING THE INSTITUTIONAL BARRIERS TO CHANGE

5.1 INTRODUCTION

This chapter examines why the step change towards more sustainable behaviour is, as yet, only happening in limited circumstances. Sustainable transport policy needs to offer new ways of addressing accessibility and new approaches to resource allocation and engagement to improve the infrastructure for slow or active modes of travel. Chapter 4 highlighted the tools that national government's have at their disposal to steer attention towards sustainability objectives. National level policies are cloaked in the rhetoric of sustainability and, often, strong targets are set to reduce consumption or emission levels. Fairly robust datasets are collected at EU and national levels that show the trends towards and away from sustainable development and sustainable behaviour patterns. Despite the policy attention to sustainability progress, in most cases, it is slow and almost due to serendipity. Since the behaviour of individuals and market actors has not noticeably changed, this chapter presumes that the opportunity agenda of constraints and incentives supplied by the state is the key to understanding this failure.

This chapter focuses on why, despite all the efforts to address profligate resource consumption in transport, there is so little progress on resource reduction. The chapter attempts to uncover the answers to the following questions by examining the findings from European research on transport policy implementation to identify where the policy failure lies.

- Is the delay in reducing our global footprint to fair global shares and reducing CO_2 emissions to 350–450 ppm due to implementation failure, and that despite political commitment to achieve the intended outcomes there have been flaws in policy design and delivery?
- Has the selection of government tools and policy instruments been naïve and inappropriate?
- Have the delivery agencies been especially obstructive?
- Or have government civil servants just underestimated the difficulties faced by lower tiers of government and local partnerships in collaborating to produce a built environment where all daily needs can be accessed without recourse to private motorised vehicles?
- Or is it just a case of tokenism to global environmental issues on the part of our leaders, based on the ease at which the Kyoto emission reductions, for much of Europe, were achieved with little need to resort to behaviour change?

The research on implementation barriers is very full, covering the barriers to achieving sustainable transport outcomes and the barriers to innovation more generally. The research categorises the barriers into the following labels: financial, organisational, cultural, legislative, political and technical, which overlap to some extent. Examples of each category are listed in Tables 5.1–5.6.

Institutional barriers are defined by Rietveld and Stough (2005: 1) as '*values, culture, interest group goals, laws and statutes, regulations, and entrenched and existing practices*'. They go on to state that:

> achieving sustainable transport always involves addressing significant and deep institutional barriers to change. But it is not clear whether institutions are more of a supporting vehicle or a barrier to solutions, even in the long run [...]. The lesson is that institutions serve both as barriers to problem solutions and as vehicles for facilitating solutions, e.g., via helping keep transaction costs relatively low.
>
> (ibid.: 13–14)

As the ECMT/OECD (2001: 4) study of barriers to achieving sustainable transport solutions in 168 cities around the world notes: '*Implementation problems are not the same, nor are they experienced in the same way in all countries. Particular economic, institutional and political structures, as well as region-specific social and cultural factors can engender particular implementation problems*'.

The remainder of this chapter is divided into two sections. The first section summarises what is known about the barriers to the effective implementation of more sustainable transport modal choices such as public transit provision and infrastructure for walking and cycling, as well as the implementation of strategies to reduce car travel demand through 'demand management' or 'mobility management'. The final section of the chapter examines the strategies that have been used at national and the city level to overcome these difficulties.

Table 5.1 Financial barriers in the implementation of sustainable transport policy

Financial:
• Different financial structures of local and national organisations
• High resource cost (skilled staff, data requirements) and high risk to secure public funding for major schemes
• Time delays and uncertainty in securing finance from private sector actors
• Few examples of the right 'pricing signals' at national or local levels
• Taxation policies and government funding tends to favour car use (company car) and business travel, i.e. few subsidies or tax deductions for cycling and bus use.

5.2 INSTITUTIONAL BARRIERS

FINANCIAL BARRIERS

As one would expect, lack of finance is the perennial problem and the number one barrier faced by transport projects (Banister 2005a: 55; KonSULT 2005). Lack of finance may mean that the most appropriate solution is not selected due to the insufficiency of staff to design the preferred project and negotiate with stakeholders (GUIDEMAPS 2003). There is extensive data collection and modelling required, justifying the business case or value for money of a major transport scheme. Using consultants, the modelling and data collection costs are in the region of £1 million (€1.2 million) (DISTILLATE 2006). Additional costs are incurred in the process of bidding for government funding, including the quantification of scheme impacts and the application of new models of finance which require private sector participation. Roughly a third of the total outlay is staff time. Major scheme bids to national government, therefore, require a high initial resource input and are a high risk strategy to gain funding when the total funds available are relatively small. But, because so much transportation funding is provided in this competitive 'top-down' way it has led to a separate administrative decision-making structure devoted to the planning and design of major transport infrastructure (essentially highways, railways and light rapid transit) (Blandford *et al.* 2008).

The control of public transit funding by higher tiers of government creates specific barriers for policy integration at the metropolitan level and for the implementation of innovatory transport measures. The major-scheme funding-bureaucracy often operates independently of the land use planning process at national and local levels which it profoundly affects. The focus on highway infrastructure for major government spending through this process heavily subsidises the viability of private car use relative to public transit. This is an example of what Stead (2003: 335) terms '*weak and perverse incentives*' for joint collaboration between organisations and professions. Other examples, besides misguided financing and investment flows, identified in the ECMT/OECD (2001) cross-Europe study were weaknesses in the pricing and fiscal frameworks for transport. For example, market incentive structures deter commercial transport operators from operating marginal services (Atkins 2003). There is also a high risk that if local politicians impose road tolling, stringent parking standards, and/or development taxes, neighbouring authorities will attract activity away through a laxer regime (Commission for Integrated Transport 2003). Perverse financial incentives operate across several public funding objectives (sustainability, technological innovation, employment growth, energy saving, health, sustainable transport, etc.), which combined with the tax-raising system can incentivise or (dis) incentivise sustainable choices (Wixey and Ruiz 2003).

Funding regimes tend to have a built-in path dependency and are rarely flexible enough to widen the scope of schemes to be selected unless the non-traditional schemes can show that they can deliver the objectives of the preferred schemes (Wixey and Ruiz 2003: 10). Hence, significant financial barriers arise for promoters of innovatory schemes, since their uniqueness does not fit within the appraisal criteria designed for major transport infrastructure such as road schemes and light rail. Often the drip-feed of funding available for sustainable transport initiatives, which often contain a package of small measures, is uncertain or insufficient to implement all the measures simultaneously, leading to incomplete delivery of the initiative (Moore 1994; Mittler 1999; Civilising Cities 2003). Some sources of funding require loans or grants to be spent within a specified, often short, period of time. This favours projects with a shorter lead-in time rather than other projects that would be more effective (DISTILATE 2006). The funding framework for transport, therefore, has a more constraining influence on the implementation of innovative schemes at the local level, which require relatively higher staff costs during the operational phase. The perception of the higher cost of sustainable options also often deters the involvement of private sector investors in these schemes (Smerdon et al. 1996).

Securing funding from private sources, through the negotiation on development proposals at specific locations, as part of local government powers to control land use and/or negotiation over private contributions to major transport projects, to recoup the resulting value uplift to private property owners is marked by uncertainty, time delays and recourse to the courts of law. Private sector involvement, generally, in the financing and implementation of transport schemes is perceived by local government transport planners as causing specific financial barriers (National Audit Office 2008; DISTILLATE 2006). These include: substantial delays in project planning while the search for private partners is carried out; lack of staff to collaborate with and manage the private sector partner; and lack of skilled staff with the requisite leadership, project management and negotiation skills (Atkins 2003, 2004). Smaller transport authorities are more likely to underestimate the time and therefore cost associated with progressing innovatory or contentious transport schemes.

So, despite government policy priorities to expand public transit facilities and encourage more active travel options, financial systems rarely change to incentivise the introduction of the new policy priorities. Often scheme promoters are faced by inflexible, and often separate, financial systems for road and rail and by necessity have to bid for funding from several different funding sources, each of which may have different requirements that need to be satisfied (Civilising Cities 2003; KonSULT 2005). The lack of connection between funding schemes and government policy undermines the coordinated delivery of a package of measures and joint working with other organisations.

ORGANISATIONAL BARRIERS

Table 5.2 Organisational barriers in the implementation of sustainable transport policy

- Incompatible objectives and targets
- Lack of clarity in targets and objectives
- Competition for limited public financial resources
- Skill resource and time limitations
- Competing objectives of external organisations dedicated to highways
- Lack of agreement within a partnership
- Organisational change
- Different organisational structures and jurisdictional boundaries that separate Local Authorities, public agencies and transport companies
- View of sustainable transport/mobility management within organisation
- Perception of 'consultation' and the need to consult with local partners, communities and transport users
- Nature of public transport in terms of quality and provision
- Private rather than public ownership of public transport leading to difficulty in imposing social rather than commercial objectives.

Vested interests

Perceived threat/competition

Disparities in staff training

Perceived loss of organisational and programme identity/strategic positions

Perceived loss of organisational–leader–staff prestige/authority/domains

Inter- and intra-professional differences

Lack of common language

Different priorities/ideologies/outlooks/goals

Differing organisational–leader–professional socialisation

Poor historical relations/image formation

Costs outweigh benefits

Bureaucratisation

Centralisation

Professionalisation

Specialisation

Infrequent/inadequate internal and external communication

Fragmentation of the environment–federal/state/local levels of government

Little or no boundary permeability/roles

Inadequately trained personnel

Structural differences

Figure 5.1 Inhibitors of organisational coordination

At the project level, problems with coordinating the input from different organi-sations and policy conflicts are the second most frequently mentioned barrier found in Banister's (2005a) review. This research was carried out by the EU-funded DANTE consortium and involved a study of 61 'sustainable' transport measures in six European cities (Aalborg, Bristol, Bucharest, Enschede, Rome and Zurich). Organisational barriers can include the distribution of resources between govern-mental bodies, the lack of incentives to work in new ways or address new issues, the fragmentation of the policy and implementation chain, and failures of communica-tion in joint working arrangements. Stead (2003), summarising the work of Halpert (1982), has identified the inhibitors to effective organisational working (Figure 5.1). These are issues that can be overcome in the short to medium term.

Many city administrations have allocated insubstantial resources to address the carbon mitigation and transport adaptation measures required to provide a sustainable transport system. In many cases they are lagging behind because insufficient interest has been accorded to transport by elected politicians and senior officials, resulting in lower priority and budget allocated, with consequent difficulties in delivering planned programmes (Atkins 2004). In other cases, city administrations lack the legal powers, responsibilities and funds to work effectively with different policy sectors to achieve sustainable transport outcomes. These difficulties manifest in lack of skilled staff, dif-ficulties in recruiting and retaining key transport planning and traffic engineering staff, or an appropriate mix and level of staff skills (Stead 2003; Atkins 2004).

Atkins' (2004) study found that the performance of local authorities reflected differences in their knowledge and capacity, which was manifested in their oversight of the key requirements in programme delivery and monitoring progress, confu-sion over the responsibilities for transport planning design and implementation, and unwillingness to explore best practice and benchmark with other local authori-ties. This is often linked to lack of clear responsibilities or ownership of the project or programme by senior staff, who delegate the management of projects and the achievement of organisational targets to inexperienced staff. Organisations were particularly vulnerable to non-performance following corporate restructuring.

Communication and trust are the key drivers for effective working across dif-ferent organisations. Cross-sector projects by nature involve partners with different professional backgrounds and thus differences in culture, language and agendas 'which present obstacles to communicating the worth of a project' (Civilising Cities 2003) unless understanding can be created between partners. Pemberton (2000) found that despite regular contact between the key players in the delivery of trans-port policy in his case study, there was still mistrust. One reason for this he suggests is that officers from transport, planning and economic development departments rarely attend each other's meetings, which might provide a more informal arena to improve understanding.

The ECMT/OECD (2001) report concluded that the main barrier to sustainable transport is the lack of policy integration due to inefficient and counterproductive roles. This research provides additional evidence of the gaps in performance integration which were discussed in Chapter 4 (Section 4.2). Road building and public transit improvements tend to have an identifiable 'home' within the highways and transportation department. But often the focus is a narrow engineering approach to the effective design and implementation of infrastructure schemes, and less on implementing corporate policies to influence travel behaviour (Stead 2003; Atkins 2004). In Atkins' (2003) survey, only a third of the transport respondents felt that transport was considered sufficiently by the social services department and only half of respondents considered that transport issues are considered sufficiently in the location and accessibility of healthcare facilities. Research by Akerman (2006) to identify the common ground between transport planners and health care planners found that the former were more likely to identify the promotion of walking and cycling and the latter as the need to improve public transit, access issues and rural isolation.

Cross-links from other services to transport tend not to be made in authorities that have weak transport policies and they, conversely, fail to acknowledge the role that transport can play in contributing to health and education objectives (Atkins 2004). Similar comments on integration have been made between transport policy and land use planning where, because of the close interaction, the consequences of failure have repercussions on sector policy delivery (Banister 2002b; Stead 2003; Hull 2005). Table 5.3 provides further empirical research evidence of the unintended policy effects from the implementation of sustainable transport measures when land use and transport planning functions are not integrated.

The implementation of demand management or mobility management (MM) projects are often jointly delivered by several organisations, and constrained by the fragmentation of responsibilities within organisations and the competing objectives of participants (Wixey and Ruiz 2003). This type of project often brings together a wide variety of organisations which may have little experience of joint working. The agencies involved could include:

> Various public agencies responsible for constructing and maintaining different types of transport infrastructure (roads, parking, cycle paths, etc.); organisations (both public and private sectors) responsible for running public transport services (buses, trams, trains, taxis, etc.); companies and other, usually private sector, organisations that manage sites where MM measures are to be applied (e.g. offices); organisations involved in marketing and publicity initiatives, or in offering certain MM services (e.g. developing travel plans).
>
> (Wixey and Ruiz 2003: 6)

Table 5.3 The unintended effects of failure to integrate land use and transport planning

Indecision	Outcomes	Example
1 Inadequate funding – fiscal constraints.	No implementation, or delayed or partial action.	Package of measures for a city accepted, but only partially introduced for financial reasons. Important to provide investment in public transport as an alternative mode prior to restrictions on the use of the car being imposed.
2 Ill-defined legal and regulatory rules – legal constraints.	Legal challenges and delays in implementation.	Road pricing could be introduced, but challenged in the courts on the basis of lack of consultation, or human rights concerns over privacy and use of information.
3 Sectorisation of policy making – no coherence.	Lack of awareness of indirect effects of policy actions.	City centre strategy of car restraint works well, but growth allowed in peripheral areas so net effect is more travel.
4 Opaqueness of responsibilities for decisions between agencies – conflict.	Partial implementation and no clear rationale for action.	Construction of new housing in peripheral locations leads to longer car based work journeys. Closure of local schools and hospitals lead to longer journeys.
5 Partial implementation – no commitment.	Unclear or inconsistent messages.	Package of measures for a city accepted, but only partially implemented for political (or other) reasons, thus reducing its effectiveness.
6 Lack of debate and involvement – no consultation.	No change in behaviour and public resentment.	Plans introduced to encourage modal shift from car to public transport or cycle, but little change takes place due to inappropriate implementation or non-acceptance by users.

Source: Table 4.1 (Banister 2005a: 61), reproduced with permission

Often, incentive and appraisal systems do not encourage or reward cross-sectoral teamwork within public sector organisations (Stead 2003). For lack of foresight, sustainable transport objectives continue to be undermined by the policies of other departments, locally (e.g. education) and nationally (e.g. education and healthcare), that generate travel or increase distances travelled (e.g. location of healthcare).

The project manager of a sustainable measure such as mobility management has to surmount both internal and external barriers to effective communication. The first barrier is that sustainable transport measures do not have an identifiable home within multipurpose local government organisations. Different tasks are inevitably carried out by officers in different departments and securing their input when needed by the project manager depends on the goodwill of all concerned. Small scale projects, like mobility management, rarely are significant enough to get the chief executive's recognition and support so, despite clear action plans and delivery dates, the project manager has no power to coopt assistance or demand delivery from partners (Civilising Cities 2003).

Without interdepartmental committees to manage inter-sector working, setting responsibilities and reconciling conflicting priorities, organisational complexities and inter-agency
rivalries will delay implementation (Stead 2001; GUIDEMAPS 2003; Atkins 2003;
Civilising Cities 2003).

Inter-sectoral partnerships on cross-sector initiatives are fragile and unless the
numerous tensions can be overcome through effective communication networks,
projects will be cumbersome and slow to deliver (Civilising Cities 2003). Each partner
has to see past their own agendas and identify with the project goals (DISTILLATE
2006). This can be problematic if the partnership's primary purpose is to access funding.
Shared objectives need to be clear, regularly communicated and consistently applied by
the management team. The partnership between central and local government in the
delivery of transport policy has often been characterised by mixed messages. On the
one hand, government strategies proclaim the need for demand restraint measures and,
on the other hand, spending decisions heavily favour road investment. Lower tiers of
government then have the task to integrate these two strands and to demonstrate how
they form a consistent approach. When local government administrations also feel that
their efforts to encourage modal shift are being constrained by central government, this
creates a severe barrier to progress (Atkins 2003).

CULTURAL BARRIERS

Many of the implementation barriers faced by the sustainable transport initiatives
mentioned above are due to the enduring norms in society which will only change
over the long term. Socio-cultural barriers were the third most frequently mentioned
barrier in Banister's (2005a) study. Examples of cultural barriers are the status of the
car in society, the esteem in which experts are held, and the values of transport professionals. These barriers emerge from, and are embedded in, specific socio-cultural
contexts and are related to geopolitical factors.

Table 5.4 Cultural barriers in the implementation of sustainable transport policy

---

- Societal trends towards increasing dependency on the car and decentralised urban form
- Human resistance to change and general lack of knowledge
- Professional barriers between organisations and academic disciplines
- Different levels of understanding of the 'technical' issues and assumptions used in transport
  and land use planning
- Consultation procedures inimical to the gender, ethnicity, disability etc. needs of different
  groups in society
- Lack of a tradition of methods for achieving consensus
- Unwillingness to take part in participative approaches on the part of major sections of the
  population and therefore dominance by unrepresentative minorities
- Inherent contradictions in people's attitudes.

The car is now seen as such an important possession for households that people are becoming 'locked-in' to using it (Dupuy 1999; Lucas and Jones 2009). This has arisen, according to Dupuy, because the continuing investment in the road network and the marketing of cars as a status symbol has created a 'virtuous magic circle', so that *'to belong to the system has become essential, and to a large extent it is the fact that many others are in the system that motivates us to enter it (or remain in it), to use a car, and thus to become dependent on it'* (Dupuy 1999: 12). This dependence has been influenced by the growth of the road network, and development of suburban and edge-of-city housing and employment making the car indispensable for cross-city journeys. Most car owners are reluctant to use public transit once they have become used to the accessibility and flexibility that the car provides, and often the perception of public transit by non-users is that it is a dirty mode of travel used primarily by the lower social classes (Lucas and Jones 2009). This, in turn, leads to a substantial mandate that influences society's approach to the enforcement of restrictions (speed cameras, illegal parking, etc.) placed on vehicles and thus the effectiveness of any demand–restraint measures. There is thus a strong motor lobby reflected in public, business and media resistance to measures that will reduce the freedom and accessibility provided by the car (ECMT/OECD 2001; Banister 2002a; Lyons and Chatterjee 2002; Atkins 2003). This has a spiral effect making it politically difficult to introduce stricter traffic restraint measures to encourage car users to consider alternative modes.

Another cultural barrier is the respect that experts have in many countries. This is often linked to centralised administrative and planning bureaucracies where government officials make decisions in secret with little engagement with external stakeholders. GUIDEMAPS (2003) found in these situations that project management was specifically weak due to diffuse internal communication within the political and official bodies, leading to uncertainty and poor linkages between the stages in the design and development process. It has been observed that the discipline of transport planning and the profession have a distinct culture, or way of doing and thinking, that creates a barrier to interaction. Drawing on the work of Allison (1971), Rein and Schon (1994) and Sabatier (1993), Ney (2001: 156) shows how different cultures produce different 'perceptual lenses', 'policy frames', or 'policy belief systems'. These are frameworks for collecting, ordering and analysing data which structure what they see as relevant. Pemberton's (2000: 25) examination of transport planning in north-east England provides an example, where:

> *any discussion of such* [environmental] *issues was framed by the transport planners in terms such as models, traffic flows and highway capacities with no reference to similar environmental capacities. Second, that the whole language of seeing areas of land as corridors suggested 'an*

implicit assumption that what's important is what's at each end' (pressure group), and not the countryside, communities and habitats that the infrastructure might pass through.

The focus on highway flows and capacities has two main political effects. First, the network of corridors is used as a spatial organising concept to connect the political entities of the member state(s); the role the TEN's concept provides for the EU (Buunk 2003; Jensen and Richardson 2004). Second, the spatial representation in policy documents secures funding and permits with relative ease for these schemes, that can be interpreted as an example of the *'structured nature of business privilege'* (Pemberton 2000: 26). The view that the health of the economy will determine voting patterns (Vigar 2000), coupled with the fear of competition from neighbouring jurisdictions (Lucas 1998), fuels the efforts to which local government supports the economic concerns of the main employers within their jurisdiction.

This culture or set of value priorities has been commented on in other studies (Bayliss 1998; Hull *et al.* 2005; Hull 2008). This manifests as a transport profession that is perceived to be interested in a narrow range of issues, tends to be wedded to certain models and techniques, is slow to embrace issues outside the traditional professional arena, and thus can field few people able to interact with other professions. When professionals are limited to certain kinds of mindsets and values, they tend to become more risk averse and unwilling to take on new approaches (Pemberton 2000; Donovan *et al.* 2005). Other disciplines react to the perceived introverted nature of transport engineers. Land use planners, so often sidelined by the scale and lack of transparency of the transport funding bureaucracy, tend to be somewhat reactive to regional transportation network policy issues (Blandford *et al.* 2008). It is well known amongst built environment professionals that a sustainable transport policy should prioritise the basic daily needs for the majority by foot, cycle and local public transit and that transport choices should respect wider economic, social and environmental objectives (Table 4.1). However, socio-cultural forces are seen as blocking any attempt to integrate policy sectors (Bayliss 1998). In the UK, a joint department of transport and land use planning which produced a 10 year strategic framework for a sustainable transport future was quickly sidelined and the departments separated.

LEGISLATIVE BARRIERS

Supportive legislation can require that certain actions or events take place. Its absence, therefore, can be crippling for the introduction of 'new' approaches to resolving accessibility issues (Wixey and Ruiz 2003). This creates several unintended side effects. First, the interlinkages between transport modes, and the synergistic effects with policy instruments in other policy sectors, are not considered. For example, large areas of public

Table 5.5 Legislative barriers in the implementation of sustainable transport policy

---

- No direct binding laws or regulations regarding sustainable transport solutions or mobility management (e.g. in terms of restricting car use)
- Lack of a supportive legislative framework to introduce local land use and transport policies
- Complex legislative procedures.

---

policy and investment, such as health and education, are only weakly influenced by the development planning system in many countries but have a major bearing on patterns of activity and transport demand (Commission for Integrated Transport 2003). Second, there is no legal requirement, or limited powers, to require or enforce the adherence to good practice, such as using sustainability criteria in decision making, or to require the implementation of an agreed multi-modal plan or strategy.

Third, the absence of a legal responsibility to take the strategic overview or split responsibilities to act, creates substantial delays and inaction until agreement is reached between all stakeholders (KonSULT 2005; Commission for Integrated Transport 2003). A permissive operating environment for privatised transport operators makes it difficult for public transit agencies to plan services over the longer term when the operators decide to cancel routes on commercial grounds giving only six weeks notice (Atkins 2003). The limited legal powers of a transport agency deter the provision of services outside the jurisdiction of the authority, inhibiting the development of wider sub-regional transport services.

Legislation can also have negative effects through deterring the most 'sensible' solutions or by creating unnecessary hurdles to be mastered before a scheme can be developed. Laws that prevent anti-competitive practices such as shared taxi schemes, integrated fares and timetables create barriers to private sector collaboration and delay the provision of higher quality public transit by public sector agencies (Atkins 2003: 3). The time and cost barriers created by adherence to legal requirements in project implementation is well documented in the literature. In Banister's (2005a) survey of 61 EU transport projects this was the fourth ranked barrier. There are two main issues of concern for infrastructure promoters. The first is where the alignment of the infrastructure causes damage to protected habitats and species, which prevents implementation (Transportation Research Board 1996). The second issue is the complexity of overlapping legislative processes, with different legislation for different modes and often different ministers in charge (Commission for Integrated Transport 2003; Eddington 2006: 56–57). The complexity of the development permit process also can involve the re-examination of the scheme in its entirety at a statutory or non-statutory inquiry in public which reviews written and oral evidence pertaining to the benefits and the drawbacks of the scheme (KonSULT 2005). Land use interventions, road building and road pricing schemes are particularly prone to scheme revisions required by the

findings of these inquiries. These perceived legal barriers raise issues about the technical justification required for projects, the role given to public participation, the scope
for legal challenge from beginning to end, the discussion and negotiation on equitable
compensation, and the number of government agencies that need to be involved in the
planning and consideration of projects.

POLITICAL BARRIERS

Political barriers to the successful implementation of sustainable transport measures
arise from changes to the power relationships between organisations, the perceived
need of politicians to implement major projects during their electoral term of office,
their desire to be re-elected, and wavering political commitment. The reorganisation
of government structures in the 1990s as neoliberal ideas on the efficacy of less
government intervention took hold across parts of Europe has reshuffled responsibilities between tiers of government, introduced new non-elected public agencies and
reduced the state's financial commitment to major infrastructure schemes. Often the
new institutional arenas are no more than '*talking shops*' since the real policy decisions are being made by higher tiers of government. In the UK, the autonomy of local
government has been curtailed and now local politicians feel that their authority, in
the eyes of the electorate, has reduced as the public funding for new road infrastructure has declined (Pemberton 2000). In the political game of winning elections
demand–restraint policies are not yet guaranteed vote winners and, moreover, as
the earlier discussion on funding constraints has shown, national government support for these schemes is erratic (Vigar *et al.* 2000; Atkins 2003).

The election cycle creates a hurdle for innovatory schemes that might be con-
troversial as politicians become more risk-averse in the run up to re-election. In some
countries there are local elections every year. The consequences of this are that
local politicians tend to adopt short-term strategies that will provide results within
their term of office and to steer clear of strategies that might prove unacceptable

Table 5.6 Political barriers in the implementation of sustainable transport policy

- Change in political direction or control of the Local Authority and/or timing of council
  elections
- Lack of long-term planning and strategic planning or belief by politicians in technical
  considerations or scientific evidence as a basis for decision making
- Long timescale of implementation and effect of measures (outside the political cycle of 4–5 years)
- Few examples of policy integration at local level and national levels
- The power and resources of different partners (e.g. monopoly positions of developers)
- Few insights on how to work with others
- Emphasis on what is publicly and politically acceptable rather than what might be most
  cost effective.

to the electorate (Donovan *et al.* 2005). A lack of public acceptability to one of the measures in the sustainable transport package may mean that the demands lobbied for by pressure groups are accepted before politicians are willing to commit themselves to the package. This can work against longer-term achievement of the transport strategy that requires a number of 'pull' and 'push' measures to change travel behaviour. Local elections may mean, also, that projects are not completed or are delayed because of changes in political direction (GUIDEMAPS 2003).

Few politicians wish to be considered as 'anti-car' so they stall on addressing the global greenhouse gas emissions from car use. There is also a strong perception that road investment aids the regeneration of the local economy, and that the reverse, traffic restraints, will deter new investment in an area and therefore conflict with economic development objectives. Local economic interests tend, therefore, to be prioritised above environmental quality and health policies without any direct lobbying from business interests. Pemberton (2000: 26) concluded from his case study that '*business gets what it wants with regard to policy because of the objectives it shares with local authorities rather than influence through direct lobbying.*'

The studies also show that local politicians have a wide remit of responsibilities that often conflict. They have to respond to the attitudes and concerns of residents and local traders who may complain that certain details of a transport scheme negatively affect them. They have to support their local party policy priorities, and the population of the municipality as a whole, which may conflict with their role in deciding on transport policy. In the Atkins study (2003: para 7.15) this led to decisions on strategic schemes, which had local disbenefits and schemes that reduced car parking or reallocated road space away from cars, being overturned or abandoned.

Without support from the public or higher tiers of government, few local administrations are prepared to take the difficult decisions to reduce private car use and traffic congestion. Yet, politicians are often more confident than their officers in their ability to tackle climate change and achieve sustainable transport targets (GUIDEMAPS 2003). However, this confidence tends to buckle around election time when politicians fail to support particular schemes in the face of public opposition. Politicians can foresee clear positive outcomes from schemes to improve road safety and increase public transit use, but remain to be convinced that motorway tolling and congestion charging will have the desired effect of changing behaviour. These latter schemes are often complicated by the need to gain political support from adjacent municipalities, since these schemes either cross political borders or have cross-boundary effects (GUIDEMAPS 2003).

The lack of a political mandate at the regional level creates a barrier for obtaining political assent for sustainable transport approaches. Regional coordination of public and private sector investment and commitment to sustainable transport schemes in legal plans can prevent lower government levels from undermining

regional strategies through the pursuit of local vested interests (e.g. on parking strategies) or by permitting major traffic generators that cause congestion on regional
infrastructure networks. In the European countries selected in the GUIDEMAPS
(2003) research, the UK had the highest severity of institutional barriers for obtaining political assent for transport schemes partly due to the absence of an elected
regional tier of government. Within the context of the central ownership of transport
policy and decision making in the UK system, it is politically easier to produce a government transport strategy that has something for all constituents, rather than make
any difficult political decisions (Vigar 2006).

TECHNICAL BARRIERS

Besides the institutional and cultural barriers discussed above, there are technical barriers around creating a more cross-sector approach to transport delivery (Stough and
Rietveld 2005). Keeping up to date with the changes in policy creates multiple new
challenges including data requirements, methodological and analytical approaches to
sustainability and resource minimisation, and the monitoring of outcomes.

Data quality and quantity on resource inputs and policy outcomes is poor in nearly
all countries, and thus creates an obstacle in the assessment of sustainable transport initiatives and in providing the technical evidence base and underlying analysis
for local transport strategies (ECMT/OECD 2001; Atkins 2004). The understanding
of '*urban travel and land use and their interactions, remain sparse, inconsistent and
often of overall poor quality*' (ECMT 2001: 9). Computerised models of land use and
transport interaction are beneficial in enhancing the decision makers' understanding
of transport problems and alternative strategic policy options, and while they help
to secure the funding for major schemes, they are expensive to construct and rely
on expensive data collection. Transport officers criticise the time and effort spent on
validating existing models using narrow criteria that provide little understanding of
the behavioural responses to new transport measures (DISTILLATE 2006). Models
are rarely used early enough in generating alternative strategies and there is a shortage of skilled personnel to provide intelligent interpretation of results (Hull 2009).
Transport officers therefore rely on their own professional judgement or suggestions
from stakeholders.

In policy circles more attention is being given to the interrelationship between
a city and its hinterland or travel-to-work region. But there are still questions concerning the understanding of how transport interactions work in a particular context
and how they are affected by transregional flows. The issue of the transportation
of goods by freight traffic is still often seen as a separate domain despite the long
distances goods are transported by road. While data availability and modelling
data representation are improving, LUTI models are not yet able to assess the

Table 5.7 Technical barriers in the implementation of sustainable transport policy

- The large scale, scope and complexity of sustainability that can be daunting
- Lack of good tools to capture, summarise and present viewpoints and discussions
- Lack of integrated assessment models/tools which reflect the specific social and economic dynamics of the impact of interventions on mobility, accessibility and exergy
- Lack of knowledge of the costs and benefits of mitigation measures and how they might change in coming decades
- Lack of research on sustainable consumption patterns and option choice
- Underdeveloped methodologies for monitoring change and policy impacts on quality of life questions
- Datasets that vary in terms of significance, comparability, consistency and administrative level of collection (local authority, regional forum, national level).

social, environmental and health benefits of alternative schemes, the influence of destination choice, and the effects of travel shifting, car sharing, or improvements to walking and cycling (Hull 2009). Surveys of urban planners across Europe have found that strategic environmental assessments and health impact assessments have made no difference to policy decisions because they lack clear definition and in the case of health impact assessments are not a legal requirement in most countries (Hull 2008a; Fischer 2009).

There is also a specific gap in the evaluation and appraisal tools for small- to medium-sized schemes covering parking controls, bus improvements, fare subsidies, travel planning, traffic management, land use, walking and cycling schemes (Barton 2004; Hull 2009). Current appraisal methodologies, such as multi-criteria analysis and cost-effectiveness appraisals, do not meet transport officer requirements for evaluating accessibility and the economic and other distributional impacts. The narrow economic 'value for money' criteria are perceived by these officers as distorting scheme selection choice (Hull 2008a). The cumulative effects assessment of demand management measures is still in its infancy (Hull et al. 2009a,b,c). Transport officers do not have much confidence in judging the biodiversity, health, noise, townscape, heritage and water pollution impacts from transport, which are seen as having a low level of importance in transport scheme appraisal (May et al. 2008; Hull 2009). This creates a barrier to understanding the mix or package of measures that are appropriate in different settlement contexts to secure more sustainable patterns of travel. The absence of in-house expertise and experience of implementing demand–restraint measures and alternative fuelled-vehicles are a further barrier to selling these policies to politicians and the public (Whitelegg 1997; Vigar 2006).

Another area of weakness in practice, which detracts from successful policy implementation, is the use of indicators. Target setting and performance monitoring of transport policy remains underdeveloped in many countries. One of the difficulties

Table 5.8 How to overcome the barriers to sustainable travel

Strategy components	Key elements
1 Establish a supportive national policy framework	Develop a national policy framework for sustainable urban travel.
2 Improve institutional cooperation and coordination	Coordinate national policy approaches on urban land use, travel, health and the environment. Decentralise responsibilities when possible; centralise when necessary. Consider all modes of travel and land use priorities when allocating government funds.
3 Provide a supportive legal and regulatory framework	Ensure that the rules and regulations for public transit clearly specify the roles of public and private sector actors. Ensure that measures to promote walking and cycling and transport demand management are supported in the legal and regulatory framework. Fully integrate air quality, greenhouse gas, noise and other environmental targets into policy requirements through adopting technical standards and rigorous monitoring.
4 Ensure a comprehensive pricing and fiscal structure	The pricing and fiscal structure should send the right messages about promoting sustainable travel.
5 Rationalise financing and investment streams	Channel revenues from pricing initiatives (e.g. road or congestion pricing, parking fines, etc.). Allocate funding (investments or other) in a balanced way. Weigh national investment and financing in capital cities against the funding needs of other cities.
6 Encourage effective public participation, partnership and communication	Involve the public early in the strategy design process. Seek partnerships with different stakeholders in the transport system. Inform and communicate with transport system clients to help them buy into behaviour change.
7 Improve data collection, monitoring and research	Improve data collection. Carry out consistent monitoring. Organise and finance research, development, and testing.

Source: Adapted from ECMT (2001: 6–9)

for local officers is distinguishing the difference between desired outcomes (objectives) and outputs (delivery on the ground) (Atkins 2004). The problem here is lack of knowledge of what evidence is most appropriate for assessing progress towards cross-cutting objectives and targets. This understanding is linked to previous barriers discussed concerning the contribution of transport to achieving the priorities of other sectors such as health, social issues, education and economic development. Yet, if the links and the shared objectives are not identified in advance of strategy implementation, side effects or unintended effects may seriously damage activities in other policy areas, or at least miss the opportunities for synergistic effects (Banister 2005a; Marsden *et al.* 2006). The unintended side effects from failing to jointly plan for sustainable transport options are shown in Table 5.7.

This section has focussed on why it appears so difficult to implement sustainable policies for urban travel. It has looked at the potential barriers under six categories: legal, financial, cultural, political, organisational and technical. The next section examines the strategies that have been used at national and the city level to overcome these difficulties.

5.3 ACHIEVING POLICY COLLABORATION ON SUSTAINABLE ACCESSIBILITY

The previous section has highlighted that despite the existence of central and local government strategies and funding for demonstration projects to implement sustainable travel options, there are severe structural barriers to mainstreaming change. Ostrom's work has shown how embedded, and therefore longstanding, societal structuring rules allocate to organisations the resources and responsibilities to act, and that for each new event these rules need to be negotiated or accepted. The barriers to change can be divided into structural barriers and operational barriers. The former include legal, financial and cultural barriers; and the latter, organisational, political and technical barriers. The former might be considered to be quite rigid constraints since they require substantial political consensus to overturn, while the latter maybe categorised as flexible barriers since they can be overcome given time and resources (KonSULT 2005). What can be achieved on the ground is shaped, however, by the key structuring variables of legal and financial powers and cultural willingness to act.

The literature on implementation provides many good practice lessons on how to overcome barriers. Some of these suggestions are more comprehensive than others. Of particular merit is the advice provided by the European Conference of Ministers of Transport (ECMT 2001) to national governments on how to promote sustainable travel in urban areas. Their strategy for overcoming barriers has seven components. Table 5.8 summarises the recommended approach. The ECMT argue for flexible, integrated policy packages covering at least the land use and transport sectors and comprising of a cross-sector mix of regulatory, pricing, and technological measures. The discussion in this section follows the order of priorities identified in the ECMT package to resolve the gaps in conceptual and performance integration identified in Chapter 4. Recommendations from the Transportation Research Board (1996), Atkins (2003, 2004), Stead (2003), Wixey and Ruiz (2003), Banister (2005a) and Hull (2008a, 2009) will be discussed where appropriate.

LEGAL REQUIREMENTS

The legal authority for the effective implementation of sustainable transport strategies is held by disparate bodies. This authority to act needs to be enjoined, through legal means, so that these resources are brought together to ensure that the central coordinating principle of a sustainable development strategy – minimising the use of natural and manmade resources (using Factor 4 and 10 principles to produce more for less) can be achieved across all policy sectors. This is a task for national and/or regional government to integrate politically the different interests, agencies and cultures around resource minimisation. This is a radical concept for most governments to undertake since traditionally working practices and government structures have separated policy sectors.

Resource minimisation in transport can best be achieved through sharing power and authority to act with lower tiers of government. Accountability and performance measurement of public sector expenditure can still be managed effectively, based on the attainment of negotiated targets for resource minimisation and other sustainability objectives. The legal framework has to ensure that elected public organisations provide the coordinating mechanism for institutions (other public bodies, private sector organisations and service providers, and individuals) to work together. Elected authorities can be held to account not only by higher tiers of government but by their electorate which give them resources of authority and probity (Office of the Deputy Prime Minister 2004). But to achieve resource minimisation effectively they need power and authority, within the governance system, to carry out the necessary actions.

As the ECMT (2001) suggest, the number one priority is for a clear and internally consistent, supportive national policy framework to secure sustainable urban travel. The transport strategy needs to be able to influence the policy agenda of other government policy sectors (e.g. land use, health and education) to ensure the horizontal coordination of policy at the national level. It also needs to set the scope of the possible and appropriate outcomes through setting transport targets (scope rules) for regional and local tiers of government. It has to be multi-modal – addressing all modes of travel including active travel – and to maximise the cross-sector synergistic effects through linking to land use, health, education, environmental and economic policies. The detailed business plan for implementation must be consistent with the transport strategy.

To enhance the vertical integration of priorities, the national policy framework should take a long-term perspective and provide clarity and consistency. Mutually supportive links with other policy areas should be identified so that it is clear to lower tiers of government where the policy synergies lie. Banister (2005a: 62) suggests the national transport framework should include the following priorities:

• Maximise the use of public transit and green modes of transport
• Manage the private car through integrated transport and mobility management
• Minimise urban sprawl
• Improve air quality through less fuel use and reductions in the emissions of pollutants.

These ideas are roughly consistent with the priorities expressed by Bayliss (1998) and Bertolini and le Clerq (2003) in Table 4.1. The key point is that the strategic objectives should be couched in broad enough terms that identify opportunities or synergies to improve the design and/or performance of schemes.

The second priority identified by the ECMT (2001) is to improve institutional coordination and cooperation to deliver the national transport framework effectively. They justify this to national governments as improving the communication between national departments of state 'so that inconsistent messages on priorities for sustainability are not handed down on a sectoral basis' (ibid.: 6). The communication of national priorities is seen as a two-way process with regional levels of government where these exist, and with local government communicating their priorities up to the national level as well. Priorities need to be developed and tested in discussion arenas with as wide a range of transport stakeholders as possible.

Pivotal to ensuring cooperation between key stakeholders is clarity concerning the position of each participant in the process. The third priority in Table 5.8 is a legal and regulatory framework that specifies the powers and responsibilities for public and private sector actors. Elected public sector organisations need the legal powers commensurate with a decision making and leadership role, and this is specifically important for the coordination role at the city-region level. Their remit should cover intermodal transportation across the city-region and clearly specify the parameters of their relationship with private sector providers. Elected city-region administrations should have operational powers to set service and network quality standards for the public transit network. Municipalities may feel that a looser grouping of metropolitan administrations to coordinate transport planning and delivery across the city-region will be sufficient. A clear legal framework for the role that private service operators are expected to play should be set by the national government, clearly specifying the balance between competition and cooperation allowed.

National government should ensure that elected local government has the resources that are commensurate with fulfilling the leadership role on sustainable transport. They must ensure that the use of other government tools such as economic incentives and taxation support resource minimisation behaviour and that the financial framework set by national government does not distort the implementation of national transport policy.

By setting the national framework clearly around resource minimisation and reviewing and streamlining laws and guidelines for sustainable transport, the national regulatory context should be simplified. Consistency and clarity of purpose at the national level can be more easily translated down the tiers of government if the financial incentives also pursue sustainable transport solutions and resource minimisation. Regional policies and more detailed city-region policies for transport should be consistent with the national strategy through the customisation of national targets to the local level and with funding clearly linked to their achievement. Within a clear structure of targets and timescales, local constituencies within the city-region should have the flexibility to decide how to achieve them based on local discussion and consensus. The range of measures preferred at the local level should not only contribute to resource minimisation but reflect community goals.

FINANCIAL REQUIREMENTS

Financial regulation can provide the 'push' and 'pull' levers to support behavioural change. If fiscal measures are used to achieve resource minimisation and translated into easily understood ideas, on ecosystem resource conservation or strategies to reduce carbon emissions, they can also play an informative role highlighting the causal effects of individual behaviour. As the ECMT (2001: 8) report advises: '*the pricing and fiscal structure should send the right messages promoting sustainable urban transport across sectors*'. There needs to be internal consistency in the taxation system that while taxes primarily raise money for the state they also, on balance, aim to make the economy more eco-efficient through reducing the resource intensity of goods and services. The ECMT (2001: 8) specifically mentions that government revenues from pricing initiatives (car restraint measures such as road/congestion pricing and parking fines) should be channelled back into '*benefits* [that] *can be felt by those bearing the costs*'. In order to justify the restraint measures the revenue raised should stay at the spatial level, where it has been obtained, to improve public transit and environmental quality of the area.

The dispensation of public sector funds in the form of grants and subsidies should be tied to the achievement of resource minimisation as well as value-added outcomes, through specified requirements in tenders, service contracts and agreements with lower tiers of government. Each tier of government can reinforce state policies through their own procurement and contract processes.

The decentralisation of powers can create the context for the ownership of sustainable transport solutions within city-regions but actual implementation is dependent on the existence of a significant local funding base. Cities with powers to raise their own revenue and those with autonomy over expenditure appear to coordinate the transport system more effectively (see the Malmö, Amsterdam and London case studies in Chapter 7). Leadership commitment, devolved powers, and control over budgets are the primary driving forces to enable city-region administrations to overcome local barriers. This provides the basis to undertake the resource-intensive (skilled staff and financial resources) coordination and cooperation with transport service operators, which is essential to the long-term implementation of sustainable transport strategies.

The discussion so far has assumed, for most states, the continuing centralised control of public finance and that distribution to localities will directly seek to support opportunities for the implementation of sustainable transport measures, and which will complement locally raised resources. The ECMT warns against the 'excessive concentration' of public resources in capital cities to the detriment of improving the transport systems in other important metropolitan areas. Similarly any public funding for transport dispensed by government organisations should prioritise project proposals equitably and objectively against environmental, economic and social equity criteria ensuring that decisions do not prevent and close down the opportunities for the effective management of travel demand.

CULTURAL REQUIREMENTS

Using regulatory and fiscal measures to drive change will only work with the public, politicians and professionals if they accept the need for behaviour change. Banister (2005a: 62) refers to the 'problems relating to inertia, professionalism, and a general resistance to change' when stakeholders feel that they will lose out from the overall package of measures. In devising the scope of the regulatory and fiscal measures, the government needs to introduce the changes so that the net effect of behaviour change is seen as positive. The marketing of any tax changes should ensure that the total tax burden is not substantially increased and that individuals are given some scope to reduce their charges (see the Netherlands case study in Chapter 7). The message should be customised to different stakeholder groups. The short-term effects of change often create winners and losers, and the government should ensure that it is not held to ransom by powerful interests.

Central to creating understanding of the need for behaviour change is ensuring that the scientific information on climate change and the costs to different groups in society and to the environment are clearly understood. Cultural resistance will not necessarily be removed through a well-developed communication strategy. However, the likely distribution of benefits and costs needs to be debated from the bottom up to engender public and private understanding of the need to respond. As Ostrom (1986) recommends, the *pay-off* rules need to be clearly debated and identified before society will be motivated to respond.

Organisational processes

Organisational issues are about how to make this process happen and to ensure that the decision-making processes efficiently and fairly address the issues. One of the tools that governments have is the provision of customised information and advice, and working with ordinary people in the community to gain an understanding of their accessibility issues and how these can be resolved using a wider range of travel modes. The community has a key role in identifying short-term achievable actions and projects. A broad base of ownership and support for sustainable action can be achieved using the existing machinery for citizen engagement or by establishing ongoing mobilisation forums (Transportation Research Board 1996).

The partnership approach can be reinforced through the media, and with advocacy groups and individuals through the preparation of city-wide plans provided they are engaged early on in the strategy generation process so that their involvement continues through to project implementation and monitoring of progress. The generation of strategic options should be informed by a baseline study to identify problems and opportunities, and data and analysis should be updated at regular intervals to support monitoring of trends and the evaluation of specific measures. Wixey and Ruiz (2003: 11) advise that the specific target group for policies should be involved in the planning phase so that the project team can '*design*[ing] *and adapt*[ing] *the services to the user needs*' and can understand the implementation barriers more fully. Elected officials should be engaged at this stage so that they can understand the benefits of integrating land use, transport, health, air quality and other environmental issues and the sustainable transport solutions available. Important actors such as businesses, employers, residential and commercial land developers and associations are the key actors in the delivery of sustainable travel policies. Again, it is the hearts and minds of ordinary people (car users and transport system clients) that have to be won over if demand management is to be implemented effectively.

A sustainable transport strategy for a city-region, designed to meet government targets for resource minimisation yet allow easy access to spatial opportunities, should be the tool to gain the cooperation of key organisations that either act as opinion-formers or potential investors. As the Transportation Research Board (1996) imply, the strategy should aim to be all inclusive, building on the goals of existing organisations, through forming strong links with transport operators, with broader community groups and environmental groups, as well as drawing in the officials from other policy sectors within the government organisation. Detailed action plans can also be a means of two-way interaction with local communities to gain their backing for the projects in their neighbourhood. The support of the community and local businesses around short-term achievable projects can engender a sense of ownership and achievement when they are implemented. Once these groups are aware of the planning and decision-making process, they can drop in at whatever stage they feel is appropriate to evaluate, test and lend their support to secure effective implementation.

The Transportation Research Board (1996), and Wixey and Ruiz (2003) specifically focus on the organisational processes necessary to introduce multi-modal and mobility management measures effectively. Their best practice advice provides a process and a list of attributes that are necessary for success. These start with getting the structures for partnership right, then move onto establishing a clear vision or mission statement with as wide a group of stakeholders as possible based on an understanding of what the problem is. The process moves on to the selection of projects, and then the monitoring and the marketing of success stories. According to the Transportation Research Board (1996: 5–10) the enabling organisation:

- resolves issues of authority and responsibility;
- establishes partnership structures;
- includes diverse interests; and
- expands the roles for existing organisations.

Innovatory approaches require their own formal structure or close links into an existing organisational structure. Whatever the structure, the organisational roles and responsibilities of the working group and its constituents, the project manager and backup support team, the partners and funding bodies should be clearly delineated (Wixey and Ruiz 2003). Wixey and Ruiz (2003) found that the most successful projects were those where the project champion was involved in the initiative from the start. Bringing the chief executive on board, or other senior managers and stakeholders, from the start was also important to project success.

The vision statement and plan provide the project team with a 'strong foundation to work from' and the strategic justification to secure funding (Wixey and Ruiz 2003: 11). The plan should set realistic and measurable objectives that relate to community needs but also should measure progress towards resource minimisation. This should cover sustainable land use/transportation goals and practices, and measure appropriate indicators from education, health and social services strategies. As Wixey and Ruiz suggest, mobility management policies should reflect the multi-modal nature of the solutions including the car. A combination of push and pull 'carrots and sticks' measures needs to be identified.

The advice on the selection of measures is to go for the 'easy wins' first, based on what key stakeholders would like to achieve with the support of the project team and back up organisation. If the funding mechanisms have been realigned with government sustainability objectives the measures chosen should be capable of satisfying funding body priorities. Attitudinal change and the impact of measures on resource use, pollution and travel behaviour should be collected and compared against the baseline. Updates should be reported in a form that is understandable to both policy makers and the public. Success should be marketed to promote sustainable travel options and tailor-made for different social and transport groups. The Transportation Research Board (1996) advise that success should be communicated through stories so that people understand why someone has changed their travel behaviour '*document*[ing] *the steps people followed and the challenges they faced and how they overcame them, as well as the results achieved*' (ibid.: 7–2).

Best practice advice on organisational change appears eminently sensible, but if radical changes to organisational practices are to occur then inter-sector/ interdepartmental interaction between individual practitioners will also need to change (Stead 2003: 344). Stead was alluding to the need to integrate land use and transportation planning but integration, arguably, needs to go much wider than this if resource minimisation opportunities are to be widely achieved. Atkins (2004) suggests that the integration of different disciplinary cultures and ways of working requires internal management arrangements that are conducive to obtaining a (corporate) collective responsibility for sustainable transport outcomes. They make several recommendations to address this issue. These include: appointing directors who have a responsibility for a wider area of service delivery than usual so that holistic objectives and priorities are better communicated; joint working and resource sharing between service areas within local government and between elected governments across the city-region; ensuring that the incentive structures, career development and the training of senior managers recognise explicitly transport's contribution to wider objectives and priorities; and more robust monitoring of programme and performance management.

TECHNICAL KNOWLEDGE

Research has shown that the tools available to transport planners tend to measure the direct impacts of single projects rather than the indirect and cumulative effects of a package of sustainable measures (Banister 2002b; Hull 2008a, 2008c). As Banister (2002: 10) states:

Policy impacts are much more complex than simple models can address. Where empirical evidence is available [...] the impacts may seem small, as many changes take time to impact and the adjustments are in several directions. Some people may travel less, but others more. Much analysis tries to assess the net effects rather than identifying and measuring the different types of linkages. Analysis must therefore begin to move away from cause and effect as a simple representation of reality to developing the full range of effects (or chains) that actually take place.

The technical capabilities of decision makers in terms of the selection of the right combination of instruments appropriate in each city context are skills to be acquired and require training and knowledge transfer (Banister 2005b).

Data collection and monitoring improvements are recommended by the ECMT (2001). Their recommendation is the development of a consistent methodology at the international level to aid the process of benchmarking progress against other similar organisations. They feel that data collection on urban travel and land use activities linking to health, ecological and environmental objectives can provide an urban barometer which could be used to engage with residents and local businesses. These improvements in data collection, and research on the synergies and the effectiveness of potential solutions, are dependent on additional funding provided by government.

A key area for improvement is the development of appraisal tools which can compare the technical case for a range of intermodal solutions objectively including a package of measures. An example of a package of measures might be the infrastructure to promote walking and cycling in an urban area and transport demand management such as car sharing, telecommuting, traffic signals responsive to buses and employer mobility plans, etc. Appraisal tools are needed at the different stages of strategic forecasting and appraisal, scheme option appraisal, impact monitoring and cumulative effects evaluation.

The European Environment Agency (2007) recommends the development of strategic impact assessment as a tool to incorporate a broader agenda from other policy areas so that the positive and negative synergies between several policy goals can be captured early on in policy design. This practical and intuitive approach to appraisal would require more research and testing in order to develop our understanding of the cumulative effects of the sustainability domains below:

- *Economic integration*: between short-term costs and long-term return to different groups
- *Environmental integration*: between pressures, media and impacts
- *Spatial integration*: between land uses, activity patterns and spatial dynamics
- *Time integration*: between trends, targets and strategies over the short, medium and long term

- *Resource integration*: between supply- and demand-side in each sector and industry (Ravetz 2000: 275).

The technical performance of city-region administrations in providing a more sustainable transport system should be measured using both quantitative and qualitative methods. Unless data collection improves to provide long-term trend data at a sufficiently disaggregated level for use in measure evaluation, more reliance will need to be placed on qualitative methods of evaluation including expert evaluation, theories of change, documentary review, causal chain methodology, risk analysis, satisfaction scores and perception analysis (Hull 2008c). Methodological advances are also required to enable the reconciliation of qualitative data with the quantitative information on air quality, greenhouse gas emissions, noise emissions, soil and river/water quality, modal split, active travel, etc.

City-region administrations need to be encouraged to plan their monitoring programme at the same time as sustainable transport outcomes are agreed, and to agree responsibilities for monitoring specific performance indicators across departments, if they are to report more accurately on progress towards sustainability. Performance monitoring could be at the corporate level as well as the service or departmental level. Traditional measures of transport monitoring have relied on data showing the flow of traffic or passengers per hour/per kilometre by mode. More creative measures might incorporate carbon allowances for different users. ECMT have suggested that technical standards for vehicles and fuels should be rigorously monitored to show the progress made in the public and private fleets.

5.4   RECOMMENDATIONS FOR OVERCOMING THE INSTITUTIONAL BARRIERS TO CHANGE

This chapter started with the question of why so little progress has been made on resource minimisation in the transport sector despite the good intentions scattered through transport strategy documents. Drawing on research from several literatures (viz. transport planning, organisational behaviour, project management, policy analysis, economics and implementation theory) the chapter sought to answer this question through an in-depth examination of the institutional barriers to innovation in transport delivery and specifically the 'weak and perverse incentives' (Stead 2003: 335) to 'change the way we do things'.

The two main findings, or recommendations, from the examination of barriers in Section 5.2 are that:

1   **National government must realign financial systems and decision-making criteria to incentivise the introduction of low energy resource solutions.** The perverse incentives in the current system of government which support this recommendation are:

- Uncertainty and delays in securing funding for sustainable transport solutions, including the insufficiency of financial resources for small scale linked proposals.
- Strategy exhortation divorced from the allocation of resources at national and local levels.
- Market pricing signals and government priorities that undervalue the maintenance of ecosystems in decision-making criteria and hence fail to support market and political actors who wish to implement sustainable solutions.
- The complexity of gaining funding from higher-tier authorities and the private sector, followed by the hurdles of justifying the 'value for money' and gaining approval for local priorities.

2   **Legal and financial resources should be devolved to government/governance at the city-region level to ensure there is strong leadership and responsibility for behaviour change at a spatial level, which can integrate the global–local resource minimisation challenge.**

The perverse incentives in the current system of government that support this recommendation are:

- Inefficient and fragmented organisational attempts to implement sustainable transport measures characterised by counterproductive roles.
- Insufficient conceptual and performance integration of the efforts by public sector officers to reduce the use of scarce resources and to add value to products, services and local environments.
- Lack of skilled staff in local government administrations.
- Poor communication vertically up to higher tiers of government and down to residents, and horizontally with key actors/stakeholders across the authority.
- Need to change the culture of risk aversion across society.

The chapter concluded by demonstrating how these recommendations could be put into practice to drive forward a step change in sustainable transport outcomes. Achieving a step change in institutional behaviour depends on the tiers of governance (national and regional, city-region and local communities) working together to steer the selection of options by the market sector and civil society. This chapter has argued that national government has the legal and financial tools to set up the opportunity agenda that will structure the context for interaction on resource minimisation. The next chapter concentrates on identifying the policy or intervention instruments that have the potential to collectively reduce both global greenhouse gas emissions and the utilisation of scarce resources.

CHAPTER 6

Intervention instruments for sustainable transport futures

6.1 Introduction

The earlier chapters in this book defined a sustainable transport system as one that prioritised the opportunities for walking and cycling in urban areas, followed by improving the opportunities for, and the environmental performance of, public transit and multi-occupancy vehicles (Section 4.2). Only when these modes are not feasible options should reliance on low polluting private cars take precedence. It was noted that this hierarchy of transport modes, although replicated in many transport policy documents, is rarely activated in practice in the Western world. One exception to this is the city of Freiburg in Germany, where the design of car-free neighbourhoods has been successfully implemented. This case study is discussed in Chapter 7 and the outcomes derive from stable political commitment and conceptual and performance integration (Section 4.2) across several public policy sectors. Chapters 4 and 5 argued that the tools of government (viz. legal, financial, development and information powers) will have to be used in new ways to achieve institutional integration (vertically and horizontally) and presented a vision, and an action plan, for an integrated multi-scalar government system (national-regional, city-region, neighbourhood/municipality).

This chapter brings together the menu of transport and land use policy instruments currently available, which are considered appropriate for securing a more sustainable and ambulant-friendly transport experience in the built environment. These specific types of interventions include legal and fiscal instruments applied by higher tiers of government to encourage resource efficiency and/or reduce noise pollution in residential areas, improvements to the physical infrastructure for active travel (walking and cycling) and educational instruments that encourage behaviour change. Those that alter the physical infrastructure in the built environment are categorised as 'hard' instruments and those that specifically seek to change the relative costs of services and behaviour are known as 'soft' instruments or measures.

As Chapter 5 has suggested, the way these instruments are combined together and the process of their selection and implementation are integral to their effectiveness. The concepts of 'accessibility' and 'exergy' introduced in Chapter 3 (Section 3.2) refocuses transport planning on the accessibility needs of residents, tourists and commuters in the most resource-efficient way. The majority of the population do not have access to a car on a daily basis and, therefore, Chapters 2 and 3 argued that the wide range of public resources should be integrated to meet their diverse travel and interaction needs in an equitable way. The presence and safety of the young child walking or cycling to school is as important as the needs of the commuter.

This chapter aims to address the following questions:

1   What combination of instruments, applied at which government levels, can effectively reduce carbon and other natural resource use while synergistically enhancing the opportunities for active travel in urban environments?
2   How can the positive synergies between instruments be maximised?
3   Against what criteria should the effectiveness of these instruments be appraised?

6.2   TRANSPORT AND LAND USE INSTRUMENTS

There are a large number of instruments that city-region administrations (elected or appointed) can implement to make urban environments more conducive to walking and cycling while moving people and freight in a more energy efficient way than presently. Table 6.1 lists the instruments that can be deployed to affect transport and land use decision choices. Most of the interventions can be deployed by lower tier government actors, but their effectiveness depends on certain financial resource requirements and performance integration powers (see Section 5.4). Often the power to raise taxes, influence decisions concerning the strategic road network and rail infrastructure, and influence the development of new forms of energy supply have not been devolved to city-region or metropolitan administrations.

The political work carried out by transnational organisations such as the EU should not be forgotten, in particular the steering role they can play in the selection and implementation of transport interventions and specific instruments. Chapter 2 has already discussed the role played by the EU in shaping the approach to problem identification through the dissemination of research on sustainable environments and transport options; however, it is the legal requirements enacted through directives and regulations (which are binding) that arguably have had the most impact on national and local transport delivery. Figure 6.1 shows the breadth of this transport legislation from the harmonisation of public transit operating standards, to standards for the control of waste, to the protection of habitats. The assessment of the direct environmental impacts of major transport projects before authorisation can be given (Environmental Impact Assessment Directives, 85/77/EEC and 97/11/EC) and certain transport plans and programmes (Strategic Environmental Assessment Directive 2001/42/EC)) have already been discussed in Chapter 2. Most notable for the discussion below is the driving role the EU has played to secure energy efficiency in the transport sector and in setting emission limits for new vehicles on European roads and standards for fuel quality.

Table 6.1 Public policy instruments to affect change in transport and land use

	Hardware instruments	Pricing/charges for use of infrastructure and services	Organisation of work	Software instruments
Energy sources	Biofuels Electricity Hydrogen based energy			Vehicle ownership taxes Fuel taxes Congestion charging
Technology	Accessible and user friendly vehicles Clean engine technology Urban traffic control systems Intelligent transport systems (ramp metering, selective vehicle priority, incident detection systems, etc.)	Parking charges Fare levels and fare structures (flat fare, off peak, etc.) Concessionary fares for certain groups	Flexible working hours	Telecommuting, teleworking and teleshopping Travel plans (company, school, individual) Workplace parking levy Guaranteed ride home schemes
Infrastructure	Heavy rail provision Light rail and trams Enhanced bus provision Guided bus Park and ride facilities Terminals and interchanges Cycle routes Pedestrian routes Pedestrian areas Off-street parking for disabled High occupancy vehicle lanes Dedicated lorry lanes and routes City distribution centres for freight Accident remedial measures (e.g. skid resistant surfacing)			*Car use* Traffic calming (speed limits, traffic cells in city centres, re-routing of traffic flows) Physical restrictions on car use (access permits, number plate restrictions) Car sharing, car clubs Reduction in car parking provision Parking restrictions with exceptions for clean vehicles/high occupancy vehicles/etc. *Public transport service levels* On demand service Door-to-door service Higher frequency of service Bus partnerships Transparent charges (especially in areas with many sub-systems)

Table 6.1 *Continued*

	Hardware instruments		Software instruments
Land use management and initiatives	Higher density of built environment		Support to community-based paratransit or jitneys
	Development pattern aligned to public transport corridors	Information provision	Real time passenger information
	Mixed development of homes, jobs and shops		Trip planning systems
	Certain sites should be protected from development		Conventional timetable
	Specify maximum parking standards for new development	Public awareness campaigns	Personalised travel planning, health campaigns, eco-labelling
	Pedestrian-oriented design		Eco-driving training

Source: Adapted from European Commission Directorate General Environment (2004a: 35–37) and Kennedy *et al.* (2005: 397)

EU Regulations relevant to surface transport

- Regulation on rules for financial aid to trans-European networks (1655/1999 amending 2236/95).
- Regulation on the prohibition of organotin compounds on ships (782/2003).
- Regulation establishing the European Railway Agency (881/2004).
- Regulation on access to the market within the European Community for road freight traffic (1791/2006 amending 881/1992 and 484/2002).
- Regulation on Community guidelines for the development of the trans-European transport network (1791/2006 amending 1692/96/EC).
- Regulation granting financial assistance to improve the environmental performance of the freight transport system (1692/2006 repealing 1382/2003).
- Regulation raising the standard for light passenger and commercial vehicles to Euro 5 and 6 (715/2007).
- Regulation setting CO_2 emission standards for new passenger cars (3741/2008 and 8041/2009).
- Regulation on public passenger transport services by rail and road (1370/2007 repealing 1191/1969 and 1107/1970).

EU Directives relevant to transport, energy and the environment

- Directive on measures to be taken against air pollution by emissions from motor vehicles (70/220/EEC).
- Directive on Waste (75/442/EEC).
- Directive on the Conservation of Wild Birds (79/409/EEC) and (91/244/EC).
- Environmental Impact Assessment Directive (85/337/EEC).
- Directive on the measures to be taken against the emission of gaseous pollutants from diesel vehicle engines (88/77/EEC).
- Directive on the development of the Community's railways (91/440/EEC).
- Directive on the Conservation of Natural Habitats and of Wild Fauna and Flora (92/43/EEC).
- Directives on the restructuring and management of rail companies (95/18/EC) and (95/19/EC).
- Directive on the interoperability of the trans-European high-speed rail system (96/48/EC).
- Directive for Integrated Pollution and Prevention Control (96/61/EC).
- Air Quality Framework Directive (96/62/EC).
- Directive on the Control of Major Accident Hazards (96/82/EC).
- Directive on the Assessment of the Effects of Certain Public and Private Projects on the Environment as amended by Council Directive (97/11/EC).
- Directive on Air Pollution (98/69/EC).
- Directive on Air Quality standards for fuel (3740/1/00/EC) and (8040/09/EC).
- Directive on Strategic Environmental Assessment (2001/42/EC).

Figure 6.1 Recent EU legislation on transport

- Directive on the introduction of noise-related operating restrictions at airports (2002/30/EC).
- Directive on noise mapping (2002/49/EC).
- Directive on maritime safety and the prevention of pollution from ships (2002/84/EC amending previous Directives).
- Directive on the promotion of the use of biofuels or other renewable fuels for transport (2003/30/EC).
- Directive on ship-source pollution and on the introduction of penalties for infringements (2005/35/EC).
- Directives on the common framework for promotion of energy from renewable sources (3736/08/EC) and (8037/09/EC).

Figure 6.1 *Continued*

The remainder of this chapter introduces the instruments that have either been given political acceptability through implementation in spatial locations throughout Europe or those that have reached the point of technical feasibility waiting further testing and implementation. The discussion revolves around two concerns. First, what evidence is available on the potential of these instruments to reduce global greenhouse gas emissions and, second, how will they, in combination, significantly enhance the infrastructure for walking and cycling in urban areas and thus impact on urban modal travel outcomes heavily balanced towards the use of the car for most journeys. The discussion below follows the ordering in Table 6.1 which first introduces the 'hardware' instruments that involve interventions to the physical and technical infrastructure and then the 'software' instruments that seek to change behaviour through service cost, quality and information availability.

6.2.1 HARDWARE INTERVENTIONS

The sustainability of a city in the future will essentially be defined by the spread, capacity and integration of the hardware or physical infrastructure. An integrated transport system connects the public transit and active travel modes with spatial opportunities providing a just in time, transparent service across the metropolitan area. Transport and land use planning, provided they work in tandem, can reshape both infrastructure and patterns of travel in our cities through a combination of land use regulation, infrastructure provision and the improvement of the public realm. The most conducive hardware instrument for sustainability is the service intensity of public transit provision, but a convenient distribution of spatial opportunities and the use of alternative renewable fuels are also important.

DEVELOPMENT OF RENEWABLE FUELS AND CLEAN ENGINE TECHNOLOGY

The development of zero-emission vehicles and alternative fuels is a technological solution to the rising levels of petroleum consumption. This is thought by many to be a less painful way of addressing CO_2 emissions, which may not require alteration to existing travel behaviour patterns (Whitelegg 1997). The redesign of the conventional car, however, has been slow, since innovators and car manufacturers are reluctant to bear the full risks associated with new product development and marketing unless they foresee a secure market for their products. The European Council of Ministers has intervened to set standards for emissions for new cars and commercial vehicles to be implemented by vehicle manufacturers and air quality standards for the built environment to be implemented by member states (Directives 98/69/EC, 96/62/EC; and Regulation 715/2007). Table 6.2 shows the new European standards for emissions from petrol cars in g/km adopted since 1998.

However, broad diffusion of new vehicle technologies still awaits the legislative and financial support required from the EU and national governments to establish favourable conditions to create the wide deployment of clean engine technologies and the associated fuels. Hybrid electric vehicles are widely available and full electric vehicles are close to market diffusion. Electric vehicles emit low emissions of CO_2, NOx and VOCs and are ideal for dense urban areas, but full deployment will increase SOx emissions from power plants unless stringent emission standards are in place or renewable fuel sources are widely used (Whitelegg 1997).

Renewable transport fuels, such as biofuels, are considered to be an intervention ready for implementation which would have a high impact on reducing CO_2 emissions (Gray *et al.* 2006: 41). Biofuel production has a strong presence in some European countries such as Germany, Slovakia and Sweden. EU funding through the CIVITAS project has supported collaboration between the fuel industry and local government

Table 6.2 EU new standards for pollution in grams/km from petrol cars

	Carbon monoxide	Volatile organic compounds	Nitrogen oxides	Particulate matter
Euro 3 (from Jan 2000)	2.3	0.2	0.15	
Euro 4 (from Jan 2005)	1.0	0.10	0.08	
Euro 5 (from Sept 2009)	1.0	0.10	0.06	0.005
Euro 6 (from Sept 2014)	1.0	0.10	0.06	0.005

Source: Adapted from White (2002) and Institute of Advanced Motoring (2009: 120)

so that issues concerning the quality of fuel and the provision of infrastructure can be addressed (Hull 2008b). The UK demonstration project in Norwich was based on the reuse of waste oils and fats. Much of this 'clean' biodiesel comes from the waste oil processing plant in Motherwell, Scotland, which opened in 2005 with a production capacity of up to 50,000 tonnes of biodiesel a year (Gray et al. 2006; Aldridge 2008). Currently biodiesel is blended with conventional petrol in up to 5–10 per cent blends, which most cars can accommodate. A key challenge for the biofuel industry is access to reliable sources of waste matter such as waste oil and fats rather than imported bioethanol (e.g. from Brazil, etc.) which removes land from food production and increases the costs of staple feedstuffs. Biodiesel from waste oil, bioethanol from grains or wood, and electricity from nuclear power all have reduced CO_2 emissions from burning conventional fuels, but also have either air pollution or waste disposal problems that need to be addressed. Continuing research on the whole-life costs (economic, social and environment) of the alternative fuels in use will be necessary to demonstrate their contribution to achieving sustainability over the long term.

The European Parliament is creating a more supportive environment for alternative fuels through the legal requirement to achieve a 10 per cent share of energy from renewable sources in each member state's transport energy consumption by 2020 (European Parliament 2009). Revisions to the Air Quality Directive also set ambitious sustainability criteria for biofuels, while facilitating the more widespread blending of biofuels into petrol and diesel. By 2020, fuel suppliers are required to decrease by 6 per cent climate harming emissions over the entire life-cycle of their products. National level support for biofuel deployment has included a capital allowance (up to 100 per cent) for biofuel plant construction and preferential fuel duty differentials applying to biodiesel and bioethanol. Establishing both the new processing technology, to extract the energy efficiently from renewable sources, and the market for biofuels are vital ingredients to their wide deployment. There are substantial savings to be made in CO_2 emissions, with the UK government estimating that it will achieve 2.6 megatonnes CO_2 savings by 2010 from the 5 per cent Renewables Transport Fuels Obligation (RTFO) introduced in 2008 (Sustainable Development Commission 2006).

In the long term, hydrogen and fuel cell systems are expected to make a higher impact on carbon savings than biofuels (Gray et al. 2006: 44). Again, market diffusion depends on public resources for research and development, and infrastructure deployment. There are economic benefits for the 'lead' countries in knowledge transfer from the testing and demonstration of the technology, and overcoming the barriers to implementation and use. These benefits have been estimated at 10,000 job opportunities per annum, £500 million per annum gross value added (GVA) to the Scottish economy and the contribution towards achieving the 40 per cent renewable energy target by 2020 (Scottish Executive 2006).

INFRASTRUCTURE

The physical infrastructure for sustainable travel needs to be planned over the long term and implemented as and when resources become available. This includes embedding the fuelling infrastructure for alternative energy vehicles into the built environment as discussed above. Table 6.2 does not include road construction or expansion despite the perceived relationship between transport infrastructure investment, economic development and economic performance. The direction of causality is unknown and is just as likely to have the unintended outcomes of promoting outward investment to competing regions (O'Sullivan 1980; SACTRA 1994; Vickerman *et al.* 1999; Banister and Berechman 2001; Ney 2001; Preston 2001; Council for the Protection of Rural England 2003; DTZ Pieda 2004; Canning *et al.* 2007; Marsden and Thanos 2008). New road investment may be required to unlock inaccessible sites in sustainable locations for development (Lucas 1998) but should not be at the expense of public transit provision.

Energy efficient transport futures require the provision of sufficient alternatives to passenger car use. Local and long distance railway systems will be an essential component in any strategy, providing efficient freight and passenger movement between, and within, regions and should be restored and strengthened in order to compete with the passenger car and domestic flights. EU intervention has principally been to harmonise the technical standards for rail, bus and coach infrastructure to enhance the interoperability between national transport systems leaving the expansion of the systems to national governments (White 2002).

There are several possible infrastructure solutions for increasing public transit patronage within urban areas depending on the existing infrastructure and the resources available (White 2002). Light rail systems are seen as an appropriate solution for large cities but are an expensive option. Trams, with a lighter modular body, are seen as more flexible since they can utilise existing rail infrastructure as well as operate on the main streets, with the ease of adding additional cars during the rush hour. Tram systems in Germany, France, Spain, Portugal and the UK have been extended over the last decade, with more recent extensions in the Netherlands and Italy. Several capital cities (Prague, Athens) have recently developed new lines. New low-floor trams have made boarding easier and allow access for passengers using wheelchairs and prams, etc.

Guided busways incorporate a 'guidewheel on concrete kerb' to provide unimpeded passage on the busway but can also run on the highway. They use less expensive technology than trams, with the most recent example in 2010 being the Cambridgeshire Busway in the UK, which incorporates a 15 mile busway (Department of Transport 2005). Trolleybuses are also making a comeback to replace diesel buses in some busy city centres. Based on electric traction and incorporating regenerative braking, which generates energy to be stored in the battery when braking, the overhead equipment has been redesigned to be visually more acceptable (White 2002). These four solutions are seen as providing a more superior image than buses and, combined with a system of road pricing, could attract a significant modal shift from the passenger car and match the car in terms of speed and comfort.

BUS INFRASTRUCTURE MEASURES

Buses and other forms of semi-public paratransit such as minibuses can provide a flexible service at a relatively low cost to passengers. Buses will always be at the centre of an integrated system, linking to key nodes in the heavy and light rail systems and serving as low cost, key links in the network (e.g. CBD to airport or connecting job seekers to isolated employment areas). Transport operators and city administrations are working together to upgrade public transit fleets and install infrastructure (e.g. bus lanes, bus gates and busways) and traffic management measures to give priority to the bus (White 2002; Hensher and Brewer 2001). Bus-based park and ride schemes have been successful in the UK (e.g. Bristol, Edinburgh, London, York and Reading) to reduce car traffic and the amount of car parking in central areas. Park and ride facilities provide car parking for passenger cars on the boundary of the urban area, where buses, often with subsidised fare structures, use bus priority routes to transport passengers directly to the city centre. These schemes tend to be well received by the public and businesses since they are perceived as supporting economic activity in urban centres and as reducing congestion, noise and air pollution. The park and ride routes often have distinctive fleets of new buses and attract more people into the city by public transit.

TERMINALS AND INTERCHANGES

An integrated system has good connections between transport modes (e.g. walking, cycling, taxis, public transit and community transport) and the main spatial opportunities in the city-region. This can be achieved through strategies that link railway termini and nearby airports and which enable cross-city journeys to be made by public transit to employment and retail centres during the peak commuting periods and weekends. This is a challenge for many cities where the major commuter interchanges within the city environment are, for historical reasons, often on different sides of the city. The main interchanges should have significant passenger-oriented infrastructure and technology, including real-time information boards, underground cycle parking and servicing, and facilities to cater for all customer needs as they wait for connections.

An integrated city transport system must also cater for the movement of goods, as well as people. The objective of a sustainable freight policy is to utilise port and waterway capacity to better avail and transfer 50–90 per cent of motorway road freight onto the railways (Hey *et al.* 1992). Sustainable strategies are also being applied to the procurement logistics process by advancing the idea of regional production systems, which would minimise the distance travelled by goods (Hey *et al.* 1992: 212). This optimises the freight movement part of the production chain by constructing shorter supply chains and also encourages the substitution of 'near suppliers' for 'far suppliers'. A city freight distribution system, provided in partnership with local government, and located close to the outer city distributor road can encourage a more efficient structure to goods handling (see Malmö case study in Chapter 7). This can start to reduce the CO_2 from the road freight sector by encouraging more direct trips to city markets, and by allowing the freight stored at the local distribution centre to be broken up into smaller loads distributing to specific locations within the city.

CYCLE ROUTES

A cycling-friendly environment is a sustainable environment economically, socially and environmentally. A dense city cycle route network connected to all the main facilities with dedicated paths can replace many of the short journeys by car, increasing both the mental and physical health of inhabitants. National government documents foresee even modest cycling initiatives as providing '*clear benefits in terms of reduced congestion, improved public health and enhanced quality of local streets and spaces*' (Department for Transport 2004e: 1). Table 6.3 below shows how the recently designated 'cycling city' of York in the UK is one of the top ten cities in the UK for cycling.

A well connected cycle network also requires facilities for secure cycle parking at appropriate locations in the city, particularly undercover parking spaces to facilitate all weather use which can be secured in all new developments through the development permit process. Where local government has required the introduction of car-free developments, 30–40 per cent of residents will rely on the bicycle for most of their journeys (Koehler 2009). The provision of separate cycle lanes in cities such as Amsterdam, Copenhagen, Malmö and Stockholm also encourage high cycling use. Even in countries such as the UK, where the culture of cycling is not yet embedded, infrastructure can be developed through the development permit process with 'standards for provision' requiring storage for one or two cycle spaces per unit of accommodation in local land use strategies. These policy requirements need to be part of a cycling strategy for the whole of the city-region cycling network. Applicants for a development permit have also been required to provide details of how secure

Table 6.3 Overcoming the main implementation issues with respect to the promotion of cycling: an example from York, UK

Promotion of cycling in the transport hierarchy – *multi-sector policy, and a key part of the York City Council Local Transport Strategy*

Rationale – *mainly to address the problem of the gaps in the cycle route network and to provide more new routes, and to improve the quality and availability of cycle parking, lighting and bike security*

Barriers	**Resource barrier** – competition for funding with other modes. Cycling must compete for investment with other modes of transport. **Social and cultural barriers**
	– national decline in cycling trips over the last decade which according to the National Travel Survey figures (2005) has fallen by 20 per cent since 1995. In 2005 only 1.5 per cent of all trips on average were by cycle. – public acceptance: 'low participant' groups i.e. females, over 45s, teenage girls, school children, those with disabilities or who are economically disadvantaged. – growing threat of obesity: in 2003, 32 per cent of boys and 28 per cent of girls aged 2–15 years were overweight and 17 per cent of boys and 16 per cent girls were obese in England and Wales. Based on current trends 12 million adults and 1 million children will be obese by 2010.
	Economic barrier – growing emissions of CO_2 and congestion in the city centre from motorised vehicles. **Technical barrier** – difficult to quantify the positive benefits to cyclists and society. The full range of benefits of cycling are not understood.
Implementation issues	**Cycling's contribution to modal share** – walking and cycling journeys between 1991 and 2001 have been maintained at 29 per cent of all journeys. **Strategic policy context** – walking and cycling have been prioritised in the local transport strategy and guide the implementation of transport policy in York. Targets include:
	• Increase cycling by 25 per cent on existing levels by 2010. • Generate a 100 per cent increase in children cycling to school. • And increase the number of trips to work by bike by 10 per cent.
	Safety Issues – only two of the main commuter routes into the city have cycle lanes. Recent accidents/fatalities question York's designation by the national government as a 'cycling city' 2008–2011.
Longer-term issues	**Long-term economic value of cycling** – Cycling England commissioned research in 2007 that found that through improvements in health, reductions in congestion and by enhancing the ambient environment, a 50 per cent increase in the number of trips by bicycle would generate benefits worth £1.3 billion by 2015. **New initiatives** – recent funding from national government for new safe cycling routes to Schools and to train school children in cycling proficiency ('Bikeability').

Source: Barnardos *et al.* (2004); City of York Council (2006, 2009); Cycling England (2009)

undercover cycle provision is to be achieved, and this intervention has become self-policing in London where it is consistently applied as part of the local cycling policy (Department for Transport 2004e: 16). If the infrastructure for cycling is to be effective to displace short car journeys it will have to provide a direct route to spatial opportunities and be given priority at junctions and sufficient close parking at main destinations (viz. railway stations and other interchanges). The city of Malmö has developed the infrastructure for priority traffic signalling for cyclists on the main commuting roads into the CBD, but political commitment so far has only been gained to use this outside of the morning commute peak (see case study in Chapter 7).

PEDESTRIAN AREAS AND PEDESTRIAN ROUTES

Many cities and towns start to make their central areas more attractive when they create mixed-use pedestrian zones through the pedestrianisation of heavily used shopping streets for certain days of the week or time periods of the day. Partial and temporary pedestrianisation are being used in the new member states to give non-car users and tourists a greater share of street space and to hold annual events and carnivals. Other cities are reallocating road space to pedestrians in the main shopping street to provide a safer and more secure shopping environment.

This is a popular intervention where the physical constraints of a historic urban form (e.g. Norwich, Oxford and York) provide the opportunity to enhance the pedestrian, and tourist, experience in the retail core as an integral element of the transport strategy. Some streets can be fully pedestrianised, others allow daytime access for cyclists, buses and taxis only, while some streets are closed to through traffic and in others two-lane traffic is reduced to one lane to allow wider pavements. Central area access restrictions must be phased in with other measures that divert car drivers to off-centre car parks, improve public transit and the cycle infrastructure. Progress can be halted where either the inner or outer distributor road network does not have the capacity for the diverted traffic.

Road-space reallocation to widen the space provided for pedestrians and public transit provides the opportunity to improve the quality and design of pedestrian-related infrastructure in areas heavily utilised by pedestrians. This can include the provision of new public spaces for social interaction (squares, play provision, seating and shelter), the extension and design of footways and new enhanced bus stops providing shelter and real-time information. The footway can be widened at bus stops to ensure that the bus does not lose its place in the traffic and thereby minimise delays and obstructions at bus stops. These interventions not only make public transit more convenient and easy to use, they also help to reduce pedestrian casualties.

Bertolini and le Clerq (2003) recommend that government infrastructure priorities should clearly state that the road hierarchy priority is to invest in the extension or maintenance of the walking and cycling environment in the city centre. Where applied, this can achieve objectives in other policy areas such as health improvements and growth in retail sales and tourism. Table 6.3 above shows how York City Council in the UK has used its local transport strategy to promote cycling within the city boundaries. The strategy states that the local authority will give priority to road users in the following order:

1   pedestrians
2   people with mobility problems
3   cyclists
4   public transport users (includes rail, bus, taxi, coach and water)
5   powered two wheelers
6   commercial/business users (includes deliveries and HGVs)
7   car-borne shoppers and visitors
8   car-borne commuters.

(City of York Council 2006: 46)

Several other interventions complement pedestrianisation, such as reduced speed limits in the central area, the re-routing of traffic away from the centre, bus priority lanes, a restrictive central area parking policy, improvements to the streetscape and pedestrian facilities, and park and ride facilities.

LAND USE INTERVENTIONS

There are a number of land use interventions that could be implemented in the short to medium term which would have significant impact on energy efficiency and quality of life in urban areas. These are concepts embedded in planning doctrine across the developed world, whereby local planning officers actively encourage new development to locate in and around transport interchange points or established centres well served by public transit. The assumption here is that: 1) higher urban density and frequent peak and off-peak public transit services will influence travel behaviour; and 2) households located in higher density mixed-use areas accessible to local activities will take advantage of the local spatial opportunities offered and decrease their travel. The soundness of these arguments depends on the quality of the local services and public transit provided.

Research in low density city regions in Australia, Canada and the USA have found that the pairing of high residential-density and quality public transit services is very difficult to achieve in practice (Rodriquez et al. 2006; Curtis and Olaru 2007; Filion and McSpurren 2007; Boarnet et al. 2008). The connectivity of higher density, mixed-use neighbourhoods in these locations to wider metropolitan spatial opportunities by public transit is often poor. The performance of the transport system across the metropolis is, therefore, integral to securing the cumulative positive effects from the land use measures of density and quality of design. The restrictions on car access and parking, the reallocation of road space to public transit and pedestrians, and improving the pedestrian experience in the city centre, as discussed above, combine to improve the accessibility of local neighbourhoods to metropolitan spatial opportunities.

The design of neighbourhoods can encourage sustainable patterns of travel behaviour. Two neighbourhood design concepts that have been used to achieve neighbourhood self-containment are the '*walkable neighbourhood*' (Perry 1929) and the '*jobs–housing balance*' (Cervero 1996, 2001). A walkable neighbourhood is one defined by a catchment of 400 metres, or a five minute walk 'pedshed', within which the residents can meet most of their daily needs, thereby minimising their need to travel further afield. The 400 metre walk is also a common threshold used to define the appropriate walk distance to a bus stop from home or employment site. As distance from home to bus stop or railway station increases, car journeys increase and non-motorised travel decreases (Kitamura *et al*. 1997; Cervero 1994). Ensuring that the jobs and housing in a defined area are balanced is another concept that attempts to secure self-containment and reduce cross-boundary commuting. As a response to the low density urban sprawl in the USA a new design movement entitled 'Smart Growth' has developed, which prioritises densification and diversity of development, infill development and the regeneration of sites rather than building on undeveloped or greenfield land.

The development permit process for new housing can be used to require the developer to fund a new bus service if the location is poorly served by bus services. This could involve the developer funding a new service for an initial five years or providing commuted payments to the local administration to enhance service provision. Increasingly, the development permit process is being used to encourage new housing without onsite car parking spaces so that the space released can be used for other purposes. Space can be freed to improve the shared environment of the development, providing an internal green space and courtyard for residents to meet and share, or to increase the housing density. Car-free developments, discussed earlier, work well in inner city areas that are highly accessible by public transit, walking and cycling. This is also an instrument to support local business by encouraging shopping on foot. To ensure that the residents of these schemes are not using a car for their daily travel needs, in cities such as London and Freiberg, they are neither eligible for an on-street car parking permit in the Controlled Parking Zone nor allowed to park in council-owned car parks. In London, there are legal restrictions attached to the development permit, with exemptions for disabled drivers (Department for Transport 2004e: 34).

The same sustainable accessibility principles can be applied to the planning of new commercial and office developments through the implementation of a travel plan with an agreed modal split as part of the development permit. The effective implementation of a travel plan will reduce the car parking spaces provided in-line with the target modal split and enhance accessibility to public transit and cycling networks (Curtis and Olaru 2007). Larger commercial developments may be able to provide a new rail link or station through a negotiated planning agreement. In the USA and Canada, developers are often allowed a 'development density bonus' when they provide desired amenities that further public policy goals. Commercial developments and hospitals should be designed to secure convenient bus access onto the site, with bus stops located in the prime location close to the main building entrance. Larger developments should be permeable so that cycle and walking networks connect through the site. Companies can also incentivise cycling and discourage car use through a workplace parking levy.

Residential street environments can be redesigned so that the streets become shared spaces for children playing and traffic that needs to gain access. The 'home zone' concept involves extending the pavement texture across the road, removing road markings, and creating landscape barrier features to reduce traffic speeds (Biddulph 2001). In a home zone project in Aberaman in Wales the traffic has been calmed by inserting tree planters in the street, thus narrowing the roadway and creating communal spaces for picnic benches and barbeques. When the local community is involved in the design of the features this leads to neighbourhood pride and proactive management by residents (Barnardos *et al.* 2004: 16). Similar quality of life improvements can be implemented through area regeneration projects. Residents' concerns about neighbourhood management, such as litter and graffiti, crime and anti-social behaviour can be addressed through physical improvements to streets and footpaths, additional community policing, CCTV surveillance in high crime areas, as well as organised leisure schemes for young children and adolescents.

6.2.2 SOFTWARE INTERVENTIONS

The key to a sustainable transport system is the ability to restrain the use and slow the speed of motorised vehicles in certain locations, such as residential neighbourhoods and central areas frequented by tourists and pedestrians. A number of software interventions such as changes to the pricing of infrastructure use and to the organisation of the work day, restrictions on the use of the car in certain areas of the city, and the promotion of more active travel through awareness-raising campaigns have a role to play in influencing the travel choices of citizens. These instruments complement the improvements to public transit and modal interchanges, the interventions which steer new development to locations well served by public transit, and reallocate land given over to motorised vehicles to other street users, and the setting of high standards for pedestrian and disabled accessibility.

Some of these interventions will incur substantial costs to the public sector and require a long process of negotiation with developers, transport operators and other government administrations. Other interventions which place restrictions on car use and access and which punish infractions effectively or which charge for the use of space, such as congestion charging, will require careful preparation and justification to gain majority political support. There are several interventions, however, that will help to make lives less car dependent and educate and inform individuals about the most energy efficient means of travel and which with organisational backing can be implemented in the short term. These interventions, which include personalised and company travel plans, the workplace parking levy, eco-driving and intelligent transport systems, can have a substantial impact in terms of changing routinised behaviour patterns particularly if their application is widespread (Gray *et al.* 2006).

TAXATION POLICY

Changing the focus of taxation policy towards conserving natural resources is a long-term task particularly since many of the incentives and subsidies given within the tax structures of many nations work against the objectives of sustainable urban transport (European Conference of Ministers of Transport 2001; European Commission Directorate General Environment 2004b). In the late 1990s, the EU introduced a fuel tax for international aviation (Rietveld and Stough 2002). However, many member states have altered fuel and vehicle ownership taxes in the last decade to favour ultra-low sulphur fuel, renewable transport fuels and clean engine technology. Taxes on larger vehicles (cars and trucks) and carbon fuels can be increased to discourage use. Taxation policy is a very political and sensitive area of government policy so that the public needs to be well informed about both the need for energy reduction and eco-efficiency, and how actual charges will affect them personally. Because of this political sensitivity, policy discussions on vehicle and fuel taxation are being conducted within the parameters of a no overall increase in taxation ('taxation neutral') policy following a spate of lobby group protests after previous interventions to increase fuel taxes (Lyons and Chatterjee 2002).

The efficient pricing of carbon consumption through taxation policy and other fiscal instruments will have a high impact on transport modal choice in the long term. Pricing mechanisms are already in place through: the EU carbon emissions trading scheme for large companies; carbon permits used to control vehicle ownership in Singapore; vehicle taxation based on the distance travelled in the Netherlands; road tolls for motorway use; and several cities (viz. London, Oslo, Bergen, Trondheim, Rome, Bologna and Durham) have implemented forms of cordon pricing (Banister 2005b: 88; Goddard 1997; Gray *et al.* 2006). The identification of the most cost effective pricing mechanism based on the actual carbon consumed and the technology to record carbon consumption will take some time to sort out. Personal or individual carbon allowances to achieve energy efficiency and taxation based on the distance travelled both conform with the concept of exergy discussed in Chapter 3, and would raise awareness of the carbon intensity of decisions to purchase and travel options as consumers choose how they spend their carbon resources (Gray *et al.* 2006; Tight *et al.* 2004).

Road user charging or road tolling is now technically feasible but there are complex institutional issues yet to be resolved in many cities (Hensher and Brewer 2001). Support for road user charging comes from the business community and higher income earners who are more likely to use their cars for commuting. Road user charging can either use satellite technology, or camera-based technology installed at the road side to identify the vehicle crossing a cordon, and allows charges to be varied according to the density of traffic (commensurate with congestion in the area) during certain periods of the day. Cordon-based charging is perceived as less intrusive and less expensive than electronic charging equipment installed in every vehicle to track origins and destinations (Glaister and Graham 2006: 1409). However, congestion charging, for using road space during peak periods when the flow of traffic is impeded by the sheer volume using the road, is also considered an effective way to remove drivers who don't need to make the journey in that particular time period. It may also deter latent demand and remove the need for additional road capacity (Hensher and Brewer 2001; Eddington 2006).

The net social and economic benefits experienced from road user charging in a congested historic market town (Durham) or a congested capital city centre (London) include reduced overall traffic flow, reduced pollution and noise, improved journey time reliability, increased use of bicycles and motorcycles, increased pedestrian flows, modal shift to public transit, increases in car sharing/pooling, improvement to public transit finances, and increased tax revenues (Department for Transport 2004b; Glaister and Graham 2006). In both of these examples, substantial improvements were made to the bus service and the street environment to complement the charging scheme. Reductions in congestion range from 30 per cent (London) to 85 per cent (Durham) (Department for Transport 2004b). The environmental benefits need to be counterbalanced by the disbenefits arising to vehicle users and their passengers during the charging period. Many drivers will change modes, use other routes, reduce the frequency of journeys made or make the journey outside the charging period. Both of these schemes sought to address a localised problem of insufficient road capacity for the demand experienced. There is the fear that if road use was rationed through a national charging mechanism this would have an unfair affect on the low income population in rural areas where there are few realistic public transit alternatives (Glaister and Graham 2006).

Table 6.4 Overcoming the main implementation issues with respect to road user charging: an example from central London

---

Cordon-based charging – single sector policy, but a key part of a complex range of strategies for transport in London and the desire to make London a liveable city

---

Rationale – mainly to address the problem of congestion in central London, but also to raise revenue for investment in transport and to achieve environmental objectives on air quality

---

Barriers	*Resource barrier* – level of charges: effectiveness of charging and use of funds.
	Social and cultural barriers
	– equity: reinvestment of revenues in public transport, but adverse impacts on shift workers and low income car users.
	– business impacts: greater efficiency and reliability, and can pass on costs.
	– public acceptance: hypothecation of revenues and extensive consultations to gain acceptability.
	Legal barrier – requirement for vehicles to display licence: legislation changed.
	Side effects – boundary pressures: eventually to be overcome by a full road pricing scheme and a flexible boundary, but at present traffic management to ease increase in traffic at boundary and to accommodate diverted traffic.
Implementation issues	*Entrance to charging area* – limit number of entry and exit points and turning movements.
	Residents – reduced rate of charging at 10 per cent of full rate.
	Cleaner vehicles – exempt.
	Cycles and motorcycles – exempt.
	Taxis and buses – exempt.
	Enforcement – fine of £80.
	Timing – introduced in Spring 2003.
Longer term issues	*Property market effects* – including land values, rent levels and returns inside and outside the charging area.
	Development effects – including pressures inside and immediately outside charging area.
	Employment effects inside and outside charging area.
	London wide impact on *image of city*.

Source: Adapted from Table 3 Banister (2002a: 8), reproduced with permission

There are several barriers that need resolution before a cordon-pricing scheme can be implemented. Table 6.4 summarises the main barriers, the nature of the problem and how it was overcome, the implementation issues and the longer-term spatial impacts the road user charge in central London may have (Banister 2002a : 8–9). In the London zone there is a fixed charge of £8 between 7am – 6pm (Monday to Friday) for vehicles crossing the cordon with exemptions for buses, taxis and motorbikes, and reductions for residents and some employee categories (see Chapter 7 for further discussion).

Any universal system of charging for the full economic, social and environmental costs of motorised travel would have to gain public support and would need to demonstrate the value added from the intervention. The negative effects can be reduced through mechanisms to ensure tax revenue neutrality (Glaister and Graham 2006) and tax credits to alleviate any hardship (Litman 1997). A revenue-neutral tax system would 'return' the additional charges from vehicle use through lower vehicle registration taxes and/or lower local taxes. A revenue-neutral national road tolling scheme may gain political acceptability, but Glaister and Graham (2006) predict that the burden of payment could fall on urban areas. They model the revenue impact of two scenarios: 1) a charging system based on low environmental damage costs; and 2) one based on full environmental costs and a charge that reflects the incremental congestion cost inflicted by each vehicle. In the latter case, charges that reflect all the costs of road use imply a reduction of only 9 per cent in national traffic levels, since the congestion element is localised (Glaister and Graham 2006: 1405). The model suggests that road user charging could be tax revenue neutral and still provide economic and environmental benefits if a medium range of environmental damage costs were recouped.

The technology to implement a universal charging system is nearly available, and will be trialled in the scheme to be introduced in the Netherlands by 2011. Satellite-based geographical positioning systems are in place and car manufacturers are now installing navigation facilities in new vehicles. The camera-based technology and the electronic payment system will need to be decided for each context. A revenue-neutral charge could be trialled for freight using a distance-based charge so that the political acceptability issues, the electronic vehicle identification equipment and other infrastructure, and the costs of administration of different systems can be assessed (McKinnon 2006).

WORKPLACE INTERVENTIONS

There are several workplace interventions such as flexible working, telecommuting, travel planning and a workplace parking levy which can encourage and sustain behaviour change (Cairns et al. 2004; Hull et al. 2009). At the company or school site, a travel plan, if widely discussed with members can help to reduce the dependence on car use and improve the physical and mental health of members through regular exercise. The essence of a successful travel plan is an evidence base on the origin of trips (homes) and modal choices that can be used for a car sharing information interface, and measures to make bicycle use more appealing by providing covered bicycle racks, shower facilities and financial incentives. The travel plan should be conceived as a tool to achieve CO_2 reductions and energy efficiency in company and employee travel and supported by an organisation policy on tele-working and teleconferencing to cut down on the need to travel (Palmoski 2008). Some companies also provide real alternatives to private car use by running their own special bus services (para-transit) to collect and return staff to rail stations or city centres, giving financial assistance with public transit costs and prioritising car parking space for car sharers (Curtis and Olaru 2007).

While company travel plans are often a condition for gaining a development permit, they soon lose momentum if they are not refreshed by company and staff commitment. If there is a financial incentive to encourage cycling, implementation of the travel plan can be led by cyclists themselves. GlaxoSmithKline in London have integrated a Bike Miles scheme into their travel plan. The incentives include a money voucher for employees who arrive by bike each day redeemable at a bike shop, access to professional bike maintenance during work time, cycle parking located in a prime position, and state of the art changing facilities (Department for Transport 2004e: 72–73). Regular cyclists have doubled in number and registered cyclists who cycle occasionally to work have risen from 50 to over 300. The scheme also benefits GlaxoSmithKline since a year's worth of vouchers costs significantly less than the value of a car parking space.

Charging for the use of workplace parking spaces is an instrument that can reduce unnecessary workplace parking spaces. This type of instrument could be imposed as a condition of a development permit. The employer would charge employees for an annual parking permit or licence to mimic the actual or opportunity cost of the parking space. This, therefore, is a financial 'stick' to encourage eco-efficiency in travel option choice and is simple to administer and highly effective in terms of reducing carbon emissions and traffic congestion (Ison 2004). The availability of subsidised and/or free car parking in urban areas has been one of the key drivers supporting commuting by car. The proviso here is that the cost of parking is passed onto employees and that too many exemptions are not negotiated. As a fiscal instrument to reduce car dependency in all large local organisations it needs to be integrated with other behaviour change policies and the income stream used to invest in public projects valued by businesses and employees.

CAR USE

There are several instruments that either restrict the access of motorised vehicles in certain urban areas or that reduce their speed. Traffic cells and mazes are used to protect residential areas in central urban areas from through traffic by re-routing the traffic away from the area and restricting direct access between specific cells or zones in the urban area. A 'zones and loops' system allows buses, taxis, delivery vehicles and cycles into through streets but restricts general traffic to the first zone chosen with no direct access to the other zones in the central area. Re-routing traffic in this way complements other interventions such as the pedestrianisation of central area streets and the introduction of reduced speed limits in the central area.

Traffic calming is another instrument used to lower traffic speeds in residential areas and areas with high pedestrian activity such as shopping streets so that walkers and cyclists feel safe to use the street space. This is the most effective intervention to improve road safety in the short term (Millward and Wheward 2003 quoted in Barnardo's *et al.* 2004: 16). The Child Accident Prevention Trust (2004) quotes research estimating that if a child is hit by a car at 20 mph (32 kmph) there is a 95 per cent chance of survival; at 30 mph (48 kmph) this drops to only 55 per cent; at 40 mph (64 kmph) 85 per cent of pedestrians are killed. Liabo and Curtis's (2003) research found traffic calming schemes had reduced childhood traffic injuries by up to 15 per cent. Slower vehicle speeds in urban areas also reduce traffic noise, induce safe play and cycling (Liabo and Curtis 2003). Barnardo's *et al.* (2004) recommend traffic calming to be implemented first in the most deprived residential areas and in inner city areas. Reducing the volume and the speed of traffic is the key to improving child safety and promoting active travel at a young age to access local facilities, and ultimately cementing healthier lifestyles. In areas where there are high numbers of children, a network of safe cycle routes should connect to schools (see Table 6.3), leisure facilities and parks.

The enforcement of existing speed limits could have a high impact nationally, reducing fuel consumption and therefore CO_2 emissions, but also road accidents, fatalities and road congestion. Gray *et al.* (2006) cite estimates that 15 million motorists exceed the maximum speed limit on UK motorways and most go unde-tected. A properly enforced motorway speed limit in the UK is calculated by Anable *et al.* (2006) to cut carbon emissions from transport by nearly 1 million tonnes per annum (quoted in Gray *et al.* 2006: 45). They estimate that a new 60 mph (96 kmph) limit would double the annual reduction by averaging 1.88 million tonnes a year of CO_2 savings, which if continually enforced would more than cover the CO_2 savings expected from the transport sector in the current national strategy.

Car clubs (car pools) have been introduced in many cities by local government to provide an alternative to car ownership. In these schemes, cars in the pool are hired out to members who can activate the vehicle through a smartcard and who subsequently return the vehicle to a dedicated car parking space. Interventions that either restrict the availabil-ity of on-street parking or that ration the available space through high parking charges are considered to be more effective than any other traffic management instrument in terms of influencing mode choice (Rye and Ison 2005). This would entail a revision of parking policy in many cities which have spent significant resources providing intelligent transport systems (ITS) to effectively manage the car driver's search for a vacant parking spot. Provided there are sufficient transport alternatives available the city administration can use the parking market as a means of reducing car dependency and securing modal shift. A restrictive car parking policy ideally should be implemented by a higher (regional) tier of government, since as Calthorp (2005) suggests efficient parking strategies are rarely set by local government because of competition with adjacent local administrations and the lobbying by special interest groups such as business interests and motorists.

BUS SERVICE IMPROVEMENTS

Energy efficient transport in urban areas relies on bus services and other forms of semi-public para-transit such as minibuses to provide a flexible service at a relatively low cost to passengers. To attract significant modal shift from the passenger car, alternatives need to match the car in terms of speed and comfort. Several infrastructure measures already discussed are being implemented by transport operators and city administrations to upgrade public transit fleets and install technology to give priority to the bus in order to reverse the decline in public transit patronage which often characterises deregulated systems of transport provision (Hensher and Brewer 2001). These partnerships are often established on the basis of a legal agreement to improve the quality of service provided including the quality standards for vehicles in use (cleaning, service frequency and reliability, CCTV), and improvements to the interchange facilities (White 2002; Hensher and Brewer 2001).

Much can be done to make bus services a reasonably attractive means of getting about in urban areas after service quality and frequency have been addressed. A city wide electronic fare/smartcard has been shown to boost public transit and provide information on trip lengths, trip ends, time and day of travel for each of the tickets (season, concessionary, etc.) sold which is invaluable for public transit planning (Balcombe *et al.* 2004; Lockhart and Scotney 2008). Well designed and lit bus stops with real-time information can also stimulate bus patronage. Clear and reliable information on service frequency is a prerequisite to provide certainty of service for passengers. On-site printed timetables are sufficient but real-time intranet facilities at workplaces and on TV monitors at transport interchanges, hospitals and leisure centres cut down the waiting time at bus stops (Curtis and Olaru 2008; Hull *et al.* 2009a,b).

AWARENESS RAISING

Clear and reliable information about the most energy efficient means of transport between home and the spatial opportunities the urban area offers will enable individuals to carefully consider the necessity and the timing of, and the mode for, each trip. Timetabling information can be provided on websites or direct to individual mobiles. At the individual level, personalised marketing of more active means of travel can be tailored to individual lifestyles with individuals provided with face-to-face advice on how to meet their travel needs in a healthy and sustainable way. These individual support programmes have been a very cost-effective way of initiating behaviour change (Hull *et al.* 2009a,b).

Eco-driving techniques have been demonstrated to local authority and freight distribution employees to show the fuel consumption savings that can be obtained through careful driving application (Hull *et al.* 2009a,b). Good practice for eco-driving includes adhering to speed limits, breaking and changing gear at the optimal time, avoiding idling, limiting the use of air conditioning, reducing drag through closing windows, ensuring tyres are filled to the optimum pressure, shedding unnecessary weight from the vehicle, and keeping a minimum distance from the vehicle ahead to avoid sharp breaking (Grey et al. 2006). Gray et al. (2006) quote research in the Netherlands, where eco-driving has been incorporated into normal driving lessons and assessed as part of the driving test, which found that drivers who had received the training drive 4–10 per cent more efficiently than other drivers. Research quoted by the Energy Savings Trust (2005) puts the potential energy efficiency savings as much higher (5–25 per cent). Fines have been introduced in some countries for vehicle idling, when engines are left running at the roadside unnecessarily. This has covered buses, taxis and commercial vehicles.

This section has tried to explain the range of instruments that will secure a more energy efficient existence in our towns and cities and to identify the ease and the timescale of implementation. There are obviously many simple, single, energy efficient interventions that could be implemented by the public sector. Proactively enforcing existing speed limits is such an obvious intervention that achieves not only carbon reductions, but meets safety and quality of life objectives too. Likewise with eco-driving and travel planning interventions. The land use measures, including cycling, pedestrianisation, and traffic calming require more thought and planning to integrate with other sector objectives, but these are relatively low cost interventions that if planned in an integrated way will have many synergistic cumulative benefits. Reducing our car dependency through the co-proximity of services, creating diversity in our suburbs, encouraging the opening of small general stores and open-air markets, and restricting road space for private vehicles will all help to stimulate walking, social interaction and increased quality of life.

A prerequisite for action to create places catering for pedestrians and cyclists of all ages and disabilities is the demonstration of will and intention, clearly signposted in strategies and plans, and implemented using the integrative tools and mechanisms available between the different levels of government. Many strategies and research activities fail to include all modes of transport when planning for accessibility in strategic long-term planning. If walking and cycling modes were given a higher profile than hitherto in transport planning this would help to link with policies for health, education and social development (European Commission Directorate General Environment 2004b). A recent report on CO_2 abatement policies for transport by the European Conference of Ministers for Transport (ECMT 2007) claimed that national policies tend to concentrate on some of the higher cost measures available, for example subsidies for biofuels, while some low cost measures are neglected. Lower cost measures such as regulation of fuel quality and some car components (such as tyre pressures), support for eco-driving and labelling were identified as lower cost options.

6.3 INTEGRATIVE MEASUREMENT TOOLS FOR SUSTAINABLE ACCESSIBILITY

The previous section has summarised a number of interventions which are appropriate in the urban location to reduce energy consumption and carbon dioxide emissions and to help create more actively used neighbourhood environments. Singularly, these interventions will have some positive impact on the sustainability of a city or neighbourhood. Linking the interventions together has the potential to secure additional or synergistic gains that are greater than the sum of each individual intervention (Hull 2008c, 2010 forthcoming). Deciding which combinations of interventions will maximise sustainability may be intuitive in each location, but actually demonstrating, against some scale, that a certain combination is the most effective is difficult to show. The real challenge in justifying which package of measures will be appropriate in the specific context is the availability of good indicators and data based on the baseline situation before the implementation of the package of instruments, and data that can track the direct and indirect effects over a period of time as well as how the instruments interact in synergistic and antagonistic ways. This is the challenge brought out by the assessment of the case studies in Chapter 7. This section, therefore, addresses this issue by seeking to review the decision support tools available, which may help to justify choices and gain the support of politicians and members of the public.

The task is to identify measures or indicators of sustainability (equity, environmental protection, exergy, economic growth) that can be relatively easily used to measure at least the direction of change across the different dimensions of sustainable development. Any appraisal or accounting system should encompass the widest definition of sustainable development. The indicators should be able to inform policy development at the local, regional, national, and supra-national scales of government. It is important to be able to model the effects of action on the indicators and to use a basket of indicators to assess the cumulative effects of a transport proposal. To be understood and used by a wide as possible clientele, the measurement has to be scientifically consistent and transparent to decision makers and members of the public (Van der Waard *et al.* 2007).

There are several indices which have been used to report on the sustainable development of nations. These include indices that have been derived to compare nation states on how 'green' their economies are (e.g. Green GDP, the Z index, Approximate Environmentally Adjusted Net National Product); or how the economy meets social needs (e.g. the Index of Sustainable Economic Welfare, the Economic Aspects of Welfare Index and Quality of Life indices); and the use of natural resources (e.g. the Ecological Footprint, Net Primary Productivity (NPP) sequestration) (see Mitchell 1996 for a review of these indices). None of these specifically relates to transport, although the ecological footprint provides a broad basis for assessing the use of resources.

Transport economic (cost) efficiency

Transport project appraisal has traditionally been assessed on the economic cost effectiveness of a project that involves an estimation of the 'social welfare benefits' emanating from the project using a number of proxies (the reduction in journey times, savings in vehicle operating costs and savings in accident costs) which are expressed as a monetary benefit and appraised in relation to the actual cost of the project (Canning *et al.* 2007). Cost benefit analysis (CBA) seeks to identify the most efficient use of public resources and assumes that travel time savings and safety are appropriate indicators of 'social welfare' and that the predicted benefits are realised and then converted into reduced wage costs, increased property values, expanded labour market and/or job catchment areas (Council for the Protection of Rural England 2003). Most studies use travel time savings as a proxy for economic growth, making authoritative statements that '*a 5 per cent reduction in travel time for all business travel on the roads could generate around £2.5 billion of cost savings – some 0.2 per cent of GDP*' (Eddington 2006: 15). In practice, small reductions in travel time for car users appear to be overstated in current transport scheme appraisal when they are factored up to the whole population of car drivers. The precise relationship between the transport network and the region's growth is unclear, but transport is considered to be an '*enabler*' of growth and '*productivity when other conditions are right*' (Eddington 2006: 15). Few studies of transport impacts actually give an idea of what these conditions are in different contexts.

The complexity of interactions between transport infrastructure investment, accessibility, regional economic performance and global economic markets impacts on our ability to understand the causal chain interaction which might be triggered by public sector investment. Part of the problem is that the key indicators used to assess the impact of transport investment on productivity (GDP, investment, freight tonnes kilometres and passenger kilometres) are positively correlated (Preston 2001: 15). The underlying assumption is that development pressure and traffic growth is benign. Tellingly, Holl (2006: 10) states:

> The distribution of benefits and impacts among different locations is often crucial in transport policies (Bristow and Nelthorpe 2000). Who benefits, where are the benefits concentrated, and who and which areas are negatively affected? CBA, in general, does not provide insights into the mechanisms that may lead to different responses by firms in different sectors of the economy, nor on spatial differences [...]. If transport projects are seen as instruments for regional development, then knowledge of how firms in different areas react to transport changes is significant for the design of an effective spatial policy.

From the late 1990s, the quantitative focus on safety and economy has been supplemented by other qualitative criteria such as the impact on the environment, accessibility and integration (Department of Environment, Transport and the Regions 1998b). Although there is parity between these different criteria in the appraisal guidance, the deciding factor on whether to proceed with a transport proposal is still made on the grounds of the perceived cost effectiveness of government spend (Department for Transport 2009; Transport Scotland 2008: 53) rather than the effective use of financial resources to reduce natural resource consumption. A significant aspect of the Scottish Transport Appraisal Guidance (STAG) is the revenue derived from the taxation of fuel. A reduction in overall fuel consumption as a result of improvements to the public transit, cycling and walking infrastructure would, therefore, count negatively in the appraisal of the economic benefits of these schemes. Environmental and social costs can be overlooked if they are outweighed by benefits to other objectives. So, although a wide range of elements pertaining to sustainable development may have been assessed for each transport scheme proposed, if the final decision on whether to proceed is reduced to a decision on predicted travel time savings or the cost efficiency of the proposal, schemes that encourage mobility will be supported. This is intuitively working against the aims of sustainable transport.

The capture of the full range of economic changes as a result of a proposed transport project is clearly still a priority in national transport appraisal policy. Eddington (2006) calls for the '*recognised problems of economic growth* [to be] *fully taken into account* [so that] *any other consequences (e.g. through more-people-in-work leading to more commuting, or higher GDP leading to increased housing demand and higher car ownership) would then be considered within the modelling process*' (ibid.: 19). He goes on to say that: '*There is a danger that the increasingly important environmental impact analysis of major transport schemes will be seen as hypocritical if it includes (for example) the benefits of smoother traffic flow but not the environmental consequences of economic impacts which are also cited as benefits*' (ibid.: 19).

TRANSPORT CARBON EFFICIENCY

Transport efficiency can also be considered from the aspect of the resource inputs and the final outcomes rather than single outputs such as reduced travel costs to car drivers. The outcome for the transport sector would then be to achieve the goal of a more efficient use of resources (carbon, air quality, land and soil, water, biodiversity, materials/minerals, financial) in transporting people and goods. When we are looking for the best set of interrelated projects to build that will reduce the resource consumption of travel, the economic efficiency of schemes is inappropriate (O'Sullivan 1980). The methodology of using carbon inputs may be a more appropriate way of appraising the value of new transport projects (www.green-alliance.org.uk; www.bettertransport.co.uk).

The concept of transport carbon efficiency (measuring the carbon intensity of transport use) has the advantage of simplicity, like the measure of transport economic efficiency, which it could replace (Gray *et al.* 2006). Transport carbon efficiency is a measure of value for money but in relation to the cost per unit of carbon saved, rather than the cost of a scheme to the government. If national governments chose to set a target for the reduction of carbon from the transport sector, this measure could help to identify the cheapest way to save carbon from transport. There is substantial work to be carried out, however, to make this appraisal system workable. Gray *et al.* (2006: 47) raise several methodological challenges:

- An indicative value for carbon needs to be set to aid broad assessment of policies within and between sectors, and policies need to be assessed according to the resources required to save an equal amount of carbon.
- The absolute and relative scale of the emissions savings expected from individual transport policy measures need to be evaluated. How much does it cost to save a gram of carbon from various transport policies compared to other sectors?

If transport projects were systematically assessed in terms of their value for money in relation to the cost per unit of carbon saved it is likely that low technology interventions, including speed management and software measures such as travel planning would show the best value for money using a carbon abatement appraisal system.

INDICATORS OF RESOURCE EFFICIENCY

There are a number of alternative indicators of resource efficiency which could be used in addition to carbon accounting to assess travel impacts and transport system efficiency (Table 6.5). The modal share of walking and cycling trips can be used as a proxy for the physical fitness of the population; the proportion of population within 400 m of a regular public transit service (e.g. every 15 minutes) can be used to assess social inclusion as well as the availability of alternatives to the car; the modal share of trips by residents is a proxy for the level of car dependence and transport energy emissions; while the average distance of travel by mode is another proxy indicator for transport energy emissions and other environmental impacts.

Accessibility to public transit, local jobs, local centres and open space is primarily assessed as a social inclusion indicator but it also has effects on walking and cycling as mode choices. These are indicators that assess multiple objectives including neighbourhood vitality and interaction and opportunities for healthy travel choices. Accessibility is already incorporated into many transport appraisals. Accessibility is, therefore, an important indication of the distribution of spatial opportunities and of problems, enabling more detailed analysis by social group

Table 6.5 Indicators of transport resource efficiency

Criteria	Indicator
Economic	
Sustainable consumption	Gross value added; cost/unit of carbon saved; consumption per capita; ecological footprint
Economic self-sufficiency	Percentage of food sourced locally; job–housing ratio
Transport efficiency	Average passenger journey time and length, per mode; occupancy rate of passenger vehicles; proportion of vehicles that meet Euro standards
Accessibility to spatial opportunities	Accessibility to jobs, services, open spaces; percentage of population within 400/800m pedsheds
Environment (natural)	
Noxious emissions	VOC and acidifying gases from transport
Greenhouse gas emissions	Global greenhouse gas from transport; modal share and average distance travelled, by car
Biodiversity	Habitat and ecosystem disruption from transport
Minerals	Consumption of mineral oil products in transport
Green space area and pattern	Quality and fragmentation of open space
Landscape	Reduction of vegetation biomass through transport
Other diffuse pollution	Polluting accidents (land, air, water) from transport
Environment (resources)	
Land use	Density of development; development of vacant, urban brownfield sites
Soil condition	Land lost to development
Energy use	Energy consumption per transport mode; use of renewable energy sources in transport; load factor for freight vehicles
Water use	Consumption of water in transport/transport products
Cultural heritage	Disturbance of heritage features
Social and health needs	
Physical fitness	Modal share of walking/biking; exposure to PM and NO_2 from transport
Traffic accidents	Persons killed/injured in traffic accidents
Noise	Exposure to noise
Security	Perceptions of safety by mode
Journey ambience	Perceptions of comfort and reliability by mode
Distance to bus stop	Percentage of population within 400m of a frequent bus service
Neighbourhood severance	Fragmentation of communities through transport

Source: Adapted from Spiekermann and Wegener (2004) and Mitchell (2005)

(see Chapter 3). Indicators could also include the job ratio in the defined area, the proportion of population within 400m and 800m pedsheds and the proportion of population within 400m and 800m of major green space.

The density of development (net or gross) is often used to assess the efficiency with which land is used. Other indices in use include the overall land-take by development, the proportion of vacant land, and the proportion of new development on brownfield (previously used land) and greenfield land. Settlement form also affects embodied energy and the demand for heating and electricity, which varies according to estate layouts, building types and construction materials used. The UK's Building Research Establishment uses an environmental assessment method (BREEAM) to measure the sustainability of buildings. It adopts a weighting scheme that systematically sums and compares, ascribing relative values to the criteria without using a common unit of appraisal. It also allows some stakeholder involvement in deciding what should be valued the most.

Table 6.5 also includes indicators for the prudent use of natural resources that should cover water, land cover, soils, energy, minerals/materials and biodiversity. Water impacts are assessed using predictions of the volumes required and how this will impact on water supplies, catchment areas, drainage and flood risk. The impact on soil quality can be assessed taking into account the land lost to transport infrastructure development. Biodiversity is assessed by examining the impact of development on protected habitats and species, nature reserves, woods, water courses, shelter belts and other environmental features.

Indicators would need to be agreed that cover other issues such as traffic noise, pollutants and danger, the visual intrusion of transport infrastructure in each neighbourhood, and the geographical disjunction of existing communities and social interactions by transport infrastructure and traffic flows. The impact of transport on the health of the nation and cultural heritage should also be assessed.

MULTI-CRITERIA ASSESSMENT

Assessing all the dimensions of sustainability requires assessment against a set of criteria and then combining the rankings or the weightings. It is difficult for all the dimensions to be scored on a universal scale and one should be wary of social and environmental factors being traded away by perceived economic benefits as happens in current practice. Local, national and international technical experts are often used in project evaluation to weight the relative importance of each of the dimensions or indicators. These indicator weights are then applied to the scores to calculate an overall score. It is much harder to interpret the cumulative effects of the interactions between transport and land use interventions, and how they in turn interact with interventions from other policy sectors. Many of the instruments in Table 6.1 only have a small impact or are implemented in an incremental way. An integrated assessment is preferable and would involve the assessment of the expected interactions (synergistic, antagonistic) between new interventions and existing system components, noting the scale and direction (negative, positive) of these interactions, and would then consider the collective effect of these interactions on the dimensions of sustainability (Tricker 2007; Hull 2008c).

There are several tools available to support the integration of the assessment and the weighting of the components of sustainability. Strategic environmental assessments (SEAs) provide an integrated approach to the assessment of how proposed plan policies will singly and collectively impact on natural resources, including the impact on air quality, water, land and soils. SEAs require a detailed environmental assessment against baseline data including the identification of problem issues, consideration of alternatives, impact prediction involving cumulative effects, mitigation and monitoring of the solution(s) and impacts. Best practice guidance (Office of the Deputy Prime Minister *et al.* 2005) recommends the use of action-indicator matrices with quantitative and/or qualitative data (the latter expressed using a variety of symbolic techniques). Assessment involves predicting the effects of proposals on evaluation criteria (identifying changes in space and time), describing them in a consistent manner, and commenting upon their significance (duration, magnitude, receptor importance, reversibility, etc.).

There are also many effective methods for engaging with local residents in a meaningful way early on in the process of option generation and appraisal. Empowering methods of interaction with members of the public include the citizen's jury, the 'planning cell' or 'planungszelle' methods, and sustainability threshold analysis (STA). These types of public interaction support local democracy and citizen engagement in the political process where hard choices have to be made. The citizen's jury is composed of a representative group of residents (30–40) invited to participate in identifying the problems in their area and appropriate solutions. They act as a jury calling expert witnesses to help them work out the solutions (Hull 2006). Similarly, the idea of composing several planning cells (25 people in each) allows several groups of citizens to work out solutions to a given planning problem. The city of Hanover used this method to identify how to improve public transit in the city. Twelve planning cells (300 citizens) worked for four days to produce their solutions which were then summarised and voted for in a citizen survey (GUIDEMAPS 2003).

STA is a specific site-based technique used with a wide range of stakeholders, with different interests in a development site, to agree the type of development appropriate for the site, assess progress and the solutions to achieve more sustainable development (Barton 2004). The process involves identifying the relevant sustainable development issues in the location and what would need to be achieved through intervention to make a significant impact on the issue or problem.

Table 6.6 shows the baseline threshold assessment of development potential against twelve criteria. The value of the threshold approach '*is that it directly relates the level and seriousness of impact to importance, and at the same time it identifies where action is needed to mitigate impacts*' (Barton 2004: 10). A traffic signal colour scheme is used to convey the level of seriousness for which action is needed:

- Red is an unacceptable level of sustainability
- Orange is highly problematic
- Yellow is a negotiable level where unsustainable practices can be overcome by practicable means
- Green is a good level of sustainability
- Blue is an excellent level of sustainability.

Having agreed the baseline issues and potential solutions, stakeholders meet to assess the degree of change and the further action which is needed. The baseline scoring system is checked to see the direction of progress: 'moving towards' or 'moving away' or 'not sure' judgements of the impact of an intervention on the sustainability of the location/solution.

Implementing sustainable accessibility (see Chapter 3) in urban areas is a learning process, where potential positive interventions are demonstrated and monitored to understand how, if at all, they have a beneficial effect on travel behaviour. Sustainable accessibility depends on the achievement of multiple priorities across several sectors (transport, energy, land use, health, etc.) and, thus, the search is on for indicators that can measure progress across several priorities. The availability of a simple transparent indicator to which sustainable transport can be reduced and measured would provide a strong tool for decision making.

This review has shown that the available tools do not yet allow a simple assessment of the contribution an instrument will make to the different dimensions of sustainable development or assess the progress that society is making towards efficient resource use. A system of carbon rating might provide one such simple mechanism, but it only measures consumption of one scarce natural resource. As Chapter 5 has shown, one of the barriers to the acceptance of behaviour change is the weak governance capacity to engage all the stakeholders who need to be influenced. Engaging stakeholders through the citizen's jury or planning cell or through using STAs are mechanisms for gaining a wide assessment of the baseline issues, potential solutions and progress with the implementation of solutions. These sorts of decision support tools have a role in sustainable development through the awareness raising and educational opportunities they provide.

6.4 CREATING THE PLATFORM FOR CHANGE

Our present mobility patterns are increasing CO_2 emissions and we are relying on the private car for the growth trips of leisure and shopping. Transport strategies in many countries specifically aim to enhance mobility rather than improving the accessibility to spatial opportunities. Gray *et al.* (2006: 19) ask the question: *'Can*

Table 6.6 Sustainability threshold assessment

Criteria	RED Development IMPOSSIBLE	ORANGE Development PROBLEMATIC	YELLOW Development CONDITIONAL	GREEN Development OK	BLUE Development PRIORITY
			Assessment of development potential		
1 Physical development potential		Contaminated land, buildings awkward to repair, steep slopes	Derelict land and buildings requiring treatment and/or rehabilitation		Previously developed land and vacant buildings capable of easy reuse
2 Market development potential	Land-locked site with no access possible	Zero/low value site, lacking appeal or potential; owner unwilling to sell	Marketable site/ buildings depending on conditions and costs imposed	Likely to be viable irrespective of conditions or S106 costs	High value sought-after location
3 Infrastructure capacity		Major threshold breached: shift in investment priorities required	Contribution needed to school/sewage treatment/roads/station etc.	No particular thresholds are breached	Spare capacity in local schools, public transport services, road system, sewage treatment
4 Pedestrian accessibility to key local facilities	No facilities within 800 m	Few facilities available within 800 m	Legal agreement could fill key gaps in facilities	Most facilities within 800 m	Choice of facilities available, most within 400 m
5 Public transport accessibility to jobs/centres	No regular public transport services accessible or planned	Only poor services accessible or planned	Poor services capable of improvement	Good quality services within 400 m	Excellent quality services within 300 m
6 Energy use and carbon fixing	Very exposed sites	Shelter belts, woodland, coppices	North-facing slopes, tree-replacement conditions		Gentle south-facing slopes, spare CHP/CH capacity

Table 6.6 Continued

Criteria	RED Development IMPOSSIBLE	ORANGE Development PROBLEMATIC	YELLOW Development CONDITIONAL	GREEN Development OK	BLUE Development PRIORITY
			Assessment of development potential		
7 Water	Areas liable to flood every 30 years or more	Marginal flood areas: high ground water vulnerability	Areas of medium ground water vulnerability	Supply, treatment, drainage okay; no flood risk	
8 Land, soils and local food production	Unstable land, areas prone to coastal erosion	Allotments, market gardens, organic farmland	High quality soils; impact on farmland		Contaminated land
9 Biodiversity	SSSIs and other national designations	Locally defined valued habitats and wildlife corridors	Locally valued but common habitats, trees and hedgerows	No threat to assets	Potential to create new habitats in degraded areas
10 Air quality and noise	Areas prone to unacceptable level of pollution	Source of pollution capable of correction – but who will pay?	Migratable noise levels		
11 Open space value or impact	Valued and well-used public open space (POS)	Common-land, valued public access land	Inadequate local open space, contribution needed	Ample supply of accessible open space locally	
12 Aesthetic and cultural heritage	Listed buildings; vulnerable landscapes of great value	Specific areas of valued landscape or great archaeological value	Conservation areas, AONBs, National Parks		Ugly or monotonous environment needing improvement

Source: Barton (2004: 14)

*a transport strategy which is largely focussed on reducing congestion and improv-
ing the efficiency of the network, therefore by definition speeding up traffic flow
and increasing capacity, be compatible with carbon reduction?'* The subsequent
question must be: how can the urgency of the required responses to climate change
be brought to bear on transport policy? It is not clear whether current policies will
stabilise car use or even reduce emissions. Few countries have set environmental
targets for the transport sector, on the basis that it would be more efficient to focus
first on other sectors of the economy which can abate more cheaply (Stern 2006).

Mobility is the cornerstone for EU and national strategic level policies to ensure
high speed connectivity between the strategic spaces favoured by higher order economic activity (banks, corporate headquarters, high-level service industries) and
market spaces overseas where key transactions are negotiated. Eddington (2006: 5)
has reaffirmed the importance of international gateways, the growing and congested
urban areas and their catchments, as well as key inter-urban corridors for facilitating
the movement of people and goods. In this conception of priorities, aviation, freight
and business car use are the important components for global connectivity.

Reviews of the potential of ICT to enable more activities to be undertaken
remotely suggest that new developments in communication will not substantially
change the perceived need for face-to-face business interaction or leisure travel
(Echenique 2005; Banister and Hickman 2007; Kohler 2007). *'There will be substitution of certain kinds of travel by telecommunications, but also it would generate
further travel demands, especially for freight, as a consequence of the increased
range of opportunities for trading created by the advances in communications'*
(Echenique 2005: 10). ICT is being used to create new global technology-based
spaces at the main airport hubs and other national transport accessible locations
(Banister and Hickman 2007).

The possibility of fossil fuel price increases and the security of energy supply
in the future are the more likely drivers to change in transport systems. The search
for new commercial fuels is developing hand in hand with new vehicle technologies *'designed with minimising emissions as a major objective, while retaining the
flexibility of the motor car'* (Kohler 2007: 19). This may lead to further development of private vehicle control and navigation systems, but is unlikely to reduce the
dependence on or distance travelled by passenger cars (Kohler 2007; Banister and
Hickman 2007), and their high cost may mean that their ownership becomes socially
divisive (Graham and Marvin 2001). Chapters 2 (Section 2.3) and 5 (Section 5.2)
identified the enduring cultural consumption practices or social norms that are
unlikely to change over the short term. ICT, however, has the potential to break down
the distinction between public and private transport if used to enable personalised
transport to be ordered for 'door-to-door' travel (Kohler 2007). Telecommunication
systems are already helping to support more 'seamless journeys' on public transit

through providing real-time information direct to mobile technologies on services, information, timetables, etc. ICT can secure resource efficient delivery of freight in metropolitan areas as hub-satellite systems track vehicles and loads using logistics platforms to improve utilisation and loading levels (Banister and Hickman 2007).

The opportunity to be more mobile with lower pollution levels is available at a price to all consumers. It is likely that these improvements to vehicle and fuel technologies coupled with some carbon-related user charges is all that the transport sector will achieve to contribute to tackling climate change. Despite calls by the EU and other stakeholders that transport users should meet all their external economic, social or environmental costs it is unlikely that there will be societal support for 'getting the prices right':

> Getting the prices right means making a comprehensive assessment of the full range of economic, environmental and social impacts of transport policies, including climate change. Not only does this ensure that full account is taken of environmental and social impacts but as these impacts have economic consequences, it also ensures that the economic assessment is sound. As expected, the evidence suggests that, on average, the inclusion of such effects reduces the returns from transport. For road schemes, the benefits are on average reduced by around £1 for each pound invested, although there is significant variation: the effect is smaller for many schemes but some see significant reductions (up to £3–4 per pound spent). Public transport schemes in urban areas can have environmental and social benefits.
>
> (Eddington 2006: 6)

To move to a low carbon technology future and one which minimises resource consumption implies a reduction in the need to travel. It will take a major shift to move from the dominant concept of mobility to accessibility and exergy.

There are technological, institutional and communication challenges to the internalisation of the external costs of transport use. Carbon accounting and cumulative effects assessment are relatively new methods, that are limited by data availability, and 'beset by potentially conflicting policy objectives [...] For example, the relationship between the goals of congestion reduction and carbon reduction are not well understood' (Gray et al. 2006: 18). The absolute and the relative scale of carbon emission savings from different policy packages would need to be compared between transport and other policy sectors. Gray et al. (2006) identify the transport policy instruments that would impact positively on carbon emissions from both freight and surface transport (Table 6.6; see also Whitelegg 1997). Substantial research is now being carried out to estimate the carbon savings from different transport policy packages (Johnson 2008), but it is unclear whether the outputs will be comprehensive enough to inform the detail of specific transport and land use strategies. Selecting the optimum package of transport policies to achieve economic, environmental and social goals is a much more difficult task. Before the cost effectiveness ('relative abatement costs') of policy packages can be assessed we need direct experience of their application and consequences. Understanding the social impacts and the potential rebound effects will take much longer. Some evaluation data on the political deliverability and policy synergies of the measures in Table 6.7, from the experience of other countries is available, but the key to the transferability of these experiences, critically, is to understand the differences in each socio-institutional context.

Table 6.7 shows that the structuring rules put in place by the EU and by national governments are important in providing the confidence and certainty that change in practices and behaviour will be a part of future government strategies. Incorporating environmental and social issues into transport policy takes a great deal of time, so the approach has to be consistent over several terms of political office:

> Without strategies that unfold with consistency over a long period and that cover a metropolitan region (or large portions thereof), it is unlikely that smart growth efforts will be successful in changing the course of urban development. Episodic and localised interventions are incapable of achieving the desired environmental objectives, in large part because they are unable to reshape behaviours in a way that conforms to these goals. For example, for car users to shift to transit, transit conducive conditions must be present at both points of origin and destination.
>
> (Filion and McSpurren 2007: 503)

Clarity and consistency of policy from higher tiers of government and with funding streams is also important. Where there is coordination between higher tiers of government and complementary strategies and budgets they can have significant leverage in effectively steering lower tier authorities (Rodriquez *et al.* 2006). Local spatial strategies, in their turn, can implement and support new approaches where policies and interventions are complementary and synergistic across policy areas. Single objective goals can impede the achievement of socially optimum goals. Any platform for change needs a clear vision, and the alignment of vision and rhetoric with policy and practice (Eddington 2006; Kohler 2007). If targets and goals are clearly communicated to delivery agencies and the general public, the '*cultural context of consumption*' (Kohler 2007: 19) can be shaped in a positive manner over the long term (see discussion in Chapter 5.2).

Many of the interventions in Table 6.7 are low cost and low technology solutions for behaviour change. They include a mixture of 'push' measures such as parking

Table 6.7 Policies to reduce carbon from 1) surface passenger transport and 2) freight transport

Policy Objective	SURFACE PASSENGER TRANSPORT		FREIGHT TRANSPORT	
	Local/regional government	National/EU level	Local/regional government	National/EU level
Reduce carbon content of fuels/ increase vehicle efficiency	• Fuel switching grants • Government purchase of alternative-fuelled vehicles • Subsidy for alternative-fuelled buses • Bus operator fleet targets for alternative fuels • Speed limit enforcement • Eco-driving • Eco-driving test • Vehicle idling campaigns	• Vehicle efficiency standards (voluntary/ mandatory agreements) • Fuel quality standards • Biofuels • Technological developments (e.g. hydrogen fuel cells)	• Freight dematerialisation • Logistics planning/load sharing • Sustainable distribution centres • Fuel switching grants • Technological developments • Eco-driving training	• Vehicle efficiency standards • Fuel quality standards
Modal switch: change to more efficient forms of transport/ using the network more efficiently	• Smart measures • Car clubs • Car free housing • Car sharing • High occupancy vehicle lanes • Investment in public transport and bus lanes • Policies to encourage walking/cycling • Pedestrianisation • Road space reallocation • Controlled parking zones • Low emission zones • Road pricing (including urban congestion charging) • High speed rail • Intelligent transport systems	• Graduated car vehicle excise duty • Company car tax • Fuel duty (+escalator) • Vehicle scrappage schemes • Eco-car labelling • Motorway pricing and national road user charging	• Goods distribution centres • Rail freight investment	• Lorry road user charging • Eurovignette • Early scrappage incentives for HGVs
Reduce the volume of travel	As above + • Teleshopping • Teleworking • Land use planning policies • Park and ride facilities	As Above + • Fuel duty (+ escalator) • Company car tax • Distance based vehicle insurance	As Above + • Development of less transport intensive industries • Local sourcing	As Above + • De-materialisation

Source: Adapted from Gray et al. (2006: 22)

controls and charges and 'pull' measures such as better bus services. These should be implemented effectively to create awareness, debate and public support for sustainable transport, to understand behaviour reactions and the likely unintended effects of policy implementation. It is unlikely that increased awareness of climate change and environmental considerations *per se* will lead to low energy resource choices unless accompanied by extensive penalties and rewards. As Chapter 5 has argued, local government administrations need the finance, legal and development tools to facilitate the production of strategies and the successful implementation of projects. It is important that strategies are based on solid research and that there are on-going corrective mechanisms to respond to unintended effects. Local government should therefore enter on a mission of partnering and joint learning with delivery agencies setting up funded programmes '*to nurture successful initiatives and encourage their replication* [and] *establishing an on-going process of review and collaborative learning*' (Kohler 2007: 19).

The experience of successful partnering in transport project delivery appears mixed across Europe. GUIDEMAPS (2003: 83) found collaboration and '*consensus making*' a key factor in overcoming barriers in the Czech Republic and France, where '*intensive communication takes place particularly between politicians and lobby groups and in most cases a constructive rather than a climate of conflict is found*'. Sweden was noted for '*strong and engaged project management*' and consensus, or a compromise was negotiated to overcome any barriers (ibid.: 84). In Spain, they found that politicians are more likely to force through a solution to overcome any barriers faced in implementation and, similarly, serious communication problems were experienced in Greece, '*caused by the lack of systematic public participation, as well as problems in achieving acceptance*' (ibid.: 84). New methods to engage with partners, such as STA (see Table 6.5) should be trialled to overcome these problems.

Changes to policy goals often require the establishment of new institutional structures or the strengthening of existing structures. There are two issues here. First, sub-national delivery agencies need to have the '*right geographical scope, powers and responsibilities*' to effectively take a leadership role on climate change (Eddington 2006: 51). GUIDEMAPS (2003) found that public authorities in the Czech Republic, UK and Greece were often constrained by lack of finance, legal powers and land ownership. Extensive land ownership and public sector power to develop housing is a key advantage in Copenhagen, Stockholm and Singapore, where the local state has '*exceptional planning capacity*' to successfully '*concentrate*[d] *growth in transit-focused communities built around subway and commuter rail stations*' (Filion and McSpurren 2007: 504). Also the effective coordination of the extension of commuter services with urban development in Tokyo is credited to the private railway companies, due to their ownership of land at the periphery of the metropolitan region (ibid.: 504).

The second issue in the effective implementation of innovative measures are the managerial and institutional hurdles that have to be overcome when a large number of partners are required to collaborate on transport project delivery, which can lead to project delays because of the need to coordinate so many partners (GUIDEMAPS 2003; Innes and Gruber 2005). Innovatory transport measures tend to be the object of constant bargaining to ensure delivery (Filion and McSpurren 2007). The cost effectiveness of having such a long planning and delivery chain is raised by Eddington (2006: 7), who found:

> In one area alone up to ten metropolitan authorities and the Passenger Transport Authority are required to cooperate to deliver the city's bus priority measures; and the delay and uncertainty of the planning system for major transport projects – the Thameslink 2000 scheme required over 30 consents under four different Acts and took over eight years – should be substantially reduced.

This chapter has examined the contribution of transport and land use instruments to bringing about more sustainable accessibility systems in city-regions. It has assessed the potential of transport instruments to achieve more social interaction on our streets, making these places safer, making the inhabitants healthier, and moreover, supporting low carbon transport modes. These instruments are relatively inexpensive to implement, and if designed and implemented simultaneously with land use planning, health, social services and education interventions they can go a long way to creating distinctive neighbourhoods in our cities once again.

There are good practices, in every country, but these are localised and not yet mainstreamed. The next chapter looks at some of these approaches to try and understand what is considered successful about their implementation and to what extent elements can be transferred to different cultural and institutional contexts.

CHAPTER 7

INTEGRATED TERRITORIAL PLANNING IN PRACTICE
CASE STUDIES

7.1 INTRODUCTION

The focus of this chapter is on innovatory approaches to the planning of development and physical accessibility to spatial opportunities using national and local case studies from across Europe. In this sense the chapter brings together the strands of debates from previous chapters and extends the discussion with examples of attempts to implement a package of transport and land use interventions. The early chapters set a challenge for society to reduce the negative impacts of transport infrastructure and use within the earth's carrying capacity in such a way that the necessary changes also serve other societal objectives such as improving health, reducing accidents and providing a better quality of life for all. Chapter 3 proposed that the concepts of accessibility (need to travel) and exergy (adding value while reducing resource input) would help to integrate knowledge across all sectors of public policy on resource minimisation ('conceptual integration'). Chapters 4 and 5 found that the capacity of government and governance to collaborate, across horizontal and vertical multi-scalar institutional structures ('performance integration'), in most countries in the implementation of policy instruments to achieve low energy development pathways is weak. Chapter 5, therefore, argued that a step change in transport resource consumption could only be achieved when the opportunity agenda of incentives and constraints for organisations and individuals was set to reduce resource consumption and waste. The chapter went on to hypothesise that change was, thus, dependent on:

1   National government action to realign financial systems and decision-making criteria to incentivise the introduction of low energy resource solutions.
2   Government institutions at the city-region level having sufficient legal and financial resources to ensure there is strong leadership and responsibility for behaviour change to integrate the global–local resource minimisation challenge.

The case studies that follow are used to test these two hypotheses and to provide the evidence base of what can be achieved in practice when land use and transport policy are integrated. The case studies document innovatory approaches to planning for future sustainability in Denmark, Sweden, the Netherlands, Germany, and the UK. There was little to differentiate these countries in 2004 in terms of the modal

Table 7.1 Modal split for land motorised passenger transport in 2004 (all journeys in percentages)

Country	Cars	Buses and coaches	Rail	Tram and metro
EU-25	82.4	9.3	6.5	1.4
Denmark	81.8	9.9	8.0	0.2
Germany	84.8	6.6	7.1	1.5
Netherlands	84.3	6.7	8.1	0.9
Sweden	83.0	7.6	7.6	1.7
United Kingdom	87.2	6.2	5.5	1.1

Source: Compiled from European Commission (2007a: 106)

split of land-based passenger transport. In Table 7.1 the slight differences can be accounted for by the geographic context and preferences for investment in rail rather than metro and tram, and with a higher dependence on road transport in the UK.

Table 7.2 shows that since 2006 the UK, Sweden and Germany have curtailed the growth in global greenhouse gas emissions from transport at below the average of the EU-27 countries. Up until 2006, emission growth in the Netherlands was substantially higher than the EU average. These figures are obviously affected by the socio-economic geography of each country. Denmark and Sweden are relatively low density countries with populations respectively of approximately 5.5 million at a density of 128/km² and 9 million at a density of 21/km². Both countries have a high proportion of agricultural employment and a well-educated workforce. Germany and the UK have much larger populations with 82 million and 61 million respectively and similar densities of 230 and 246/km² respectively. The Netherlands, with a population of approximately 16.5 million has a much more densely populated, low lying terrain, at around 400 people/km². Both Germany and the UK have witnessed a decline in the proportion of workforce engaged in manufacturing and an increase in labour employed in service industries. Since industrial output has not reduced in either country, this could be interpreted as a product of improved efficiency and/or de-industrialisation. Many believe that the reduction in CO_2 emissions in Germany since the 1990s, most notably from the industrial and commercial sectors of the economy, is based on de-industrialisation and reunification of East and West Germany[2].

Case studies can serve as tools of learning, if sufficient information is presented about the physical and policy context, to enable the reader to understand the theories used by local politicians and officers to organise physical accessibility within the city environment. The combination of tools and instruments chosen may provide useful lessons and best practice[3] models for other policy makers (Banister and Hickman 2007: 15). Data sources for the case studies in this chapter use both primary and secondary material to understand the factors that influence policy

Table 7.2 Growth in greenhouse gas emissions from transport 1990–2006
(all figures in million tonnes)

Country	1990	2006	Percentage change 1990–2006
Netherlands	26.4	36.1	37 %
Denmark	10.7	13.6	27 %
EU-27	779.1	992.3	27 %
United Kingdom	118.9	136.7	15 %
Sweden	18.4	20.2	10 %
Germany	164.4	162.0	−1.5 %

Source: Compiled from European Commission (2009: 172)

change and practice. The understanding is enriched through delving 'deep', using a historical interpretative institutional approach to both the analysis of the academic research material written in English and ethnographic research that compares the case studies against a template of implementation issues discussed in Chapter 5 (Table 5.8). A substantial body of research since the late 1990s has examined the take up and implementation of innovatory practices and initiatives by local government administrations. Much of this research has focused on the implementation barriers to delivering new social welfare policies by lower levels of government. This chapter seeks to theorise on the innovatory approaches towards more sustainable and transport resource-efficient environments and structures, and the discussion around five broad institutional questions that are seminal to interpreting the outcomes of innovatory programmes of change. These are:

1   Clear national rules that prioritise sustainability principles, including resource minimisation, across policy sectors
2   Structures that support problem solving and coordination at the local level
3   A framework for the coordination of public and private sector interaction
4   Engagement with civil society to understand the factors that affect transport behaviour and, thus, public acceptability of transport demand management
5   Evaluation of the effectiveness of interventions and adaptation measures to correct systemic problems.

There are, however, a few caveats to be aware of in learning from what appears to be 'exemplary' practices from abroad. First, we need to understand the contextual explanatory variables in each case study (Stough and Rietveld 2005). As discussed in Chapter 4, these include the tools of governance (resources, legal competencies, public sector development capacity, coordination and information provision) available to public sector actors and how these are shared between agencies and different tiers of government (Vigar *et al.* 2000). It requires substantial research to understand the drivers for initiating change and where the responsibility and power to act lies in the (often) long chain of implementation (Ostrom 1986). In the analysis, it is therefore important to track how the strategic framing is carried out at supra-local levels and how this has been justified and developed through the testing of different scenarios, the setting of targets and the choice of instruments to implement those strategic goals.

The task of interpreting why a particular package of measures works to address a particular societal issue and the process of how this is achieved over a period of time requires an interdisciplinary approach informed by political economy, institutional and policy analysis. The second caveat in policy transference is, therefore, to check the interpretation of the contextual structuring factors, the policy goals and drivers, and the outcomes with local experts. This will help to establish 'context comparability or differences' in approach and implementation consistency between case studies (Stough and Rietveld 2005: 7). The documentary material and the specific examples quoted have been validated against loosely structured policy-maker interviews in the case study cities. The validation of author interpretation has not attempted to be comprehensive, and the reader must note that comparative case study analysis as a methodology is still in its infancy.

7.2 MULTI MODAL PLANNING IN DENMARK

Denmark has a relatively small, highly educated, prosperous population residing in small settlements in a flat, predominantly agricultural country. The strong values placed on education and health and a strong culture of local governance have been central to the implementation of innovative approaches to development and energy efficiency. One example of how this political culture has produced local solutions to local issues follows the decline in the demand for agricultural engineers in the 1980s (Hau 2006: 25). Their skills were reused to kick-start a renewable energy industry, with engineers (re)employed, designing and testing wind turbine components and the developing locally owned wind farms. The localisation of renewable energy was initially kick-started by the national government through income tax allowances for household energy generation. The municipalities have been strong local actors in service delivery in the past, owning municipal energy supply companies, spawning community wind farms and the development of high-efficiency combined heat and power (CHP) networks in the urban areas. Most local public spending is financed by local taxes. Denmark is, now, credited with having five of the world's ten largest central solar-heating plants used for district heating.

National government spend until recently has been characterised by equal rights for all citizens, delivered through the universal welfare system that has virtually eliminated regional imbalances in Denmark (Jørgenson et al. 1997). The 1992 Planning Act delegated much of the responsibility for spatial planning to the then 275 municipalities and 14 county councils. Plans were based on the principle of '*frame-work control*': that local plans must not contradict the planning decisions made at higher levels (Østergård 1994: 8). Central regulations mainly took the form of guiding principles (Tengström 1999: 133), although the national state retained the power to veto the decisions of the municipalities that compromise national interests.

Spatial planning has been innovative in Denmark too. Local government has traditionally had substantial autonomy over development strategies in the local plan, which gives landowners the right to develop in line with the plan. The 1947 'finger-plan' for Copenhagen sought to control urban sprawl through concentrating development along the finger-axes, each served by a railway line, in order to protect the landscape and biodiversity between each finger (see Figure 7.1). The national spatial strategy *Denmark towards the year 2018*, produced in 1992, outlined an equally visionary agenda with six spatial development goals (Østergård 1994: 12):

1   Denmark's cities will be reinforced in Europe
2   The Øresund region will be the leading urban region in the Nordic countries
3   Denmark's cities will be beautiful and clean and will function well
4   Denmark's cities will be efficiently linked to the international transport axes in a environmentally sound manner
5   Denmark's landscapes will be varied and the rural areas will flourish
6   Denmark's coasts and cities will keep their distinctive qualities and will be attractive tourist destinations.

Underpinning this strategic perspective is the conceptual integration of environmental protection and economic growth; that they can reinforce each other. This optimism is supported by extensive data collection and close monitoring of the impact of development on ecosystem management with strong feedback mechanisms into decision making at the municipality level. Cross-sector integration has been a driving force in stabilising global greenhouse gas emissions from the industrial and commercial sectors through capitalising on the development of clean technology industries. Denmark is now seem as a world leader in clean technology innovation, with clusters of research institutions and clean technology companies, many located in Copenhagen, which hosted the UN Climate Change conference in 2009.

The issue of noise pollution has been a sensitive political issue since the 1970s when surveys identified that '*every third dwelling in Denmark is exposed to non-acceptable traffic noise*' levels exceeding 65 dB(A) (Whitelegg 1997: 164). Knowledge of the impacts of development on environmental sustainability strongly influenced the national Transport Action Plan of 1990, which called for action to reduce environmental problems caused by transport. The targets set in 1990 include:

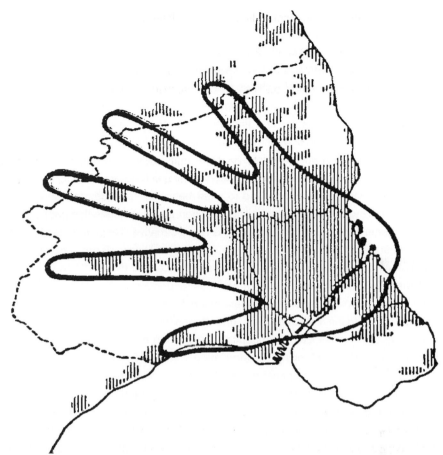

Figure 7.1 Copenhagen Finger Plan of 1947. Source: Knowles (2006) Figure 3, p.418, reproduced with permission

1   Energy consumption and CO_2 emissions should be stabilised by the year
     2005 and reduced by 25 per cent by 2030
2   Emissions of NOx and HC should be reduced by at least 40 per cent by 2000
     and 60 per cent by 2010
3   Emissions of PM_{10} particulates should be halved in urban areas by 2010
4   A reduction in noise levels in dwellings exposed to unacceptable traffic noise
     (>55 dB(A)) so that by 2010 no more than 100,000 dwellings are exposed to
     noise levels of 65 dB(A) (Tengström 1999: 69–70).

The stabilisation of CO_2 emissions has yet to be achieved (Table 1.1). Following the publication of the national transport plan, the central municipalities of Copenhagen and Frederiksberg in the Greater Copenhagen Area (GCA) embarked on a 30 year programme to reduce central and inner area parking by 3 per cent each year (Newman and Kenworthy 2000). Table 7.1 shows that by 2004, Denmark had a lower share of car travel in the modal split for land-based passenger transport than the other case study countries in this chapter and that the share of bus travel was much higher. While capping traffic growth during this period, the central GCA municipalities also upgraded bicycle and pedestrian infrastructure and activities. However, in the early stages of implementing a sustainable national transport system, little support from the national government was provided to steer behaviour towards more sustainable transport choices, partly due to prevailing transport planning norms that public transit was complementary to the car rather than a real alternative (Tengström 1999: 124). Also, in rural areas, the high level of cycling, above the national 18 per cent trip-share, turned attention away from further bus service enhancement (Naess 2006a).

Strategic spatial planning in Denmark has responded positively to evolving EU spatial planning policy, generating substantial debate on the role of Copenhagen in Europe. This led to the realisation that Copenhagen would need to grow and develop to keep pace with other European capitals (Jørgenson et al. 1997; Danish Ministry of Environment 1997). Planning modernisation in the early 1990s relinquished the long-standing paradigm of spatial equality between the municipalities to pave the way for the accelerated growth of Copenhagen. Around a third (1.8 million) of the population of Denmark resides in the GCA, which was governed by 51 municipalities (Naess 2006b) before local government modernisation in 2007. The change in the strategy of equal entitlement for each municipality also included a weakening of the responsibilities of the county councils to set minimum benchmarks for welfare service provision delivered by the municipalities (Jørgenson et al. 1997). Physical planning has historically been characterised by strong service sector integration with the welfare services, with provision initiated by the municipalities in collaboration with key stakeholders.

The 1990s local government modernisation programme also gave more power to the national government to become an active player in the realisation of major projects, with the Ministry of the Environment in 1992 calling for the integration of the Danish transport system with the European TEN, in an environmentally benign way (Tengström 1999). The realisation of the fixed Øresund bridge and tunnel combining rail and road access between the cities of Copenhagen and Malmö in 2000 was the most significant outcome of the modernisation programme, which sought to invest in the integration of the rail and road systems.

This marked a distinct shift in policies from the 1990s, for transport and spatial planning policy, from the conceptual integration of environmental quality and economic values to realignment around economic objectives (Tengström 1999; Tietjen 2007). Local government reform in 2007 streamlined the number of municipalities from 275 down to 98 and created five regional councils to replace the county councils (Tietjen 2007). The new regional councils are directly elected but have no finance-raising powers. The growth-orientated national strategy now calls for the development of the fastest growing urban regions on Zealand and Eastern Jutland (Tietjen 2007). Transport and spatial policies have been actively developed to support these economic objectives through concepts of 'transnationality', linking cities to networks across national borders. Jørgenson et al. (1997: 50) highlight the aspiration of the Ministry of Environment that Copenhagen should become the 'new Europole in Scandinavia [at] the centre of the new Øresund region'. New rail and road links across the Øresund have transformed the industrial decline of Malmö (see Swedish case study later) and bolstered Copenhagen airport as the only large international traffic gateway to the Baltic (Matthiessen 2004: 198). A joint port complex has also been formed between the two cities.

The Øresund region is shown in Figure 7.2 and comprises Sjilland and Bornholm in Denmark and Skåne in south west Sweden located on either side of the Øresund. The Øresund link in 2000 increased the catchment area of Copenhagen airport for international travel and removed the barriers for road and rail access between Stockholm and Copenhagen (Matthiessen 2004: 201). Passenger numbers have increased on the heavy train system by 7 per cent between 2000–2004 mainly due to long distance travel to/from Sweden and Jutland and Funen (Vuk et al. 2007: 15). The continuing status of Copenhagen airport depends, to some extent, on the support of Scandinavian Airlines (SAS), which is owned 50 per cent by three governments (Denmark with 2/7, Norway with 2/7 and Sweden with 3/7) (Matthiessen 2004: 199). The one-hub strategy employed by SAS focuses on Copenhagen despite the lobbying for direct services out of Oslo and Stockholm.

The Øresund link has, therefore, been one of the drivers behind the attraction of international investment and business to the area and the creation of regional partnerships for commercial and social development in the Øresund region (Hull et al. 2009a). These include the Øresund Committee, comprising politicians from both countries (Tietjen 2007), The Øresund bridge has also had a positive influence on cementing the identity of the GCA and in steering investment into public transit. Greater Copenhagen is about 100 km in distance from north to south and about 60 km in the west–east direction (Figure 7.2). The first phase of the GCA new metro system opened in 2002, the second phase in 2003, the third phase in 2007, and €2 billion for the fourth phase was approved by the Danish Parliament in 2007 (Vuk et al. 2007). A new train ring-line has also opened serving areas across the city.

Both population and car use increased in the GCA in the period 2000–2004. Population increased by 1.5 per cent and car passengers by nearly 5 per cent. The latter is mainly attributed to the travel behaviour of residents outside the central municipalities

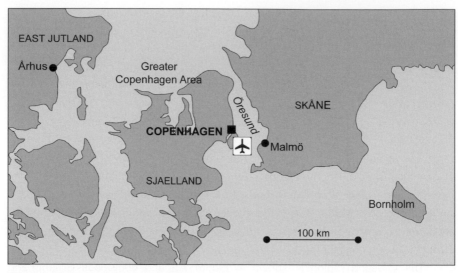

Figure 7.2 Map of the Øresund region

of Copenhagen and Frederiksberg. '*The inner city of Copenhagen still has an unchal-lenged status as the dominant centre of the city-region*' (Naess 2006a: 633). The central municipalities accommodate one third of the residents of the metropolitan area and a much higher proportion of workplaces (Naess 2006a). Comparing the trends in commuting since 1982 using national travel survey data, Nielsen and Hovgesen (2004) found that by 2002 commuting distance around Copenhagen had increased significantly. Within the GCA in 2004, 6.2 million person trips were made on an aver-age workday with approximately 50 per cent made by car and 25 per cent by each of public transit, and walking and cycling (Vuk *et al.* 2007: 7). The drop in bus passenger numbers is quite substantial with more than a 20 per cent reduction across the GCA during 2000–2004 (Vuk *et al.* 2007: 15). Bus services have been reorganised as a con-sequence of the metro, with the introduction of a new service concept of high frequency buses (A-buses) to attract more passengers from cars.

   An explanation for the detrimental changes in the modal split in the GCA can be found from within national transport policy. Vehicle speed limits in 2002 were increased on 50 per cent of the roads from 110 km/h to 130 km/h (Nielsen and Hovgesen 2004: 15). While petrol prices during 2000–2004 reduced, public transit fares '*rose quite dramatically*' (Vuk *et al.* 2007: 14). Denmark has historically had high registration vehicle taxes and VAT of 25 per cent, which combined were intended to discourage car ownership. One of the unintended effects of this policy has been the increased purchase of old energy-inefficient cars, particularly from Germany, which introduced policies in the late 1990s to improve the energy efficiency of their vehicle fleet. EUROSTAT data for 2006 shows Denmark as the least expensive member state in terms of pre-tax prices for cars, with the average price in 2006 being 8.4 per cent below the EU-25 average (European Commission 2007a: 34. The Danish government introduced a vehicle tax policy in 2007 with preferential treatment for environmentally friendly cars, with little positive reported effect so far. Substantial investment has also been committed to providing 20,000 recharge points for a nationwide system of electric cars (Whitelegg (2009).

This case study demonstrates the importance of the national structuring rules to set the agenda for resource minimisation. Up until the 1990s Denmark can be characterised as having a strong governance capacity for resource minimisation. This was built on conceptual integration of economic, social and environmental sustainability principles across public policy sectors and strong structures to support problem solving at the local level. The growing realisation of the potential for Copenhagen to play a leading role in the Baltic region, and globally, led to national policies that promoted economic competitiveness over environmental and social values and established stronger powers for regional and national government agencies. Increasing mobility in the networked functional space of Denmark is now perceived as a key factor to support economic competitiveness and to attract the knowledge industries of the future. While there are clear national rules to capitalise on the existing renewable energy expertise to develop environmentally friendly vehicles of the future, such as intelligent battery systems and plug-in vehicles, the contribution of demand management to achieving a 25 per cent reduction in global greenhouse gas emissions from the transport sector by 2030 is not yet apparent in national government policy. Table 1.1 shows that global greenhouse gas emissions from transport in 2006 are still at the EU-27 average of 1.5 per cent annual growth.

7.3 ENVIRONMENTALLY LED SPATIAL PLANNING IN SWEDEN

Sweden has been described as a centralised democracy until the end of the 1980s when a new approach to the decentralisation of policy implementation to the regional and local government was introduced. A strong central steer is still provided through clear statements of national environmental priorities, environmental quality standards in the environmental code and the enforcement of environmental penalties when environmental legislation is contravened (Seaton and Nadin 2000). This has infiltrated the public sector conscience as a paradigm of ecological sustainable development interpreted as:

1   Protection of the environment – to reduce environmental impact to a level that does not exceed the environment's natural capital to deal with it

2   Sustainable supply – to conserve the long-term productive capacity of for-
       ests, soils and water resources, and to use a higher proportion of renewable
       raw materials
3   *'Efficient resource utilisation – to use energy and other natural resources much
       more efficiently than we do today'* (quoted in Seaton and Nadin 2000: 40).

Despite the success of these policies in halting urban sprawl in the 1990s Naess
(2006b: 244) and Tengström (1999: 120) suggest that Sweden has been slow to
incorporate environmental sustainability into other areas of policy and to address
global warming. This hesitancy, Tengström explains, is accounted for by the national
importance of the car industry and car lobby groups. The new government elected in
1992 with Green party support put more emphasis on responding to global warming
and one of its first tasks was to produce an integrated, comprehensive environmental
code. However, Seaton and Nadin (2000: 37) suggest that the system remains characterised by single sector administration with little horizontal coordination.

Local government has the competency for autonomous action on many aspects of
the Swedish comprehensive welfare system and services to its electorate (Elander *et al.*
2005). This includes a clearly defined policy making role with fiscal and legal powers
to tax private income, own companies, buy and expropriate land from private owners.
These rights are constitutionally established in laws regulating relations with central government and the 9 million citizens. For example, Malmö and Skåne region, discussed
later, receive 100 per cent of the basic income tax, the municipal tax (Malmö) amounts
to 20.84 per cent and the county council tax (Skåne) 10.39 per cent, which produces
a total municipal imposition of 31.23 per cent (City of Malmö 2006: 57). Municipal
taxes in Malmö provide 56 per cent of revenue, government grants 24 per cent and the
remainder comes from operating incomes (City of Malmö 2006: 17). Fund raising and
dispensing powers give Swedish municipalities independence to make infrastructure
decisions they consider right for their area, without having to compete with other authorities for a limited pot of national resources (Hull *et al.* 2009a).

The 280 municipalities have responsibility to plan the use of land and water
within the framework set out in the 1987 Planning and Building Act (currently being
revised). They are required to prepare a general comprehensive plan and more
detailed local plans for areas undergoing change. The local plans are site-specific
design briefs specifying land zoning, the provision of public spaces and parking
areas, as well as construction materials, design and conservation requirements (Hull
et al. 2009). The local plan is legally binding (Elander *et al.* 2005) and, therefore,
development planning is a proactive tool which can be used to negotiate with private owners and developers when buying land for future projects and entering into
contracts for land development. Elander *et al.* note that due to this high level of dis-
cretion and autonomy at the local level in Sweden, there is great variation between

municipalities. This was confirmed by the findings of Reneland (2000) in his 'ped-shed' analysis of the proportion of potential service users living within 400m of specific welfare services in the 45 largest Swedish towns.

Other important actors in spatial planning include the 21 regions, the Ministry of Environment, the National Board of Housing, Building and Planning, the Ministry of Sustainable Development, and the Swedish Environmental Protection Agency. In the last decade, Sweden has been experimenting with different forms of regional government and the spatial scale best able to integrate approaches to secure sustainable economic growth. Stockholm has its own elected regional government and is required to produce a regional plan. There are nine municipality regions testing out a federation approach to regional government, with other regions remaining as national County Administrative Boards. The regional plan produced by the County Boards is advisory only and is focused on economic development and service provision. The Boards normally have a Spatial Planning Unit which provides advice and comments to the municipalities during the drafting of plans (Hull *et al.* 2009).

The framework and structure for local planning is provided in national general policies on natural resources, the environment and biodiversity, which apply across the country, and policies that are spatially specific for particular topics such as infrastructure. The National Resources Act 1987 established an emphasis on ecological sustainability in the use of land and water resources. Preservation of the long-term productive capacity of the ecosystem is one of the five basic values underpinning Swedish environmental policy. The other four are related to people's health, preservation of cultural historical values, securing efficient management of the natural resources and biodiversity. Implementation of this programme in terms of sewerage and waste treatment, recycling, green public purchase, green consumption, green accounts and biodiversity is dependent on local government and citizen action. The Planning and Building Act 1987 promotes decentralisation, resource management and better plan implementation (Elander *et al.* 2005). Since the early 1990s participation and consensus formation has been strengthened in the planning system with a strong and important role for actors from the commercial and industry sectors. In many ways, this may have narrowed the scope of local independence, with local government now working more cooperatively with business interests and national and extra-national actors.

Local government is bound by the application of national environmental regulations, amalgamated in 1999 into a single Environmental Code. On environmental issues there is clear vertical integration with the Swedish Environmental Protection Agency monitoring the implementation of pollution tolerance levels, working closely with the municipalities. Sweden has a system of regional environmental courts that deal with land and water management issues, including compensation (Government Offices of Sweden 2001). The nesting of responsibilities fits within the wider set of environmental objectives (and targets) adopted by the Swedish Parliament in 1999 (Rubin and Nilsson 2003).

The policy steer from national government has broadened out from ecological principles since the mid-1990s to include the conservation of biodiversity and a widening vision of sustainable development, which incorporates the economic and social dimensions (Ministry of Sustainable Development 2006). Specific grants have been made available by the government for local investment programmes that deliver ecologically sustainable development and for the mitigation of climate impacts. A partnership approach between municipalities and local companies has been central to securing these funds. The Ministry of Environment reported to the Swedish Parliament in 2006 that the critical sustainable development challenges of the future were '*building sustainable communities, encouraging good health on equal terms, meeting the demographic challenge and encouraging sustainable growth*' (Elander *et al.* 2005: 290). The report also presented 12 headline indicators to measure sustainable development. A new coalition government was elected in autumn 2006, raising some uncertainty about how these emerging issues would be incorporated into the revised Swedish Planning and Building Act (Elander *et al.* 2005).

The institutional political context of strong local autonomy tempered by 'national supervised control' on environmental issues and sustainable development is monitored by annual national auditing to assess the progress of local efforts to integrate these issues into corporate programmes. Elander *et al.* (2005) report that a single sector perspective is still being taken at the local level to cross-cutting issues and that the treatment of social welfare issues and new emerging environmental issues such as biodiversity is very general. Though they found innovatory approaches, such as green structure plans often integrated into the comprehensive plan, there was little evidence of a '*deeper reflection*[s] *on potential problems or difficulties*' (ibid.: 296).

Sweden is regarded as unique amongst EU member states in having a long history of transport policy making and a nationwide system of regional public transit coordination (Tengström 1999; Hårsman and Olsson 2003). Tengström (1999: 86) notes, however, that this distinction has been built on a cultural discourse that '*automobility*' is a positive outcome allowing more '*freedom of choice of where to live and where to work*'. The 21 Public Transit Authorities (PTAs) decide supply, headway, and fares (Armelius and Hultkrantz 2006: 21). The Deregulation Act 1989 introduced controlled competition, with the PTAs bearing the revenue risk and the private operators the cost risk. Successive phases of deregulation were intended to increase competition (Tengström 1999). Deregulation initially reduced costs through competition and reduced subsidies but price competition has since led to heavy losses.

Tengström (1999) notes a subtle shift of direction at the end of the 1980s, when policies to strengthen the role of public transit were introduced. However, despite the increasing levels of public subsidy, fares have increased since 1989 by an average of 8 per cent (Armelius and Hultkrantz 2006). From the late 1980s onwards specific measures to promote energy efficient vehicles, stimulate car pooling and the development and use of alternative fuels were introduced, including the production and distribution of biogas and incentives to speed up the introduction of motor alcohols based on biomass (Tengström 1999: 126). Several other measures also stem from this period: the levying of a progressive fuel tax; the environmental classification of vehicles and fuels; and the introduction of environmental zones in urban areas. These policies sat within a national transport plan that set out a huge investment programme for road and rail in order to reduce the peripherality of Sweden from the rest of Europe.

By 1998, the principle national policy instrument to steer behaviour towards resource efficiency focused on variable taxes on cars and fuel cost based on the internalisation of externalities. This was seen as a key element in the new strategy to achieve an ecologically sustainable transport system based on the use of IT, the promotion of alternative fuels, and better coordination between transport and urban planning to promote soft modes and public transport (Tengström 1999). In addition, national tax exemptions were introduced for public transport commuter tickets and car-pooling expenditures (Sjöstedt 2005).

The national government has also secured commitments to CO_2 reduction from the car industry for new car models. Every new car has a fuel consumption and CO_2 value (Olsson 2007). Specific progress had been made by 2005 in the purchase of fuel-flexible vehicles, with 10,000 vehicles sold in Sweden in 2005 running on E85 (85 per cent ethanol/15 per cent gasoline) and the number of filling stations selling E85 rising to 320 (European Environment Agency 2007: 20). National taxes are also backing the introduction of renewable fuels and alternative-fuelled cars (Sjöstedt 2005), with the new government in 2006 giving SEK10,000 to those buying a new 'clean' vehicle. This cashback/rebate has lead to dramatic changes in car purchase, with over 17 per cent of new vehicles purchased and registered in Sweden being 'environmental' or 'clean' in 2007 (SMILE 2008a). Malmö, Göteborg and Stockholm jointly run a website promoting clean vehicles and alternative fuels (www.miljofordon.se). Nationally, less attention has been given to the transport efficiency of heavy vehicles (trucks and buses), mainly using diesel fuel, from which CO_2 emissions increased by 26 per cent between 1990–2004 (European Environment Agency 2003, quoted in Olsson 2007: 4). Roughly 60 per cent of goods traffic goes by road in Sweden, much lower than other EU countries (Olsson 2007: 2). Media attention on environmental issues has grown in Sweden since 2006 and, in particular, reporting on climate change. Two approaches are being recommended to abate CO_2 emissions from vehicles. The first is to address fuel efficiency through logistics, load factor and driving habits. The second is to transfer to renewable fuels, and low blend or higher concentrations of biofuel (Olsson 2007: 5).

CITY OF STOCKHOLM ROAD TOLLING

Stockholm is covered by an advisory regional plan that integrates land use and transport matters, agreeing future scenarios based on the consensus reached with its 26 municipalities (Hårsman and Olsson 2003). Road tolling was introduced in Stockholm in August 2007 following a full-scale trial in January 2006 to test public acceptance of the idea. Motorcycles, taxis and clean fuel cars are exempt from charges. The rationale behind the introduction of road tolling was to deal with 'severe congestion' downtown causing environmental deterioration (Armelius and Hultkrantz 2006).

Before the toll, the average traffic speed during the rush hour was 60 per cent below the limit, with buses taking 30 per cent longer to come in from the suburbs compared to off peak. Thirty per cent of downtown commuters came by car. As part of the trial, which was funded by the central government, 197 new buses and 16 new routes were implemented to provide fast peak hour services from the surrounding municipalities to inner Stockholm. The road toll trial was intended to last for 12 months but legal delays meant that the trial lasted only 7 months. A pre-toll poll found 50 per cent were against the toll, with approximately three quarters of car commuters against a permanent toll, while 50 per cent of commuters by public transit were in favour (Armelius and Hultkrantz 2006: 4). Only 30 per cent of those polled realised that public transit would be improved.

Charges are made for passing into and out of the inner city cordon boundary during week days from 06.30–18.30, with increased charges during peak periods. The highest one-way charge is SEK 20 (€2) and the maximum charge incurred by a vehicle in any one day is set at SEK 60 (€6) (Armelius and Hultkrantz 2006: 4). Verification and payment are electronic, and a free-of-charge transponder is mounted on the front window of vehicles. Electronic vehicle identification detectors automatically log number plates crossing the cordon boundary in each direction and car owners are billed at the end of each month (Armelius and Hultkrantz 2006). Late payment penalties range up to SEK 500 (€49) after 4 weeks of non-payment. The charges are collected by the national government with net revenues reinvested locally. There are several exemptions as noted above and the tax is not levied during July or public holidays. The tax payments are deductible from income tax bills for journeys to work of over 5 km, and all congestion charges incurred by businesses are deductible.

Early evaluation of the congestion tax suggests that it has reduced the number of vehicles entering the zone and reduced CO_2 by an estimated 15–20 per cent (Olsson 2007). While the testing of a congestion tax in Stockholm raised the issue of how to respond effectively to public suspicion of both the tax and the invasion of privacy it has shown that taxes on car use in the central area, proportionately related to their CO_2 emissions, are effective in enhancing the energy efficiency of the transport system.

MALMÖ CASE STUDY

Malmö is the third largest city in Sweden, situated in the more densely populated, southern part of the country, surrounded by intensively cultivated agricultural land. As Figure 7.2 shows, the Øresund link in 2000, connecting southern Sweden with mainland Europe moved the hinterland boundary of Malmö to encompass the international airport at Copenhagen (Vuk *et al.* 2007: 201). This new connectivity has provided the opportunity to improve economic growth and recover from the closure of large employers in the docks (Kockums closed in 1986) and car manufacturing (SAAB closed in 1988). Over the last twenty years Malmö has moved from a major industrial centre to a service centre for the Øresund region. The population of Malmö at the end of 2005 was 271,271, an increase of nearly 8,000 since 2001, mainly due to in-migration (City of Malmö 2006: 5). The increase in service jobs has gone mainly to residents in neighbouring municipalities since the skills required are not always possessed by Malmö jobseekers (Lannerheim 2007). Economic and social exclusion is, therefore, experienced by a significant section of the population.

Swedish local government is a significant land owner. By 2000, Malmö City Council owned 13,500 hectares, much of which was bought in the 1960s and more recently with the infilling of the Western dock in 1987 and the purchase of the SAAB site in 1996 (Hull *et al.* 2009a). The municipality also has a stake in several private companies (parking, insurance, housing, arts and leisure) and therefore has significant influence over these companies. It thus has the tools and resources to master plan new developments, such as the regeneration of the 140 hectare Western Harbour district, setting the technical design standards, supervising and monitoring construction contracts.

In line with national government environmental objectives, the *Environmental Programme for the City of Malmö 2003–2008* comprises 58 environmental targets (Rubin and Nilsson 2003). The City has been under pressure from regional level actors to bring newer concerns regarding biodiversity, particulates and noise into local political debates (Elander *et al.* 2005). The Environmental Programme warns that: '*It is important to note that these are actions that really must be implemented rather than being considered as recommendations as in earlier programmes*' (Rubin and Nilsson 2003: 4). The main built environment priorities in the Environmental Programme concern traffic noise and pollution, which over the long term, are expected to increase as a result of the Øresund bridge. The *Traffic Environment Programme for the City of Malmö,* adopted in September 2005, has the goal of taking a '*decisive step in the direction of an environmentally adapted transport system when the City Tunnel finally opens in 2011*' (City of Malmö 2006: 41). One of the principle aims of the Traffic Environment Programme is to make it easy for Malmö residents to leave cars at home, by using the cycleway network and public transit.

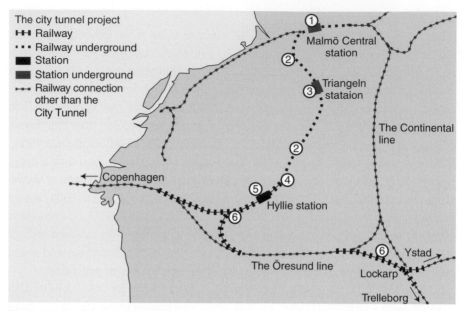

Figure 7.3 The City Tunnel in Malmö. Source: © www.malmotunnel.se, reproduced with permission from Bilfinger Berger Ingenieurbau GmbH

Since 1995, considerable investment has been spent on transport connectivity. First, the Øresund bridge, which opened in 2000, and second, the City Tunnel, due to open in 2011. The City Tunnel began construction in 2004–05 and is managed by the National Rail Administration. The Swedish State Railways, the City of Malmö and Region Skåne are partners to the project. The City Tunnel is linked to a number of strategic station redevelopment projects identified in Figure 7.3 above.

Two departments within the municipality, the Streets and Parks Department responsible for the city's environment and infrastructure, and the Environment Department responsible for implementing national environmental laws, have collaborated to deliver the *Traffic Environment Programme for the City of Malmö 2005–2010*. Funding has come from within the City budget, local companies (Skånemejerier, Sunfleet, E-on), the regional transport authority (Skånetrafiken), national government, and the EU. Table 7.3 shows the range of 'green' transport measures the City has implemented and/or tested between 2004 and 2008. The municipality set several targets in the *Traffic Environment Programme*. These include:

- Implement a sustainable transport system linked to the City Tunnel
- Secure a 10 per cent increase in bus travel by end of 2006 and a 30 per cent increase by end of 2010

- Introduce a new municipal definition of a clean vehicle: to include electric cars, hybrid electric cars, natural gas, biogas, ethanol, diesel and petrol cars (small amounts)
- Secure 100 per cent clean vehicles in the municipal fleet
- Expand the cycle network, improve secure parking facilities and information.

At the start of the implementation of a more 'environmentally adapted transport system', the modal split from a survey of 5,081 residents between the ages of 18 and 75 in 2003 was 50 per cent of trips made by car, 20 per cent by bicycle, 14 per cent by foot, 10 per cent by bus and 3 per cent by rail. The initiatives implemented in Malmö (2004–2008) are discussed below by type of initiative.

Table 7.3 New 'green' transport initiatives implemented in Malmö

Type	Initiative
Improving the quality of bus services	Marketing of new bus route system
	Bus priority measures and other bus improvements
	On street ticket vending machines
	Improved security and safety on buses
	Demand Responsive Transport System
	Integration of cycling with public transport
Improving information about public transport	Improved public transport information
	Linking individual passenger transport information with healthcare appointments
	Provision of real-time passenger information
	Automatic stop calls and information signs in buses
	Mobile internet services in connection to bus information
Mobility management	Managing the mobility needs of SMEs, schools and new movers to Malmö
	Priority at junctions for cyclists
	Eco-driving for municipal employees, hospital employees, and heavy vehicle drivers
	Travel planning and individual travel advice
	Development of car pooling
Clean and energy efficient vehicle fleets	Clean municipal fleet
	Biogas on the net
	Clean heavy vehicles with CO_2 cooler
	Alternative fuel bus fleet
	Extended environmental zone for heavy vehicles and enforcement

Source: Compiled from SMILE (2005: 31–32)

IMPROVING THE QUALITY OF BUS SERVICES

The regional transport agency Skånetrafiken revised the bus route network in 2005 in an attempt to increase patronage and reduce waiting time. The network was simplified from the previous 20 lines with branches to other areas to eight main lines and six supporting lines. During peak periods the bus frequencies on the main lines are every 5–6 minutes. Skånetrafiken undertook proactive marketing of the new routes through press releases and customised bus information to all residents, with the strapline 'Greener, faster and more often' and signs on buses with the headline 'Now it will be harder to miss the bus'. With Skåne region the City has implemented bus priority at traffic signals and improved safety on buses. All of the 185 city buses were equipped with four security cameras in 2007. As this would breach Swedish civil liberty laws, the City had to obtain approval from the national and regional government. A total of 129 real-time information monitors were installed or upgraded at bus stops, shopping centres and other strategic locations during this period, and at the same time all the city buses and some regional buses were equipped with GPS and onboard computers.

IMPROVING INFORMATION ABOUT PUBLIC TRANSPORT

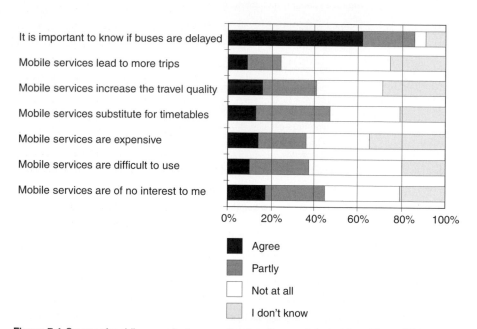

Figure 7.4 Survey of mobile users for journey planning. Source: Adapted from Figure C2.5.4 SMILE (2008b: 12), reproduced with permission

Prior to 2004, the Skånetrafiken website provided real-time information on bus services using web cameras on the street. They have now developed their travel planning tool so that it provides information direct to people's mobiles to give bus passengers more flexibility to plan a linked bus journey or change buses when a service delivery problem arises. The system shows all departures from the location where the traveller connects with their mobile, it provides maps with route information, and enables the purchase of tickets from the mobile. Surveys (Figure 7.4) have shown that around 17 per cent use their mobile for journey planning and that users tend to be young (26 per cent under 18 years; 35 per cent between 18–25 years).

Malmö's bicycle-net travel planner is now integrated with Skånetrafiken's travel planning internet tool, thus connecting the cycle and public transit infrastructure. A tool to calculate the environmental, health and economic costs of each planned trip by different modes is also being developed.

MOBILITY MANAGEMENT

The City Council initiated a comprehensive and more focused campaign on managing mobility from 2005, developing a 'brand' approach. A previous campaign in 2001 for the Western Harbour area did not consider the importance of 'soft' behaviour change instruments. It has two strands: environmentally friendly ways of getting to work and to school; and eco-driving. In the first strand the initial target was managing the mobility needs of SMEs. SMEs have been targeted to promote the use of bicycles by their employees. Employees in 80 SMEs have purchased 173 bikes and early surveys suggested around 60 per cent of bike trips replaced car journeys. This project grew to 91 companies in 2006. More emphasis was then put on travel to school to reduce the percentage of parents driving children to school, which was around 75 per cent in some of the schools targeted. This project has reduced driving by around 10 per cent. At the same time new movers to Malmö were also targeted. By 2008, 20–30 per cent of new movers replying to surveys said that they now drove their car less in Malmö compared with their previous residence.

Part of the brand has been to market Malmö as a 'cycling city'. In 2003, 20 per cent of all trips were by bike, 90 per cent of residents owned a bicycle and the city had 390 km of cycle lanes. The aim of the 1996 City Bicycle Programme was to extend the cycle lanes so that they integrate more effectively with public transit and to improve facilities for cyclists. During 2007–2008, they piloted a bicycle radar system at 20 busy (high safety-risk) intersections. The bicycle radar detects a cyclist approaching and changes traffic lights to give priority to the cyclist during off-peak hours of the day. Another initiative is to provide better signage and maps along bicycle routes, and providing air pumps and other services. Cycling was heavily promoted by the City Council in a series of campaigns in 2007 and 2008, using cyclists wearing sandwich boards with slogans, street signs and adverts. A follow up survey found that 143 people were 'affected' or 'affected quite a lot' by the campaigns, equivalent to 8 per cent of respondents.

The City of Malmö offered newcomers to the city, who were motorists, the option of using a bike or travelling on public transit for free for one month. Only 1 per cent of those contacted by telephone took up the offer and 40 per cent of those who regularly used other transport options during this month continued with these options after the demonstration period. A similar trial that targeted employees in SMEs was more successful, with 228 employees taking up the offer. Twenty per cent of the 133 trialists who replied to a survey 6 months after the trial said that they now used public transit daily (SMILE 2008e).

The City of Malmö has trained nearly all their own employees and 16 heavy vehicle drivers in a private company in fuel-efficient driving skills and habits. Fuel savings after two months of the training are typically within the range of 10–15 per cent. Seven car sharing (car pools) sites have been established by the City and Sunfleet, a subsidiary of Hertz and Volvo. The 20 vehicles in use in 2008 included biofuel/flexifuel cars (Toyota Aygo), electric hybrids and gas-hybrid cars. A telematic device is installed in every vehicle enabling wireless link between cars, mobile phones and the Sunfleet data base. Booking is through the internet and the cars are unlocked using a mobile phone. Based on the assumption that the car pool members had been car users before the scheme was introduced, it is estimated that the replacement journeys using Sunfleet cars would have reduced CO_2 pollution by 42 per cent, NOx by 60 per cent and PM_{10} by 12.5 per cent (SMILE 2008c: 29). While only 10 per cent of the 223 individual and company members completed all questionnaire surveys including a travel diary, these respondents doubled the distances travelled by car at the expense of public transit travel after joining the car club.

Clean vehicles

The average fuel consumption of new cars in Sweden was well above the EU average in the 1990s and several initiatives have been taken by the national government to reverse this trend. Beginning in 2005, the City of Malmö initiated a demonstration programme of 'clean' vehicles, supported through demand management and marketing campaigns to change people's perceptions about clean vehicles. This involved the purchase of 250 clean vehicles for the municipal fleet by 2008, all of which displayed information about the fuel used. This increased clean vehicles as a percentage of the municipal fleet from 24 per cent in 1999 to 33 per cent in 2004 and to nearly 70 per cent at the end of 2008. During the same period, Skånemejerier (milk-product company) introduced 10 new heavy vehicles, which run on a 50–50 mixture of natural gas and biogas, into its fleet. When planned in 2004 this was an innovative approach in Sweden but is now fairly commonplace for large road freight haulage firms.

Malmö has been proactive in using local opportunities to reduce the consumption of petroleum and diesel as a transport fuel since the 1980s. Since 1988 all the city buses in Malmö have run on natural gas, which is 90 per cent methane, supplied through the natural gas grid between Göteborg and Malmö. More recently the Malmö municipality, Skånetrafiken and the sewerage company have developed biogas using waste from the food industry, from slaughterhouses and manure. The gas produced is 60 per cent methane and has to be cleaned to remove the CO_2, water and sulphur. By 2008, 90 per cent of the filling stations in Malmö supplied natural gas and there were four filling stations supplying methane. The extension of the environmental zone in Malmö and the new regulation that only allows access for heavy duty vehicles above 3.5 tonnes using biofuel was the impetus Skånemejerier needed to start greening its vehicle fleet. To further encourage the ownership and use of alternative-fuelled cars, parking charges have been reduced in public car parking spaces. The first hour of parking is free for these vehicles provided the vehicle is not more than 3 years old. Officers had hoped to get local political approval for entirely free parking for clean vehicles, but politicians changed their minds after the national government decided to give a cash bonus to purchasers of clean vehicles.

The investment in the bus service and active travel modes in Malmö are designed to complement the improvements to the Skåne rail system in an integrated public transport system. The City intends to connect car sharing to public transit and to provide rented bicycles at all the main rail stations.

Figure 7.5 shows significant increases in bus usage in Malmö since 2002, which demonstrates that the measures in Malmö to market public transit to residents through information campaigns and travel planning measures in combination make a difference. The national legal and fiscal context is also important in respect of travel options since these increases in bus usage mirror those in other Swedish cities. There is currently no political support for the use of separate bus lanes or for cyclist priority on key commuter routes in the peak hours in Malmö. In 2007, interest in cycling has risen in Sweden in many locations but there is yet no evidence of this in Malmö. Surveys show that compared with five years ago the 3,000 respondents are travelling a little less by car, using buses more but cycling less.

In conclusion, this has been a very detailed study of Sweden and Malmö, which has demonstrated conceptual integration between environmental issues and urban design of neighbourhoods. There are sufficient resources and responsibilities for local government to make a difference, supported by regional structures for problem solving. There are also clear national rules that prioritise environmental sustainability and resource minimisation. There are suggestions in this case study, however, that local level enthusiasm' to improve the quality of urban environments is being held back by the reticence of politicians to disturb car commuters. The congestion charging pilot was initiated by the national government in Stockholm and two low energy initiatives in Malmö were reduced

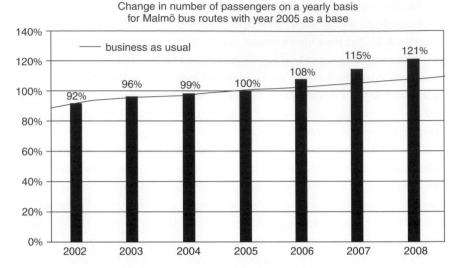

Change in number of passengers on a yearly basis
for Malmö bus routes with year 2005 as a base

Figure 7.5 Trends in bus passengers in Malmö 2002–2008. Source: Figure C1.3.1 SMILE
(2008b: 7), reproduced with permission from Trafikutvecklare Skånetrafiken

by local politicians. The civil engineering profession in Sweden has particular authority,
witnessed by the Skåne region's perception of transport infrastructure (road and rail) as
the solution to the peripherality of the region in relation to European markets. There is
also a hint of an inward-looking preoccupation on behalf of local government, embarking
on collaboration with private sector actors and the empowerment of citizens.

7.4 INTEGRATED CITY-REGION PLANNING IN THE NETHERLANDS

The Dutch system of spatial planning has been held up as an exemplar of good practice, with a longstanding capacity to integrate land use and infrastructure development
(Selman 1996; Salet 2003; De Boer 2007; Healey 2007). A number of factors have
been noted that contribute to this perception. First, the government structure is highly
regulated with central government holding the executive power on environmental
policy, transport policy and spatial policy (Seaton and Nadin 2000; De Boer 2007).
For example, tough targets were set by central government in the early 1990s for
reductions to pollution and resource usage, using integrated life-cycle management
techniques (Selman 1996: 25). Second, a conceptually strong vision of spatial planning with '*innovative*' steering concepts and techniques has been used to classify
locations based on their accessibility (Geurs and van Wee 2006). This has '*reformed*

transportation planning' according to De Boer (2007: 397). Third, there is strong local autonomy through the preparation of the land use plan (*bestemmingsplan*), which is legally binding. A fine balance between central steering through legal requirements, national planning documents and finance for infrastructure and local policy making based on perceived local needs has therefore been achieved. This is currently set to change in the new Planning Bill, with central government keen to reduce what are perceived as delaying tactics by local government over the implementation of major infrastructure projects (Needham 2005).

The regulation of spatial development in the Netherlands has evolved through several phases of national policy. Schwanen *et al.* (2004) identify three distinct changes in policy up to 2004:

1   *Concentrated decentralisation* in the 1970s and 1980s, which sought to elimi-nate urban sprawl by channelling new urban growth into designated overspill or growth centres outside these areas. This approach drew on the experience of new town development in the UK (Priemus 2007b).

2   *Compact urban growth* from the 1980s attempted to address inner city decline through policies to upgrade the housing stock and protect local retail facilities (Healey 2007). As part of this approach, new housing growth was guided first towards urban brownfield sites and then greenfield extensions of the urban area (the VINEX locations selected by the Netherlands government). This sequential approach to retail and residential location has overall proved successful (Geurs and van Wee 2006). However, most of the new housing growth locations were developed outside of urban areas with a dominant mix of single-family owner occupied houses and few urban amenities (Priemus 2007a). Schwanen *et al.* (2004) also note that the focus solely on housing and retail gave little thought to the renewal of employment in urban areas. As a result '*the majority of jobs in many cities can now be found in new employ-ment concentrations outside the old original city centres*' (ibid.: 582).

3   *ABC firm location policy* came to the fore in the 1990s, following criticisms of the VINEX approach, underpinned by an understanding that different types of eco-nomic activity have specific accessibility demands. This policy sought to control mobility by matching the mobility profiles of different activities to the accessibility of different locations. Commercial development was classified according to whether car access was an essential requirement for employees and clients. Development not directly dependent on car access was encouraged to locate at either the cen-trally located 'A' locations well connected to public transport or the 'B' locations at development nodes reasonably accessible by public transit and by car. Only those activities that have a high spatial reach and low intensity of use by members of the public should locate at 'C' locations which have good motorway access.

Rigid implementation of the ABC policy has been difficult to achieve. Companies have been able to locate at 'C' locations and to secure parking facilities for employees even where public transit is well provided (Martens and van Griethuysen 1999; Snellen *et al.* 2002; Schwanen *et al.* 2004; Straatemeier 2006; Banister and Hickman 2007). These deviations can be accounted for by:

a   Local political concern to attract new employment
b   Insufficient number of 'A' locations reserved for people-intensive uses such as offices
c   Difficulty in predicting the scale of employment growth in the office sector, which as a result of a) and b) has led to either office development in 'C' locations or development sites recategorised as 'B' types to maximise the opportunities this classification gives for mobility choice
d   Insufficient attention paid to regional accessibility needs and the competition between cities for employment growth
e   Fragmentation of political jurisdictions covering the wider metropolitan area.

4   *Development-oriented strategy* since 2004 which breaks away from the 'compact city' policy to embrace the development initiatives of private investors and public–private partnerships around key nodes in the transportation network (Priemus 2007b). This marks a distinct fourth phase in spatial planning in moving away from the single urban integrated framework for development led by public sector land purchases to a public–private partnership to open up 'rural' development opportunities once protected. Part of the rationale is to overcome inter-municipal conflict through giving more authority and a stronger mediating role to the regional (provincial) level.

The Dutch rules for spatial planning reflect a general situation of substantial autonomy for municipalities up until the new millennium, although these began to unravel from the late 1990s when the powers of national infrastructure agencies increased (Healey 2007). Local government authority stems from preparation of the only spatial plan that is legally binding (*bestemmingsplan*), a public monopoly in acquiring land for development and the granting of permits for building in conformity with the plan (Needham 2005). The municipal development plans (the indicative plan or *structuurvisies*) and the implementation plan (*bestemmingsplan*) are approved by the Province to ensure that they conform to EU Directives and national legislation. Dutch municipalities and provinces, however, have few tax raising powers.

Transport policy is contained in the National Mobility Plan, which is prepared by both the Minister of Transport, Water Management and Public Works and the Minister of Housing, Physical Planning and Environment. This sends a strong signal concerning the interrelationship between transportation and spatial planning policies. The focus of national transport policy has oscillated between supply side and demand restraint measures since the 1960s. Struiksma *et al.* (2008) discern four clear phases:

1   *Planning and construction of road infrastructure* from 1960s–1980s. During this phase new roads were developed to accommodate the demand for mobility from cars and freight. The singular focus on new road infrastructure was questioned in the 1980s with the growth in traffic congestion. Other concerns emerging at this time were the growth of car use for leisure, the increase in traffic accidents, the reduction in air quality and long-term dependence on imported oil. A more balanced policy approach emerged comprising infrastructure improvements, and the use of economic policy instruments and congestion as a way of regulating traffic (Tengström 1999: 8).

2   *Accessibility and the environment* in the late 1980s until 2001. This phase demonstrated a growing commitment to reduce the need for car use through significant investment in public transit infrastructure and measures to restrain car use. Central government funding for transport during this phase could be spent by local government exclusively on public transit (Veeneman *et al.* 2007). The 1990 national transport plan echoed the spatial planning focus on the compact city and location planning at the time (Tengström 1999: 124). As a result of this policy integration a more comprehensive approach to transport planning emerged with a raft of policies, which included taxes on the use of cars rather than ownership, and measures to influence the technical standards for cars and a focus on travel behaviour (Tengström 1999). Tengström refers to the intensity of debates at this time on how to respond to climate change in a densely urbanised country of over 16 million people where much of the land is below sea level, while preserving the quality of life and accessibility.

3   *Network management* policies came to the foreground in national government policy from 2001 to 2006. It was influenced by the network city ideas voiced in EU transport policy and the integration of member states through the TENs railway network of high speed rail lines (Tengström 1999). This phase catered for the demand for mobility once again through road improvements, more efficient use of existing infrastructure, and with substantial funding for the expansion of the *Mainpoorts* of Rotterdam and Amsterdam Schiphol as the key ports in the national network (Priemus 2007b).

4   *Infrastructure as a necessary condition of economic development* from 2006 onwards. The more recent focus is reducing congestion through enlarging road capacity to enhance reliability and reduce travelling time. Road congestion is reported to have increased five-fold between 1985 and 2000. The main solution in the latest Mobility Plan is a 20 per cent extension of the highway network by 2020 (Struiksma *et al.* 2008: 3).

The Ministers of Transport and Environment determine the final route and design of infrastructure projects and this is legally binding on all levels of government with respect to land use. Until recently, national and provincial projects have been dependent on municipality cooperation for their implementation through the building and environmental permit processes, often requiring alterations to the legally binding local land use plans first (Struiksma *et al*. 2008). Proposals for new road infrastructure tend to meet with huge local public resistance delaying any hope of implementation (Needham 2005). Despite the existence of '*powerful*' national legal and financial steering tools (Struiksma *et al*. 2008) infrastructure projects take on average nine years from approval to final completion, not including those that stagnate in the bureaucracy. Prior to 2008 anyone could make an objection or an appeal against municipality decisions, which gave innumerable possibilities for the local level to delay national government policies they did not like (Needham 2005).

The planned expansion of road infrastructure, the need for collaboration at the city-region level, and the stagnation in the highly controlled Dutch housing market provide the institutional context for shifting the strategic overview of infrastructure investment to the Provinces in the 2008 Planning Act with some loss of autonomy at the municipality level. The new Act aims to speed up the process of plan-making through (Needham 2005):

- Introduction of powers for national and provincial government to make legally binding land use plans and to grant building permits for the locations covered by these plans
- Introduction of national and provincial guidance to municipalities for plan making and powers to comment on draft plans
- Land use plans to have a limited life of 10 years before revision and further approval
- Infrastructure projects to be allowed as major deviations from the *bestemmingsplan*
- Appeal against planning decisions to be limited to those with a legally protected interest in the outcome (e.g. property owners).

The significance of these potentially radical changes in the Dutch planning system will become apparent when defined in the detail of planning decrees. Irrespective of what these may contain, the broad details of the Planning Act represent a strong drawing in of powers back to national government, or centralisation, with specific new legal powers delegated to the 12 Provinces. These are additional to the disbursement of central government funds to Provinces, which have encouraged a more development-oriented role, and powers to regulate regional public transit following privatisation in 2001 (Needham 2005; Veeneman *et al*. 2007).

Public transport has essentially been a 'public monopoly' in the Netherlands, with virtually all operators owned by the municipalities or central government until the introduction of competitive tendering in 2001, when the national bus company was sold to Arriva, Veolia and Connexxion (Veeneman *et al.* 2007). Competitive tendering has been introduced gradually to allow a learning process for the operators and the passenger transport authorities (PTAs) established to plan public transport and to award tenders for periods '*up to 8 years in the bus sector and 15 years in the railway sector*' (Veeneman *et al.* 2007: 1). The 12 Provinces and seven urban area governments established as PTAs were given powers to decide on their own fares and to stimulate innovation in service delivery (Cheung 2007; Veeneman *et al.* 2007).

The graduated approach to the introduction of competitive tendering has allowed different tendering approaches towards incentives and control to emerge (Veeneman *et al.* 2007). Veeneman *et al.* note three positive outcomes: 1) that service levels are much more clearly specified than before, with contracts won on the basis of patronage and frequency levels as well as on the basis of price; 2) that the regional transport authorities have monitored services diligently providing evidence to secure fines against operators; and 3) for those services tendered out the improvement in quality perception has increased by 5 per cent for earlier contracts and by 8 per cent for the later contracts by 2006. De Boer (2007: 3) notes that unless tenders were specific on requirements such as wheel chair accessibility, operators based their cost calculations '*on the cheapest and worst possible vehicles*'. The obligation to tender services competitively did not apply to the national railway network or the major urban areas of Amsterdam, Rotterdam, The Hague, and Utrecht.

The Netherlands has had an integrated ticketing system since 1980, when the strip ticket and the season ticket replaced the differentiated local system of fares and tickets. These can be used anywhere in the country on bus, tram and metro and some railway lines around the larger cities (Cheung *et al.* 2007). A public transport electronic smartcard (*OV-chipkaart*) was introduced at the end of 2005 in the Rotterdam region and then on the Amsterdam metro and several lines of the National Rail network. This has taken seven years of planning by all the major public transport operators and has been introduced on a commercial basis to be gradually installed on the buses and trams in the main Dutch cities and the regional and rural routes, as well as in all Netherlands railway stations by 2009 (Cheung *et al.* 2007).

The main advantages are two-fold: first to increase public transport usage by '*providing seamless travel and one-step shopping*' (Cheung *et al.* 2007: 1); and second to provide detailed information on ridership at route level to refine the fare structure which the stripticket was unable to provide. The smartcard serves as an electronic purse, requiring the rider to touch the card reader on entry and exit from each station for the fare to be deducted. Loading is possible at special ticket vending and auto-loading facilities with agreement reached with the banking sector. It is intended to extend the technology to pay for other transport services, such as car and bicycle hire, and car parking. This will overcome some of the criticisms of the focus on prestige high-speed rail projects in the Netherlands and the lack of attention and statistics on the entry and exit modes at train stations (Rietveld 2000).

Table 1.1 shows global greenhouse gas emissions from transport increasing at an annual rate of over 2 per cent; a 37 per cent increase between 1990 and 2006. The national government first set a target of 20 per cent reduction in all sectors by 2020, doubling the target to 40 per cent in 2008/09. The growing emissions from the transport sector have been a source of embarrassment for the environmental credentials of the Netherlands government. Since the late 1990s there have been policies to tax the use of motorised vehicles via road user charging. A proposal in 2002 was dropped, however, to re-emerge in legislation that was passed in 2009. KLM, the national airline, has also introduced measures to offset 10 per cent of its CO_2 emissions through a tax on passengers. The national government is funding 25 energy efficient projects as part of its Innovation Action Agenda. These are intended to be iconic, innovatory projects to serve as exemplars and include the deployment of electric cars fuelled from wind energy, the design for a climate neutral and climate-proof floating city in Almere and climate-neutral initiatives in Rotterdam (Haccoû 2009). Central to this innovation strategy is the vision to have by:

•   2014: 1,000 CO_2 neutral streets
•   2019: all new houses are CO_2 neutral
•   2024: first floating city
•   2029: all roofs are green roofs.

AMSTERDAM EXAMPLE

Amsterdam brands itself as the 'network city', a metropolis with an international focus. It forms the northernmost cornerstone of the Randstad Holland, with Rotterdam and The Hague providing the other two cornerstones (see Figure 7.6). The environmental protection of this green heart has been a leading concept in Dutch spatial planning for over fifty years. Careful planning of resource use has had a lasting legacy with public transport dominating the movement between these cities, with car and bicycle modes dominant for journeys within these settlements, and the car dominant for all other long distance journeys (Bertolini and le Clerq 2003; Geurs and van Wee 2006).

Amsterdam is presented as an exemplar of the integrated and comprehensive approach by many European planners. From the City's own account this seems to have been the case following on from the single sector approach that prevailed in the 1960s and 1970s (Jolles et al. 2003). The continuing search for housing development sites to satisfy housing need first within the city and then outwith in ancillary growth cores, which were later incorporated within the boundary of the city, has dominated political priorities. These annexations ensured that the City held onto the population and tax base (Faludi and Van der Valk 1995). In this way, Amsterdam's concentric layout of canals was extended by '*rhizome-like lobes of ancillary development cores and wedge-shaped fingers*' of open space until the end of the 1960s (Jolles *et al.* 2003: 7). Negotiations with neighbouring municipalities on housing land were later abandoned in the 1970s, when the national government designated 15 new growth centres in a policy of concentrated deconcentration. As a result of this policy, Amsterdam lost young and middle-class households and jobs to the growth centres (Salet 2003). The 1985 structure plan responded with a more integrated spatial approach to planning with a focus on compact development within the city with high densities and mixed-use developments. Salet (2003: 180) comments that '*this policy was designed to stop the forces of the City from draining away by encouraging them to remain within the metropolitan district*'.

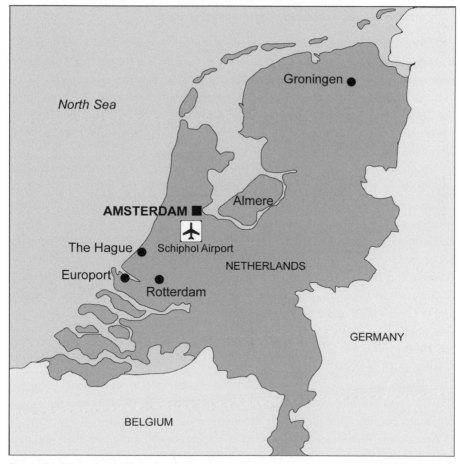

Figure 7.6 Amsterdam in the national context

The City planners have had to respond to many unanticipated opportunities over the last hundred years and revise their policies accordingly:

*   The nineteenth century construction of the Central Station on a group of artificial islands
*   Relocation of dock and service facilities on the IJ from east of the city to the west, freeing space for new housing and creative industries
*   The growth of the rapidly expanding Schiphol airport to the south west, whose environmental contour was found to contravene the Noise Abatement Act 1979 noise limits for residential areas (Whitelegg 1997: 168). This prevented planned housing sites on the western side of Amsterdam from being used and highlighted the need for better public transit links to the airport
*   The development of the headquarters of the ABN-AMRO Bank close to the Zuid/WTC station has speeded up the development of the Zuidas (South Axis) and the dispersal of employment across the region.

The City has been like an accordion expanding out in search of more space for housing to relieve the 'tight' housing market in the city. Each breath out has incorporated valuable landscape resources for city dwellers such as urban parks. Some of these incursions have been repelled by neighbouring municipalities. These activities have been punctuated by sharp breaths inwards when the focus has been on the regeneration of existing residential areas through improvements to the housing fabric, the public realm and accessibility within the city.

Amsterdam scores highly in surveys for having the most attractive residential environments in the Netherlands (Romein and Trip 2008). The historic inner city of canals and bridges is a small-scale human landscape with high densities of cultural heritage and amenities, with strong competition for space from the leisure, tourist and economic clusters (Bertolini and Salet 2003). However, the City Council is criticised for creating a '*congested monofunctional tourism area*' in the historic core (Romein and Trip 2008: 11) and monofunctional areas of subsidised social housing (Jolles *et al.* 2003). Eighty per cent of housing in Amsterdam is subsidised (Bertolini and le Clerq 2003) and the City now acknowledges that the lack of affordable private housing accounted for the loss of higher income households from the city in the 1960s and is still holding back economic growth of the city (Jolles *et al.* 2003; Romein and Trip 2008).

Integrated planning has stabilised the modal split in the Randstad region (Bertolini and le Clerq 2003). The combination of density, diversity and the supply of good public transport has clearly reduced car use in the residential environments of Amsterdam, Rotterdam and The Hague compared with more suburban and rural settings in the Randstad (Dieleman *et al.* 2002: 524). The population of Amsterdam grew to 676,000 in 1984 and reached 735,000 in 2002 (Jolles *et al.* 2003: 71). In the context of population and employment growth, public transport and cycling have held onto a significant share and are growing in Amsterdam. The modal split in Amsterdam, in 1997, was 35 per cent cycling, 25 per cent public transport and 40 per cent car. Bertolini and le Clerq (2003) note that the growth rate of car trips has been lower than the growth in population and jobs but that the average distances travelled by car are increasing and the car is now the dominant mode in post-war Amsterdam.

Within its administrative area, the ABC policy of allocating development to locations based on accessibility needs and location characteristics has worked. This has helped to accentuate the different characteristics of nodes in the transport network and led to a hierarchy of stations on the metro network (Jolles et al. 2003). Several institutional and policy factors have worked positively to bring this about. First, the City has been a significant land owner and from the late nineteenth century the City has only released land in leasehold to 'trusty investors and developers' (Jolles et al. 2003: 40). Second, the city has gained new responsibilities for regional coordination devolved from the provincial government. There has been an absence of metropolitan government in the Amsterdam region, despite attempts by the City of Amsterdam to negotiate a sub-provincial coalition with neighbouring municipalities (Jolles et al. 2003). In 1990 the Province agreed to allow the City to perform the physical and spatial planning provincial tasks under the Province's supervision and monitoring through a joint Planning Committee (Jolles et al. 2003: 13). This led to some devolution from the City during the 1990s downwards to the 18 Boroughs (16 with their own administrations, the City Centre and Westpoort). A large number of tasks have been devolved including the drafting of zoning plans (Jolles et al. 2003: 166).

The third contributing factor has been continuity in land use policy despite a meandering spatial gaze. Specifically, this has included the office location policy linked to public transit nodes (ABC policy); the regulation of car use and the accessibility of locations through parking restrictions; and the expansion of the dedicated cycle infrastructure. Parking policy since the 1960s has attempted to 'maintain the character and aesthetic quality of the city centre' (Jolles et al. 2003: 112). Towards the end of the century it was thought that higher parking fees and the introduction of resident parking permits could selectively reduce 'the out-of-control volume of motorized road traffic' (Jolles et al. 2003: 127). Residents and companies apply for a parking permit which is only valid in their area.

The City planners found in the late 1960s that cycling trips were reducing. The City responded in 1968 with a memorandum calling for dedicated routes for cyclists, segregated from motorised traffic, wherever possible. In the memorandum, the Chief Executive is quoted as saying that: 'the interaction between people and the city must form a constant consideration in all our measures' (Jolles et al. 2003: quoted on 116). 'A finely meshed network of safe routes was required for pedestrians along which there would be less nuisance from *motorised traffic. Such routes should, wherever possible, be set out through quieter areas, should include the main attractions, and should serve the residential and university districts* (Jolles *et al.* 2003: 114).

In the late 1960s, as well, the issue of accessibility was uppermost in planners' minds as the Metro Plan was presented to City leaders in 1968. Substantial investment has been directed to public transit since then, for example the new Ring line and the connection between Schiphol airport and the city centre. The City has been allowed to postpone the introduction of competitive tendering until 2012 as far as the concessions currently held by the municipal company GVB are concerned (Veeneman *et al.* 2007). Public transport is the fastest growing mode in Amsterdam, helped by substantial investment in infrastructure and, since 2000, a policy of mixed use to create attractive and better quality neighbourhood environments (Louw and de Vries 2002). The electronic smartcard was introduced on the metro system in 2006 (Cheung *et al.* 2007).

The 2003 outline Structure Plan is entitled 'Opting for Urbanity'. The new approach is explained by planners in the following way:

> The choice fell on urbanity because urbanity is an extraordinary important anchor for market-oriented urban planning. In economic terms, opting for urbanity means that the focus is on differentiation in environments and the mixing of functions. After all, in order to gain a competitive advantage, the 'new economy' business activities sought after by Amsterdam's mandarins are dependent on constant innovation and synergy. Finely intermeshed systems in a compact setting with a high interaction density (exchange of knowledge and information) are important for the new economy. [...] This is also relevant for the 'incubator' function for the new economy [...] Opting for urbanity also means − in socio-cultural terms − opting for finely intermeshed systems in a compact setting with a high density of social interaction (integration, tolerance, social dynamic).
>
> (Jolles *et al.* 2003: 193−194)

It is with this backdrop of political support for enhancing the quality of life in the city that the 2007−2010 Economic Programme pays more attention to the regional and international scale of development and quality of life amenities such as the creative arts, culture, tourism, leisure, sports, education and hotel accommodation (Romein and Trip 2008). Large-scale cultural venues are now part of all area redevelopment programmes in order to distribute tourists around the city. Examples are the Music Building in the eastern docklands and the recently constructed Film Museum on the northern bank of the river IJ.

The urban region of Amsterdam is evolving into a 'network city' with a much greater spatial spread and influence across Europe (Salet 2003). In this sense, the city is looking outwards once again. Bertolini and Salet (2003: 132) question '*how its scattered areas of urbanity can remain connected within the networks of urban interaction, the focus of which is partly outside the traditional municipal boundaries. This gives rise to a new situation, where Amsterdam will have to exchange its traditional "inside-out" policy (planning its expansion) for an "outside-in" approach, where the focus shifts to positioning itself in the networks of multiple centres in a broader spatial field.*'

The pressures are for Amsterdam to function at an increasing scale of operation outside its jurisdiction, and to address the growing mobility and road congestion in the region. '*Market processes* [have] *generat*[ed] *a ring of subcentres on the peripheral transport ring*' (Healey 2007: 48) within the city limits, while other transport nodes such as Schiphol airport have developed outside the city territory. '*New spatial concepts* [have] *emerg*[ed] *based on transport axes*' (Healey 2007: 66) and nodes. Zuidas is one of the new nodes or junctions in the south of Amsterdam, a location for international business and driven by the Dutch commercial company ABN AMRO. Involvement in this public–private partnership has been a challenge for the public sector (Priemus 2007b). Around 10,000 homes will be provided on the 300 hectare site to help solve the housing shortage with infrastructure, such as high speed train links to Schiphol and the international rail network, in the underground dock zone (Projectbureau Zuidas, no date: 7).

Accessibility by public transit is being developed at two levels in the Amsterdam city-region. At the regional level public transit connections are being developed using high-speed rail networks between the complementary multiple urban centres in the metropolitan region and to other European cities. This builds on the local neighbourhood scale, accessibility that has been achieved through the densification and the diversification of land use. Bertolini and le Clerq (2003) identify two policy challenges for the city. First, to develop the critical mass of destinations or '*spatial opportunities*' (e.g. workplaces and facilities) within short distances to maintain the high levels of cycling and walking in the city. Second, to significantly increase the share of public transit for the longer inter-regional trips through applying demand restraint measures to car use such as road pricing, which currently has little political support (Bertolini and le Clerq 2003: 585, 588).

Local air pollution ($PM_{10}/2.5$, NOx, CO_2) from the 5,000 freight lorries operating in Amsterdam has been reduced since 2007 with the introduction of cargo trams operating from a freight distribution centre, adjacent to the Zuid station. Initially, City Cargo Amsterdam introduced two cargo trams delivering from the distribution centre to an inner city hub from where electric trucks deliver to the final destination. The aim is to expand the operation to a fleet of 52 cargo trams distributing from four peripheral 'cross docks' to 15 inner-city hubs by 2012 (ELTIS 2007).

This case study of the Netherlands has demonstrated longevity in integrated infrastructure and land use planning. There have been shifts in national priorities based on perceptions of how best to secure locations for housing growth and to enhance competitiveness. Throughout there has been a strong steer through the dispensation of national financial resources and spatial planning documents, which have served to coordinate the actions of lower tier governments. The power of the municipalities, particularly the cities, to coordinate the public sector at the local level is a feature of the Amsterdam case study and the faltering steps to relinquish some of this autonomy to the private sector. The City of Amsterdam has certainly shown a problem solving and adaptive capacity in the face of globalisation pressures, renewing the spatial strategy to integrate with wider city-region developments. In terms of the cultural acceptance of demand restraint measures, the high national trip-share of cycling at around 30 per cent of all journeys and the highway laws protecting cyclists are relevant to the urban design achievements in Amsterdam. Recent legislation on road user charging and the strengthening role of the provincial tier of government for infrastructure decisions suggests an acceptance of the need for national government action on minimising transport global greenhouse gas emissions and integrated city-region government.

7.5 LEGISLATING FOR QUALITY OF LIFE IN GERMANY

Germany has a reputation for striving to innovate and implement cutting edge environmental technology. There is a perception amongst German environmental managers that they are ahead of other European cities (Löffler 2005). On the one hand, this is driven by high expectations from customers that products they purchase are environmentally friendly (Löffler 2005). On the other hand, the Federal (national) Government has provided a strong steer in the protection of species, in the reduction of energy consumption and CO_2 emissions. Environmental management is narrowly regulated by federal and regional legislation. While German states are constituents of the Federal Republic, there is considerable state autonomy to initiate action as well as to exercise a strong regulatory function at the municipal level (Löffler 2005; Salet and Thornley 2007). This formal hierarchical approach to environmental protection has been criticised as very technocratic (Freund 2003) and strongly legalistic (Fürst and Rudolph 2003) leaving little room for the development of the bottom-up consensus approach.

Germany has a population of over 82 million and is constituted as a federal republic with three tiers of government: Federal (Bund), regional (Länder) and local government. Traditionally, the regions have had a strong role in regional economic planning with land use planning decentralised to local government (Fürst and Rudolph 2003). Local government has constitutional rights of local self-administration within the limits set by law, which includes land use planning (Freund 2003). Local self-determination is bolstered by the right to raise local business taxes, as well as receiving a share of general wage and incomes taxes imposed by central government. This leads to competition between municipalities for enterprises and high income population (Freund 2003: 136). Additional funds in the form of block grants are received from the Bund and Länder (Löffler 2005).

Most responsibilities are delegated to local government. These include land use planning, public transit, the provision of water, electricity, gas, housing and construction (Löffler 2005). In one sense there is no need for cooperation with other authorities (Löffler 2005) although the lack of inter-municipal cooperation is an issue for city-region and regional planning (Freund 2003: 136). The Land government does have powers to require cooperation by relevant authorities but 'out of respect for municipal autonomy' uses these powers sparingly (Freund 2003: 141). The margin of action on the environment is limited for local authorities as already discussed. The environmental and landscape protection objectives and measures are defined in landscape plans (Seaton and Nadin 2000). Generally, landscape plans are prepared in parallel with transport and the more comprehensive spatial plans (Seaton and Nadin 2000). This approach to integrated spatial planning, where the focus is on planning the settlement structure in relation to public transit, based on concepts of decentralised concentration, as well as conserving open space and natural resources has been strongly supported by the Green movement from the 1980s (Fürst and Rudolph 2003: 155). Spatial plans are binding at the local level and are considered by many as setting 'restrictive' and 'inflexible spatial ordering concepts' on how space can be used (Fürst and Rudolph 2003: 159).

The administrative responsibilities for spatial planning have been changing since the 1990s as a result of several factors. First, rapid motorisation and suburbanisation fuelled by post-war reconstruction has resulted in more and more people living in suburban and peripheral areas outside local jurisdictions (Freund 2003; Fürst and Rudolph 2003; Heeg 2003). Despite proactive policies by the transport authorities, public transit patronage declined during the 1990s in most city-regions. Second, EU policies on integration and economic competitiveness have led to a growing realisation by regional actors that spatial planning at the local government level is unlikely to 'optimis[e the] economic efficiency' of German city-regions (Heeg 2003: 169). Third, the unification of East and West Germany from 1990 has merged two very different systems of planning.

Attempts to break down the artificial separation of economic policy at the regional level and spatial planning at the local level have resulted in a number of metropolitan or city-region associations being established to manage the economic and spatial development of more functional city spaces. Some are informal groupings, while others are formally established as a regional county with an elected president and representatives (Fürst and Rudolph 2003). There is differentiation in the formal groupings, between those elected by the population and associations elected by the state parliament (Heeg 2003).

Their tasks are not only to strategically plan for the city-region but to achieve this in a more consensual way, working with economic agents and the different tiers of government (Heeg 2003; Fürst and Rudolph 2003; Löffler 2005). Although there are different approaches, the metro-region associations have gained more powers, which include regional planning, public transit coordination, recreational facilities, and the marketing of regional economic opportunities and potentials (Heeg 2003).

Nearly all German city-regions have a functional agency coordinating public transit delivery (Heeg 2003) working with associations of local transit providers who set the prices, routes and frequency of public transit (Häussermann 2003). All major metropolitan areas now use integrated ticketing for all transit modes, and the Federal Government has promoted vehicle fleet modernisation and real-time information, and other quality measures. However, investment in the Federal Transport Infrastructure Plan 2003 was heavily biased towards railways, motorways and federal highways. Germany still has an extensive network of tramways, which have been upgraded to light rail standards (*Stadtbahn*) in suburban and peripheral areas and converted to the underground rapid transit (*U-bahn*) in city centres. Germany also has a suburban railway system or S-Bahn.

Most German cities have a car modal share of up to 55 per cent (Buehler 2008: 4), which reflects an extensive autobahn network, high car ownership and driving licence rates. Eighty-one per cent of households owned a car in 2001 while 27 per cent of households owned two or more vehicles (Buehler 2008: 4). From 1970 to 2005, car passenger kilometres increased by more than 50 per cent, but the rate of growth has reduced to 5 per cent in the last decade (Buehler 2008: 5). The Federal Government has been very proactive on reducing the environmental pollution from vehicle use. The Air Quality Control Act 1990 and the Traffic Noise Protection Law 1990 set strict limits to regulate the noise from road construction, trams and trains. As a result much of the high-speed train network has either been constructed underground or in enclosed structures on the surface (Whitelegg 1997: 167). Legislation in 1995 was introduced to address high concentrations of short-lived ozone (O_3) pollution, providing powers to '*ban vehicles from the road and impose speed limits should the concentration of O_3 exceed 240μg/m³ at three separate measuring stations in one region over a one hour period*' (Whitelegg 1997: 162).

At the same time, the Federal Government instigated policies for '*less/non-polluting vehicle propulsion technologies; innovative electronic technology, life-cycle analysis; climate protection and rational energy use; and integrated corporate management systems for sustainability*' (Heeg 2003).

In terms of the internalisation of the costs of motorised transport the Federal Government effectively gave a large subsidy to car and lorry drivers in the twentieth century. Whitelegg (1997: 187) quotes research by the Umwelt- und Prognose-Institut in Heidelberg, which estimated that taxation of car purchase and use in Germany only covered 25 per cent of the costs of road infrastructure, air and noise pollution, and accidents imposed by cars. They estimated that the equivalent figure for lorries was approximately 18 per cent. Scheiner (2006: 295) quoting Bovy et al. (1993) makes the same point that transport costs by private motorised vehicles in Germany are comparatively low based on relative purchasing power across 16 European countries. On the other hand he notes that housing costs are comparatively high.

Since this research was carried out, the Federal Government has used fiscal measures more effectively to increase the degree of internalisation of external costs. Petrol tax has increased using the fuel escalator as part of an '*environmental tax reform*' which between 1999 and 2004 increased the petrol tax from $0.15 per gallon every year to a total of $0.75 (Buehler 2008: 9). Between 1960 and 2007 the tax increased from 60 to 65 per cent of the petrol price (Buehler 2008: 9). Between 1999 and 2004 sales of motor fuel in Germany reduced and car vehicle miles travelled grew by only 2 per cent (Buehler 2008: 9). Since the 1990s the Federal Government has promoted more energy efficient vehicles through annual vehicle registration fees that increase with tailpipe emissions and engine size and the car sales tax, which was 19 per cent in Germany in 2007 (Buehler 2008: 8). The more energy-efficient vehicles meeting the Euro IV and V standards receive large tax reductions (Banister 2006: 7). The Federal Government also offers tax breaks for the purchase of energy efficient vehicles, with electric cars being completely tax-free for the first five years. These measures combined have helped to reduce CO_2 emissions from cars by 3 per cent between 1999 and 2003, increased the fuel efficiency of the vehicle fleet by 6 per cent during this period, and increased the members in car sharing schemes (Buehler 2008: 9). This compares favourably with the preceding ten year period when the consumption of motor fuel in Germany increased by 10 per cent and CO_2 emissions from transport increased by 12 per cent (Reckien et al. 2007: 340).

Comparing the costs of car ownership and use in the USA and Germany in 2006, Buehler (2008: 9) found that they were roughly 50 per cent higher in Germany. In this equation the operating costs per kilometre were 2.5 times higher in Germany, partly accounted for by the price of petrol, which was twice as expensive in Germany as in the USA. He estimates that in 2005 revenues from road users exceeded the cost of road construction and maintenance by 2.6 to 1, though this figure does not include the external negative costs (Buehler 2008: 11). In Germany, car taxes have traditionally not been ring-fenced for transport investment but are used to finance all government policies including social security. In 2009, the Federal Government introduced a new base rate combined with a CO_2 motor vehicle tax (European Automobile Manufacturers' Association 2009) further strengthening the internalisation of the external negative costs of transport use.

At the beginning of 2005, the Federal Government initiated a heavy goods vehicle (HGV) toll on the entire motorway network (12,000 km) based on distance travelled (Federal Ministry of Transport, Building and Urban Development 2009). This user charge is designed to promote the transport of goods by waterways and rail based transport, to promote more efficient use of HGVs and to secure funding for the maintenance and operation of motorways from users. Most of the funding is invested into the federal trunk roads sector, the remainder used to modernise road, rail and waterway networks. In compensation, the HGV vehicle tax has been reduced and incentives to purchase cleaner HGVs introduced. Lower toll taxes were first introduced in 2005, with increases in 2007. Statistics collected suggested that HGV's are responsible for roughly half the costs of motorway maintenance and the toll is designed to recoup these. Toll collection is automatic using satellite technology and an onboard unit calculating the toll due based on the number of axles and the emission class of the HGV. There are automatic and stationary enforcement checks at control bridges and spot checks on the motorway and the haulier's premises. This scheme not only integrates freight transport and environmental policy but also provides a more level playing field between road and rail modes.

Since the early 1970s, local government in Germany has promoted energy efficiency in the transport system by restraining the use of the car in city centres and enhancing alternative modes of transport (Heeg 2003; Buehler 2008). This includes restrictions on car parking since the 1980s in German cities, comprising both a reduction in supply and the increase in parking charges. Parking restrictions are generally applied area wide, set maximum parking time limits and provide exemptions for residents (Buehler 2008: 13). Plan permit requirements set maximum parking space rules and often require developers to finance the provision of public parking garages. Local government also has strong powers to set maximum limits for the speed of traffic within their jurisdiction. Particularly notable is the reduction of speed limits on most urban roads to 30 kmph and in many residential areas to 6 kmph (Buehler 2008: 13). Car restrictive policies and the improvements to public transit have helped to achieve an increase in public transit patronage of six per cent from 1999 to 2003 (Buehler 2008: 9). Cycling as a proportion of all trips is currently around a 9 per cent trip-share, and the national cycling strategy 2002–2012 aims to increase this. Substantial funding was made available in 2008 to extend existing cycle tracks as well as measures to enhance safety.

In the city of Freiburg, in south-west Germany, there is a deep-rooted awareness of the environment and transport sustainability (Koehler 2009). Between 1996 and 2009 the dependence on nuclear power has halved to 35 per cent of energy needs while CHP has expanded from 3 per cent to 52 per cent. Renewable energy provides the remainder. Since 2002, the city has been proactively promoting solar power through installing solar systems on the roofs of all school buildings and using these as a means to provide vocational training in the energy sector. Freiburg has reduced CO_2 emissions by 13 per cent since 1996 and has set a target of 40 per cent reduction by 2030 (Koehler 2009).

Freiburg, with a population of 215,966, is a compact city which can be crossed quickly with a 20 minute pedshed (Koehler 2009). The main objective of transport policy is traffic avoidance, protecting residential areas from motorised traffic through extensive traffic calming (30 kmph) and expensive parking fees (FWTM Freiburg, no date). The transport sector contributes 20 per cent of total CO_2 emissions. Compared with other major German cities Freiburg has the lowest motor vehicle density, with 423 vehicles per 1,000 people (FWTM Freiburg 2009). Neighbourhood policies which aim to increase the quality of life and to increase walking and cycling have been commonplace in German cities. These include car-free housing developments, car-free pedestrian zones in city centres, cycle lanes and traffic calming in residential neighbourhoods (Buehler 2008: 13). The redevelopment of the Vauban Quarter, a former military area on 38 hectares, in Freiburg was achieved using the ideas of car-free housing and high building insulation standards, with many houses producing their own energy. The car ownership ratio in Vauban is 85 per 1000 inhabitants with some parking provided in shared parking lots. In another new housing district, Rieselfeld, the municipality provided a tram system early on in the development. The municipality has very favourable conditions to implement new energy initiatives in all new development since it is a developer and regulator, with the Green Party having a strong presence on the local council including the mayor.

This shorter case study on progress in reducing resource use in Germany has shown the effectiveness of strong structures for coordinating action between the vertical tiers of government. Critics would argue that these are too restrictive and rigid, but their existence has enabled the Federal Government to implement fiscal instruments to increase the cost of private motorised vehicles (cars, HGVs) generally and radical tax breaks for ownership and use of low-polluting vehicles. The combination of fiscal instruments and demand restraint instruments implemented in towns and cities has increased the attractiveness of rail and tram use and helped to stabilise, and now reduce, global greenhouse gas emissions from transport (Table 7.2). The contribution of the reunification of Germany to the reduction in global greenhouse gas from transport is an unknown factor. Car ownership levels between eastern and western Germany since reunification have nearly 'harmonised' in terms of ownership per person over 18 years of age. Data on global greenhouse gas emissions from all sectors collected by the European Environmental Agency (European Union 2009) shows that the reduction of emissions in Germany from 1990–1995 was only 7.8 per cent compared with 21.3 per cent over the period 1990–2007. Comparable figures for the UK are 7.6 and 17.4 per cent. In the latter case, these reductions were mainly due to structural changes in the energy industry, with the replacement of coal-fired stations with gas-fired plants. There were slight increases in global greenhouse gas emissions from all sectors in Denmark, Sweden and the Netherlands between 1990–1995.

Germany is a prosperous nation with a well educated population that accepts the need to regulate on environmental matters. In August 2007, the Federal Government adopted the goal of reducing CO_2 emissions by 40 per cent by 2020. There appears to be acceptance of strong rules on resource minimisation that coordinate problem solving and action down to the local level. The phased implementation of the distance toll for HGVs is just one example of the Federal Government's ability to achieve integrated policy objectives. However, the recent moves to set up metro-region associations of local government acknowledge the need to strengthen the horizontal integration of policy and particularly the coordination of public and private sector interaction to enhance economic competitiveness at this wider spatial scale. While local government, within its boundaries, has good local autonomy and significant resources to manage the use of space, restrain car use and enhance neighbourhood environments within its jurisdictions, it has little influence over the investment strategies of the powerful infrastructure agencies, particularly the Land agency for road building and Deutsche Bahn (the national railway company). It remains to be seen whether more effective working relationships with these agencies can be resolved through integrated strategic infrastructure planning at the metro-region level.

7.6   BEST PRACTICE IN THE UK

The urban areas of the UK were particularly affected by a neo-liberal approach to government intervention from the 1980s onwards and structural changes to energy supplies in the 1990s. These wider economic developments changed the context for the regulation of land use and infrastructure and led to a cautious approach to land use regulation of private sector development proposals. The strategic city-region integration of public policy and regulation provided by the urban metropolitan counties was removed in the 1980s with the abolition of the county councils in urban areas. By removing this technical capacity from an elected tier of government more emphasis was placed on the lowest tier of elected government (Districts and Boroughs), whose boundaries rarely enclosed the whole of an urban area, to work in unison with public and private sector developers to enhance the quality of life in their jurisdictions.

This new socio-cultural philosophy was seen to boost the economic competitiveness of the UK economy but at the expense of the structural decline of many urban areas reliant on heavy industry. By the mid-1990s, the local land use plan had become more a tool to record the planned investment decisions of the public sector, identifying opportunities for private sector investment, than a visionary document of aspirations and legal requirements. The local plan still remained an advisory document to be taken into account in development permit decisions, though the involvement of stakeholders at different stages of the production was given legal status. The local plan, essentially, became a document for coordinating the investment proposals of key local and national developers. By this stage, the production of a regional spatial strategy to coordinate infrastructure and housing growth locations assumed more strategic importance with collaboration between local and regional public sector agencies to provide detailed advice to the national government. The local plan was the means to implement the strategic regional spatial ordering of priorities at the local level guided by advice notes on different topics produced by the appropriate national government department (there were several reorganisations of the civil service at national government level). There were, obviously, many local authorities that rose above the national government focus on procedural regularities to proactively agree visionary policies to provide for better quality lived experience in their jurisdictions. The absence of an elected tier of government at the city-region or regional level has reinforced the competition between neighbouring local administrations, not helped by national government monitoring, and performance tables, on the speed of development-permit decision making.

Compared to the national government tinkering the land use planning system has been subject to, transport policy planning has had a much more stable and evolutionary development. Since 1973, local government has been required to produce a transport plan that later became the main mechanism for bidding into central government funding for strategic transport schemes (May *et al.* 2008). From 2000, the transport plans developed into integrated modal strategies, delivering national government objectives for increasing accessibility and road safety and reducing air pollution and traffic congestion. The system of representative democracy in the UK elects a national government administration that has substantial power over lower tiers of government through the dispensation of public resources raised through taxation and the powers to change the decision rules on how this funding is used. This, in effect, transfers any oversight in national policy making down to the local level and leaves little autonomy or sense of ownership of the resulting strategy (May *et al.* 2008). Devolution to Wales and Scotland in the late 1990s, however, transferred public sums and the right to enact secondary legislation on some topics to their elected governments.

National government and private sector stakeholders have become increasingly critical of what they perceive as the slowness in the delivery chain for strategic or national transport projects. Several eminent economists and civil servants have examined these claims and recommended that the appropriateness of these schemes should be taken at the national level by an Independent Planning Commission of appointees, rather than through the lengthy highways inquiry process involving national and local stakeholders. The need for a national transport plan also became evident to overcome the time consuming deliberation in these inquiries to determine how specific proposals might contribute to the modal-specific national policies. Eddington (2006: 52) considered that a national transport plan would '*focus*[ing] *on objectives and deliver*[ing] *high return schemes, rather than modes or technologies*'.

A longstanding weakness of transport planning and the process for levering funding for local transport projects has also been the lack of integration with land use planning and other public policy sectors (Stead 2003; Atkins 2003; Hull 2005). Large quantities of advice issue from the Department of Transport and the departments dealing with land use planning and health on sustainable development and good practice guidelines but their translation to the conurbation or city-region is hampered by the administrative and political vacuum. This makes the development of a cross-modal strategy for the travel-to-work area, working with privatised transit operators, a difficult challenge for the public sector. In addition to the administrative hurdle of working across jurisdictional boundaries, the national government's appraisal criteria and the indicators to monitor transport policy interventions are too narrowly defined on the flow of traffic on the transport infrastructure (see the concept of 'mobility' in Section 3.2) to support the evaluation of sustainable strategies and schemes (Hull and Tricker 2005; Marsden *et al.* 2006). The main impediment that Vigar (2006: 283) identifies is that the national transport strategy is still '"*double-barrelled", with demand management policies and extensive infrastructure investment in supply side capital projects in evidence*'.

When the resourceful elected urban county councils were abolished in the 1980s, public transport authorities were established to encourage public transit coordination across the sub-region with appointees from the municipalities as their executive. This functional solution, lacking sufficient funding, has had to work through voluntary agreements with the private operators and other constituencies to achieve a level of public transit integration. Recent legislation will, however, strengthen the coordination powers of these sub-regional authorities in England, with accelerated powers for some to introduce the London system of bus franchising alongside bus priority measures. Local authorities, since 2000, do have discretionary powers to manage road space demand and raise local funds to improve public transit services through road tolling and workplace parking charges. Few have used these powers so far. Greater London is the exception where 13 per cent of the 61 million UK population reside.

Greater London is unique in England and Wales in having an elected strategic level body, which covers the area of the 33 London Boroughs. The Greater London Authority (GLA) is governed by a directly elected Mayor and was established by Act of Parliament in 1999, following the abolition of the former Greater London Council in 1986. The GLA has several stand-alone agencies for key aspects of its work. One of these, Transport for London (TfL), created in 2000, is the transport authority for the whole of London tasked with managing London's transport system and the growing demand for travel. TfL has a remit that covers the strategic management of the buses, the Underground, Docklands Light Railway, London Overground, Croydon Tramlink,

London River services, Victoria Coach Station, and 580 km of main roads. In addition, their responsibilities include the traffic lights, regulating the city's taxis and private hire vehicles, and promoting walking and cycling (Osborne 2008: 1).

The special treatment of London as the nation's capital has secured an integrated public transit system for the city with an electronic smart card for payment (Oyster card). This level of coordination of payment for travel services impacts positively on travel behaviour. London has the highest level of bus availability: 99 per cent of households live within 13 minutes of a bus stop with a service hourly or better (Department for Transport 2006b), considerably above the national average of 89 per cent (Watters *et al*. 2007). Car ownership in London is much lower than the national average: 38 per cent of households do not have a car compared to the national average of 25 per cent (Watters *et al*. 2007). London also has the lowest proportion of two car owning households at 16 per cent (Department for Transport 2006b). Households in central London are thus less car-dependent than households in outer London and the rest of the country and much more likely to travel by public transit (Watters *et al*. 2007).

TfL has delegated powers to regulate the bus market in London by setting the service specification for type of vehicle, the frequency of services, the route and interworking requirements with other services, which are unique to TfL (Hensher and Brewer 2001). This gives TfL considerable purchasing power in contractual negotiations over service provision in London and more generally in the market for new buses (Watters *et al*. 2007). Sustained growth in population and economic activity in the city in the 1990s had highlighted the transport challenges the city must address in the twenty-first century (Figure 7.7). These include, first, the need for additional investment and coordination of public transit services. Second, the status of London as a global city is seen as dependent on a transport system that is both interconnected and operates without 'traffic congestion'.

The first London mayor Ken Livingstone was elected in 2000 as an independent with a new, politically risky mandate that included substantial investment in the capital's public transit system using revenue raised from a cordon road tolling scheme. The cordon around a relatively small area (21 square kilometres) of Greater London (see Figure 7.8), was eventually implemented in February 2003 following delays as two inner boroughs tested the justification for such a scheme through judicial review (Kollamthodi *et al*. 2005). The scheme has four main objectives:

- to reduce congestion levels in central London;
- to improve journey time reliability for car drivers;
- to improve bus services (through revenues generated); and
- to make the distribution of goods and services more efficient (Glaister and Graham 2006).

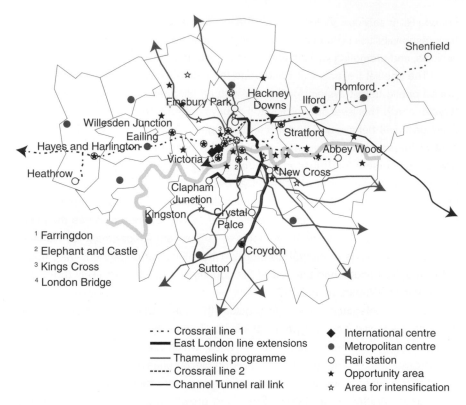

¹ Farringdon
² Elephant and Castle
³ Kings Cross
⁴ London Bridge

---- Crossrail line 1   ◆ International centre
━━ East London line extensions   ● Metropolitan centre
── Thameslink programme   ○ Rail station
---- Crossrail line 2   ★ Opportunity area
━━ Channel Tunnel rail link   ☆ Area for intensification

Figure 7.7 New development opportunities and rail infrastructure schemes in London. Source: Mayor of London (2004: 130), reproduced under licence

The charge area is bounded by the London inner ring road, which allows traffic with no need of access to avoid the zone, while drivers of non-exempt vehicles who need to travel within the zone must pay the fixed daily charge of £8 (increased from £5 in July 2005) (Transport for London 2007: 126).

The defined scheme operation hours are working weekdays between 07:00 and 18:00. Buses, coaches, licensed taxis, minicabs and two-wheeled vehicles are automatically exempt from the charge. Many of the potentially chargeable vehicles (cars, vans and lorries) are eligible for discounts or exemptions including residents of the charging zone, vehicles used by disabled people, vehicles with nine or more seats, and certain alternative-fuelled vehicles (Watters *et al.* 2007: 13). The scheme is enforced by a network of automatic number plate recognition (ANPR) cameras that monitor all vehicles entering and circulating within the zone. The number plates of vehicles are read and stored on a database. Drivers found to be evading payment

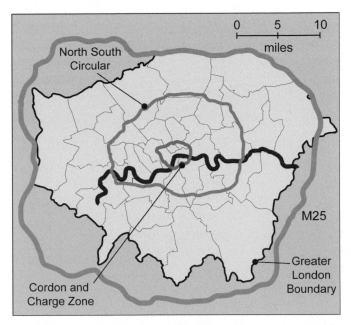

Figure 7.8 Area covered by the London Congestion Charging Scheme in relation to the Greater London area.

are issued with a penalty charge notice which fines them £50 (€57) or £100 (€114) depending on the promptness of payment.

Politically, for the new mayor, it was important to implement the scheme quickly using existing camera technology (ANPR) to enforce compliance rather than testing the reliability of transponder units and satellite technology. It is reported that in the first eight months of operation the scheme generated over 100,000 licence issues a day and that more than 900,000 penalty charge notices were issued (Glaister and Graham 2006: 1413). The costs for operating the first ten years of the scheme were estimated at £1,247 million (€1,416 million) (Kollamthodi *et al.* 2005). This estimate included the start-up costs, the operating and management costs, traffic management costs, the costs of additional public transit services, and the scheme compliance costs to road users. The annual monitoring reports show that the toll collection costs are substantial. The annual operating expenses between 2002/03 and 2005/06 were £289 million (€428 million)[4] (European Environment Agency 2008c: 37). This figure does not include the start-up costs or the annualised cost of the ANPR camera system.

The scheme is self financing, and produced net revenues in 2002/03 of around £2 million increasing to £122 million in 2006/2007 for reinvestment in transport improvements across London (Transport for London 2007: 5, 129; European Environment Agency 2008c: 37). Traffic flows by the end of the second year had reduced by 21 per cent, which equates to 70,000 fewer vehicles entering the charging zone (Transport for London 2007). This has contributed to an estimated 16 per cent reduction in NOx and PM_{10} emissions. Around 25 per cent of this improvement is due to changes in the vehicle fleet which would have happened without the scheme (Kollamthodi et al. 2005). The scheme is estimated to have led to savings of 19 per cent in traffic related CO_2 emissions and a 20 per cent reduction in fuel consumed by road transport within the charging zone. At the end of 2006/07 the reduction in traffic using the charge area has been maintained although traffic congestion had increased due to the disruption caused by the maintenance activities of utility companies on the highway network (Transport for London 2007).

Overall, after five years of operation, congestion is down eight per cent, underground light rail patronage has increased slightly, bus patronage has increased substantially and substantial investment from the road tolling revenues has been invested in hybrid-fuel buses, Euro IV standard buses and increased bus frequencies. In parallel with these service improvements, TfL have equipped 8,000 vehicles with GPS tracking and installed 500 passenger information signs. This included installation of bus priority technology at half of the signalled junctions in London to allow virtual bus detection (Osborne 2008). Public transit has increased its capacity and successfully accommodated any displaced car users. Of the 65,000 to 70,000 car trips that are no longer made to the zone during charging hours, 50–60 per cent are now made by public transit, 20–30 per cent have diverted around the zone, and 15–25 per cent have changed the timing of their trip. Panel surveys indicate that journey-time savings for all vehicles average 14 per cent, with an increase in the reliability of journey times (27 per cent improvement for outward journeys, 34 per cent for return journeys). Kollamthodi et al. (2005) estimate that on a typical average trip of 80 minutes this equates to mean travel-time savings of about 10 minutes. Road traffic accidents have reduced. It is estimated that congestion charging directly leads to between 40 and 70 fewer personal injury road traffic accidents in the charging zone per year (Transport for London 2007).

Several compromises had to be made by TfL to achieve speedy implementation, including a reduction in charges and a large number of discounts (29 per cent of vehicles) and exemptions (26 per cent). Banister (2006) considers that these exemptions reduce the effectiveness of the policy and will create future problems if they are to be reassessed. Generally Londoners are more supportive of the scheme since implementation with support growing from 40–49 per cent in the first two years, while over 40 per cent of residents within the charging zone consider their area as a better place to live since implementation. Originally, businesses were

neutral to the scheme but following implementation the impact appears differentiated with finance and business sectors gaining from the reduction in journey times,
while the retail and leisure sectors argue that the charge has detrimentally affected
business (Kollamthodi *et al.* 2005). Transport for London (2007: 130) compares
these perceptions with British Retail Consortium figures that show that the central
London economy has performed particularly strongly since the introduction of road
tolling, with recent retail growth (value of retail sales) in central London at roughly
twice the national growth rate.

The Mayor's Transport Strategy in 2004 included a proposal for a western
extension of the charge area. Following evaluation this was implemented in February
2007, but later cancelled by the new Mayor on election in May of that year (Transport
for London 2007: 120). According to Glaister and Graham (2006: 1398) the financial benefits of the extension, in terms of raising new capital for transport investment
were '*less persuasive than the original scheme – partly because it would quadruple
the number of residents entitled to a 90 per cent discount, most of whom must pay
the charge currently.*'

In 2005, TfL issued their 20 year strategy for transport in their report *Transport
2025: Transport Vision for a Growing World City* (Transport for London 2005). The
main objectives are to:

*   Support economic development by improving public transit and managing the
    road network to reduce traffic congestion
*   Tackle climate change and enhance the environment by reducing CO_2
    emissions, improving air quality, reducing noise and improving the urban
    environment
*   Improve social inclusion by making transport more accessible and secure for
    users (Osborne 2008).

Road tolling in London complements several London-wide strategies including
the 20 year transport plan, the Mayor's London Plan (2004) and the Mayor's Climate
Change Action Plan (Greater London Authority 2007). The London Plan is a conurbation wide spatial plan to address the challenges from major population and employment
growth in London and to coordinate major development in East Thameside and the
channel tunnel rail link at Stratford. It takes an integrated approach to transport provision and development through improving accessibility, making major improvements to
public transit and tackling traffic congestion. The Mayor has set targets to increase the
capacity of public transit by 50 per cent from 2001 to 2022 (Greater London Authority
2004: 136). Specific schemes include bus priority measures, tram and busway transit
schemes to improve capacity, support regeneration benefits and urban realm improvements (Greater London Authority 2004: 145).

A key component of the public transit strategy is to make the interchange between modes less complex and more convenient through better coordination. Approximately 80 per cent of all rail trips in London involve an interchange (either between rail services or with another mode), similarly 60 per cent of underground (main mode) trips and 20 per cent of bus trips involve interchanges. This equates to over 2 million passengers in London interchanging in the morning peak period every weekday (Osborne 2008: 1). The Oyster card is one element of this, the other is the provision of real-time information. These measures have contributed to a 38 per cent increase in bus patronage between 1999 and 2007 (Osborne 2008). Recent legislation has opened up the potential for the Mayor to have more influence on national rail services in London and, thus, ensure better integration between all transport modes, and major development areas (see Figure 7.6) (Transport for London 2004: 125).

The Mayor's Climate Change Action Plan (Greater London Authority 2007) sets in train an ambitious plan to achieve a 60 per cent reduction in emissions by 2025. This is more ambitious than the UK government's policy of a 60 per cent reduction by 2050 (Department of Environment, Food and Rural Areas 2006; Department of Trade and Industry 2007). A mixture of public transit, travel demand management, active travel and alternative-fuel measures are being implemented to achieve this target. Initiatives include schemes such as workplace and school travel planning activities to encourage motorists to leave their car at home and use more sustainable methods of transport, as well as the development of car clubs to deter the private ownership of vehicles. TfL is implementing a 900 km continuous network of principle cycle routes to increase provision by 200 per cent by 2010. Osborne (2008) quotes figures that suggest for an average Londoner, switching from driving to work to taking the bus will save 0.6 tonnes of carbon per year; taking up cycling instead would increase these savings to 1.1 tonnes. Research by both the GLA and Commission for Integrated Transport (CfIT) suggest that increased efforts in the areas of car vehicle technology, behavioural change and sustainable distribution could secure considerable additional carbon savings. CfIT quantified the reduction by 2020 on 1990 levels as around 14 per cent (Commission for Integrated Transport 2007).

London is way ahead in terms of energy efficient transport practices compared to the rest of the UK. This is partly because of the institutional advantages it has but also because national government policy to encourage vehicle efficiency through fiscal measures is generally poorly marketed (Watters et al. 2007). TfL are funding a £1 million trial of low carbon technology in London's taxi fleet, the introduction of a fuel efficient driving campaign aimed at both taxi and private hire drivers, and establishing an electric vehicle partnership to support greater uptake of electric vehicles, which have zero tailpipe emissions. Greater London is designated as a low emission zone to remove the most polluting lorries over 3.5 tonnes, buses and coaches from the city. Many London boroughs are supporting these approaches through subsidised parking charges for cleaner vehicles. When progress towards sustainability depends on local action it is vulnerable to local political changes. In London's case the election of a new mayor in 2008 has put a temporary halt on the progress of these green initiatives with the cancellation of the extension to both the charging zone and the low emission zone regulation for smaller vans and minibuses which was scheduled for 2010.

To conclude the UK case study, we must note that substantial national government funding is targeted to public transit but that there is little modal integration at national level to reap the synergies from public subsidy to the private train and tram operators, the private bus operators and the transport funding dispensed to local transport authorities. Local government is left with the job to negotiate with the private sector operators and powerful public sector highways and rail agencies to attempt to coordinate infrastructure provision. London is a separate case, with a highly educated, prosperous electorate and with the political clout of a national capital. Generous public sector funding, which sustains large policy and delivery agencies such as TfL, and legal powers to organise a regulated private market for bus provision show the positive action that follows.

There is deep distrust of local government in the centralised government system of the UK with tight *ultra vires* rules or boundary markers to the agency of local government. Where substantial power and resources are held by national government it stifles the leadership role of local level actors and the responsibility for behaviour change to integrate the global–local resource minimisation challenge. The UK context is, therefore, characterised by weak national rules and guidance on how to prioritise sustainability principles in resource decision making. This leads to a weak capacity to integrate policy sectors at the different levels of government and, therefore, the absence of strong structures to support problem solving at the local, and city-region levels. London, of course, is the exception to this conclusion.

7.7 CONCLUSIONS ON THE LESSONS TO BE LEARNT

This chapter has sought to test the hypotheses that behaviour change towards transport resource minimisation is dependent on: 1) strong national government action to incentivise the introduction of low energy resource solutions through the use of financial and legal powers; and 2) the existence of well-resourced government institutions at the city-region level to provide strong leadership to local level actors and undertake the responsibility for behaviour change.

The approach to the analysis of each case study in this chapter has focused on the presence of five key themes:

1   Clear national rules that prioritise sustainability principles, including resource minimisation, across policy sectors

2   Structures that support problem solving and coordination at the local level
3   A framework for the coordination of public and private sector interaction
4   Engagement with civil society to understand the factors that affect transport
     behaviour and, thus, public acceptability of transport demand management
5   Evaluation of the effectiveness of interventions and adaptation measures to
     correct systemic problems.

The remainder of this chapter considers each of these themes in turn, drawing on the case study analysis of the historical changes in the scope of concern, the responsibilities of organisations, and their legal and financial competencies to carry out strategic spatial planning.

7.7.1 CLARITY OF NATIONAL RULES

Clear national rules on how to prioritise sustainability principles, including resource minimisation, across policy sectors clearly account for the differences in these five case studies. Sweden and Germany have longstanding strict environmental legislation and have exploited, and even driven, EU regulations and directives on local air noise pollution and clean energy developments, and used these concepts and standards to steer civil society action and local government strategies. Denmark, too, has had strong legislation to protect rural areas, to reduce noise pollution and promote renewable energy. The specific nuances of the historical, social, legal and cultural contexts in each case clearly influence the development pathways in each country. Denmark, Sweden and Germany have invested heavily in a low-emissions transport infrastructure. In Denmark's case the focus has been placed on electric vehicle technologies and the investment in electric charging points in the built environment. Germany and Sweden have moved on to invest in second generation biofuels based on agricultural and food waste and have invested in the infrastructure required, reaching the two per cent reference value set by the EU Biofuels Directive in 2005 and a 5.75 per cent share in 2010 (European Commission 2009: 163).

All the case study nations have established different classes of vehicles for taxation purposes related to their CO_2 emission profiles. In Germany and Sweden the incentives and constraints have gone much further. In both these countries, income tax reductions apply where the daily commute is by public transport. There are also generous rebates for the purchase of low energy vehicles in both countries and in Germany radical policies for tax-free electric vehicles, higher petrol fuel prices, and an HGV motorway road toll based on distance travelled and the efficiency of the vehicle. In the case of Germany all these national policies work synergistically to increase the demand for fuel efficient vehicles and reduce the number of journeys made.

The Netherlands case study has demonstrated a high level of integration between policy sectors at the national level with ecological principles integrated with transport and land use in government spatial planning strategies. In this small, densely populated country these principles are embedded across natural and built environment professionals. The national government has instigated strong policies to improve the modal integration of, and investment in, public transit and more recently passed legislation to implement a road charging system based on distance travelled. In comparison with the other case studies, the UK government has prevaricated such that there is an absence of clear framing for sustainable transport outcomes using the legal and financial structures available.

7.7.2 STRUCTURES TO SUPPORT INTEGRATED PROBLEM-SOLVING AT THE LOCAL LEVEL

All the countries outlined in the case studies, except the UK, have some form of elected regional government. Regional government has had more longevity in the German example, whilst the recent regional competencies in Denmark, Sweden and the Netherlands have, arguably, still to establish themselves as authoritative institutions. Several attempts in the Netherlands, Germany and in the UK have been made to strengthen the government capacity across city-regions, or the functional travel-to-work areas, through voluntary or legal coalitions of elected local government to enhance the capacity for integrated problem solving at this spatial scale.

It is noticeable that in Sweden and Denmark local government raises most of its spending through local taxation, and in the case of Germany a significant proportion through business rate taxation. These powers are not available to local government in the Netherlands and in the UK. Local government in Sweden, the Netherlands, Denmark and Germany also has a substantial portfolio of land and business interests. The case studies have not been able to explore the extent of the ownership of resources in these countries, which give local government authority to negotiate with other public and private interests operating within their jurisdiction. However, these institutional preconditions influence the approach to local problem-solving in each country.

The absence of these powers and resources for policy making, raising taxes, enacting legal requirements and land ownership create barriers for proactive and timely delivery of new approaches to resource minimisation. The Greater London Authority had to choose a low technology and more expensive approach to road tolling to be able to implement the instrument in a timely fashion. Even where local government has autonomy over ample resources, the effect of transport (related) prices and taxes set by higher tier levels of government may work antagonistically with local initiatives creating sub-optimal outcomes. In the Malmö case study, the

Swedish government's payback to individuals purchasing alternative energy cars, on the one hand, gave legitimacy and support to the investment in biofuel infrastructure and the low emission zone, but caused the elected councillors to water down their generous proposal of free parking for clean vehicles in the city centre.

On the other hand, the German case study demonstrates a vertical consistency of approach towards transport policy with national prices and taxes on transport efficiency supporting local policies on traffic calming, car parking and the priority to walking and cycling in neighbourhood strategies. This has reduced distances travelled by car more effectively than the other case study countries since 1995 despite high car ownership. Germany also demonstrates that a consistent policy of car restraint applied incrementally at all levels of government has positive synergistic effects on health and energy consumption. This has given a clear message to businesses and individuals, and provided the right institutional context to emphasise the social welfare benefits that will accrue from restrictions on energy consumption (Ubbels and Verhoef 2005).

7.7.3 COORDINATING PUBLIC AND PRIVATE INTERACTION

The case studies of Sweden, and to a lesser extent Germany and the Netherlands, suggest that strong, inward looking, local government at the municipality level can also be a hindrance to the effective coordination of public and private investment strategies and the synergies that can flow from the integration of future investment plans. There are many intervening variables that can affect the achievement of positive synergies, including the effectiveness of national steering policies and the adaptive capacity of local government, which will play out differently in different contexts. A strong national political commitment to resource efficiency sets a renewed challenge for public sector and market actors to revise their practices to maximise new opportunity agendas. Great skill and commitment are required by spatial planners, at all levels of government, to gain local consensus for the implementation of the more 'radical' instruments discussed in Chapter 6 from public and private sector actors. Without the ability to use legal tools or financial incentives to bring together new partners to work together in long-term partnerships it will be difficult to work in tandem with all other public sector and private actors to prioritise walking and cycling first, followed by public transport and then access by other modes.

7.7.4 ENGAGEMENT WITH CIVIL SOCIETY

It is difficult, for several reasons, to make a straight comparison between these case studies on how they have effectively engaged with members of the public to understand the factors that affect transport behaviour and, thus, public acceptability of transport demand management. First, the information provided in these vignettes is not necessarily comparable. While the data search has been informed by a common thematic template, the analysis for reasons of research funding has explored to greater depths in the cases of the cities of Amsterdam and Malmö. More importantly, the comparison is made more complicated by the differentiation in the geopolitical and cultural contexts in the cities chosen. The public perception of the safety of cycling clearly differs in the UK and Germany, with trip-shares of two and nine per cent respectively, in comparison to the Netherlands, Denmark and Sweden where cycling has a trip-share of 20 per cent and above. Household location choices are made on the basis of this physical settlement pattern, the characteristics of accommodation, the living environment in each neighbourhood and the available transport services, trading off one factor against another within their budget constraints. Their travel behaviour and long-term housing mobility are closely linked to their own life-cycle and family responsibilities (Scheiner 2006). Once settled their travel behaviour will be influenced by the density of the urban form and accessibility of facilities, but also by the non-monetary costs of each travel mode. If the physical patterns are different, then we may expect travel behaviour outcomes to be different. The latter includes their sensitivity to time taken to reach their destination, including the time in transportation, waiting period and the perceived quality of the travel option (Boucq 2007; Sun *et al.* 2009).

7.7.5 MONITORING THE EFFECTIVENESS OF INTERVENTIONS

The capacity to monitor the effectiveness of interventions influences the ability to adapt and implement corrective mechanisms when 'experiments' go wrong. Often the data requirements to satisfy national comparative indicators on transport, which reflect the mobility concept of flows and outputs such as length of new highway construction, etc., give little indication of the natural resource efficiency of investment. Table 7.4 illustrates these issues by comparing the performance of the case study countries on several quantitative indicators of transport efficiency over a 16 year period. The UK lags behind the other nations in terms of reducing car ownership and road fatalities over the period 1990–2005, although is on a par in terms of the increase in the distances travelled. Germany appears to have significantly increased passenger car kilometres since 1990, but this is tempered by an increase of only 6.6 per cent since 1995. Germany's most notable achievement is in reducing global greenhouse gases from transport, at least since 2000. Sweden and the UK are on a par in terms of the percentage increase in distance travelled by passenger cars, the growth in global greenhouse gas emissions, and the growth in rail transport. Sweden, however, has a much higher percentage of railways electrified, a lower increase in passenger car numbers during this period, and declining bus patronage levels.

Table 7.4 Comparison of case study countries on selected transport indicators

	Denmark	Sweden	Netherlands	Germany	United Kingdom
Percentage increase in passenger cars 1990–2006	27	17	31	45	38
Percentage increase in pkm by passenger cars 1990–2006	13	13	8	27	17
Percentage change in road fatalities 1990–2006	−4.5	−3.4	−3.9	−4.7	−3.0
Percentage increase in pkm by bus and coach 1990–2006	17	-10	-8	-9	8
Percentage of railways electrified in 2003	27	69	73	55	31
Percentage increase in pkm by rail 1990–2006	20	46	32	30	41
Percentage increase in pkm by tram and metro 1990–2006	0.2	10	15	3	40
Percentage growth in greenhouse gas emissions from transport 1990–2006	27	10	37	−1.5	15

Source: Various tables from European Commission (2007, 2009)
Note pkm person kilometres travelled. All figures above '5' are rounded up

Interesting as these differences and similarities are, they do not explain how action in different policy sectors to utilise resources more effectively interact to produce these outputs. Moreover, the introduction of a specific policy measure in one city may have different effects in another due to the differentiation in socio-economic preferences of the population and the pattern of spatial opportunities. For example, the introduction of a car club in one city may increase car travel and reduce bus patronage, while in another city the discernible effects are a reduction in total kilometres travelled by car. Measures designed to reduce average trip distance may be effective in one city but result in increases in another simply due to the physical configuration of each city (Marshall 2004). Few city-regions collect sufficient baseline information at a disaggregated level consistently over time to show the impact of transport, land use and health interventions.

Chapter 8 concludes the discussion of these transferable lessons on how to achieve the institutional capacity at the level of city-regions so that ecological systems thinking can be used to integrate actions horizontally and vertically across the spatial scales. Discussion will focus on how energy efficient futures must enthuse all levels of society, not just the formal government structures and will draw out how to change societal paradigms on mobility and accessibility.

CHAPTER 8

IMPLEMENTING A SUSTAINABLE TRANSPORT PACKAGE

8.1 INTRODUCTION

This book has argued that government action has to be undertaken in new ways to integrate the resources invested in urban areas so as to enhance the capacity and resilience of communities to respond to global environmental challenges. Transport resource consumption has been identified as expansive and profligate in developed countries with national governments responding to the perceived social preferences for motorised private transport. Powerful national transport agencies have been established, particularly for highways, to invest in network improvements, thus fuelling the phenomenon of 'hyper-mobility', which has become institutionalised in some societies to the extent that measures to manage travel demand and suppress mobility are believed to breach human rights and create a brake on economic growth. It is for reasons of economic competitiveness that the governments of the UK, the Netherlands and Denmark have all recently centralised decision making on strategic transport network investment to further shrink space–time to global markets. There are, thus, strong socio-political forces supporting the continuance of old investment practices that have, over time, led to spatial fragmentation, the dispersal of activities, and the growth of energy intensity.

Changes to policy goals require either the establishment of new institutional structures or the strengthening of existing structures to be effective. Central to the implementation of innovative approaches are the roles given to individual actors and the structures which incentivise human behaviour (Lindblom 1990; Hanf and O'Toole 1992); otherwise a gap between policy intent and policy delivery may arise. A key question for the behaviour change and climate resilience debates is, therefore, how to change the institutionalised practices and structures in society, which lead to profligate resource consumption through incentivising new behavioural practices. Mechanisms to coordinate multi-scalar public and private interaction to achieve dematerialisation and resource efficiency will be a vital component in behaviour change strategies. Integral to this new investment focus on low energy solutions will be a complete overhaul of our implicit values on consumption and decision making practices so that the environment is valued in our business models.

The biggest challenge in reducing carbon emissions and resource consumption from transport is, therefore, to institutionalise new ways of working and decision rules throughout all levels of governance. Achieving a step change in institutional behaviour depends on the tiers of governance (national and regional, city-region and local com-munities) working together to steer the selection of options by the market sector and civil society. Chapter 4 has shown that national government has the legal and financial tools to set up the opportunity agenda that will structure the context for interaction on resource minimisation. Chapter 3 charted the path towards greater sustainability, drawing on the ecological principles of 'exergy' or the minimum input of resources required to resolve a systemic problem. Chapter 5 neatly listed the structural changes that will put transport in the twenty-first century on the path to sustainability:

1   National government must realign financial systems and decision-making criteria to incentivise the introduction of low energy resource solutions

2   Legal and financial resources should be devolved to government/governance at the city-region level to ensure there is strong leadership and responsibility for behaviour change at a spatial level, which can integrate the global–local resource minimisation challenge.

This chapter focuses on the institutional structures that will need to be put in place if member states are going to create a platform which integrates sustainability princi-ples into public and societal decision making. The case studies in Chapter 7 provide the evidence of how land use and transport policy can be integrated and there-fore sets benchmarks against which to monitor progress. In discussing the national structuring rules that will be required to kindle low energy transport futures through collaborative action at the city-region level specific examples from the Chapter 7 case studies will be used.

8.2   NATIONAL INTERVENTIONS AND INSTRUMENTS

The imperative is for national and transnational governments to exert their agency by setting an opportunity agenda of incentives and constraints that will both lever flows of private capital for low energy projects and encourage citizens to reduce resource consumption and waste. It seems likely that a combination of legal, fiscal, land use and behavioural interventions will be necessary to secure greater accessibility to spatial opportunities without increasing mobility. How the deployment of tools should be shared between higher levels of government to be effective at implement-ing the low energy paradigm is debateable and relative to existing structures in each nation. Section 8.3 argues that the functional city-region level has to have sufficient resources, authority and autonomy to coordinate across public policy sectors and public and private actors to ensure that there is strong leadership and responsibility for behaviour change. This section argues that agency at this level must be set within structuring rules that prioritise the introduction of low energy resource solutions to local development needs.

The EU has given a strong policy steer to national and local policy practice by regulating across a wide area of economic and environmental issues in member states (see Chapter 2). The emphases of EU transport and energy policy since 2001 have been on reducing the material and energy intensity of production processes and transport of people and goods (Commission of the European Communities 2007a). The European Parliament adopted two new targets in 2009: 1) to reduce EU CO_2 emissions from 1990 levels by 20 per cent by 2020; and 2) to achieve a 20 per cent share of energy from renewable sources by 2020 in the EU's final consumption of energy (European Parliament 2009). The Council of Ministers (CoM) has been reticent about setting a specific carbon reduction target for the transport sector considering this to be a subsidiarity issue best decided by member states themselves. But the CoM has set pollution standards for fuel and new vehicles, culminating in a legal requirement to produce a 10 per cent share of energy from renewable sources in each member state's transport energy consumption. This regulation gives legal effect to the EU's existing goal of reducing average emissions from new cars to 120 grams CO_2/km, to be phased in from 2012 (Olsson 2007; Commission of the European Communities 2009). The package of measures also included stricter environmental standards and a reduction of global greenhouse gas emissions for fuel by 2020. These improvements to the technological efficiency of vehicles will, however, only achieve significant reductions in energy consumption over the medium to long term (Watters *et al.* 2007; see also Chapter 6).

Behaviour change will, therefore, need to be orchestrated at national government level to ensure first of all that a common purpose permeates all central state departments. The concept of exergy – increasing the value added through lower input of natural and material resources – can provide the fulcrum for pan-departmental policy. This is at the core of sustainability discussed in Chapter 3. National government priorities need to be consistent across policy sectors with a clear structure that aligns the rhetoric with the practice of decision taking. Higher tiers of government should use their legal tools to set CO_2 and resource minimisation targets which not only reduce environmental impacts but also achieve second order objectives such as improving health, reducing accidents and providing a better quality of life. Clear outcomes, which are time specific, should be set and monitored, and decision-making criteria introduced to encourage market and local political actors to invest in ecosystem maintenance and the capabilities of the population.

One of the findings from the Chapter 7 case studies was the recent success of the interventions initiated by the Federal Government in Germany to reduce energy consumption and to support longstanding sustainable localised spatial planning practices. The clear articulation of national legal requirements for the maintenance of environmental ecosystems, the realignment of taxation systems to prioritise energy minimisation and substantial federal investment in projects that reduce energy intensity have significant synergistic causal interactions that warrant further research.

It has been argued that a 60 mph (96 kmph) speed limit on motorways and trunk roads in the UK would produce the CO_2 reductions from transport required in the Government's climate change strategy, if properly enforced, according to the modelling carried out by Anable et al. (2006). Similarly, influencing travel behaviour, and regulatory policies supporting high densities and smaller distances between residences, work places and public facilities, results in resource efficiency, connectivity and social interaction. Legal tools and contracts that specify energy efficiency and waste reduction targets in procurement policies at all levels of government have a role to play in organisational behaviour change and to embed closed loop systems of local consumption of resources.

Public investment in infrastructure is also central to achieving national CO_2 targets and has longstanding implications for the built form and economic, environmental and social sustainability. Funding criteria needs to make explicit the ecosystem, health, and quality of life outcomes that will be monitored. Information and awareness raising to identify problems and possible solutions and good practice examples should be led by national government, with national public broadcasts and other media slots to encourage and influence debates. Policy objectives have to be consistent and clearly articulated, with broad party political support to instil confidence in lower tiers of government that the approach to ecosystem maintenance and dematerialisation, and the commitment, will not waiver over the medium to long term.

Establishing the decision-making criteria to evaluate and calculate the contribution of a transport project to ecosystem and social sustainability must include the whole productive cycle (viz. the abstraction of raw materials including fuel, vehicle production and maintenance, infrastructure construction and maintenance, and the disposal of wastes). New option-generation and appraisal tools will need to be developed to support the generation of alternative approaches to achieve strategic 2050 visions and meet national targets for energy efficiency and resource reduction. These are tools that will help politicians and civil servants to clearly identify the life cycle resource-reduction opportunities, the benefits and costs, and the risks and uncertainties inherent in the investment choices, so that the outcomes and distributional impacts are more transparent and can, therefore, be clearly understood (Marsden et al. 2006; van der Waard et al. 2007; Fischer 2009). An adapted strategic environmental assessment tool offers the potential to assess the cumulative effects of policies and development proposals provided the ecological impacts and the resource efficiencies are accorded the same attention as the broad environmental concerns.

Combined with clear legal requirements for resource minimisation, national and regional fiscal policies can kick-start the adoption of the most energy efficient and environmentally friendly behaviour and technology possible. The tax system influences travel behaviour. A tax system that raises revenue on the basis of the carbon consumed or the energy consumed per work performed (energy efficiency) in transport will influence both the choice of mode and the design and use of that mode in ways different to a system that encourages consumption of carbon-based fuel. Similarly, a tax system that subsidises the car commute to work will have a different impact on the built form to one that subsidises active travel. Fiscal policy is, therefore, a key driver of how urban form evolves, influencing the type of infra-structure constructed, the location decisions of investors and households as well as individual decisions on mode choice.

There are also a number of mode pricing mechanisms that could be intro-duced to encourage a better distribution of transport across the modes both spatially and temporally (Ney 2001). For example, Sweden and Germany have used both 'carrots' (viz. national subsidies and tax incentives) and 'sticks' (road tolls) as part of their holistic agenda on energy efficiency. In both countries there are personal income tax exemptions for public transport commuter tickets and car-pooling expenditures, and subsidies for the purchase of new low CO_2 emis-sion cars. Over recent decades the cost of owning and using a car has reduced in real terms while the cost of public transport has been increasing. Moving towards a vehicle taxation system that taxes vehicle use and modal energy efficiency would help car owners become aware of the true costs of using their vehicles (Zuckerman 1991; Whitelegg 1997; CEC 2007a).

The recent significant reductions in global greenhouse gas transport emis-sions in Germany have come from making car travel more expensive. This has included several elements. First, a comprehensive fuel-duty escalator designed to reflect the environmental damage caused by petrol and diesel consumption with annual price increments that have been sustained. Second, the Federal Government in Germany increased the differential in motor vehicle taxes between conventional and alternative-fuelled vehicles until 2009, when a base tax to cover administration costs and a CO_2 motor vehicle tax was introduced (European Automobile Manufacturers' Association 2009). Third, the Federal Government introduced a distance-based motorway toll for HGVs in 2005 to cover the main-tenance costs of HGV use of this network, to incentivise operators to run their vehicles more fuel efficiently and to encourage freight travel by train and waterway. The financial and external costs of the journey are reinforced through a highly visible in-vehicle metering system that makes the link between the energy effi-ciency of the vehicle, travel speeds and distance, and carbon emissions. German research on the evaluation of different policy scenarios (also including land use policies, maximum car speeds and subsidisation of public transport fares) has shown that only vehicle pricing policies that increased costs between 100–200 per cent had a significant effect on vehicle distances travelled (car-km per capital per day) (Spiekermann and Wegener 2003: 56–57).

Table 8.1 Examples of mobility planning and accessibility planning instruments

Mobility planning	Accessibility planning
Road construction and expansion	Land use management and initiatives
Motorways, freeways, beltways, interchanges, rotaries	Compact development
	Mixed uses
Arterial expansion	Pedestrian-oriented design
ITS, smart highways and smart cars	Transit villages
On-board navigational systems	Telecommunication advances
Vehicle positioning systems	Telecommuting/teleworking
Real-time informational systems	Telecommunities
Transportation system management	Teleshopping
One-way streets	Transportation demand management
Rechannelising intersections	Ride sharing
Removing curbside parking	Preferential parking for high occupancy
Ramp metering	vehicles
Large-scale public and private transport	Parking management and pricing
Heavy rail transit and commuter rail	Guaranteed ride home programmes
Regional busways	Community-scale public and non-motorised
Private tollways	transport
Road user charging schemes	Light rail transit and trams
	Community-based paratransit or jitneys
	Bicycle and pedestrian paths

Source: Adapted from Kennedy *et al.* (2005) Table 2 page 397

Road tolling has been successfully implemented in the USA and Norway to raise money locally for transport infrastructure projects and in London and Stockholm to alleviate traffic congestion. These schemes have produced travel time savings for commercial traffic and private motorised travel as unnecessary journeys are removed from the road. Used in this way, they can be considered as 'mobility' instruments since they reinforce existing mobility patterns and access to dispersed spatial opportunities in the city-region (see the classification in Table 8.1). Collectively, mobility instruments cater for private motorised vehicles and can make it harder to offer any viable transport alternatives.

When road tolling is implemented simultaneously with a combination of the accessibility instruments in Table 8.1 it can be an appropriate element of an integrated transport and land use strategy capable of achieving more efficient use of the road network, through reducing air pollution and energy consumption as a result of induced changes in modal choice and travel demand (Hensher and Brewer 2001; Glaister and Graham 2006). In combination with other demand management measures, road tolling can provide the revenue benefits to reinvest in improving the density and frequency of coverage of public transport services. This, to some extent, will assuage public sensitivities to what can be perceived as just another tax (Kollamthodi *et al.* 2005) and enable some distribution of revenues to residents and low income households. The case studies in Chapter 7 demonstrate that when accessibility instruments are central to both transport and land use strategies and are consistently maintained over a decade or two they can have a positive influence on the modal split.

To implement the accessibility instruments in Table 8.1 in a way that reinforces the synergistic effects requires each level of spatial governance to act in unison to move towards jointly held resource minimisation outcomes. Clear national requirements for dematerialisation, ecological investment and annual monitoring will help to knit the tiers of governance together through a clear and consistent strategy that allows flexibility and learning. Chapter 5 finds that the net-like supportive structure is not yet in place in most countries because of weak governance capacity to integrate at national spatial levels and the city-region. These deficiencies of governance capacity lead to gaps in deliberation between strategic or forward thinking, the policy generation stage and local level strategies, and the operational delivery of services. As a result, issues that deserve attention, but are outwith the current policy priorities, fall through the gaps between policy sectors.

This book has argued strongly that sub-national delivery agencies need to have the '*right geographical scope, powers and responsibilities*' to effectively take a leadership role on climate change. The organisational behaviour literature identifies clarity of responsibility and powers to act as being integral to implementation success. Many of the proactive local authorities on ecological sustainability have the autonomy to make their own policy decisions and are substantial land owners. This applies to local government in Sweden, Denmark, the Netherlands and Germany. Local government in Sweden, Denmark and Germany also have taxation powers. By comparison, the devolved governments in the UK (Greater London Authority, Welsh Assembly and Scottish Government) have certain legal competencies to make policy, sometimes through enacting secondary legislation, but have few powers to raise finance. A culture of strong political autonomy enables local administrations to set strong local targets (e.g. reduction of carbon emissions), take the leadership role in planning and implementation (e.g. develop high efficiency heating networks/combined heat and power), and introduce new laws (e.g. ban polluting vehicles).

Where political control is not devolved, lower tier governments have to make substantial efforts to partner and secure commitment from a crowded set of actors across the city-region to secure an integrated and more energy efficient transport system for local people. The effort to influence agendas of a wide set of actors often dissipates the energy and commitment of political leaders and civil servants. Having a mandated political institution at the city-region level will enable this functional level of governance to make highly political decisions and, with key city-region stakeholders, '*engage with a skilled technical debate about what might work for the region in transport terms'.* [This will] *build a sense of ownership of the strategy and commitment among stakeholders'* (Vigar 2006: 284).

For this to ensue, national and regional government must devolve sufficient legal and financial resources to city-region level governance structures, to take the leadership and responsibility for behaviour change and implement national resource minimisation policies.

8.3 CITY-REGION INTERVENTIONS AND INSTRUMENTS

The task of securing sustainable accessibility and connectivity through low energy spatial interaction has to be a localised task. Top-down strategies should only set the broad structuring principles of sustainability to secure low energy development pathways that provide equitable opportunities for all social groups. The city-region must be planned from the 'inside-out' by local people and not from afar. The particular sensitivities of local people and the geographic and infrastructure context cannot be ignored. Pan-European and national governments can set the general direction of change using fiscal and legal interventions but the detail of the sustainable future to be aimed for, and how to get there, must be decided locally. The city-region is the scale at which one organisation can efficiently plan a more sustainable transport system and integrate private and public investments to reduce the use of scarce resources and to add value to products, services and local environments. This requires structures that support problem solving and coordinated approaches that are continuously capable of absorbing corrections, to overcome inefficient, fragmented attempts to initiate change characterised by counterproductive roles. Structures with sufficient authority and resources are needed to communicate effectively up to higher tiers of government and down to residents, and horizontally with key actors/stakeholders across the city-region.

The city-region government must agree a broad framework for change across the city-region to control the location of strategic developments that will have a structural impact on travel behaviour and investment across the city-region. Development projects that shape urban form should be managed through the strategic plan to ensure that all the opportunities for exploiting integration, ecosystem investment, energy efficiency and community participation are captured. These may include the renewal of railway station neighbourhoods, inner city development, large scale mixed-used development, new housing projects and industrial parks. A four-pronged resource minimisation strategy is needed that:

- makes car travel no longer a necessity,
- brings the spatial opportunities closer to home;
- increases the energy efficiency of public transit; and
- provides information on the environmental and health impacts of travel choices.

Changing established practices can only be accomplished through a joint journey of learning with all stakeholders. This is a multi-scalar endeavour and involves long-term strategic planning to identify the low energy futures and a plan of implementation that has broad public support. City-region government must engage long and wide to identify appropriate (to the context) scenarios of desirable energy efficient futures and work out how to get there. This future visioning should be carried out with as many different constituencies in the local area as possible to identify lifestyle aspirations and how these can be influenced through waste reduction and energy efficiency principles. This is a key part of the awareness-raising task and involves explaining at a personal level the likely energy supply options and climate change scenarios society will face in the future. These visioning exercises provide the arena for debates amongst all city or settlement inhabitants of the goals they would like the city to achieve by 2050. These debates should take place in schools, community centres and neighbourhoods as well as in the city council chambers, with each constituency identifying how they could contribute to achieving resource efficiency (Factor 4, Factor 10 in Chapter 3).

Sustainable city-region futures depend on new ways for public and private sector services to work together to systematically articulate clear long-term strategies and short-term actions with detailed implementation plans supported by the local electorate. Transport and infrastructure is just one element of the total package. Backcasting techniques can help stakeholders to work back from the agreed end date targets to identify the behaviour changes that will be required to attain future goals and the government interventions which will be needed to support low energy lifestyles (Quist 2007).

Just as in Freiburg, frequent public transport services should link the neighbourhood to the city centre, to job locations and other commercial services, and to leisure opportunities and open spaces. At the city-region level the public transport interconnections should be organised so that local public transport services and cycleways connect to the mainline rail and coach services with secure cycle parking garaging. The need to own, and use, a car should be removed for everyday travel needs for all but transporting the very young, the very elderly and the disabled. Freiburg brands itself as the 'city of short trips'. To emulate this the sustainable travel infrastructure has to be pre-planned and not left as an afterthought, and should be a central preoccupation for land use planning, transport planning, healthcare, education and other community services working cooperatively.

These deliberations and future planning should be guided by the latest 'scientific' information on stocks of natural resources (viz. clean air, water quality, soil quality, tranquility, biomass, biodiversity and minerals), people resources (viz. skills, employment, health and fitness) and energy supply reserves. Sustainability is about using these resources to add value and is a long-term venture thus requiring investment in these resources as well. The resource stock implications of all decisions must be clear so that the social implications and the ecological effects are adequately recognised. Where information is not available, the precautionary principle should be employed so that present decisions should not restrict the scope of future action. Decisions should be framed by the broad sustainability principles of 'minimising resource use' and 'the polluter pays', the proximity principle and the best practicable environmental option. We must ensure that society can adapt to future challenges: '*solutions that succeed in serving more goals at the same time will invariably be the ones with the greatest chance of success*' (Bertolini *et al.* 2005: 209).

Few of the instruments implemented in the case study cities to enhance the sustainability of the local transport system are new and all have been widely deployed. What is new is the way they have been combined to maximise their positive synergistic effects and consistently applied over a period of time to have affect.

A practical and effective way of reducing the time benefits that cars enjoy and the negative emissions in urban areas is to slow down these vehicles to the speed of buses and bicycles. A zero tolerance attitude to speeding would need to be marketed and justified just as zero tolerance to smoking in public places was introduced. A second effective instrument for reducing CO_2 emissions and leveraging a more sustainable modal split is to reduce the space benefits enjoyed by motorised private vehicles through reducing the availability of on- and off-street car parking spaces and increasing the charges for parking. A staged approach might involve the use of differentiated fees as a first step to reflect the limited availability of public space in urban areas and to create incentives to reduce car use (e.g. free parking spaces at the periphery and high fees in the centre) (CEC 2007). This could be introduced to cover public spaces or municipality controlled parking places first followed by workplace car parking and then commercially run provision. An effective parking management policy across the city is the key to behaviour change, reducing CO_2 emissions and liberating space for other activities. The provision of shared garages '*that are only as accessible as public transport stops – at all origins and destinations*' (Knoflacher 2006: 398) would start to even out the accessibility to spatial opportunities by different modes. There would need to be strong incentives to use these centralised garages through a differentiated pricing system that charges a higher rate for the privilege of parking at home. The same principle of charging for parking should be introduced for all other spatial opportunities (work, shopping, leisure, etc).

Good neighbourhood design can reduce the demand for mobility through increasing densities and bringing spatial opportunities closer to the home (Dunatov 2008). This can be the central purpose of the spatial planning task marrying the planning for active travel, the design of energy efficient buildings with empowerment of the existing and future residents. Space normally reserved for roads and on-site parking spaces can be reallocated to cycling and walking, meeting places for residents and landscaped green spaces. This builds on the Dutch 'woonerf' and new urbanist ideas to implement the living streets design concept. In the new neighbourhoods in Freiburg the streets are designed as shared streets for play and access, cycle ways or pedestrian paths. On-street parking is only permitted on the main neighbourhood street. Garages are provided on the edge of each neighbourhood and on-site parking spaces are discouraged in new housing developments.

Researchers have found that the co-orchestration of dense land development with a mix of public and commercial facilities is correlated with neighbourhood live-ability (Jacobs 1961), the propensity to walk to shops (Spiekermann and Wegener 2003; Boarnet et al. 2008; Buehler 2008) and bus service profitability and service frequency (White 2002). The liveable neighbourhood concept relies on high quality public transport and cycling infrastructure to provide the dense web of links within neighbourhoods and between neighbourhood centres. Freiburg is branded as a city of 'short trips' enclosed within a 20 minute walk isochrone (Koehler 2009). If urban areas are to be retrofitted for short trips to occur, economic instruments (viz. road tolling and high parking charges) would need to be in place to gradually charge for the preferential access the car provides. There would need to be a grand vision and long-term action plan with wide discussion on what it would mean for different neighbourhoods and social groups. Road space would be reallocated to dedicated public transport lanes with more frequent services, dedicated cycle lanes and pave-ment widening. Car parking areas can be converted back to vegetation biomass or built on to increase the amount and range of housing in central areas of towns and cities, depending on which is the greater need. If the retrofitting is planned well it will have a momentum and dynamism of its own with an increase in local services and other spatial opportunities.

As part of the resource minimisation strategy, public transit must invest in low emission fleets, low emission zones in the city should be introduced to accelerate freight vehicle fleet turnover and the built environment equipped with the infrastruc-ture for electric and biofuel technologies. Denmark has started to implement an ambitious project of installing on-street electric vehicle charging points in urban areas. Most cities have focused on shifting the modal split towards collective trans-port modes. These involve relatively cost effective improvements to bus services including new energy efficient buses, new bus stops with raised platforms and real-time information, new timetables and routes, and new marketing/branding. If coordinated well these have positive immediate effects in the short term which can be sustained until longer-term interventions take effect.

Eco-driving techniques, workplace and school travel plans, and personalised travel planning are central to any marketing and communications programme to change travel behaviour. Personalised travel advice is the lynchpin of travel behaviour change since one-to-one engagement is necessary to explain the consequence of current transport behaviour and the personal and societal benefits of change to more energy efficient modes. Behaviour change initiatives need to be coordinated with incentives (viz. trial subsidised travel passes; free cycle training and maintenance, etc.) to start and sustain behaviour change even over the short term. Where these initiatives are not coordinated so as to reinforce their synergies the benefits will be dissipated, since continual reinforcement of low energy choices is required to embed new behaviour patterns across the palette of modal and lifestyle choices (see Chapter 7). The Malmö case study also demonstrates that effective monitoring of instrument effects on behaviour change is also important to inform future measures and to celebrate the success of any resource reduction achievements.

Behavioural change initiatives, working with individuals or households, to promote more energy efficient means of travel and driving style have shown promising reductions in energy consumption over the short term (6–18 months) where effectively monitored. Cairns et al. (2004) estimate that a behaviour change programme could cut traffic in urban areas by 3 per cent overall and 5 per cent in peak times if upscaled, while in the high intensity scenario these reductions are 14 and 21 per cent respectively. Well-designed instruments will have a significant impact during peak journeys to work, reducing congestion and carbon dioxide emissions (Anable 2005). Cairns et al. (2004) quote estimates that suggest, on average, every €1 spent on well-designed soft measures could bring about €10 of benefit in reduced congestion alone. Table 8.2 below summarises the instruments discussed above noting their relative implementation costs and acceptance by the public.

The system of land use development planning and management provides a mechanism to secure synergies across policy sectors and to resolve the conflicts over the distributional impacts of policies and projects. To do this effectively, the traditional land use planning system will have to take on a much wider agenda. The new tasks will include the coordination of the long-term health and integrity of natural ecosystems the city-region depends on, through protecting natural capital and ensuring resource consumption is at sustainable rates, and assessing development proposals against natural ecosystem and human quality of life impacts (Whitelegg 1997: 100). The development management and planning system also has an evangelical role in changing social behaviour through raising awareness of environmental destruction and waste and through promoting community action to improve local neighbourhoods.

Table 8.2 Key instruments of a sustainable transport programme

Instrument	Description	Public acceptability	Financial cost
Road tolling	Charge for use of road space for private vehicles	Medium	High initial costs, but long-term revenue stream
Vehicle taxation	Taxation of vehicles on basis of energy efficiency and pollution levels	High	Low
Speed enforcement policy	Zero-tolerance of existing speed limits	High	Low
Regulation of speed limits	Reduce speed limits on motorways and in residential areas	Low	Low
Parking charges	Match charges to the scarcity of spaces and that perceived to users	Low	Low
Parking provision	Reduce parking spaces	Low	Low
Play streets	Incorporate play streets in all new development, which allow occasional access for vehicles	Medium	Low
Land use regulation	Increase gross densities	Medium	Low
Reduce space available to cars in urban areas	Reallocate road space to dedicated public transport and cycling lanes; living streets	Medium	Low
Energy efficiency incentives	Tax incentives to encourage public transport use and cycling to work; low energy vehicle fleets	High	Medium
Behaviour change and training initiatives	Personalised travel advice (eco-driving, travel planning, etc.)	High	Low

Understanding of the public acceptability of demand management measures will be integral to the marketing of low energy lifestyles. This will entail more detailed understanding of public perception of comfort, access and security of alternative transport modes and the institutional barriers to change. Measures that discourage car travel are likely to receive significant initial opposition from the public and businesses and should be anticipated and an agreed marketing strategy implemented to deal with hostile reactions.

It is unlikely that society will have the capacity to deliver the energy and resource reduction targets to stabilise climate change in an equitable way unless the energy of local people is harnessed to bring about the behaviour change required. While governments must take the lead and provide the right incentive structures, local people caring about their own patch must be the driving force behind change.

In the short term, while there are some interventions that are sustainability proofed (for example, returning land to biomass and social interaction), achieving the connectivity between transport modes and spatial opportunities in an energy efficient way will be a learning process. Understanding the benefits that can be gained from different combinations of instruments in each specific context will have to be learned through trial and error to ensure that the benefits of more energy efficient strategies can be 'locked in' for future generations. Education and reinforcement of the benefits of energy and resource efficiency will need to be shared widely to secure public acceptability of behaviour change.

8.4 THE CHALLENGE AHEAD

Solving future challenges in a sustainable and equitable way requires a complete break from existing systems of decision making. Although there is no overriding consensus on whether city-region and metropolitan scale organisations require additional powers to formulate and implement plans to achieve significant resource consumption reductions (compare Salet *et al.* 2003 with O'Sullivan 1980 and Filion and McSpurren 2007), the cases studies show the value of strong city or unitary powers, such as finance raising, legal and development tools to facilitate the production of strategies and the successful implementation of projects. Tough resource efficiency targets laid down by higher tiers of government can be the mechanism to secure alliance building and collaboration between local stakeholders. The paradigm change, at the same time, requires strong local government with sufficient political stability to consistently implement the unfolding of the package of resource efficient measures over the long term. Decoupling resource consumption from economic growth trajectories entails a 'U' turn of gigantic proportions.

Discussing the new challenges for spatial planning at the city-region scale, Salet *et al.* (2003: 377) argue that:

> The institutional problem is not so much the fragmentation of policy actors as the disconnectedness of learning practices and policies. [...] The main challenges to metropolitan policies are to find the keys to unlock the connections between different spheres of action.

The administrative tasks to achieve this level of integration should not be underestimated. New ways of organising connectivity between spatial opportunities (Salet *et al.* 2003) and between policy sectors will require multidisciplinary teams of civil servants working with politicians, and resourcing through standing innovation networks composed of scientists, researchers, and local experts (practitioners and local residents) to ensure that mutual learning from other practice contexts is maximised. This will obviously require new working practices for local and central government officers and politicians and more policy engagement by scientists and academics. Dealing with future uncertainties will require more robust approaches to *ex ante* assessment of policy choices followed by *ex post* evaluation of economic, social and environmental impacts. Evaluation research should focus on understanding the mechanisms and dilemmas in cross-sectoral decision making and policy implementation for low energy futures. The implementation of demand management policies need to be underpinned by robust evidence of the motives that encourage individual and organisational responses to fiscal and regulatory instruments of government control. We still lack understanding of whether individuals and organisations will respond according to 'objective' economic rules of behaviour, will become carbon counters, or whether habitual institutionalised practices will be maintained (Spiekermann and Wegener 2003; Reynolds-Feighan 2005).

The scale of change required to really begin to make an impact on the global and local environment means that a deeper understanding of travel behaviour is needed. Behaviour change is the solution to the environmental, social and health issues society is facing and involves releasing individuals from the systems and norms around them (Anable *et al.* 2006). Government has to lead from the front and instigate change supported by knowledge makers and distributors, who should first understand and address the acceptability of change for decision makers (e.g. politicians and transport planners) as well as members of the public, so that the benefits to individuals of various elements of the package can be understood and marketed to them. Personal and social gains must be considered as one, rather than divorced as in the past. Specific tools will be needed to engage more effectively members of the public and local politicians on issues of climate change and travel behaviour so that the debates embrace reasoned actions that examine the whole process in terms of societal benefits, where all options and implications are considered.

The big question is: have we got the capacity to deliver significant resource reductions to meet the needs of individuals now and in the future? If we just examine the feasibility of meeting the current accepted stable level of 350 ppm of global greenhouse gas emission reductions by 2030, the verdict must be that collectively across Europe this target is unlikely to be met in time. Significant progress is being made to address the energy efficiency of building and vehicle design, which will have an impact by 2030, but the question is whether the impact will be widespread enough to make a substantial dent in our growing consumption demands. The 'business as usual' scenario suggests not. Transport behaviour has to be controlled more strongly through fiscal and regulatory tools so that the savings made in other sectors are not whittled away by our increasing demand to travel. The global greenhouse gas emissions from transport so far have not been factored into climate change adaptation plans. This must change and the transport sector must deliver their share of the carbon reduction targets. Most governments have been reluctant to break the link between the growth in average incomes and longer journeys since fuel duties provide a secure stream of income to the government exchequer. Coupled with fears of unpopularity and economic decline it has been difficult within government circles to create the momentum and motivation to change accepted ways of working. These fears of unpopularity also seem to have engendered a fear of open debate and transparency in decision making. There is wide acknowledgement that effective resource reduction will require a collaborative effort across government departments for delivery. The task seems too large to attempt successfully.

Much greater action is still required to make a real difference, and certainly to deliver transport's share of carbon reduction. As this book has suggested in Chapter 6, an easy 'win–win' first move would be to use public funds to achieve sustainable rates of resource efficiency. This would require the consistent use of transport project appraisal methodologies and funding schemes that promote energy and resource minimisation. By changing the rules of the game for infrastructure funding the onus is then placed on the scheme promoter to demonstrate through systematic appraisal whether the scheme proposed will induce a reduction in resource use as well as to assess impacts on demand, distances travelled and the environment. If consistently applied, this will lead to more schemes being promoted and justified on the basis of energy efficiency and travel time reductions for public transport and external health benefits.

Funding streams can have a powerful impact on the developments proposed by public and private sector agencies. It is hard to influence private sector spending but substantial change can be instigated through the use of public spending. The public sector can through joint working and complementary and synergistic actions create significant leverage through the use of legal and regulatory powers. The effectiveness of any government policy depends on the extent to which local planning agencies administer the sustainability and climate change strategies in the spirit of the government's original intent and interest. There are two possible solutions here: 1) using legal requirements for lower tiers of government to deliver required outcomes as in Swede; and 2) the signing of national–local or national–regional contracts (e.g. annual or five-yearly) for the delivery of specific projects as in France (Salet *et al*. 2003). But this does not necessarily mean that key strategic objectives will be realised. Filion and McSpurren (2007) highlight the importance of ensuring strategies are based on solid research and that on-going corrective measures during implementation should overcome any difficulties. To meet the global greenhouse gas emission target dates, national governments must proactively use their available powers to garner the energy and enthusiasm of all constituencies in society, including public interest groups in societal learning. Government should therefore enter on a mission of partnering and joint learning with delivery agencies setting up funded programmes '*to nurture successful initiatives and encourage their replication* [and] *establishing an on-going process of review and collaborative learning*' (Kohler 2007: 19).

Rather than relying on single issue solutions to societal problems a package of measures is required which should be implemented in stages, with the 'win–win' measures first to build up positive attitudes to change. These could be improvements to the public realm (parks, public squares), financial incentives to use public transport and to cycle to work, and improvements to public transport services. These are part of a long-term campaign to sell a new brand of 'low energy and healthy lifestyles' with the strapline '*Look after yourself and the planet*'. As in any promotional campaign for a new product, the benefits of the product have to be sold to consumers. The focus should be solely on the positive aspects of the package so that the public is aware of how they will gain and why collectively we need to consume less energy and fewer resources. An information and marketing campaign needs to be sustained throughout the implementation of the measures and until public acceptability has been gained. Information concerning the impact of resource consumption on the environment and social welfare, and awareness raising of alternative travel options should be made available to everyone using modern methods of communication (viz. Facebook, YouTube, flickr, podcast, twitter, etc.). Role models such as entertainment and sporting heroes should be used to reinforce healthy walking and cycling lifestyles. Involvement and communication can be encouraged through workplace and personal travel planning so that the aims and means of reaching healthier and more energy efficient lifestyles become clear to ordinary people. Peer group pressure also has a key role to play.

Within the context of this book, climate change adaptation and mitigation measures require a sophisticated mix of action across several policy areas including energy, construction, transport, food and waste. The EU policy of carbon trading, for example, in this context is focusing too narrowly on reducing emissions rather than reducing resource consumption and investment in ecosystem stability. The Council of Ministers intends to force the issue of pollution reduction by requiring the major industrial polluters to compete for pollution allowances through the auction of phase 2 Emissions Trading Scheme allowances. This narrow focus on the market and financial transactions (cost minimisation criteria) undermines efforts to ensure that all resources (natural, human, physical and financial) are used efficiently and not wasted.

There has been a recent trend across several EU states for the central executive to claw back the power and responsibilities to prioritise and approve strategic infrastructure decisions in an attempt to speed up the implementation of national policies on road and airport expansion, with some transport experts claiming that it is for central government to decide '*the balance between national needs and possible local impacts*' (Eddington 2006: 57). Despite the aspiration to consult widely on transport strategies, this centralisation will bypass longstanding administrative processes of deliberation and consensus, which although time consuming and expensive encourage engagement and debate, and provide legitimacy. The UK response to the cumbersome system of representative democracy is to remove strategic infrastructure decision making from the democratic system altogether and to rely on appointed 'experts' to interpret national policy, which neatly bypasses the elected representatives.

It appears that by removing the strategic infrastructure decisions from the democratic decision making arena will not only curtail discussion on the major 'structuring' decisions in the built environment but also close down one 'high profile' media arena that could provide an opportunity to openly debate what future sustainability might mean with as wide a section of civil society as possible. Participation in decision making empowers ordinary individuals, is a learning and awareness raising process and can engender commitment to neighbourhood quality. Opportunities to debate and discuss cannot be squandered, otherwise a fatalistic approach to affecting future change may take hold.

The question still remains of identifying the optimum package of interventions for each city-region that builds on the knowledge gained through impact measurement of 'innovatory' approaches, and which builds up resilience to global environmental hazards and strongly reduces pollutants and resource inputs. The way forward has been charted by the case studies in Chapter 7, through refocusing the legal and financial structuring rules to encourage resource reduction and through targets to embed low energy behaviours. Others must follow.

NOTES

1   The OECD is a global organisation that champions effective governance and works with national governments to improve economic development and living standards principally through the dissemination of research findings.

2   Personal communication with Michael Wegener.

3   The primary data on the case studies has been collected mainly by the author funded through the EU CIVITAS demonstration and evaluation programme and the UK research council (EPSRC) funded programme on sustainable urban environments.

4   2006 conversion rate.

REFERENCES

Adamowicz, W. (2003) Valuation of Environmental Externalities, in Hensher, D.A. and Button, K.J. (2003) *Handbook of Transport and the Environment*, Elsevier Ltd, pp. 375–389.

Akerman, P. (2006) Moving towards better health: A survey of transport authorities and primary care trusts in South West England, *Public Health,* **120**, 213–220.

Aldridge, S. (2008) Scotland: Riders fuel their own buses, *Biodiesel Magazine*, April 2008 [online]. Available at: http://www.biodieselmagazine.com/article.jsp?article_id=2253 (Accessed 04/09/2009).

Anable, J. (2005) 'Complacent Car Drivers' or 'Aspiring Environmentalists': Identifying travel behaviour segments using attitude theory, *Transport Policy,* **12**, 65–78.

Anable, J. and Bristow, A.L. (2007) *Transport and Climate Change*, CfIT, London.

Anable, J., Lane, B. and Kelay, T. (2006) *An Evidence Base Review of Public Attitudes to Climate Change and Transport Behaviour*, Department of Transport, London.

Anderson, D. (2006) *Costs and Finance of Abating Carbon Emissions in the Energy Sector*, Prepared for the Stern Review, Imperial College, London.

Anforth, E., Denton, A., Revill, M. and Barrett, J. (2008) *Regional Transport Policy and Climate Change: Is Being Good, Good Enough?*, paper presented to the Transport Practitioners Meeting 14–15 July, Reading, UK.

Apparicio, P. and Sequin, A. (2006) Measuring the Accessibility of Services and Facilities for Residents of Public Housing in Montreal, *Urban Studies,* **43** (1), 187–211.

Armelius, H. and Hultkrantz, L. (2006) The politico-economic link between public transport and road pricing: An ex-ante study of the Stockholm road-pricing trial, *Transport Policy,* **13**, 162–172.

Association of County Councils, Association of District Councils, and Association of Metropolitan Authorities (1996) *The Future of the Planning System: A Consultation Paper*, Association of Metropolitan Authorities, London

Atkins (2003) *Local Authority Survey. Final Report,* Department for Transport, London.

Atkins (2004) *Working with Weaker Local Authorities, Final Summary Report on Findings*, report to Department for Transport, London.

Atkins (2007) *Review of the Future Options for Local Transport Planning in England*, Department for Transport, London.

Audit Scotland (2006) *Scottish Executive: An Overview of the performance of Transport in Scotland*, Audit Scotland, Edinburgh.

Axhausen, K.W. (2005) Social Factors in future travel: A qualitative assessment, *Arbeitsbericht Verkehrs – und Raumplanung,* **294**, IVT, ETH Zürich, Zürich.

Bachrach, P.S. and Baratz, M.S. (1963) Decisions and non-decisions: an analytical framework, *American Political Science Review*, **57**, 642–51.

Baeten, G. (2000) The Tragedy of the Highway: Empowerment, Disempowerment and the Politics of Sustainability Discourses and Practices, *European Planning Studies*, **8** (1), 69–86.

Balcombe, R., Mackett, R., Paulley, N., Preston, J., Shires, J., Titheridge, H., Wardman, M. and White, P. (2004) *The demand for public transport: a practical guide*, TRL Report, **593**, TRL Ltd, Berkshire.

Balloch, S. and Taylor, M. (eds) (2001) *Partnership Working: Policy and Practice*, The Policy Press, Bristol.

Banister, D. (1996) Energy, quality of life and the environment: the role of transport, *Transport Reviews*, **16** (1), 23–35

Banister, D. (1997) Reducing the need to travel, *Environment and Planning B*, **24** (3) 437–449.

Banister, D. (2002a) *Transport Planning*, 2nd edition, Spon Press, London.

Banister, D. (2002b) *Overcoming Barriers to Implementation*, Paper for Presentation at the STELLA Focus Group 5 on Institutions, Regulations and Markets in Transportation Meeting in Brussels, 26–27 April.

Banister, D. (2005a) Overcoming barriers to the implementation of sustainable transport, in Rietveld, P. and Stough, R.R. (eds) (2005) *Barriers to Sustainable Transport: Institutions, Regulations and Sustainability*, Spon Press, Oxford, pp. 54–68.

Banister, D. (2005b) *Unsustainable Transport. City Transport in the new century*, Routledge, Oxford.

Banister, D. (2006) City Futures and Transport, *paper presented at Transport Planning – A Design Challenge? conference, 14–16 June, University of Amsterdam, Amsterdam.*

Banister, D. and Berechman, Y. (2001) Transport investment and the promotion of economic growth, *Journal of Transport Geography,* **9**, 209–218.

Banister, D. and Hickman, R. (2005) Reducing travel by design: What happens over time? in Williams, K. and Burton, E. (eds) *Spatial Planning, Urban Form and Sustainable Transport*, Ashgate, Aldershot, pp.102–119.

Banister, D. and Hickman, R. (2007) *How to Design a more Sustainable and Fairer Built Environment* (JU5): *Transport and Communications*, report to Foresight Intelligent Infrastructure Systems Project, Office of Science and Technology, London.

Barnardo's, Transport 2000 and the Local Government Association (2004) *Reduce Speed Now. Stop, Look and Listen: children talk about traffic*, Barnardos, Ilford, Essex.

Bart, I.L. (2009) Urban sprawl and climate change: A statistical exploration of cause and effect, with policy options for the EU, 2010, *Land Use Policy,* **27** (2), 283–292.

Barton, H. (2004) SOLUTIONS: Assessing Local Urban Form, *Paper for the first SOLUTIONS Symposium, December 2004.*

Bayliss, D. (1998) Integrated Transport and the Development Process, *Journal of Planning Law*, pp. 38–51.

Beale, H.B.R. (1993) Notes on the concepts of Secondary and Cumulative Impacts. *Newsletter of Committee A1F02*, TRB, X(2).

Begg, D. and Gray, D. (2004) Transport policy and vehicle emission objectives in the UK: is the marriage between transport and environment policy over? *Environmental Science and Policy*, **7**, 155–163.

Bell, M. (2006) Policy issues for the future intelligent road transport infrastructure, *Foresight Intelligent Infrastructure Systems Project* [online]. Available at: http://www.foresight.gov.uk/OurWork/CompletedProjects/IIS/Index.asp

Bertolini, L. (1999) Spatial Development Patterns and Public Transport: The Application of an Analytical Model in the Netherlands, *Planning Practice and Research,* **14** (2), 199–210.

Bertolini, L. (2003) Transport and cities: exploring the need for new planning approaches, *paper presented to the Third AESOP–ACSP conference, 11–14 July, Leuven.*

Bertolini, L. and Salet, W. (2003) Planning Concepts for Cities in Transition: Regionalization of Urbanity in the Amsterdam Structure Plan, *Planning Theory and Practice*, **4** (2), 131–146.

Bertolini, L., le Clercq, F. and Kapoen, L. (2005) Sustainable accessibility: a conceptual framework to integrate transport and land use plan-making. Two test-applications in the Netherlands and a reflection on the way forward, *Transport Policy,* **12**, 207–220.

Bhat, C.R., Handy, S., Kockelman, K., Mahmassani, H.S., Chen, Q. and Weston, L. (2000) *Accessibility Measures: Formulation Considerations and Current Applications*, Report 4938–2, prepared for the Texas Department of Transportation, September 2000.

Biddulph, M. (2001) *Home Zones: A Planning and Design Handbook*, Bristol.

Black, W.R. (2001) An unpopular essay on transportation, *Journal of Transport Geography*, **9**, 1–11.

Blandford, B., Grossardt, T., Ripy, J. and Bailey, K. (2008) Integrated Transportation and Land Use Scenario Modeling using Casewise Visual Evaluation: Case Study Jeffersonville, IN., *paper presented to the TRB 2007 Annual Meeting, Washington, USA.*

Boarnet, M.G. and Crane, R. (2001) *Travel by Design: The Influence of Urban Form on Travel,* Oxford University Press, Oxford.

Boarnet, M.G., Joh, K., Siembab, W., Fulton, W. and Nguyen, M.A. (2008) What Next for the Land Use–Travel Behavior Link? Re-Centering the Suburbs, *paper presented at the ACSP–AESOP conference, Chicago, July 2008.*

Bohme, K. (2002) *Nordic Echoes of European Spatial Planning*, Nordregio, Stockholm.

Bonsall, P., Shires, J., Link, H., Becker, A., Papaioannou, P. and Xanthopoulos, P. (2007) Complex Congestion Charging – An Assessment of Motorists' Comprehension and the Impact on their Driving Behaviour, *paper presented at the European Transport Conference, 17–19 October, Leeuwenhorst, Netherlands.*

Boucq, E. (2007) The Effects of Accessibility Gains on Residential Property Values in Urban Areas: The Example of the T2 Tramway in the Hauts-de-Seine Department, France, *paper presented at the European Transport Conference, 17–19 October, Leeuwenhorst, Netherlands.*

Bouwman, M.E. and Voogd, H. (2005) The urban–rural continuum and Dutch mobility patterns, *paper presented at AESOP congress, Vienna.*

Bovy, P., Orfeuil, J.P. and Zumkeller, D. (1993) Europe: A Heterogenous 'Single Market', in I. Solomon, P. Bovy and J.P. Orfeuil (eds) *A Billion Trips a Day, Tradition and Transition in European Travel Patterns,* Kluwer, Dordrecht, pp. 21–32.

Bradbury, A., Tomlinson, P. and Millington, A. (2007) Understanding the Evolution of Community Severance and its Consequences on Mobility and Social Cohesion over the Past Century, *paper presented at the European Transport Conference 17–19 October, Leeuwenhorst, Netherlands.*

Brake (2003) Brake Survey of 11–14 year olds [online]. Available at: http://www.brake.org.uk

Breheny, M. and Rookwood, R. (1993) Planning the Sustainable City Region, in Blowers, A. (ed.) *Planning for a Sustainable Environment,* Earthscan, London, pp. 150–189.

Brenner N. (1999) Globalisation as Reterritorialisation: The Re-scaling of Urban Governance in the European Union, *Urban Studies,* **36** (3), 431–451.

Bristow, A.L. and Nelthorpe, J. (2000) Transportation Project Appraisal in the European Union, *Transport Policy,* **7** (1), 51–60.

Brodde Makrí, M-C. (2002) Accessibility indices and planning theory in Sucharov, L.J., Brebbia, C.A. and Benitez, F.G. (eds) *Urban Transport VIII: Urban Transport and the Environment in the 21st Century,* WIT Press.

Buehler, R. (2008) Towards More Sustainable Transportation: Do Policies Matter?, *paper presented at the ACSP–AESOP conference, July 2008, Chicago.*

Buunk, W. (2003) *Discovering the Locus of European Integration,* Eburon, Delft.

Byron, H., Treweek, J.R., Sheate, W.R. and Thompson, S. (2000) Road developments in the UK: An analysis of Ecological Assessment in EISs produced between 1993–1997, *Journal of Environmental and Planning Management,* **43** (1), 71–97.

Cabinet Office (2000) *Reaching Out: the role of central government at regional and local level,* Central Office for Information, London.

Cairns, S., Sloman, L., Newson, C., Anable, J., Kirkbride, A. and Goodwin, P. (2004) *Smarter Choices – Changing the Way We Travel. Final Report of the Research Project – The Influence of Soft Factor Interventions on Travel Demand,* Report to the Department for Transport, London.

Cairns, S., Sloman, L., Newson, C., Anable, J., Kirkbride, A. and Goodwin, P. (2008) Smarter Choices: Assessing the Potential to Achieve Traffic Reduction Using 'Soft' Measures, *Transport Reviews,* **28** (5), 593–618.

Calthorpe, P. (1993) *The next American Metropolis. Ecology, community and the American Dream*, Princetown Architectural Press, New York.

Calthorpe, P. and Fulton, W. (2001) *The Regional City. Planning for the End of Sprawl*, Island Press, Washington D.C.

Calthrop, E. (2005) Institutional issues in on-street parking, in Rietveld, P. and Stough, R.R. (eds) (2005) *Barriers to Sustainable Transport. Institutions, regulation and sustainability*, Spon Press, London, pp. 130–142.

Campaign for Better Transport (2002) *UK Bus Priorities Modal Shift* [online]. Available at: http://www.cfit.gov.uk/docs/2002/psbi/lek/pdf/appendix6.pdf (Accessed 16/07/2008).

Campaign for Better Transport (2008). *Getting Transport Right* [online]. Available at: http://www.bettertransport.org.uk/node/927 (Accessed 08/07/2008).

Canning, S., Leitham, S., Dobson, A. and Simmonds, D. (2007) Transport, Economic Development and Regeneration, *paper presented at the European Transport Conference, 17–19 October, Leeuwenhorst, Netherlands.*

Cervero, R. (1988) Landuse mixing and suburban mobility, *Transportation Quarterly*, **42**, 429–446.

Cervero, R. (1994) Transit-based housing in California: evidence on ridership impacts, Transport Policy, **1** (3) 174–183

Cervero, R. (1996) Mixed land uses and commuting: Evidence from the American Housing Survey. *Transportation Research A*, **30** (5), 361–77.

Cervero, R. (2001) Efficient Urbanisation: Economic Performance and the Shape of the Metropolis, *Urban Studies*, **38** (10), 1651–1671.

Cervero, R. (2002) Induced Travel Demand: Research Design, Empirical Evidence and Normative Policies, *Journal of Planning Literature,* **17** (1), 3–32 [online]. Available at: http://sagepub.com (Accessed 15/04/2008).

Cervero, R. and Gorham, R. (1995) Commuting in transit versus automobile neighbourhoods, *Journal of the American Planning Association,* Spring 95, **61** (2), 210–231. [online]. Available at: http://weblinks2.epnet.com/DeliveryPrintSave.asp?tb +1&_ ua=bo+B_+shn+1+db+buh... (Accessed 12/08/2004).

Chang, Ha-Joon, (2002) *Globalization, Economic Development and the Role of the State*, Zed Books, London.

Chapin, F.S. and Kaiser, E.J. (1979) *Urban Land Use Planning*, 3rd edition, University of Illinois Press, Urbana, Chicago.

Chatterjee, K., Harman, R. and Lyons, G. (2004) *Local Strategic Partnerships. Transport and Accessibility*, Report to the Department of Transport, London.

Cheung, F. (2007) Nationwide Implementation of Public Transport Smartcard in the Netherlands, *paper presented at the European Transport Conference, 17–19 October, Leeuwenhorst, Netherlands.*

Child Accident Prevention Trust (2004) *Child road accidents factsheet [online].* Available at: http://www.capt.org.uk

City of York Council (2006) *Local Transport Plan 2006–2011*, City of York, York, UK.

City of York Council (2009) York – a cycling city [online]. Available at: http://www.york. gov.uk/transport/cycling/cyclingcity/about/

City of Malmö (2003a) *Environment Department*, Folder no. 7, Miljöförvaltningen, Malmö.

City of Malmö (2003b) *The Streets and Parks Department*, Folder no. 4, Miljöförvaltningen, Malmö.

City of Malmö (2006) *Annual Report 2005*, Miljöförvaltningen, Malmö.

Civilising Cities (2003) *The 'Civilising Cities' Initiative An Overview: 1999–2002*, Draft version 2, University of Westminster Transport Studies Group.

CIVITAS SMILE (2005) *Inception report*, Streets and Parks Department, Miljöförvaltningen, Malmö.

Clark, J.M., Hutton, B.J., Burnett, N., Hathway, A. and Harrison, A. (1991) *The appraisal of community severance*, Contractor Report 135, Transport and Road Research Laboratory, Crowthorne.

Cole-Hamilton, I. (2002) *Something good and fun: children's and parents' views on play and out-of-school provision*, Children's Play Council, London

Commission for Integrated Transport (2001) *European Best Practice in Delivering Integrated Transport*, Commission for Integrated Transport, London.

Commission for Integrated Transport (2003) *Second Assessment Report: 10 Year Transport Monitoring Strategy*, Commission for Integrated Transport, London.

Commission of the European Communities (2004) *Towards a thematic strategy on the urban environment*, COM (2004) 60 final, European Commission, Brussels.

Commission of the European Communities (2007a) *An Energy Policy for Europe*, COM (2007) final, European Commission, Brussels.

Commission of the European Communities (2007b) *Green Paper. Towards a New Culture for Urban Mobility*, COM (2007) 551, European Commission, Brussels.

Commission of the European Communities (2009) *White Paper: Adapting to Climate Change*, COM (2009) 147/4 [online]. Available at: http://ec.europa.eu/health/ph_ threats/climate/docs/com_2009_147_en.pdf

Committee for Spatial Development (1999) *European Spatial Development Perspective*, Final Draft, Luxembourg, Commission of the European Community.

Cooper (2003) *Draft Guidance on Cumulative Effects Assessment of Plans* [online]. Available at: http://www.env.ic.ac.uk/research/epmg/CooperCEAGuidance.pdf

Coppens, T. (2006) Effectiveness and efficiency in realising urban regeneration projects in Flanders; a neo-institutional perspective, *Paper presented to the AESOP PhD workshop, July, Bristol.*

Council for Environmental Quality (1997) *Considering Cumulative Effects Under the National Environmental Policy Act* [online]. Available at: http://www.nepa.gov/ nepa/ccenepa/ccenepa.htm

Council for the Protection of Rural England (2003) *Economic Impact Reports for Road Schemes*, Council for the Protection of Rural England, London.

Council of Ministers (2001) *Strategy for Integrating Environment and Sustainable Development into the Transport Policy,* adopted by the Ministers responsible for Transport and Communications at meeting of the European Union's Council of Ministers, April 4–5, Luxembourg.

Council of the European Union (2001) *European Council meeting in Gothenburg: Presidency Conclusions 16 June 2001*, Brussels [online]. Available at: http://ue.eu.int/uc/Docs/cms_Data/docs/pressData/en/ec/00200-rl.en1.pdf.

Council of the European Union (2009) *Council adopts climate-energy legislative package*, Brussels, 6 April, 8434/09 (Presse 77).

Cowell, R. and Martin, S. (2003) The joy of joining up: modes of integrating the local government modernisation agenda, *Environment and Planning C: Government and Policy,* **21**, 159–179.

Crane, R. and Crepeau, R. (1998) Does neighborhood design influence travel? A behavioral analysis of travel diary and GIS data, *Transportation Research, Part D: Transport and Environment,* **3** (4), 225–238.

Crass, M. (2001) Presentation of the Key Preliminary Findings of the ECMT–OECD Project on Implementing Sustainable Urban Travel Policies (1998–2001), *paper presented to World Bank Urban Transport Strategy Review Consultation Workshop, February 28–March 1, Budapest, Hungary.*

Curtis, C. and Headicar, P. (1994) *The Location of New Residential Development: Its Impact on Car-Based Travel I. Research Design & Methodology*, Oxford Brookes University working Paper No. 154.

Curtis, C. and Olaru, D. (2007) Travel Minimisation and the Neighbourhood, *paper presented at the European Transport Conference, 17–19 October, Leeuwenhorst, Netherlands.*

Cycling England (2009) Cycling News. It pays to invest in bikes *Cycling England* tells councils [online]. Available at: http://www.bikeforall.net/news.php?articleshow=613

Danish Ministry of Environment (1997) National Planning Report, Ministry of Environment, Copenhagen.

David Simmonds Consultancy, University of Leeds, MVA Consultancy and Oxford Brookes University (1998) *Accessibility as a Criterion for Project and Policy Appraisal*, Department of Environment, Transport and the Regions, London.

Davies, P. (2003) *The Magenta Book. Chapter 1: What is Policy Evaluation?,* Background Document, Cabinet Office Strategy Office, London.

Dawkins, R. (1989) *The Selfish Gene*, Oxford University Press, Oxford.

De Boer (2007) The Modern Urban Dus. Accessible, Attractive and Efficient? Integrated accessibility as a challenge, *paper presented at the European Transport Conference 17–19 October, Leeuwenhorst, Netherlands.*

De Bok, M. and Sanders, F. (2005) Firm Relocation and Accessibility of Locations, Empirical Results from the Netherlands, *Transportation Research Record, Journal of the Transportation Research Board, No. 1902,* Transportation Research Board of the National Academies, Washington, D.C., 35–43.

De Groot, J. and Steg, L. (2006) Impact of transport pricing on quality of life, acceptability, and intentions to reduce car use: An exploratory study in Five European countries, *Journal of Transport Geography,* **14**, 263–270.

De Jong, M., Lalenis, K. and Mamdouh, V. (2002) *The theory and practice of institutional transplantation: Experiences with the transfer of policy institutions,* Kluwer Academic Press, Dordrecht.

Department for Transport (2003) *Road casualties in Great Britain 2002,* DfT, London.

Department for Transport (2004a) *Accessibility Planning in Local Transport Plans: Technical Guidance,* Department of Transport, London.

Department for Transport (2004b). *Feasibility Study of Road Pricing In The UK* [online]. Available at: http://www.dft.gov.uk

Department for Transport (2004c) Road casualties in Great Britain: main results: 2003, *Transport Statistics Bulletin* SB(04)30 [online]. Available at: http://csrb.drdni.gov.uk/statistics/details.asp?publication_id=92 (Northern Ireland statistics)

Department for Transport (2004d) *Transport Analysis Guidance* [online]. Available at: www.webtag.org.uk (Accessed 17/11/2004).

Department for Transport (2004e) *Walking and Cycling: successful schemes,* DfT, London.

Department for Transport (2005) Cambridgeshire Guided Busway: Inspectors Report, [online]. Available at : http://www.dft.gov.uk/pgr/twa/ir/cambridgeshireguidedbuswayin5647?page=7

Department for Transport (2006a) *Transport Statistics Bulletin: National Travel Survey 2006,* DfT, London.

Department for Transport (2006b) *Transport Appraisal, Wider Economic Benefits and Impacts on GDP,* DfT, London.

Department for Transport (2007a) *Transport Statistics GB 2007,* DfT, London.

Department for Transport (2007b) *Local Transport Planning. The Next Steps. A consultation,* DfT, London.

Department for Transport (2007c) *Long Term Process and Impact Evaluation of the Local Transport Plan Policy,* Prepared by Atkins in association with Price Waterhouse Coopers and Warwick Business School.

Department for Transport (2009) *NATA Refresh. Appraisal for a Sustainable Transport System,* DfT, London.

Department of the Environment (1993) *Reducing Transport Emissions Through Planning,* HMSO, London.

Department of Environment, Transport and the Regions (1998a) *Sustainable Development Policy Statement*, HMSO, London.

Department of the Environment, Transport and the Regions (1998b) *Guidance on the new approach to appraisal*, DETR, London.

Department of Environment, Transport and the Regions (1999a) *Good practice guide on sustainability appraisal of regional planning guidance* [online]. Available at: http://www.planning.dtlr.gov.uk/gpgsarpg

Department of Environment, Transport and the Regions (1999b) *Planning Policy Guidance Note 12, Development plans*, HMSO, London.

Department of the Environment, Transport and the Regions (2000a) *Transport 2010*, DETR, London.

Department of Environment, Transport and the Regions (2000b) *Tomorrow's roads: safer for everyone*, DETR, London.

Department of Environment, Transport and the Regions (2000c) *Local Quality of Life Counts: A handbook for a Menu of Local Indicators of Sustainable Development*, TSO, London.

Department of the Environment, Food and Rural Affairs (2005) *Climate change and the greenhouse effect: a briefing from the Hadley Centre* [online]. Available at: http://www.metoffice.com/research/hadleycentre/pubs/brochures/2005/climate_greenhouse.pdf

Department of the Environment, Food and Rural Affairs (2006) *The Climate Change Programme*, DEFRA, London.

Department of the Environment, Transport and the Regions, and Transport, Research and Consultancy (2000) *Social Exclusion and the Provision and Availability of Public Transport*, DETR, London.

Department of Trade and Industry (2007) *The Energy White Paper*, DTI, London.

Dieleman, F.M., Dijst, M. and Gurghouwt, G. (2002) Urban Form and Travel Behaviour: Micro-level Household Attributes and Residential Context, *Urban Studies*, **39** (3), 507–527.

Dijst, M., de Jong, T. and van Eck, J.R. (2002) Opportunities for transport mode change: an exploration of a disaggregated approach, *Environment and Planning B: Planning and Design*, **29**, 413–430.

Directorate General for Energy and Transport (2007) *Towards a New Culture for Urban Mobility*, European Commission, Brussels.

DISTILLATE (2006) Project E Funding Workshop, 19 October 2006, accessed from www.distillate.ac.uk

Docherty, I. (2000) *Making Tracks: The politics of local transport*, Ashgate, UK.

Docherty I., Shaw, J. and Gather M. (2004) State intervention in contemporary transport, *Journal of Transport Geography*, **12**, 257–264.

Donovan, R.G., Hunt, D.V.L. and Porter, E.J. (2005) Barriers to achieving sustainability: reflections from Eastside, Birmingham. *Proc. SUE: Vision into Action Conference, March 2005, Birmingham, UK*.

DTZ Pieda (2004) *Economic Effects of Road Infrastructure Improvements*, DTZ Pieda, Edinburgh.

Du, H. and Mulley, C. (2007) *Transport Accessibility and Land Value: a case study of Tyne and Wear*, RICS Research paper series, **7** (3), RICS, London.

Dudley, G. (2003) 'Can accessibility planning gel transport and locational policies?' *Local Transport Today*, 2 October 2003, pp. 10–11.

Dunatov, A. (2008) Where has the 'Sustainability' gone in Transport Planning?, *paper presented to the Transport Practitioners Meeting, June, Reading, UK.*

Dupuy, G. (1999) From the 'magic circle' to 'automobile dependence': measurements and political implications, *Transport Policy*, **6**, 1–17.

Echenique, M. (2005) Mobility and Income, *paper presented to the SOLUTIONS conference, December 2005, Cambridge.*

ECOTEC (1993) Reducing transport emissions through land use planning, London, HMSO.

Eddington, R. (2006) *The Eddington Transport Study. The case for action: Sir Roy Eddington's advice to Government*, HM Treasury, London.

Edén, M., Falkheden, L. and Malbert, B. (2000) The Built Environment and Sustainable Development: Research Meets Practice in a Scandinavian Context, *Planning Theory & Practice*, **1** (2), 260–272.

Egebäck, K.E., Ahlvik, P. and Westerholm, R. (1997) *Emissionsfaktorer för fordon drivna med fossila respektive alternativa bränslen*, The Swedish transport and Communications Research Board, Stockholm.

Elander, I., Alm, E.L., Malbert, B. and Sandström, U.G. (2005) Biodiversity in Urban Governance and Planning: Examples from Swedish Cities, *Planning Practice and Research*, **6** (3), 283–301.

Emmerson, G. (2007) Statutory quality partnerships – a contradiction in terms?, *Local Transport Today*, **463**, 21.

Energy Savings Trust (2005) *Ecodriving Manual,* accessed from www.carplus.org.uk

European Automobile Manufacturers' Association (ACEA) (2009) *Overview of CO₂ Based Motor Vehicle Taxes in the EU* [online]. Available at: http://www.acea.be/images/uploads/files/20090428_C02_taxation_overview.pdf (Accessed 14/09/2009).

European Commission (1997) *Amended EIA Directive* (97/11/EC).

European Commission (1999) *European Spatial Development Perspective. Towards Balanced and Sustainable Development of the Territory of the European Union*, Office for Official Publications of the European Communities, Luxembourg.

European Commission (2001a) *European Transport Policy for 2020: Time to Decide* COM (2001) 370, Office for Official Publications of the European Communities, Luxembourg [online]. Available at: http://www.europa.eu.int/comm/off/white/index_en.htm.

European Commission (2001b) *INTERNAT project final report*, Office for Official Publications of the European Communities, Luxembourg.

European Commission (2001c) *Directive 2001/42/EC on the assessment of the effects of certain plans and programmes on the environment,* Official Journal of the European Communities, 21/07/2001, L197/30.

European Commission (2003) *External Costs. Research results on socio-environmental damages due to electricity and transport,* Report no. EUR 20198, DG Research, Brussels/Office for Official Publications of the European Communities, Luxembourg.

European Commission (2005) *Communication from the Commission to the European Parliament and the Council on a Thematic Strategy on the Urban Environment,* COM (2005) 718 final, Brussels.

European Commission (2006) *Keep Europe Moving. Sustainable Mobility for our Continent. Mid-term review of the European Commission's 2001 White Paper,* Office for Official Publications of the European Communities, Luxembourg.

European Commission (2007a) *Eurostat statistical books. Panorama of Transport,* Office for Official Publications of the European Communities, Luxembourg.

European Commission (2007b) *An Energy Policy for Europe* [online]. Available at: http://eur-ex.europa.eu/smartapi/cgi/sga_doc?smartapi!celexplus!prod!DocNumb er&lg=en&type_doc=COMfinal&an_doc=2007&nu_doc=1

European Commission (2008) *Communication from the Commission to the European Parliament and the Council on Greening Transport,* COM (2008) 433 final, Brussels.

European Commission (2009) *Panorama of Transport,* Office for Official Publications of the European Communities, Luxembourg.

European Commission Directorate General Environment (2004a) *EU Expert Group on the Urban Environment Meeting of 24 September 2004 Minutes* [online]. Available at: http://ec.europa.eu/environment/urban/pdf/minutes_04_09_24.pdf

European Commission Directorate General Environment (2004b) *EU Expert Group on Transport and the Environment, Working Group on Sustainable Urban Transport,* Final report.

European Conference of Ministers of Transport (2001) *Implementing Sustainable Urban Travel Policies. Key Messages for Governments,* CEMT/CM (2001) 12/FINAL.

European Conference of Ministers of Transport (2007) *Cutting CO_2 Emissions from Transport. What Progress?,* ECMT, Paris.

European Conference of Ministers of Transport /OECD (2002) *Implementing Sustainable Urban Travel Policies: Key Messages for Governments,* Final Report, ECMT, Paris.

European Environment Agency (2003) *Overall energy efficiency and specific CO_2 emissions for passenger and freight transport,* Indicator factsheet, TERM 2003, EEA.

European Environment Agency (2004) *Ten key transport and environment issues for policy-makers* [online]. Available at: http://reports.eea.eu.int/TERM2004/en/ TERM2004web.pdf (Accessed 24/03/2005).

European Environment Agency (2005) *European Environment: State and Outlook,* State of the Environment Report No. 1/2005 [online]. Available at: http://www. eea.europa.eu/publications/state_of_environment_report_2005_1   (Accessed 07/09/2009).

European Environment Agency (2006a) *Urban sprawl in Europe, the ignored challenge,* EEA Technical Report No. 10/2006, Office for Official Publications of the European Communities, Luxembourg.

European Environment Agency (2006b) *Greenhouse gas emissions trends and projections in Europe,* EEA Technical Report No 9/2006, Office for Official Publications of the European Communities, Luxembourg.

European Environment Agency (2007) *Transport and environment: on the way to a new common transport policy. TERM 2006: indicators tracking transport and environment in the European Union,* Office for Official Publications of the European Communities, Luxembourg.

European Environment Agency (2008a) *Impacts of Europe's changing climate* [online]. Available at: http://www.eea.europa.eu/themes/climate (Accessed May 2009).

European Environment Agency (2008b) *Climate for a transport change. TERM 2007: indicators tracking transport and environment in the European Union,* EEA:Copenhagen.

European Environment Agency (2008c) *Success stories with the road transport sector on reducing greenhouse gas emissions and producing ancillary benefits,* EEA Technical Report No 2/ 2008, Office for Official Publications of the European Communities, Luxembourg.

European Local Transport Information Service (ELTIS) (2007) Goods delivery by carg tram: efficient, clean and safe, Amsterdam, Netherlands [online]. Available at: http://www.eltis.org/cs_search.phtml?search_start=1&concept_id=3

European Parliament (2009) *EU Climate Change and Energy Package,* [online]. Available at: http://ec.europa.eu/environment/climat/climate_action.htm

European Union (2009) *Energy, transport and environment indicators,* Publications Office of the European Union, Luxembourg.

Evans, A. (1990) Competition and the structure of local bus markets, *Journal of Transport Economics and Policy,* **24** (3), 255–82.

Evans, R., Guy, S. and Marvin, S. (2001) Views of the City: multiple pathways to sustainable transport futures, *Local Environment,* **6** (2), 121–133.

Evans, S.R. and Hutchins, M. (2002) The Development of Strategic Transport Assets in Greater Manchester and Merseyside: Does Local Governance Matter?, *Regional Studies,* **36** (4), 429–438.

Faludi, A and Van der Valk, A. (1995) *Rule and Order: Dutch Planning Doctrine in the Twentieth Century,* Kluwer Academic Publishers, Dordrecht.

Farthing, S., Winter, J. and Coombes, T. (1997) Travel behaviour and local accessibility to services and facilities, in Jenks, M., Burton, E. and Williams, K. (eds) *The Compact City. A Sustainable Urban Form?*, E & FN Spons, London, pp. 181–189.

Federal Ministry of Transport, Building and Urban Development (BMVBS) (2009) *Heavy goods vehicle tools in Germany* [online]. Available at: http://www.bmvbs.de/en/ Transport/Roads/HGV-toll-,2075.978565/Heavy-goods-vehicle-tolls-in-G.htm

Feitelson, E. (2001) Introducing environmental equity dimensions into the sustainable transport discourse: issues and pitfalls, *Transportation Research,* **7D** (2) 99–118.

Feitelson, E. (2002) Packaging Policies to Address Environmental Concerns, in Hensher, D.A. and Button, K.J. (2003) *Handbook of Transport and the Environment,* Elsevier Ltd, 757–769.

Ferguson, E. (2000) *Travel Demand Management and Public Policy*, Ashgate, Aldershot.

Fernie, P. and McKinnon, A.C. (2003) The grocery supply chain in the UK: improving efficiency in the logistics network, *The International Review of Retail, Distribution and Consumer Research,* **13** (2), 161–174.

Ferrary, C. (2008) What practical steps can we take now to reduce Greenhouse Gas Emission from Transport, *paper presented to the Transport Practitioners Meeting 14–15 July, Reading, UK.*

Filion, P. and McSpurren. K. (2007) Smart Growth and Development Reality: The Difficult Co-ordination of Land Use and Transport Objectives, *Urban Studies,* **44** (3), 501–523.

Fischer, T.B. (2009) *On the role(s) of (strategic) environmental assessment in 'greening' decision making*, Copernicus lecture, 2 March, Utrecht University.

Flyvberg, B. (1998) *Rationality and Power: Democracy in Practice*, University of Chicago Press, Chicago, IL.

Frank, J.D. and Engelke, P.O. (2001) The Built Environment and Human Activity Patterns: Exploring the Impacts of Urban Form on Public, *Journal of Planning Literature,* 16, 202–218.

Frank, L.D. and Pivo, G. (1995) Impacts of mixed use and density on utilization of three modes of travel: single-occupant vehicle, transit, and walking, *Transportation Research Record,* **1466**, 44–52.

Franke, J. (2007) The Revival of Rail Freight Transport in the Netherlands?, *paper presented at the European Transport Conference, 17–19 October, Leeuwenhorst, Netherlands.*

Freund, B. (2003) The Frankfurt Rhine-Main region, in Salet, W., Thornley, A. and Kreukels, A. (eds) (2003) *Metropolitan Governance and Spatial Planning. Comparative case studies of European City-Regions,* Spon Press, London.

Fürst, D. and Rudolph, A. (2003) The Hanover metropolitan region, in Salet, W., Thornley, A. and Kreukels, A. (eds) (2003) *Metropolitan Governance and Spatial Planning. Comparative case studies of European City-Regions*, Spon Press, London.

FWTM Freiburg Wirtschaft Touristik und Messe (2009) *Freiburg Green City. Approaches to Sustainability*, FWTM, Freiburg, www.freiburg.de/greencity.

Gaffron, P., Benecke, J. and Flämig, H. (2007) Hinterland Traffic of the Port of Hamburgh. Keeping the Gateway Open, *paper presented at the European Transport Conference, 17–19 October, Leeuwenhorst, Netherlands.*

Gaffon, P., Hine, J.P. and Mitchell, F. (2001) *The Role of Transport in Social Exclusion in Urban Scotland: Literature Review*, Central Research Unit, Scottish Executive Development Department, Edinburgh.

Gärling, T., Loukopoulos, P. and Lee-Gosselin, M. (2003) Public attitudes, in Hensher D.A. and Button K.J. (eds) *Handbook of transport and the environment,* Elsevier, Amsterdam.

Geerlings, H. and Stead, D. (2002) The integration of land use planning, transport and environment in European policy and research, *Transport Policy,* **10** (3), 187–196

Geurs, K.T. and van Wee, B. (2006) Ex-post evaluation of Thirsty years of compact urban development in the Netherlands, *Urban Studies,* **43** (1), 139–160.

Giddens, A. (1984) *The Constitution of Society,* Polity Press, Cambridge.

Giddens, A. (1990) *The Consequences of Modernity*, Polity Press, Cambridge.

Gifford, J. (2005) A research agenda for institutions, regulations and markets in transportation and infrastructure, in Rietveld, P. and Stough, R.R. (eds) (2005) *Barriers to Sustainable Transport. Institutions, regulation and sustainability*, Spon Press, London, pp. 102–110.

Gilbert, R. (2005) *Defining Sustainable Transport*, prepared for Transport Canada, Centre for Sustainable Transportation, Toronto.

Giuliano, G. and Narayan, D. (2004) A comparison of work and non-work travel: The US and Great Britain, in Rietveld, P. and Stough, R.R. (eds) *Barriers to Sustainable Transport,* E & FN Spon Press, London.

Giuliano, G. and Small, K. (1993) Is the journey to work explained by urban structure?, *Urban Studies,* **30** (9), 1485–1500.

Glaister, S. and Graham, D. (2006) Proper Pricing for Transport Infrastructure and the Case of Urban Road Congestion, *Urban Studies,* 43 (8), 1395–1418.

Glasson, J., Therivel, R. and Chadwick, A. (1999) *Introduction to Environmental Impact Assessment Principles and Procedures, Process, Practice and Prospects*, UCL, London.

Goddard, H.G (1997) Using Tradeable Permits to Achieve Sustainability in the World's Large Cities, *Environmental and Resource Economics,* **10**, 63–99.

Golob, T.F. and McNally, M.G. (1997) A model of household interactions in activity participation and the derived demand for travel, *Transportation Research,* 31B, 177–194.

Goodwin, P. (1996) Road Traffic Growth and the Dynamics of SustainableTransport Policies, in Cartledge, B. (ed.) *Transport Policy and the Environment,* Oxford University Press, Oxford.

Goodwin, P. (2003) Unintended Effects of Policies, in Hensher, D.A. and Button, K.J. (2003) *Handbook of Transport and the Environment*, Elsevier Ltd, pp. 604–613.

Goodwin, P. (2004). Solving congestion (1997 inaugural lecture), in Terry, F. (ed.) *Turning the Corner? A Reader in Contemporary Transport Policy*, Blackwell Publishing.

Gordon, P. and Richardson, H.W. (1995) Geographic Factors Explaining Worktrip Length Changes. Chapter 2 in 1990 NPTS Report Series: Special Reports on Trip and Vehicle Attributes, U.S. Government Printing Office, Washington, D.C., U.S. Department of Transportation, Federal Highway Administration .

Gordon, P., Kumar, A. and Richardson, H.W. (1989) Gender differences in metropolitan travel behaviour, Regional Studies, **23** (6), 499–510.

Government Offices of Sweden (2001) *Environmental Code: Ordinance (2001: 527) on Environmental Quality Standards on Ambient Air* [online]. Available at: http://www.sweden.gov.se/sb/d/5400/a/43486 (Accessed 15/01/2008).

Gradinger, K. (no date) *Streets Wiki Beta* [online]. Available at: http://www.livablestreets.com/streetswiki/vauban-freiburg-germany (Accessed 30/07/2009).

Graham, S. and Marvin, S. (2001) Splintering Urbanism. Networked infrastructures, technological mobilities and the urban condition, Routledge, London.

Gray, D. (2009) Rural Transport: Finding an Angry Crofter, *paper presented at Transport Infrastructure workshop, 26 March, Edinburgh, Scotland.*

Gray, D., Anable, J., Illingworth, L. and Graham, Wendy (2006) *Decoupling the link between economic growth, transport growth and carbon emissions in Scotland*, Scottish Executive, Edinburgh.

Grayling, A., Hallam, K., Graham, D., Anderson, R. and Glaister, S. (2002) *Streets ahead: safe and liveable streets for children,* Institute for Public Policy Research, London.

Greater London Authority (2004) *The London Plan*, Greater London Authority, London.

Greater London Authority (2007) *Press Release. Reprieve for small businesses as Mayor suspends phase three of Low Emission Zone*, 2–2–2009 056.

Gudmundsson, H. (2000) Driving Forces of Mobility, in Dolin, J., Ehlers, P. and Poulsen, S. (eds) *Geografiske Verdensbilleder*, Gyldendal, Copenhagen.

GUIDEMAPS (2003) *Deliverable D2: Review of common practice in decision-making in local and regional transport schemes. User needs for a good practice handbook, Gaining Understanding of Improved Decision Making and Participation Strategies,* EU contract no. GRD2-2000-30128.

Grübler, A. (1990) *The Rise and Fall of Infrastructures, Dynamics of Evolution and Technological Change in Transport*, Physica-Verlag, Heidelberg.

Grübler, A. (1998) *Technology and Global Change*, Cambridge University Press, Cambridge

Haanpää, S. (2008) Climate Change Adaptation In The Context Of Spatial Planning – Institutional Means Of Reducing Local Vulnerability In The Baltic Sea Region, *paper presented to ACSP-AESOP 4th Joint conference, 8 July, Chicago, USA.*

Haanpää, S. and Peltonen, L. (2007) *Institutional vulnerability of spatial planning systems against climate change in the BSR,* YTK Centre for Urban and Regional Studies, 40.

Haccoû, H. (2009) Changing Land Use to Mitigate Climate Change. A Transatlantic Collaboration, *paper presented to Changing Land Use to Mitigate Climate Change. A Trans-Atlantic Collaboration symposium, 7–9 May, Dubrovnik, Croatia.*

Hacking, T. (2004) The 'Right Hand Rule' for Impact Assessment: A Framework for Clarifying the Meaning of Integrated, Triple Bottom-Line and Sustainability Assessment, *Paper presented at the International Association for Impact Assessment conference, 24–30 April 2004, Vancouver.*

Halden, D., McGuigan, D., Nisbet, A. and McKinnon, A. (2000) *Accessibility: Review of Measuring Techniques and their Application,* Scottish Executive Central Research Unit.

Hall, P. (1988) Conclusions, in Banister, D. (ed) *Transport Policy and the Environment,* London, Spon Press, pp. 333–336.

Hall, P. (1995) A European perspective on othe spatial links between land use, development and transport, in Banister, D. (ed) *Transport and Urban Development,* E. & F.N. Spon, London, pp. 65–88.

Hall, R., Piao, J. and McDonald, M. (2007) *CIVITAS Guard. Transferability of Measures,* Transportation Research Group, University of Southampton.

Halpert, B.P. (1982) 'Antecedents', in Rogers, D.L. and Whetten, D.A. (eds) *Interorganizational Coordination: Theory, Research and Implementatio,* Iowa State University Press, Ames, pp. 54–72.

Handy, S. (1992) Regional versus local accessibility: Neo-traditional development and its implications for non-work travel, *Built Environment,* **18**, 253–267.

Handy, S. (1993) Regional versus local accessibility: neo-traditional development and its implications for non-work travel, *Built Environment,* **18** (4), 256–267.

Handy, S. (1996a) Methodologies for exploring the link between urban form and travel behavior, Transportation Research D, **1**, 151–165.

Handy, S. (1996b) Understanding the link between urban form and nonwork travel behavior, *Journal of Planning Education and Research,* **15**, 183–198.

Handy, S. (2003) Amenity and Severance, in Hensher D.A. and Button K.J. (eds) *Handbook of Transport and the Environment,* Elsevier Amsterdam.

Handy, S. (2005) Smart Growth and the Transportation-Land Use Connection: What Does The Research Tell Us?, *International Regional Science Review,* **28** (2), 146–167.

Handy, S.L. and Niemeier, D.A. (1997) Measuring accessibility: An Exploration of Issues and Alternatives, *Environment and Planning A,* **29** (7), 1175–1194.

Hanf, K. and O'Toole, L. (1992) Revisiting old friends: networks, implementation structures and the management of inter-organisational relations, *European Journal of Political Research,* **21**, 163–180.

Hansen, J. (2007) *Climate change and trace gases* [online]. Available at: http://pubs. giss.nasa.gov/abstracts/2007/Hansen_etal_2.html

Hanson, S. (1982) The determinants of daily travel-activity patterns: relative location and sociodemographic factors, *Urban Geography*, **3** (3), 179–202.

Hårsman, B. and Olsson, A.R. (2003) The Stockholm region: metropolitan governance and spatial policy, in Salet, W., Thornley, A. and Kreukels, A. (eds) (2003) *Metropolitan Governance and Spatial Planning. Comparative case studies of European City-Regions*, Spon Press, London.

Hau, E. (2006) *Wind Turbines. Fundamentals, Technologies, Application, Economics.* 2nd edition, Springer, Berlin.

Häussermann, H. (2003) Berlin, in Salet, W., Thornley, A. and Kreukels, A. (eds) (2003) *Metropolitan Governance and Spatial Planning. Comparative case studies of European City-Regions*, Spon Press, London.

Hayat, J. and Atkins, S. (2007) Sustainable Development and the Railway in Great Britain, *paper presented at the European Transport Conference, 17–19 October, Leeuwenhorst, Netherlands.*

Headicar, P. (1997) Targeting travel awareness campaign, *Transport Policy*, **4** (1), 57–65.

Headicar, P. (2003) The contribution of Land Use Planning to reducing traffic growth: the English experience, *European Journal of Transport Infrastructure and Research*, **3** (2).

Healey, P. (1997) *Collaborative Planning: Shaping Places in Fragmented Societies*, MacMillan, London.

Healey, P. (2007) *Urban Complexity and Spatial Strategies. Towards a relational planning for our times*, Routledge, London.

Heeg, S. (2003) Governance in the Stuttgart metropolitan region, in Salet, W., Thornley, A. and Kreukels, A. (eds) (2003) *Metropolitan Governance and Spatial Planning. Comparative case studies of European City-Regions*, Spon Press, London.

Hensher, D.A. and Brewer, A.M. (2001) *Transport. An economics and management perspective*, Oxford, Oxford University Press.

Hensher, D.A. and Button K.J. (eds) (2003) *Handbook of Transport and the Environment*, Elsevier, Amsterdam.

Hensher, D.A. and Goodwin, P. (2004) Using values of travel time savings for toll roads: avoiding some common errors, *Transport Policy*, **11** (2), 171–182.

Hensher, D.A., Button, K.J., Haynes, K.E. and Stopher, P.R. (eds) (2004) *Handbook of Transport Geography and Spatial Systems*, Elsevier, Amsterdam.

Hey, C., Hickmann, G., Geisendorf, S. and Schleicher-Tappeser, R. (1992) *Dead End Road: Klimaoohutz im euiupäischen Güterverkehr, Ein Greenpeace Szenario*, EURES, Freiburg, Germany.

Hibbs, J. (2000) *Transport Policy: The myth of integrated planning*, Institute of Economic Affairs, London.

Hickman, R. (2005) *Reducing Travel by Design: A micro analysis of new household location and the commute to work in Surrey*, Unpublished PhD thesis, Bartlett School of Planning, University College London, London.

Hickman, R. and Banister, D. (2007) Transport and Energy Consumption: Does Co-location of Housing and Workplaces occur over time?, *paper presented at the European Transport Conference, 17–19 October, Leeuwenhorst, Netherlands.*

Hillman, S., Henerson, I. and Whalley, A. (1976) *Transport Realities and Planning Policy: Studies of frictions and freedoms in daily travel*, Vol. XLII, Broadsheet No. 567, Political and Economic Planning, London.

Himanen, V., Lee-Gosselin, M. and Perrels, A. (2005) Sustainability and the interactions between external effects of transport, *Journal of Transport Geography,* **13**, 23–28.

Hine, J.P. and Mitchell, F. (2001) *The Role of Transport in Social Exclusion in Urban Scotland*, Central Research Unit, Scottish Executive Development Department Edinburgh.

HMSO (2004) *The Environmental Assessment of Plans and Programmes Regulations,* HMSO, London.

HM Treasury (2006) *The Eddington Transport Study The case for action: Sir Rod Eddington's advice to Government,* HM Treasury, London.

HM Treasury (2007) *The Green Book: Appraisal & Evaluation in Central Government* [online]. Available at: http://www.hm-treasury.gov.uk./media/3/F/green_book_260 907.pdf (Accessed 04/07/2008).

HM Treasury (2008) *Budget 2008: Stability and opportunity: building a strong, sustainable future* [online]. Available at: http://www.hm-treasury.gov.uk/media/9/9/bud08_completereport.pdf (Accessed 20/07/2008).

Hoejer, M. (1996) Urban transport, information technology and sustainable development, *World Transport Policy and Practice,* **2** (1.2), 46–51.

Holden, E. and Norland, I.T. (2005) Three Challenges for the Compact City as a Sustainable Urban Form: Household Consumption of Energy and Transport in Eight Residential Areas in the Greater Oslo Region, *Urban Studies,* **42** (12), 2145–2166.

Holl, A. (2006) A Review of the Firm-Level Role of Transport Infrastructure with Implications for Transport Project, *Journal of Planning Literature,* **21**, 3–16.

Holmans, A. (1996) Housing demand and need in England to 2011: the national picture, in Breheny, M. and Hall, P. (eds) *The People – Where will they go?*, Town and Country Planning Association, London, pp. 7–15.

House of Commons (2006) *Bus Services Across the UK,* Minutes of Evidence taken before Transport Committee, HC 1317-i.

Hull, A.D. (2004) Major housing developments: density and design in appeal decisions 2000–2003, *Journal of Environment and Planning Law*, pp. 379–393.

Hull, A.D. (2005) Integrated Transport Planning in the UK: From concept to reality, *Journal of Transport Geography,* **13**, 318–328.

Hull, A.D. (2006) Structures for communication and interpretation in Neighbourhood Regeneration: mainstreaming the Housing Action Trust philosophy, *Urban Studies*, **43** (12), 2317–2350.

Hull, A.D. (2008a) Policy Integration: What will it take to achieve more sustainable transport solutions in cities?, *Transport Policy*, **15** (1), 94–103.

Hull, A.D. (2008b) Searching for the Truth: Knowledge and evaluation of sustainable cities, in Khakee, A., Hull, A.D., Miller, D. and Woltjer, J. (eds) *New Principles in Planning Evaluation*, Ashgate.

Hull, A.D. (2008c) Evaluating the cumulative effects of transport projects, *paper presented at ACSP–AESOP Fourth Joint Congress, 6–11 July 2008, Chicago.*

Hull, A.D. (2009) Implementing Innovatory Transport Measures: What Local Authorities in the UK say about their problems and requirements, *European Journal of Transport and Infrastructure Research*, **9** (3), 202–218.

Hull, A.D. (2010) *Evaluating the cumulative effects of transport projects*, forthcoming.

Hull, A.D. and Tricker, R. (2005) Sustainable urban environments: Assessing the barriers to sustainable transport, *Engineering Sustainability*, **158**, 171–180.

Hull, A.D. and Tricker, R. (2006) *Project A: Findings of the 'Phase 1' Survey on the Barriers to the Delivery of Sustainable Transport Solutions* [online]. Available at: http://www.distillate.ac.uk/reports/reports.php

Hull, A.D., Thanos, S. and Morgan, J. (2009a) CIVITAS SMILE: Malmö Context and Cumulative Effects Assessment Report [online]. Available at: http://www.sbe.hw.ac.uk/prag

Hull, A.D., Morgan, J. and Thanos, S. (2009b) CIVITAS SMILE: Norwich Context and Cumulative Effects Assessment Report [online]. Available at: http://www.sbe.hw.ac.uk/prag

Hull, A.D., Morgan, J. and Thanos, S. (2009c) Assessing the impact of behaviour change policies in Norwich and Malmö, *paper presented at the AESOP congress, 15–18 July, Liverpool, UK.*

Hull, A.D., Tricker, R. and Hills, S. (2006) *Interactions between policy sectors and constraints on cross-sector working in the delivery of Sustainable Urban Transport Solutions*, DISTILLATE Consortium project report [online]. Available at: http://www.distillate.ac.uk/reports/reports.php

Hutton, B. (2007) We need to fundamentally rethink transport models so they represent the reality experienced by travellers, not network providers, *Local Transport Today*, **463**, 18.

IEA (2004) *World Energy Outlook 2004*, IEA, Paris, France.

Innes, J.E. and Gruber, J. (2005). Planning styles in conflict: the Metropolitan Transportation Commission. *Journal of the American Planning Association*, **71** (2), 177–188.

Institute for Road Safety Research (SWOV) (no date) National Travel Survey [online]. Available at: http://www.swov.nl/uk/research/kennisbank/inhoud/90_gegevensbro nnen/inhoud/ovg.htm (Accessed 04/09/2009).

Institute of Advanced Motoring (2009) *Motoring facts*, IAM, London.

Ison, S. and Wall, S. (2004) Market and Non-Market Based Approaches to Traffic-Related Pollution: The Perceptions of Key Stakeholders, *International Journal of Transport Management*, **1** (4), 133–143.

Jaarsma, C.F. and van Dijk, T. (2005) The paradoxical role of infrastructure in the use of metropolitan green areas by urban residents, *paper presented in the AESOP congress*, July 2005, Vienna.

Jacobs, J. (1961) *The Death and Life of Great American Cities*, Random House, New York.

Jenks, M. (2000) The acceptability of Urban Intensification, in Williams, K., Burton, E. and Jencks, M. (eds) (2000) *Achieving Sustainable Urban Form*, Spon Press, London, pp. 242–250.

Jenks, M., Burton, E. and Williams, K. (1996) *The Compact City: A sustainable urban form?* Spon Press, London.

Jensen, O.B. and T. Richardson (2004). Making European Space: mobility, power and territorial identity, Routledge, London.

Johnson, E. (2008) Goodbye to carbon neutral, getting biomass footprints right, Environmental Impact Assessment Review, **29** (3), 165–168.

Jolles, A., Klusman, E. and Teunissan, B. (eds) (2003) *Planning Amsterdam: Scenarios for Urban Development 1928–2003*, NAi, Rotterdam.

Jones, P., Boujenko, N. and Marshall, S. (2007) *Link and Place. A Guide to Street Planning and Design*, Landor Books.

Jones, S.R. (1981) *Accessibility measures: a literature review*, Report no. TRRL LR 967, Transport Road Research Laboratory, Berkshire.

Jonsson, D.K. and Johansson, J. (2006) Indirect Effects to Include in Strategic Environmental Assessments of Transport Infrastructure Investments, *Transport Reviews,* 26 (2), 151–166.

Jørgenson, I., Kjœrsdam, F. and Nielsen, J. (1997) A plan of hope and glory. An example of development planning in Denmark after Maastricht, in Healey, P., Khakee, A., Motte, A. and Needham, B. (eds) *Making Strategic Spatial Plans. Innovation in Europe*, UCL Press, London.

Kennedy, C., Miller, E., Shalaby, A., Maclean, H. and Coleman, J. (2005) The Four Pillars of Sustainable Urban Transportation, Transport Reviews, **25** (4), 393–414.

Kirkpatrick, C. and Lee, N. (2002) *Further Development of the Methodology for a Sustainability Impact Assessment of Proposed WTO Negotiations. Final Report,* IDPM, University of Manchester.

Kitamura, R., Mokhtarian, P. and Laidet, L. (1997) A Micro-analysis of land use and travel in five neighbourhoods in the San Francisco Bay Area, Transportation, **24**, 125–158.

Knieling, J. (2008) Climate Change Governance: Mitigation Strategies as a Challenge for Metropolitan Regions, *paper presented at the ACSP–AESOP Joint Congress, July 2008, Chicago.*

Knoflacher, H. (1981) Human energy expenditure in different modes: implications for town planning, in *International Symposium on Surface Transportation System Performance* Vol II, US Department of Transportation, Washington DC.

Knoflacher, H. (2006) A new way to organize parking: the key to a successful sustainable transport system for the future, *Environment and Urbanization*, **18**, 387–412.

Knowles, R.D. (2006) Transport shaping space: differential collapse in time–space, *Journal of Transport Geography*, **14** (2006), 407–425.

Koehler, B. (2009) What land use and climate change actions are being taken at the local level?, *paper presented to Changing Land Use to Mitigate Climate Change. A Trans-Atlantic Collaboration symposium, 7–9 May, Dubrovnik, Croatia.*

Köhler, J. (2007) *Transport and the environment: Policy and Economic Consideration,* report to Foresight Intelligent Infrastructure Systems Project, Office of Science and Technology, London.

Kollamthodi, S., Alanko, J. and Middlemiss, I. (2005) *Assessing the Environmental, Social, and Economic Impacts of the Thematic Strategy on the Urban Environment,* Report prepared for the European Commission Directorate General Environment.

KonSULT (2005). The KonSULT Knowledgebase. (http://www.konsult.leeds.ac.uk)

Korthals, W. (2007) Stagnation in housing production and the changing role of provinces in the Dutch planning system, *Regional Studies*, **39** (6), 1497–1512.

Kovács, G. and Spens, K.M. (2006) Transport infrastructure in the Baltic States post-EU succession, *Journal of Transport Geography,* **14**, 426–436.

Krizek, K. (2003) Operationalizing Neighborhood Accessibility for Land Use–Travel Behavior Research and Regional, *Journal of Planning Education and Research,* **22**, 270–287.

Kuby, M. (2006) Prospects for geographical research on alternative-fuel vehicles, *Journal of Transport Geography,* **14**, 234–236.

Kwan, M-P. (1998) Space-Time and Integral Measures of Individual Accessibility: A Comparative Analysis Using a Point-based Framework, *Geographical Analysis,* **30**, 191–216.

Kwok, R.C.W. and Yeh, A.G.O. (2004) The use of modal accessibility gap as an indicator for sustainable transport development, *Environment and Planning A*, **36** (5), 921–936.

Lakshaman, T.R. and Anderson, W.P. (2005) Evolution of transport institutions that facilitate international trade, in Rietveld, P. and Stough, R.R. (eds) (2005) *Barriers to Sustainable Transport. Institutions, regulation and sustainability*, Spon Press, London, pp. 158–182.

Lannerheim, P.H. (2007) Employment and Development Centres in Malmö, *Local Economy,* **22** (2), 201–206.

Lautso, K., Spiekermann, K., Wegener, M., Shepphard, I., Steadman, P., Martino, A., Domingo, R. and Gayda, S. (2004). *PROPOLIS: Planning and Research of Policies for Land Use and Transport for Increasing Urban Sustainability*, EVK4-1999-00005, EC RTD 5th Framework.

Lenschow, A. (ed.) (2002) *Environmental Policy Integration: Greening Sectoral Policies in Europe*, Earthscan, London.

Lewis, A. and Poole, F. (2005) *CIVITAS SMILE D3.1 Evaluation Plan*, Transport and Travel Research Ltd, Nottingham.

Liabo, K. and Curtis, K. (2003) Traffic calming schemes to reduce childhood injuries from road accidents and respond to children's own view of what is important: evidence nuggets, *What Works for Children Group Evidence Nugget,* April 2003 [online]. Available at: http://www.whatworksforchildren.org.uk/nugget_summaries.htm

Lindblom, C.E. (1990) *Inquiry and Change: The Troubled Attempt to Understand and Shape Society*, Yale University Press, New Haven, Conn.

Litman, T. (1997) Using road pricing revenue: economic efficiency and equity considerations, *Transportation Research Board Record,* **1558**, 24–28.

Litman, T. (2002) Evaluating Transportation Equity, *World Transport Policy & Practice*, **8** (2), 50–65

Lloyd, C. and Shuttleworth, I. (2005) Analysing commuting using regressions techniques: scale, sensitivity, and geographical patterning, *Environment and Planning A*, **37**, 81–105.

Löffler, P. (2005) *Strategic collaboration between local authorities and business actors for sustainable development: a cross-national study*, unpublished PhD thesis University of the West of England, Bristol.

Louw, E. and De Vries, P. (2002) Working at Home: The Dutch Property Dimension, *Planning Practice & Research,* **17**, (1), 17–30.

Lowndes, V. (2001) Rescuing Aunt Sally: Taking Institutional Theory Seriously in Urban Politics, *Urban Studies,* **38** (11), 1953–1971.

Lowndes, V. and Skelcher, C. (1998) The dynamics of multi-organizational partnerships: an analysis of changing modes of governance, *Public Administration*, **76** (2), 313–329.

Lucas, K. (1998) Upwardly mobile: Regeneration and the quest for sustainable mobility in the Thames Gateway, *Journal of Transport Geography*, **6**, 211–225.

Lucas, K. and Brooks, M. (2005) *Appraisal of Sustainability. Social Indicators, Institute of Transport Studies*, University of Leeds.

Lucas, K. and Jones, P. (2009) *The Car in British Society*, The Royal Automobile Club Foundation for Motoring, London.

Lyons, G. and Chatterjee, K. (eds) (2002) *Transport Lessons from the Fuel Tax Protests of 2000,* Ashgate, Aldershot.

Lyons, G., Marsden, G., Beecroft, M. and Chatterjee, K. (2001) Transportation Requirements, Reports from the Transport Visions Network, Landor.

MacDonald, L.H. (2000) Evaluating and Managing Cumulative Effects: Process and Constraints, *Environmental Management,* **26** (3), 299–315.

McKinnon, A.C. (1998) Logistical restructuring, freight traffic growth and the environment, in Banister, D. (ed.) *Transport policy and the environment*, Routledge, London.

McKinnon, A.C. (2006) Government plans for lorry road-user charging in the UK: a critique and an alternative, *Transport Policy*, **13**, 204–216.

Macnaughten, P. and Urry, J. (1998) *Contested Nature*, Sage, London.

Malmö stad website [online]. Available at: http://www.malmo.se/servicemeny/cityofmalmo (Accessed 19/09/2006) and pollution information can be obtained from http://www.ekostaden.com/extra/malmose/luft/dagensluft.htm

Manners, E. (2008) Islington's comprehensive approach to reducing transport emissions, *paper presented to the Transport Practitioners Meeting, 14–16 July, Reading, UK.*

Marsden, G. and Thanos, S. (2008) Measuring wider economic benefits of transport. A case study in good practice for indicator selection, DISTILLATE, deliverable C2 [online]. Available at: http://www.distillate.ac.uk/outputs/C2report_020806.pdf

Marsden, G., Kelly, C. and Snell, C. (2006) Selecting indicators for strategic performance management, *Transportation Research Record*, 1956, 21–29.

Marshall, S. (1999) Restraining mobility while maintaining accessibility: an impression of the 'city of sustainable growth', *Built Environment*, 25 (2), 168–179.

Marshall, S. (2004) Urban Pattern Specification, *paper presented to the SOLUTIONS conference, December 2004, Cambridge.*

Martens, M.J. and van Griethuysen, S. (1999) *The ABC Location Policy in the Netherlands: The Right Business at the Right Place*, INRO-TNO, Delft, Netherlands.

Martín, J.C., Gutiérrez and Román, C. (2004) Data Envelopment Analysis (DEA) Index to Measure the Accessibility Impacts of New Infrastructure Investments: The Case of the High-speed Train Corridor Madrid–Barcelona–French Border, *Regional Studies*, **38** (6), 697–712.

Matthiessen, C.W. (2004) International air traffic in the Baltic Sea Area: Hub-gateway status and prospects. Copenhagen in focus, *Journal of Transport Geography*, **12**, 197–206.

May, A.D., Page, M. and Hull, A.D. (2008) Developing a set of decision-support tools for sustainable urban transport in the UK, *Transport Policy*, **15**, 328–340.

May, A.D., Liu R., Shepherd S.P. and Sumalee, A. (2002) The impact of cordon design on the performance of road pricing schemes, *Transport Policy*, **9**, 209–220.

Mayor of London (2004) *The London Plan, Updated to 2008*, City of London, London.

Metropolitan Transport Authority and New York City Transit (2004) Fulton Street Transit Center Draft Environmental Impact Statement, Volume 1 [online]. Available at: http://www.mta.nyc.ny.us

Meurs, H. and Haaijer, K. (2001) Spatial Structure and mobility, *Transportation Research*, **6D** (16), 429–446.

Meyer, A. (2009) *Contraction and convergence. Why Scotland should lead the way?*, presentation to the Carbon Accounting Conference, 11 March, Heriot Watt University, Edinburgh.

Meyer, M.D. and Miller, E.J. (2001) *Urban Transportation Planning*, 2nd Edition, McGraw Hill, New York.

Miller, H.J. (1991) Modeling accessibility using space-time prism concepts within Geographical Information Systems, *International Journal of Geographical Information Systems,* **5**, 287–301.

Millward, A. and Wheward, R. (1997) Facilitating play on housing estates, *Findings Housing Research,* **217** [online]. Available at: http://www.jrf.org.uk/knowledge/findings/housing/H217.asp

Millward, L.H., Morgan, A. and Kelly, P. (2003) P*revention and reduction of accidental injury in children and older people: evidence briefing,* Health Development Agency, London.

Minister for Environment and Energy (1997) *Denmark and European spatial planning policy. National planning report for Denmark,* Copenhagen, Ministry of Environment and Energy [online]. Available at: http://www.mem.dk/lpa/publikationer/lpr97/land per cent2Deng/index.htm.

Ministry of Sustainable Development (2006) [online]. Available at: http://www.sweden. gov.se/sb/d/2066

Mitchell, G. (1996) Problems and Fundamentals of Indicators of Sustainable Development, *Sustainable Development,* **4** (1) 1–11.

Mitchell, G. (2005) Sustainability of Land Use and Transport in Outer Neighbourhoods (SOLUTIONS): A Proposed Appraisal Framework, *paper presented at EPSRC SOLUTIONS conference, December 2005, Cambridge.*

Mittler, D. (1999) Environmental Space and Barriers to Local Sustainability: evidence from Edinburgh, Scotland, *Local Environmen*t, **4** (3), 353–365.

Mogridge, M.J.H. (1997) The self-defeating nature of urban road capacity policy. A review of theories, disputes and available evidence, *Transport Policy,* **1** (4), 5–23.

Mokhtarian, P. and Saloman, I. (2001) How Derived is the Demand for Travel? Some conceptual and measurement considerations, *Transportation Research Part A*, **35**, 695–719.

Morris, P. and Therival, R. (1995) *Methods of Environmental Impact Assessment*, UCL Press, London.

Moudon, A.V., Kavage, S.E., Mabry, J.E. and Sohn, D.W. (2005) A Transportation-Efficient Land Use Mapping Index, *Transportation Research Record: Journal of the Transportation Research Board, No. 1902,* Transportation Research Board of the National Academies, Washington, D.C. 2005, pp. 134–144.

Naess, P. (1993) Transportation energy in Swedish towns and regions, Housing, Theory and Society, **10** (4), 187–206.

Naess, P. (1997) *Fysisk planlegging og energibruk* (Physical planning and energy use), Tano Aschehoug, Oslo.

Naess, P. (2003) Urban Structures and travel behaviour: experiences from empirical research in Norway and Denmark, *European Journal of Transport Infrastructure and Research*, **3**, 155–178.

Naess, P. (2006a) Accessibility, activity participation and location of activities. Exploring the links between residential location and travel behaviour, *Urban Studies*, **43** (3), 627–652.

Naess, P. (2006b) *Urban Structure Matters: Residential Location, Car Dependence and Travel Behaviour*, Routledge, Abingdon, Oxfordshire.

Naess, P. (2006c) Cost-benefit analyses of transportation investments: neither critical nor realistic, *Journal of Critical Realism*, **5** (1), 32–60.

Naess, P. (2006d) Self-selection, car ownership and indirect effects of urban structure on travel, *paper presented to the World Planning Schools Congress, July 11–16, Mexico City.*

Naess, P. and Jensen, O.B. (2004) Urban Structure Matters, Even in a Small Town, *Journal of Environmental Planning and Management*, **47** (1), 35–57.

Naess, P. and Sandberg, S.L. (1996) Workplace Location, Modal Split and Energy Use for Commuting Trips, *Urban Studies*, **33** (3), 557–580.

Naess, P., Sandberg, S.L. and Mogridge, M.J.H. (2001) Wider Roads, More Cars, *Natural Resources Forum*, **25** (2), 147–155.

Nash, C.A., Matthews, B. and Nellthorp, J. (2003) *UNITE Unification of accounts and marginal costs for transport efficiency: Final Report*, ITS, University of Leeds, Leeds.

National Audit Office (2008) *Transport and the Environment. Options for Scrutiny*, National Audit Office, London.

National Board of Housing, Building and Planning (2005) *Legislation*, Boverket (National Board of Housing, Building and Planning) [online]. Available at: http://www.sweden.gov.se/content/1/c6/04/35/93/35281ea1.pdf (Accessed 15/01/2008).

National Centre for Social Research (2008) *British Social Attitudes 2006*, UK Data Archive [online]. Available at: http://www.data-archive.ac.uk

Needham, B. (2005) The New Dutch Spatial Planning Act: Continuity and Change in the Way in Which the Dutch Regulate the Practice of Spatial Planning, *Planning, Practice and Research*, **20** (3), 327–340.

Neuman, M. and Hull, A.D. (2009) The Futures of the City-region, *Regional Studies*, **43** (6), 777–788.

Newman, P. and Kenworthy, J. (1989) Gasoline consumption and cities: a comparison of US cities with a global survey, *Journal of the American Planning Association*, **57** (3), 65–73.

Newman, P. and Kenworthy, J. (1999) *Sustainability and Cities: overcoming automobile dependence*, Island Press, Washington DC.

Newman P. and Kenworthy, J. (2000) Sustainable Urban Form: *The Big Picture,* in Williams, K., Burton, E. and Jencks, M. (eds) (2000) *Achieving Sustainable Urban Form*, Spon Press, London, pp. 102–120.

Ney, S. (2001) Understanding Accessibility, in Giorgi, L. and Pohoryles, R.J. (eds) Transport Policy and Research: What Future?, Ashgate, Aldershot.

NICHES (2007a) *Facilitating urban transport innovation on the European level. Research and policy recommendations*, accessed from www.niches-transport.org

NICHES (2007b) *MobilityTrends and Visions, accessed from* www.niches-transport.org

Nielsen, T.S. and Hovgesen, H.H. (2004) Urban fields in the making: new evidence from a Danish context, *paper presented at the AESOP congress, July 1–4, Grenoble, France.*

Nijkamp, P., Ubbels, B. and Verhoef, E. (2003) Transport Investment Appraisal and the Environment, in Hensher, D.A. and Button, K.J. (2003) *Handbook of Transport and the Environment*, Elsevier Ltd, pp. 333–355.

Noland, R.B. (2007) Transport planning and environmental assessment: implications of induced travel effects, *International Journal of Sustainable Transportation,* **1** (1), 1–28.

North, Douglass C. (1990) *Institutions, Institutional Change and Economic Performance*, Cambridge University Press.

North Lanarkshire Partnership (2006) G*lobal Footprint Project: Footprint Reduction Report*, North Lanarkshire Council, Motherwell, Scotland.

Oberholzer, Gee F. and Weck-Hannemann, H. (2002) Pricing Road Use: politico-economic and fairness considerations, *Transportation Research Part D*, **7D** (5), 357–372.

Office of the Deputy Prime Minister (2003) *Making the Connections: Final Report on Transport and Social Exclusion*, ODPM, London.

Office of the Deputy Prime Minister (2004) *The Egan Review. Skills for Sustainable Communities*, ODPM, London.

Office of the Deputy Prime Minister, Scottish Executive, Welsh Assembly Government and Northern Ireland Department of the Environment (2005) *A Practical Guide to the Strategic Environmental Assessment Directive: Practical guidance on applying European Directive 2001/42/EC*, ODPM, London.

OECD (2009) OECD Factbook 2009. Economic, Environmental and Social Statistics, OECD [online]. Available at: http://www.oecd.org/statsportal/0,3352,en_2825_293564_1_1_1_1_1,00.html (Accessed 27/07/2009).

Olsson, L. (2007) *Trading Road Transport CO$_2$ Emissions. To Get to Grips with Climate Change Impact of Heavy Vehicles; While Further Controlling Pollutant Emissions,* Swedish Environmental Protection Agency, Stockholm.

Olsson, M. and Rosberg, G. (2005) 'Malmø', *Arkitektur DK Magazine*, May 2005 Denmark.

Osborne, E. (2008) Interchange Best Practice Guidelines TFL's Findings, *paper presented to the Transport Practitioners Meeting, 14–16 July, Reading, UK.*

Østergård, N. (1994) *Spatial Planning in Denmark*, Ministry of Environment and Energy, Spatial Planning Department, Denmark.

Ostrom, E. (1986) A method of institutional analysis, in F.X. Kaufmann, G. Majone and V. Ostrom, (eds) *Guidance, Control and Evaluation in the Public Sector*, Walter de Gruyter, Berlin, pp. 459–475

Ostrom, E. (1990) *Governing the Commons: The Evolution of Institutions for Collective Action*, Cambridge University Press, Cambridge, MA.

Ostrom, E. and Ahn, T.K. (2003) *Foundations of Social Capital*, Edward Elgar Publishing, Cheltenham.

O'Sullivan, P. (1980) *Transport Policy. An interdisciplinary approach*, Batsford Academic and Educational Ltd, London.

Owens, S. (1998) Urban transport and land-use policies in East and West: learning from experience?, *International Journal of Environment and Pollution*, **10** (1), 104–125.

Palmoski, J. (2008) Connecting the dots. Moving from Travel Plans to Carbon Reduction Plans, *paper presented to European Transport Conference, 6–8 October, Leeuwenhorst, The Netherlands*.

Parkhurst, G. (2004) Air quality and the environmental transport policy discourse in Oxford, *Transportation Research Part D*, **9**, 419–436.

Parkinson, S. (2001) A summary of Environmental Justice – Mapping Transport and Social Exclusion in Bradford, Friends of the Earth, London.

Pemberton, S. (2000) Institutional governance, scale and transport policy – lessons from Tyne and Wear, *Journal of Transport Geography*, **8**, 295–308.

Perry, C. (1929) *Housing in the machine age, volume 7 of regional survey of New York and environs*, Regional Planning of New York and its Environs, New York.

Petersson, O. (1991) Shifts in Power, in Fredlund A. (ed.) *Swedish Planning in Times of Transition*, Swedish Society for Town and Country Planning, Gavle.

Pooley, C.G. and Turnbull, J. (2000) Modal choice and modal change: the journey to work in Britain since 1890, *Journal of Transport Geography*, **8**, 11–24.

Pooley, C.G., Turnbull, J. and Adams, M. (2006) The impact of new transport technologies on intraurban mobility: a view from the past, *Environment and Planning A*, **38**, 253–267.

Poundstone, W. (1992) *Prisoners' Dilemma*, Doubleday, New York.

Pratt, A.C. (1996) Coordinating Employment, Transport and Housing in Cities: An Institutional Perspectives, *Urban Studies*, **33** (8), 1357–1375.

Preston, J. (2001) Integrating transport with socio-economic activity – a research agenda for the new millennium, *Journal of Transport Geography*, **9**, 13–24.

Preimus, H. (2005) Decision-making on large infrastructure projects. The role of Parliament: Dutch evidence, *paper presented at the AESOP conference, July 13–17, Vienna, Austria*.

Priemus, H. (2007a) The Network Approach: Dutch Spatial Planning between Substratum and Infrastructure Networks, *European Planning Studies*, **15** (5), 667–686.

Priemus, H. (2007b) System Innovation in Spatial Development: Current Dutch Approaches, *European Planning Studies,* **15** (8), 992–1006.

Priemus, H., Nijkamp, P. and Banister, D. (2001) Mobility and spatial dynamics: an uneasy relationship, *Journal of Transport Geography,* **9**, 167–171.

Projectbureau Zuidas (no date) *Zuidas. Amsterdam*, Projectbureau Zuidas, Amsterdam.

PROSPECTS (2002) Deliverable No 3: Key Modelling Issues European Commission EU contract no EVK4 – 1999 – 00013 (Timms, P. and Minken, H.) [online]. Available at: www-ivv.tuwien.ac.at/projects/prospects/Deliverables/del3v6.pdf

Quinet, E. (2003) Evaluation of Environmental Impacts, in Hensher, D.A. and Button, K.J. (2003) *Handbook of Transport and the Environment*, Elsevier Ltd, pp. 357–373.

Quist, J.N. (2007) *Backcasting for a Sustainable Future. The impact after 10 years*, Eburon Academic Publishers, Delft.

Ravetz, J. (2000) *City-region 2020. Integrated Planning for a Sustainable Environment*, Earthscan Publications, London.

Ray, D. (2008) As Yogi Berra would say: It's déjà vu all over again, *Institute of Agriculture and Trade Policy* [online]. Available at: http://www.agobservatory.org/headlines.cfm?refID=102797

Reckien, D., Ewald, M., Edenhofer, O. and Lüdeke, M.K.B. (2007) What parameters influence the spatial variations in CO_2 Emissions from Road Traffic in Berlin? Implications for Urban Planning to Reduce Anthropogenic CO_2 Emissions, *Urban Studies*, **44** (2) 339–355.

Reid, A. (2005) *Environmental Assessment (Scotland) Bill*. SPICe briefing 05/21, 18 April, Scottish Parliament, Edinburgh.

Reneland, M. (2000) Accessibility in Swedish Towns, in Williams, K., Burton, E. and Jencks, M. (eds) (2000) *Achieving Sustainable Urban Form*, Spon Press, London, pp. 131–138.

Reynolds-Feighan, A. (2005) Institutional issues in transatlantic aviation, in Rietveld, P. and Stough, R.R. (eds) (2005) *Barriers to Sustainable Transport. Institutions, regulation and sustainability*, Spon Press, London, pp. 143–157.

Rietveld, P. (2000) The accessibility of railway stations: the role of the bicycle in The Netherlands, *Transportation Research D*, **5**, 71–75.

Rietveld, P. and Stough, R.R. (2002) Institutional dimensions of sustainable transport, *presentation to STELLA meeting Amsterdam, Vrije Universiteit Amsterdam*.

Rietveld, P. and Stough, R.R. (eds) (2005) *Barriers to Sustainable Transport. Institutions, regulation and sustainability*, Spon Press, London.

Rodrigue, J-P. (2006) Transport geography should follow the freight, *Journal of Transport Geography,* **14**, 386–388.

Rodriguez, D.A., Targa, F. and Aytur, S.A. (2006) Transport Implications of Urban Containment Policies: A Study of the Largest Twenty-five US Metropolitan Areas, *Urban Studies,* **43** (10), 1879–1987.

Romein, A. and Trip, J.J. (2008) Theory and practice of the creative city thesis: the cases of Amsterdam and Rotterdam, *paper presented at the ACSP–AESOP 4th Joint Congress, July 6–11, Chicago, USA.*

Royal Commission on Environmental Pollution (1994) Eighteenth Report. Transport and the Environment, London: HMSO.

Rubin, A. and Nilsson, C. (2003) *Environmental Programme for the City of Malmö 2003–2008*, The Environment Department, City of Malmö.

Runhaar, H., Driessen, P.P.J. and Soer, L. (2009) Sustainable urban development and the challenge of policy integration. An assessment of planning tools for integrating spatial and environmental planning in the Netherlands, *Environment and Planning B*, **36** (3), 417–431.

Ruston, D. (2002) *Difficulty in Accessing Key Services*, Office for National Statistics, London.

SACTRA (1994) Trunk roads and the generation of traffic, Department of Transport, London.

SACTRA (1999) *Transport and the Economy: Full Report,* SACTRA, London.

Sager, T. (1999) Rhetoric of economic rationality: The foundation of Norwegian transport planning, *European Planning Studies*, **7** (4), 501–518.

Salet, W. (2003) Amsterdam and the north wing of the Randstad, in Salet, W., Thornley, A. and Kreukels, A. (eds) (2003) *Metropolitan Governance and Spatial Planning. Comparative case studies of European City-Regions*, Spon Press, London.

Salet, W. and Thornley, A. (2007) Institutional Influences on the Integration of Multilevel Governance and Spatial Policy in European City-regions, *Journal of Planning Education and Research,* **27**, 188–198.

Salet, W. Thornley, A. and Kreukels, A. (eds) (2003) *Metropolitan Governance and Spatial Planning. Comparative case studies of European City-Regions*, Spon Press, London.

Sassen, S. (2001) *The Global City: New York, London, Tokyo*, 2nd edition, Princeton University Press, Princeton.

Schade, W., Wietschel, M., Helfrich, N., Hasenauer, U., Krail, M., Kraft, M., Scholz, A., Martino, A., Fiorello, D., Fermi, F., Christidis, P., Schade, B. and Purwanto, J. (2007) TRIAS – Sustainability Impact Assessment of Strategies Integrating Transport, Technology and Energy Scenarios, *paper presented to the European Transport Conference, 17–19 October, Leeuwenhorst, The Netherlands.*

Scheiner, J. (2006) Housing mobility and travel behaviour: A process-oriented approach to spatial mobility. Evidence from a new research field in Germany, *Journal of Transport Geography*, **14**, 287–298.

Scheiner, J. and Kasper, B. (2005) A Lifestyles approach to investigating residential mobility and travel behaviour, in Williams, K. (ed.) *Spatial planning, Urban Form and Sustainable Transport*, Ashgate, Aldershot.

Schwanen, T., Dijst, M. and Dieleman, F.M. (2002) A microlevel analysis of residential context and travel time, *Environment and Planning A*, **34**, 1487–1507.

Schwanen, T., Dijst, M. and Dieleman, F.M. (2004) Policies for the Urban Form and their Impact on Travel: The Netherlands Experience, *Urban Studies*, **41** (3), 579–603.

Schwanen, T., Dijst, M. and Dieleman, F.M. (2005) The Relationship between Land Use and Travel Patterns: Variations by Household Type, in K. Williams (ed) *Spatial Planning, Urban Form and Sustainable Transport*, Ashgate, Aldershot, pp. 17–41.

Schweitzer, L. and Valenzuela, A. Jnr. (2004) Environmental Injustice and Transportation: The Claims and the Evidence, *Journal of Planning Literature,* **18** (4), 383–398.

Scott, A. (ed.) (2001) *Global city-regions: Trends, theory, policy,* Oxford University Press, Oxford.

Scott, D.M. (2006) Embracing activity analysis in transport geography: Merits, challenges and research frontiers, *Journal of Transport Geography,* **14**, 389–392.

Scottish Executive (2001) Rural Accessibility [online]. Available at: www.scotland.gov. uk/cru/kd01/blue/ruac-03.asp

Scottish Executive (2002) *Scotland's transport delivering improvements: Transport indicators for Scotland*, The Stationery Office, London.

Scottish Executive (2004) *Environmental Assessment of Development Plans: Interim Planning Advice,* Scottish Executive, Edinburgh.

Scottish Executive (2005) *Congestion on Scottish Trunk Roads 2003*, Scottish Executive, Edinburgh.

Scottish Executive (2006) *Hydrogen and Fuel Cell Opportunities for Scotland: The Hydrogen Energy Group Report* [online]. Available at: http://www.scotland.gov. uk/Publications/2006/09/01153642/15 (Accessed 04/09/2009).

Scottish Government (2009a) *Scottish Environmental Attitudes and Behaviours Survey 2008*, Scottish Government, Edinburgh.

Scottish Government (2009b) *Scotland's People. Annual Report Results from the 2007/2008 Scottish Household Survey* [online]. Available at: http://www.scotland.gov.uk/Publications/2009/08/26090221/0 (Accessed 14/09/2009).

Scrase, J.I. and Sheate, W.R. (2002) Integration and integrated approaches to assessment: what do they mean for the environment?, *Journal of Environmental Policy and Planning,* **4** (4), 275–294.

Seaton, K. and Nadin, V. (eds) (2000) *A comparison of environmental planning systems legislation in selected countries*, Centre for Environment and Planning, University of the West of England, Bristol.

Selman, P. (1996) *Local Sustainability. Managing and Planning Ecologically Sound Places*, Paul Chapman, London.

Sermons, M.W. and Seredich, N. (2001) Assessing traveller responsiveness to land allocation based accessibility and mobility solutions, *Transportation Research 6D* (6), 417–428.

Shepherd, S. Shires, J., Koh, A., Marler, N. and Jopson, A. (2006) *Deliverable F2: Review of modelling capabilities* [online]. Available at: http.//www.distillate.ac.uk (Accessed 14/09/2009).

Shuttleworth, I.G. and Lloyd, C.D. (2005) Analysing Average Travel-to-Work Distances in Northern Ireland Using the 1991 Census of Population: The Effects of Locality, Social Composition, and Religion, *Regional Studies*, **39** (7), 909–921.

Silverman, R.M. (2003) Progressive reform, gender and institutional structure: a critical analysis of citizen participation in Detroit's community development corporations, Urban Studies, **40** (13), 2731–2750.

Sjöstedt, L. (2005) A conceptual framework for analyzing policy-maker's and industry roles and perspectives in the context of sustainable goods transportation, in Rietveld, P. and Stough, R.R. (eds) (2005) *Barriers to Sustainable Transport. Institutions, regulation and sustainability*, Spon Press, London, pp. 198– 222.

Smerdon, T., Pinney, C. and Kilford, S. (1996). *Sustainable Construction: The United Kingdom viewpoint. Report 13 BSRIA* [online]. Available at: http://www.sustainable-design.com/sustain/uk.pdf.

SMILE (2008a) *Measure 5.1 Evaluation Report for CIVITAS SMILE project*, City of Malmö, Malmö.

SMILE (2008b) *Measure 12.3 Evaluation Report for CIVITAS SMILE project*, City of Malmö, Malmö.

SMILE (2008c) *Measure 9.1 Evaluation Report for CIVITAS SMILE project*, City of Malmö, Malmö.

SMILE (2008d) *Measure 7.1 Evaluation Report for CIVITAS SMILE project*, City of Malmö, Malmö.

SMILE (2008e) *Measure 11.1S Evaluation Report for CIVITAS SMILE project*, City of Malmö, Malmö.

Smith, A. and Wheat, P. (2007) A Quantitative study of Train Operating Companies cost and efficiency trends 1996 to 2006: Lessons for future franchising policy, *paper presented at the European Transport Conference, 17–19 October, Leeuwenhorst, Netherlands.*

Snellen, D., Borgers, A. and Timmermans, H. (2002) Urban form, road network type and mode choice for frequently conducted activities: a multilevel analysis using quasi-experimental design data, *Environment and Planning A*, **34**, 1207–1220.

Social Exclusion Unit (2003) *Making the connections: final report on transport and social exclusion,* SEU, London.

Sperling, D. (2003) Cleaner vehicles, in Hensher D.A. and Button K.J. (eds) (2003) *Handbook of Transport and the Environment*, Elsevier, Amsterdam.

Spiekermann, K. and Neubauer, J. (2002) *European Accessibility and Peripherality: Concepts, Models and Indicators*, Nordregio Working Paper 2002–9, Nordregio, Stockholm.

Spiekermann, K. and Wegener, M. (2003) Modelling Urban Sustainability, *International Journal of Urban Sciences*, **7** (1), 47–64.

Spiekermann, K. and Wegener, M. (2004) Evaluating urban sustainability using land use transport interaction models, *European Journal of Transport and Infrastructure Research*, **4** (3), 251–272.

Stanilov, K. (2003) Accessibility and Land Use: The Case of Suburban Seattle 1960–1990, *Regional Studies*, **37** (8), 783–794.

Stead, D. (2001) Relationships between land use, socioeconomic factors and travel patterns in Britain, *Environment and Planning B: Planning and Design*, **28** (4), 499–528.

Stead, D. (2003) *Transport and land-use planning policy: really joined up?*, *ISSJ* 176 Unesco, Blackwell Publishing Ltd., pp. 333–347.

Stead, D. and Bannister, D. (2001) 'Influencing mobility outside transport policy', *The European Journal of Social Science Research*, **14** (4), 315–330.

Stead, D., Williams, J. and Titheridge, H. (2000) Land Use, Transport and People: Identifying the connections, in Williams, K., Burton, E. and Jenks, M. (eds) *Achieving Sustainable Urban Form*, E & FN Spon, London.

Steg, L. and Tertoolen, G. (1999) Sustainable Transport Policy: The Contribution from Behavioural Scientists, *Public money and Management*, Jan–March 1999, 63–69.

Stern, N. (2006) *The Economics of Climate Change*, HM Treasury, London.

Stewart, M., Goss, S., Gillanders, G., Clarke, R., Rowe, J. and Shaftoe, H. (1999) *Cross-cutting Issues Affecting Local Government*, Department of Environment, Transport and the Regions, London.

Storey, P. and Brannen, J. (2000) *Young people and transport in rural areas*, Joseph Rowntree Foundation, York.

Storper, M. (1996) Institutions of the learning economy, in Lundvall, B.A. and Foray, D. (eds) *Employment and growth in the knowledge-based economy*, Organisation for Economic Cooperation and Development, Paris, pp. 255–286.

Straatemeier, T. (2006) Potential accessibility: an interesting conceptual framework to address strategic planning issues in the Amsterdam region?, *paper presented at Transport Planning – A Design Challenge? conference*, 14–16 June, *University of Amsterdam*, Amsterdam.

Straatemeier, T. and Bertolini, L. (2008) Joint Accessibility Design: a framework developed for and with practitioners to stimulate the integration of regional land-use and transport strategies in the Netherlands, *paper presented at Transport Research Board Annual Meeting*, 10–12 January, *Washington, USA*.

Struiksma, R., Tillema, T. and Arts, J. (2008) Space for mobility: towards a paradigm shift in Dutch transport infrastructure planning?, *Paper presented to the ACSP-AESOP 2008 congress*, 6–11 July, *Chicago, USA*.

Sultana, S. (2006) What about dual-earner households in jobs–housing balance research? An essential issue in transport geography, *Journal of Transport Geography*, **14**, 393–395.

SUMMA (2003) *Deliverable 2: Setting the Context for Defining Sustainable Transport and Mobility* [online]. Available at: http://www.tmleuven.be/project/summa/summa-d2.pdf (Accessed 01/02/2010).

Sun, Y., Waygood, E.O.D., Fukui, K. and Kitamura, R. (2009) The Built Environment or Household Lifecycle Stages: Which Explains Sustainable Travel More? The Case of Kyoto-Osaka-Kobe Built Area, *Transportation Research Record*, **2135**, 123–129.

Sustainable Development Commission (2006) *Sustainable Development Commission's Response to the Department of Transport on Biofuels and the Renewable Transport Fuels Obligation* [online]. Available at: http://www.sd-commission.org. uk/publications/downloads/Biofuels_SDC.pdf (Accessed 04/09/2009).

Sustainable Transport in Sustainable Cities project (no date) *Why Travel, Warren Centre for Advanced Engineering* [online]. Available at: http://www.warren.usyd.edu.au/ transport

Sustrans (2004) *Safe Routes to Healthcare*. Information Sheet FH05, Sustrans, Bristol.

Sutherland, A. (2009) *To What Extent Can The Concepts and Ideas Used in Planning Naples' Regional Metro System (RMS) be Transferred to the UK?*, Dissertation submitted as part of the MSc Urban and Regional Planning, Heriot-Watt University, Edinburgh.

Swedish Ministry of the Environment (2006) Critical challenges – a Further Elaboration of The Swedish Strategy for Sustainable Development, http://www.sweden.gov.se/

Taaffe, E.J., Gauthier, E.L. and O'kelly, M.E. (1996) *Geography of Transportation*, Prentice-Hall Inc, New Jersey.

Taylor P.J. (2004) *World City Network: A Global Urban Analysis,* Routledge, London.

Tchang, G.S. (2007) Parking Policy to Improve Accessibility in Industrial Areas, *paper presented to the European Transport Conference, 17–19 October, Leeuwenhorst, Netherlands.*

Tengström, E. (1999) *Towards Environmental Sustainability? A comparative study of Danish, Dutch and Swedish transport policies in a European context*, Ashgate, Aldershot.

Territorial Agenda (2007) *Territorial Agenda of the European Union: Towards a More Competitive and Sustainable Europe of Diverse Regions* – Agreed at the occasion of the Informal Ministerial Meeting on Urban Development and Territorial Cohesion, *24–25 May, Leipzig* [online]. Available at: http://www.bmvbs.de/ Anlage/original_1005295/Territorial-Agenda-of-the-European-Union-Agreed-on-25-May-2007-accessible.pdf (Accessed on 24/07/2009).

Therivel, R. (2004) *Strategic Environmental Assessment in Action*, Earthscan, London.

Thomas, G. and Thompson, G. (2004) *A child's place: why environment matters to children,* Demos & Green Alliance, London [online]. Available at: http://www.demos. co.uk/catalogue/achildsplacebook

Thrift, N.J. (1996) *Spatial Formations*, London, Sage.

Tietjen, A. (2007) Imagining urban identity in a shrinking Danish Region, in Wang, C.Y., Sheng, Q. and Sezer, C. (eds) *International Forum on Urbanism*, Delft, pp. 183–191.

Tight, M.R., Delle-Site, P. and Meyer-Ruhle, O. (2004) *Decoupling Transport from Economic Growth – Towards Transport Sustainability in Europe,* University of Leeds [online]. Available at: http://ejtir.tudelft.nl/issues/2004_04/pdf/2004_4_2.pdf

Timmermans, H., Arentze, T. and Joh, C. (2002) Analysing space-time behaviour: new approaches to old problems, *Progress in Human Geography,* **26** (2), 175–190.

Transport for London (2004) *Central London Congestion Charging. Impacts Monitoring. Second Annual Report, July 2004,* Transport for London, London.

Transport for London (2005) *Transport 2025: Transport Vision for a Growing World City,* Transport for London, London

Transport for London (2006) *Central London Congestion Charging. Impacts Monitoring. Fourth Annual Report, June 2006,* Transport for London, London.

Transport for London (2007) *Central London Congestion Charging. Impacts Monitoring. Fifth Annual Report, July 2007,* Transport for London, London.

Transport Scotland (2008) *Scottish Transport Appraisal Guidance* [online]. Available at: http://www.transportscotland.gov.uk/reports/publications-and-guidance/corporate/j9760-00.htm (Accessed 08/07/2008).

Transportation Research Board (1996) *Institutional Barriers to Intermodal Transportation Policies and Planning in Metropolitan Areas,* TCRP Report 14, National Academy Press, Washington, DC [online]. Available at: http://onlinrpubs.trb.org/Onlinepubs/tcrp/tcrp_rpt_14-c.pdf

Transportation Research Board (1998a) *Funding Strategies for Public Transportation.* TCRP Report No. 31, National Academy Press, Washington, DC.

Transportation Research Board (1998b) *Transit-friendly Streets: Design and Traffic Management Strategies to Support Livable Communities,* TCRP Report No. 0309062659, National Academy Press, Washington, DC.

Transportation Research Board–National Research Council (2002) Desk Reference for Estimating the Indirect Effects of Proposed Transportation Projects. Slide show [online]. Available at: http://trb.org/news/blurb_detail.asp?id=668.

Tricker, R.C. (2007) Assessing cumulative environmental effects from major public transport projects, *Transport Policy,* **14** (4), 293–305.

Trip, J.J. (2007) Assessing quality of place: a comparative analysis of Amsterdam and Rotterdam, *Journal of Urban Affairs,* **29** (5), 501–517.

Tsamboulas, D.A. (2005) Intermodal transport markets and sustainability in Europe, in Rietveld, P. and Stough, R.R. (eds) (2005) *Barriers to Sustainable Transport. Institutions, regulation and sustainability,* Spon Press, London, pp. 223–244.

Ubbels, B. and Nijkamp, P. (2002) Unconventional funding of urban public transport, *Transportation Research Part D, Transport and Environment,* **7D** (5), 317–330.

Ubbels, B. and Verhoef, E. (2005) Barriers to transport pricing, in Rietveld, P. and Stough, R.R. (eds) (2005) *Barriers to Sustainable Transport. Institutions, regulation and sustainability,* Spon Press, London, pp. 69–93.

United Nations Intergovernmental Panel on Climate Change (2007a) *Fourth Assessment Report. Climate Change 2007*, accessed at http://www.ipcc.ch/.

United Nations Intergovernmental Panel on Climate Change (2007b) *Climate Change 2007: Synthesis Report*. Contribution of Working Groups I, II and III to the Fourth Assessment Report of the IPCC Core Writing Team, Pachauri, R.K. and Reisinger, A. (eds), Geneva.

United Nations Statistics Division (2005) *The Millennium Development Goals Report*, United Nations Statistics Division.

United Nations World Commission on Environment and Development (1987) *General Assembly Resolution 42/187, 11 December 1987* [online]. Available at: http://www.un. org/documents/ga/res/42/ares42-187.htm

United Nations World Commission on Environment and Development (1992) *Rio Declaration* [online]. Available at: http://www.unep.org/Documents.Multi lingual/Default.asp?DocumentID=78&ArticleID=1163 (Accessed 01/02/2010).

Urry, J. (2000) *Sociology Beyond Societies*, Routledge, London.

Van der Heijden, R.E.C.M., Van der Elst, A. and Veeneman, W.W. (2002) Inter-organisational co-operation in improving access to activity centres by public transport, in Sucharov, L.J., Brebbia, C.A. and Benitez, F.G. (eds) *Urban Transport VIII: Urban Transport and the Environment in the 21st Century*, WIT Press.

Van der Vlist, A., Gorter, C., Nijkamp, P. and Rietveld, P. (2003) Residential mobility and local housing – market differences, *Environment and Planning A*, **34**, 1147–1164.

Van der Waard, J., Tuominen, A., Van der Loop, H. and Eijkelenbergh, P. (2007) TRANSFORUM, Recommendations on Tools for Policy Impact Appraisal, *paper presented to the European Transport Conference, 17–19 October, Leeuwenhorst, Netherlands*.

Van Timmeren, A. (2007) Autonomy & Heteronomy: urban sustainability through decentralisation and interconnection, *paper presented to the International Conference on Whole Life Urban Sustainability and its Assessment, Glasgow*.

Van Timmeren, A., Kristinsson, J. and Röling, W. (2005) The Interrelationship of Sustainability and Resilience: Vulnerability of Networks, Related to the Critical Steams in Society: A Future Deadlock?, *paper presented at the SB05 Tokyo: Action for Sustainability, The 2005 World Sustainable Building Conference, 27–29 September, Tokyo, Japan*.

Van Vliet, D. (2000) Development/Demonstration: An Adaptive Strategy, in Williams, K., Burton, E. and Jencks, M. (eds) (2000) *Achieving Sustainable Urban Form*, Spon Press, London, pp. 189–201.

Van Wee, B. (2002) Land use and transport: research and policy challenges, *Journal of Transport Geography*, **10**, 259–271.

Veeneman, W., Van der Velde, D. and Schipholte, L.L. (2007) Competitive Tendering in the Netherlands: 6 Lessons from 6 Years of Tendering, *paper presented at the European Transport Conference, 17–19 October, Noordwukerhout, Netherlands*.

Verhetsel, A. (2001) The impact of planning and infrastructure measures on rush hour congestion in Antwerp, Belgium, *Journal of Transport Geography*, **9**, 111–123.

Vickerman, R. (2005) Public and Private Initiatives in Infrastructure Provision, in Rietveld, P. and Stough, R.R. (eds) (2005) *Barriers to Sustainable Transport. Institutions, regulation and sustainability*, Spon Press, London, pp. 18–36.

Vickerman, R., Spiekermann, K. and Wegener, M. (1999) Accessibility and economic development in Europe, *Regional Studies*, **33** (1), 1–15.

Vigar, G. (2000) Local 'Barriers' to Environmentally Sustainable Transport Planning, *Local Environment*, **5** (1), 19–32.

Vigar, G. (2006) Deliberation, Participation and Learning in the Development of Regional Strategies: Transport Policy Making in North East England, *Planning Theory and Practice*, **7** (3), 267–287.

Vuk, G., Hansen, C.O. and Fox, J. (2007) The OTM Model and its Application at the Metro City Ring Project in Copenhagen, *paper presented to the European Transport Conference, 17–19 October, Leeuwenhorst, Netherlands*.

Vigar, G., Healey, P., Hull, A.D. and Davoudi, S. (2000) *Planning, Governance and Spatial Strategy in Britain, An Institutionalist Analysis*, Macmillan, London.

Walker, T.W., Gao, S. and Johnston, R.A. (2007) UPlan: A GIS, Integrated, Land Use Planning Model, *paper presented to the Transport Research Board 2007 Annual Meeting, 10–12 January, Washington, USA*.

Warren Centre for Advanced Engineering (no date) *Why Travel. Sustainable Transport in Sustainable Cities Project*, accessed from www.warren.usyd.edu.au/transport

Watters, H., Tight, M. and Bristow, A. (2007) Achieving Low Carbon City Transport Systems: A Case Study Based on London, *paper presented to the European Transport Conference, University of Loughborough, Loughborough*.

Weber, J. (2006) Reflections on the future of accessibility, *Journal of Transport Geography*, **14**, 399–400.

Wetzel, D. (2007) Innovative Ways of Financing Public Transport, *paper presented at the European Transport Conference, 17–19 October, Leeuwenhorst, Netherlands*.

Wheeler, S. (2010) Regions, Megaregions, and Sustainability, in Hull, A.D. and Neuman, M., *The Futures of the City Region*, Routledge forthcoming.

While, A. (2009) Seeing the City as a space of Carbon Flows, *paper presented to the Planning Academics Conference, 2 April, Newcastle*.

White, P. (2002) *Public Transport. Its planning, management and operation*, 4th edition, Spon Press, London.

Whitelegg, J. (1997) *Critical Mass. Transport, Environment and Society in the Twenty-first Century*, Pluto Press, London.

Whitelegg, J. (2009) Brown's electric cars won't wash – not without clean electricity and bold new transport policy, says Green Party [online]. Available at: http://www.greenparty.org.uk/news/16-04-2009-electric-cars.html

Wild, A. (2000) Planning for Sustainability: Which Interpretation are we delivering?, *Planning Theory & Practice,* **1** (2), 273–284.

Williams, J. (1998) *How Big is Sustainable? The Interaction Between Settlement Size and Travel Behaviour*, European Transport Conference Proceedings, PTRC.

Williams, K., Burton, E. and Jencks, M. (eds) (2000) *Achieving Sustainable Urban Form*, Spon Press, London.

Witten, K., Exeter, D. and Field, A. (2003) The Quality of Urban Environments: Mapping Variation in Access to Community Resources, *Urban Studies,* **40** (1), 161–177.

Wixey, S. and Ruiz, M. (2003) Barriers to Successful Implementation of Mobility Management: Evidence from the EU MOST Project, *paper presented to the Regional Studies Association conference, April, Pisa, Italy.*

Wood, F.R., Burgan, M., Dorling, S. and Warren, R. (2007) Opportunities for Air Pollutant and Greenhouse Gas Emission Reduction through Local Transport Planning, *Land Use Planning,* **22** (1), 40–61.

World Bank (2002) *Cities on The Move: A World Bank Urban Transport Strategy Review,* World Bank, Washington, DC.

World Business Council for Sustainable Development (2001) *Mobility 2001– World Mobility at the end of the twentieth century and its sustainability*, World Business Council for Sustainable Development, Geneva, Switzerland.

World Health Organisation (2000) *Guidelines for Community Noise*, World Health Organisation, Geneva.

World Wildlife Fund (1991) *Caring for the Earth – A Strategy for Sustainable Living,* World Wildlife Fund, Gland, Switzerland.

Xu, K.T. (2002) Usual Source of Care in Preventive Service Use: A Regular Doctor versus a Regular Site. *Health Services Research,* **37** (6), 1509–29.

Young, O.R. (1995) The problem of scale in human/environment relationships, in R.O. Keohane and E. Ostrom (eds) *Local Commons and Global Interdependence: Heterogeneity and Cooperation in Two Domains*, Sage Publications, Thousand Oaks, CA, pp. 27–45.

Zandvliet, R. and Dijst, M. (2006) Short-term Dynamics in the Use of Places: A Space-Time Typology of Visitor Populations in the Netherlands, *Urban Studies,* **43** (7), 1159–1176.

Zuckermann, W. (1991) *End of the Road: the world car crisis and how we can solve it,* The Lutterworth Press, Cambridge.

INDEX

accessibility 19–20, 52–56, 65–70; activity-based 5, 20; audit 54, 68, 82–83; catchment analysis 53, 67, 287; cumulative opportunity 52–54; GIS modelling 52–53, 65–70, 257, 287–289; local 12, 67; maps 67; measures 19, 54–55, 66, 105, access 54, threshold 54–56, continuous 54–56, 70; pedshed 150, 164, 187, 215, 289; physical barriers 20, 53, 189; point to point 50–54, 66, 189; population potential 52; requirements 19; site characteristics 19; space–time 52–56; topological 52–53; transportation-based 20

active travel 63–66, 85, 104–105, 111, 127, 134–137, 141, 151, 157, 197, 224, 236, 241; cycling 2, 11, 29, 31, 45, 224, 228–229, 241–244, 248; walking 150–151, 159, 162–164, 173, 184, 209, 215, 219, 228, 241, 248

aviation 6, 10, 25, 36, 100, 152, 170, 279; warming effect 6, 36

behavioural change 8, 128, 224, 243; car clubs 11, 148, 157, 173, 224; car pools 11, 157, 196; company/workplace travel plans 11, 104, 114, 138, 152, 156, 243; cost effective measures 11; drivers of change 156, 170, 178–179, 183; home working 11; initiatives 193, 224, 243–244; personalised travel/journey planning 11, 139, 152, 243; school travel plans 11, 138, 243; teleworking 11, 46, 138, 187, 237; travel awareness 11

benchmarking 17, 133

biodiversity 123, 162–165, 169, 180, 187–191, 240, 260; habitats, fragmentation and loss 5, 9, 28–29, 37, 83, 118–119, 137, 140, 165, 169

built environment 122, 139–144, 191, 226–227, 242, 249; form 18

business as usual scenario viii, 6, 7, 198, 246

car 142–162; access 150, 199; access advantages 12; access restrictions 15, 148; culture 29; ownership 25–26, 43–48, 61, 68, 112–115, 157, 162, 184, 219, 229–229; regime 13; speeds 236; speed restrictions 30; travel 15, 20–22, 29, 41, 44, 48, 109, 182, 230, 236, 239; trips 22, 41–42, 207

car-free 11, 136, 146, 150, 173, 215; housing 11, 173, 215; zone 11

car parking 33, 59, 72, 90, 104, 121, 138, 145, 150–151, 156–157, 197, 204, 214, 228, 241; charges 16, 50, 138,157,197, 214, 218, 224, 242, 244; controlled parking zone 150, 173; revenue 33; workplace parking levy 138, 151, 152, 155

carbon 105, 113, 128, 134, 137, 142–143, 152–153, 156–160, 162–173, 224, 232, 236, 246–248; allowances 15, 57, 98, 134, 153; credits 16

carbon dioxide viii, 4–5, 160, 243; concentration levels 36, 102; price 10, reduction 36, 75, 100, 159, 170–171, 234, 247

cities 229, 241–242; compact 41; global 104

city-region 7, 15–16, 38–40, 45–47, 65–67, 73–74, 89, 102–107, 127–137, 145–146, 149, 175–176, 184, 198, 209–212, 216–218, 225–233, 239–249; associations 211

CIVITAS project 37, 142, 250

climate change 189, 201, 223–224, 235, 238, 240, 244–248; adaptation 100, 104, 248; anthropogenic causes 2; global 36; market failure 7; mitigation 17, 37, 82, 97, 101,104, 113, 123, 166, 188, 248; reduction targets 36, 75, 100, 234–235, 244

communication 171, 174, 243, 248

communities 63–64, 74, 76, 112, 131, 135, 164–165, 174

consumerism 25

costs 7–8, 11, 16, 19–20, 24, 26, 28–30, 32, 34, 36–39, 49–50, 57, 62, 66, 81, 86, 89–92, 99, 109–112, 123, 128, 130, 133, 136, 143, 151, 154–156, 161–162,

168, 171–172, 188, 195, 212–214, 221,
  236, 243–244, external 29, 34, 36, 57,
  86, 92, 99, 171, 213, 236, health 62,
  pollution 44–46, 62–64, 83–85, 96, 123,
  143, 145, transaction 24, travel 162, 180,
  209, 212–213, 217
context comparability 179
culture 16, 29, 32, 46, 79–83, 109, 113, 117,
  126, 132, 135, 146, 179, 208, 238, 256;
  professional 14

demand ix, 8, 25–26, 29–33, 36, 38, 40,
  46–47, 119, 129, 153, 162, 165, 170,
  193, 201, 218, 226, 232, 237, 241,
  246–247; restraint 31, 35–36, 105,
  109,114, 116–117, 120–124, 130, 133,
  178, 185, 196, 201, 209–210, 215, 218,
  224, 226, 228, 237, 244, 246
Denmark 7, 13, 103, 176–185, 215, 226–
  230, 232, 238, 242; Copenhagen 146,
  174, 180–191; Copenhagen airport 183;
  Copenhagen Finger Plan 1947 181;
  Frederiksberg 184; Greater Copenhagen
  Area 182–184; Øresund region 183,
  191–192; Transport Action Plan 1990
  180
development 4, 9, 11, 13, 16, 19, 27, 33–40,
  42, 44, 48, 59, 70–75, 84–86, 90,
  94, 96–99, 103–106, 111, 117, 139,
  144, 146, 149–154, 161, 164–180,
  191, 199–210, 215, 220, 223–224;
  management 73–74, 94, 119, 146, 150,
  156, 216–217, 233, 235, 239, 242–245,
  247; planning 45, 70, 119, 186, 243;
  spatial 23, 27–31, 199, concentrated
  decentralisation 199, compact urban
  growth 237

eco-efficient 11, 128; driving 11
ecological footprint 2, 80, 82, 160–161
economic 155, 160–164, 170–172, 177,
  182–183, 185, 187–191,195, 199, 201,
  206, 208, 211–212, 216, 219, 223,
  232, 234–235, 242, 246–247; benefits
  153, 162, 165; efficiency 162–163, 211;
  growth 160–161, 180, 187, 191, 205,
  232, 245, decoupling 35, 245; market
  161; market signals 31; productivity
  160–161
ecosystems 2, 15, 18, 35, 74, 76, 79–80, 83,
  135, 234, 243; health 34–35, 235
efficiency 234–247; energy 36–37, 41, 44,
  47, 51, 56–57, 72, 81, 101–102, 137,

143–144, 149, 152–155, 158–159,
  179, 184, 189–190, 213–214, 224,
  231, 236–247; fuel 8, 10, 189, 213;
  resource 240, 245, 247; supply side 36;
  technological 23, 234
energy 12–18, 32–37, 41–47, 51, 56, 79–82,
  85, 88–89, 95–97, 100–107, 110,
  134–145, 163–179, 186, 193, 197,
  204, 212–216, 225–227, 232–234,
  238–240, 243–249; consumption 31,
  35, 41–43, 57, 95, 98, 143, 164, 184,
  210, 228, 234–237, 243; transport 36,
  41, 43, 57, 143, 234; pollution 29, 31,
  44, 46, 64, 72, 80, 85, 96, 142, 153,
  171, 196, 198, 248; reduction12, 152,
  160; security 29
environment viii–xi, 2–4, 9, 11, 15–19, 29–39,
  44–51, 56–57, 59, 61–62, 64, 66, 69,
  72–78, 81, 83, 85–87, 98–102, 105–
  106, 108, 112, 117–119, 121–124,
  127–131, 133, 135–137, 143–150,
  153–155, 160–166, 169–172, 174,
  178, 180, 182, 185–193, 195, 197–198,
  201, 204, 206–208, 210–214, 216,
  223, 226, 229, 232, 234–236, 239, 241,
  243, 246–248; hazard 15–16, 65, 249;
  health-promotive 12, 146; protection 185,
  187, 204, 210–211
environmental assessment 48, 86, 137, 140,
  162; strategic environmental assessment
  48, 73, 86, 123, 137, 140, 166, 235
environmental capacity 16
environmental integrity 16
European Commission 37; Air Quality
  Framework Directive 140; Directive on Air
  Pollution (98/69/EC) 140; Environmental
  Impact Assessment Directive 37, 77, 96,
  140; Strategic Environmental Assessment
  Directive 37, 77, 96, 140
European Conference of Ministers of Transport
  22–23, 125, 159
European Parliament 143, 234
  Council of Ministers 34–35, 87, 142,
  234, 248
European Union 4, 34; Climate Change Action
  Plan 20096, 223–224; Directives 5,
  33, 35, 77, 102, 137, 140–142, 200,
  226; Emissions Trading Scheme 16;
  EURO standards 142, 164; model of
  subsidiarity 35, 103, 234; regulations
  140, 226; Renewable Road Transport
  Fuel Obligation10; Transport White Paper
  200135; Working Group on Sustainable
  Urban Transport 86

exergy ix, 3–4, 19, 49–50, 56–58, 67, 77,
    79, 123, 136, 153, 160, 171, 176,
    233–234; energy efficiency viii, 37, 44,
    47, 51, 56–57, 72, 81, 101–102, 137,
    149, 153, 155, 159, 179, 184, 190, 214,
    235–236, 239–240, 244, 246–247;
    Factor 4/10 principles 56, 58, 79, 126,
    240; growth in value 56, 79; low energy
    design principles 57; resource input 56,
    79, 110, 122, 162, 176, 249; resource
    minimisation 185, 197, 216, 225–227,
    233–235, 238–239, 242, 247

flooding 5, 46; sea-level rise 46; surface
    impermeability 5

Germany 6–7, 10, 13, 23, 30–31, 44, 103,
    136, 142, 144, 176–178, 184, 210–216,
    226–229, 236, 238; Air Quality Control
    Act 1990 212; car parking restrictions
    214–215; City–region Associations 211;
    Environmental Tax Reform 213; Federal
    Government 212–216; Freiburg 136,
    214–215, 240, 242, car-free housing
    215, Rieselfeld 215, Vauban Quarter
    215; Traffic Noise Protection Law 1990
    212
globalisation 26, 47, 210
Gothenburg European Council 2001 34
governance viii–xi, 4, 14, 16, 76,81, 83,
    87–89,95, 101–103, 107, 126, 135,
    167, 176, 178–179, 185, 232–233,
    238–239; scales of governance 76, 83,
    88–89, 176, 231, horizontal 83, 176,
    231, vertical 83, 176, 231
government x, 2–4, 11–13, 18, 29–30,
    36, 38, 44, 52–53, 72–78, 79–89,
    94–106, 120–122, 125–132, 134–137,
    233–240, 244–249
greenhouse gas emissions 164, 177–178,
    180, 185, 204, 210, 215, 229–230,
    234, 246; abatement costs 7, 172;
    adaptation 82, 99–100, 104, 113, 178,
    226, 247–248; carbon dioxide viii, 4–5,
    160, 243; charging 220–227; mitigation
    17, 37, 82, 97, 101, 104, 113, 123, 166,
    188, 248; tipping point 5, 36
gross added value 143
gross domestic product 16, 27–28, 31, 41,
    80, 160–162

health 1–5, 12, 15–18, 26–37, 46, 49, 53,
    61–77, 82, 85, 106, 110, 114–139,

146–149, 155–159, 163–167,
    175–176, 179, 187–188, 193, 195, 218,
    228, 230, 234–235, 239–248; costs 62;
    ecosystem 34–35, 235; human 5, 36;
    public 3, 18, 29, 35, 146
household 95, 117, 149, 179, 205–206, 212,
    219, 229, 236, 243; incomes 206, 238;
    size 226, 43

impacts 2–12, 14–15, 23, 28–31, 37–38,
    41–42, 48, 64–77, 81, 87, 110, 123,
    132–133, 137, 154, 161–167, 171–
    172, 176, 180, 188, 219, 234–235,
    239, 243, 246–249; cumulative impacts/
    effects 3, 18, 37, 73, 76, 88, 105, 123,
    132–133, 160, 165–166, 171, 235;
    direct 38, 69, 132, 137; indirect 38, 69,
    132
information 10, 16–17, 25, 51–56, 61–70, 78,
    81, 88, 95, 98–134, 136, 139, 141, 155,
    158, 171, 177–178, 193–197, 203, 208,
    222, 224, 228, 230, 235, 239–242, 248;
    information communications technology
    25, 86, automatic vehicle guidance 25,
    intelligent speed control 25, dynamic
    route real–time information 25; intelligent
    information systems 25; real-time 145,
    148, 158, 171, 193, 195, 212, 222, 224,
    237, 242
Institute of Economic Affairs 8
institutional ix–x, 3–4, 10–16, 32–33, 49,
    76–82, 88–89, 103, 107, 127, 136, 153,
    171–179, 188, 202, 207, 224–228,
    231–232, 244–246; barriers 4, 108–
    125, 134–135, cultural 116–118, 122,
    125, 147, 154, 242, financial 109–111,
    legislative 118–120, organisational 12,
    112–116, political 120–122, technical
    122–125; structures 16, 79–105,
    174–176, 232–234
institutions 2, 14, 77, 80, 83, 89, 93,
    99, 109, 126, 176, 180, 225–227;
    decision networks 14; formal rules 89;
    organisations 2, 10, 14, 34, 50, 53,
    76–83, 86–90, 95–102, 106, 109–115,
    120, 125–133, 137, 156, 176, 226,
    245–246; ways of acting informal rules
    ix, 89, 100
instruments 17, 38, 81,103, 108, 118,
    133–141, 165, 175–179, 195, 215,
    228, 233–246; awareness-raising
    150–159; hardware 136–151; land use
    137, 141, 148–151, 155–156, 175;

policy/intervention 108, 118, 135–176, 201; software 136, 138–141, 151–159; transport 137–149, 153–158
integration ix–x, 1, 3–4, 17, 26, 30, 47–53, 67, 78–90, 93, 102–105, 114, 120–137, 141, 162, 166, 176–197, 201, 208, 211, 216, 218, 224–245; conceptual 4, 83–84, 176, 180, 182, 185, 197; European 26, 47; integrated policy framework 2, 71–78; integrated territorial policies 1, 74–77; mechanism 75, 78, 81–87, 89, 92, 95–107, 132, 152, 155, 159, 161, 167, 174, 180, 225–232, 233–243, 246, accessibility ix, 3, 19–20, 52–56, 67–71, 92, spatial planning 71–74, 75–77, 101–107, strategic environmental assessment 48, 73, 86, 123, 137, 140, 166, 235; performance 4, 83–88, 114, 126, 135–137, 176
inter-linkage 1, 4, 83

Kyoto Protocol viii, 5

land use 9, 15, 38–49, 60–62, 65–87, 104–107, 124, 132–133, 137, 190, 198, 202, 216, 230, 233; artificial areas 27, 41; Corinne land use data base 27; density 27–46, 50, 57–59, 66–67, 78, 84–86, 97, 139, 149, 165, 177, 206, 208, 229, housing/residential 27–28, 41–46, 150, workplace 27, 59; land take 31, 37, 65, mix 42–45, 59, 66, 73, 84–86, 104, 139, 148–149, 205, 208, 237, 239, 242, urban sprawl 16, 29, 41, 45, 72, 127, 150, 180, 186, 199
low carbon economy 9; dematerialisation 16, 56, 79, 173, 232, 235, 238
low energy development pathways 13–17, 44, 79, 102–105, 176, 226, 239

management 16, 31–36, 44–51, 86, 91–94, 100, 104, 109–133, 134–139, 145, 151, 154, 157, 163, 174, 178–201, 210–212, 218–246
market 7, 10, 20, 23, 31–33, 38–39, 44–45, 57, 66, 70–73, 79–82, 92–93, 95–104, 108–110, 135, 142–143, 146, 154, 157–161, 168, 170, 198, 202, 206, 200–209, 219, 225, 228, 232–233, 248; incentive structures 110, 132, 244
Millennium Summit 15
mobility ix, 2–3, 12, 18–20, 23, 25, 27, 32–43, 46, 53, 57–64, 71–82, 88, 91, 98, 123,

133, 149, 162, 167, 170–171, 185, 188, 193, 199–209, 229–231, 232–241; EU Green Paper on Mobility 2007 52; hyper-38, 46–47, 232; macro 20; management 91, 109–119, 127–132, 193–196; micro 20; sustainable urban mobility 51–52
model viii, 2, 11, 15, 49–62, 98, 110, 117–118, 122–123, 133–155, 235; geographic information system models 53, 65, 70–73; land use and transport integrated models 50–52, 60, 65–66, 122; simulations 26
modes 6, 11, 25–32, 34–40, 44, 51, 53, 58–66, 70, 72–76, 85, 90, 99, 104–106, 108, 117–119, 124, 127, 130, 141, 145, 147, 153, 159, 175, 189–204, 212–217, 224–228, 236, 241–244, 255; modal choice 41–43, 58, 109, 152–155, 237; modal split 41–42, 134, 151, 177, 182, 184, 193, 206–207, 238, 241–242; sustainable 12, 90

natural capital 9, 37, 185, 243
natural hazard 15–15, 46, 65, 249
neighbourhood 2, 12, 19–20, 29, 40–46, 57–64, 67–71, 75–76, 85, 106–107, 130–131, 134, 149–151, 160–164, 175, 208–209, 215–216, 239–249; design 12, 43, 150, 241, jobs–housing balance 150, walkable neighbourhood 99, 150; liveability ix, 66, 242; self-containment 42, 150
Netherlands, the 6–7, 11, 31, 75, 84–85, 129, 144, 152, 155, 159, 176–178, 198–210, 227–238; ABC Location Policy 84, 199–200, 207; Amsterdam 207–210, 229, Economic Programme 2007–2010 208, Metro Plan 1968 208, Parking policy 207, Schiphol airport 206–209, Structure Plan 2003 208, Zuid/WTC station 206–209; compact urban growth 199; concentrated decentralisation 199; integrated ticketing system 203; Planning Act 2008 202
new urbanism 84
Norwich 143, 148

Office for Fair Trading 92
Office of Rail Regulation 92
Organisation for Economic and Community Development 22
Ostrom 88–95, 125, 130, 179; model of interaction 91; structuring rules 90–95, 125, 172, 185, 233, 249

partnerships 14, 30, 38, 89, 99–101, 108,
    116, 124, 138, 158, 183, 228, 250;
    enabling 101; maintaining 101
pedestrian 40, 51, 63–64, 74, 138–139, 148–
    149, 159, 168, 173, 182, 207, 215, 237,
    242; areas 138, 148–149; infrastructure
    182; routes 138, 148
planning 2–5, 23–46, 48–50, 54, 77,
    90–94, 101–109, 119–128, 141, 159,
    175–225; land use ix, 3, 18, 35, 66–67,
    72–73, 82, 84–90, 98, 103, 110, 114,
    118, 175, 209, 211, 217–218, 240,
    243, development permit process 45,
    243; spatial viii, 53, 71–74, 179–182,
    185–198, 200–201, 204, 207, 209, 211,
    226–227, 234, 240–241, 245; strategic
    12, 73, 98, 120, 216; urban ix 15, 35,
    45, 208
policy ix–x, 2–35, 44–45, 52–53, 59, 64, 67,
    70–90, 95–107, 108–174, 232–249;
    demand management 36, 47, 94, 109,
    114, 124, 133, 196, 218, 224–227,
    237, 246; domain 66, 82, 87; framework
    31, 87, 124, 126–127; Government
    78, 85, 111, 126, 152, 185, 201, 224,
    247, perverse effects 31, 33, 114–115;
    instruments/measures 17, 108, 136–159;
    land use 136, 173, 176, 189, 201,
    207; location 84, 199–200, 207, ABC
    Location policy 84, 199–200, 207; sector
    3, 18, 73–76, 79, 87–88, 99, 103, 105,
    107, 113, 118, 126, 131, 136, 165, 171,
    178, 185, 218, 225–234, 238; taxation
    30–32, 152–155, 185; transport ix, 2, 8,
    13–14, 29, 31, 34–35, 40, 44, 48–91,
    108–123, 128, 162–163, 172, 176,
    184, 188, 198, 200–207, 215, 217, 228,
    233–234
pollution 2–17, 29, 31, 35–38, 44, 46, 62–65,
    72, 80, 83, 85, 123, 132, 140–142, 153,
    164, 169, 171, 187, 198; air 16, 36–37,
    62, 96, 140–145, 209, 212–213, 217,
    226, 237, 245–249; emissions 2–16,
    20, 27, 31, 35–37, 41, 44, 49–52,
    57, 60, 67, 72–77, 79–82, 85, 87,
    95–98, 108, 121, 127–128, 134–135,
    140–147, 152, 156–157, 160–163,
    167–178, 180–182, 189–190, 204,
    210, 213–216, 222–224, 226, 229–
    230, 232–249; noise 36, 47, 63, 136,
    153, 180, 191, 213, 226
power 28, 33, 35, 71–72, 78, 80, 88–95,
    101–105, 110–129, 136–137, 174,

178, 180–183, 185–186, 196, 200,
    202–203, 210–214, 217–219, 225,
    227, 232, 238, 241, 245, 247–249;
    covert 78; overt 78
precautionary approach 80
privatisation 32–33, 202
project 10, 14, 37, 46, 79, 92, 106, 114–115,
    119, 125, 130, 142–143, 151, 175, 182,
    192, 195, 199, 202, 205, 234, 239, 242,
    247, appraisal processes 17, 38, 48, 69,
    129, 131–132, 137, 161–165, 235, 247;
    Scottish Transport Appraisal Guidance
    29, 162
public engagement 2, 4, 73, 103, 106, 166,
    198
public good 32, 73, 82, 90–91
public sector 159, 161, 174, 178, 185,
    200, 209–210, 216–225, 228, 24;
    accountability 33, 87, 92, 126; autonomy
    129, 180, 186–188, 199–202,
    210–211, 216–217, 277, 233, 238;
    fragmentation x, 5, 33, 46, 62, 83,
    112–114, 164, 200, 232, 245
public transit x, 30, 35, 50–74, 104–105, 109,
    111, 114, 117–128, 136–137, 141,
    144–153, 156–158, 162–163, 166,
    171, 182–184, 188, 190–191, 194–
    202, 206–211, 218–227, 239–242;
    Bus Rapid Transit 11; integration 209,
    212, 218–219, 225, modal 30, 106,
    225, 227, ticketing 30, 103, 171, 196,
    203, 212; timetables 30, 68, 119, 158,
    171, 194, 242; interchange 105, 145,
    151, 223–224; interoperability 30–34,
    51, 67, 75, 140, 144; light rail 11, 103,
    111, 138, 144–145, 212, 218, 222, 237;
    Metro 22, 177, 183–184, 203, 207–208,
    230; modes 30, 104, 145; park and ride
    72, 138, 145, 149, 173; patronage 30,
    144, 158, 211–214; service 82, 94, 149,
    219–221, frequency 163, 212, quality
    119, 127–128, 137, 145, 148–149, 151,
    158, 166, 194–195, 201, 214, 218, 223;
    smartcards 11; tram 21–22, 69, 82, 114,
    138, 144, 177, 203, 209, 212, 215, 218,
    223, 225, 230, 237

quality of life 151, 159–160, 176, 201, 208,
    210, 215–216, 234–235, 243

regulation 9, 13–14, 32–36, 44, 73, 89–102,
    109, 119, 124–126, 137–142, 159, 180,
    187–189, 199, 207, 216, 225–226, 234,

244; deregulation 32, 288; institutional
32; public 14; regulated collaboration 2
renewable energy 97, 143, 164, 179, 185,
214, 224; renewable road transport fuel
obligation 10
resilience x–xi, 16–17, 63, 232, 249
resource vii–x, 2–19, 28–37, 39, 47–50;
consumption vii–ix, 2, 79–80, 96–108,
162, 176, 232, 235, 243–248, equitable
resource consumption 2, personal
responsibility for consumption 2,
impacts 3–4, 9, 29, 31, 38, 48, 66, 69,
71, 76–87, 123, 133, 137, 163–167,
176–188, 234–239, 246–249; depletion
2, 15, 31; efficient vii–viii, 4–9, 56–58,
67, 82, 105–107, 136, 163–165, 167,
171; material 16, 79–80, 126, 163, 176,
189, 229, 232–235, dematerialisation
16, 56, 79, 173, 232, 235, materials
intensity 128–129; minimisation ix,
14–19, 48, 57–58, 73–75, 78, 81, 95,
102, 107, 122, 126–135, 171, 176, 178,
185, 197–198, 215–216, 225–227,
233–243, 247; natural viii, 9, 12, 37,
49, 72–74, 79–83, 137, 160, 162, 166,
185–187, 206, 211, 229, 234, 240, 245,
247, rates of regeneration 35
road 1, 5–6, 8–20, 23, 45, 48–52, 62–66,
86–94, 104, 106, 110–111,114–124,
128, 137–141, 145–159, 161, 168,
171–173, 177, 182–184, 189–190,
196–198, 201–204, 207, 209–210,
212–214, 216–227, 229–230, 235–
238, 241–242, 244; hierarchy 148;
network 11–13, 29, 31, 58, 86, 90, 117,
137, 148, 223, 237; user charging/
pricing 11, 16, 26, 153–155, 173, 204,
210, 237

Scottish Transport Appraisal Guidance 29,
162
settlement size 45, 84
spatial ix–x, 1–3, 19, 23, 27, 28, 43–56,
59–78, 81–87, 93, 95, 98, 101–107,
118, 128, 130–135, 141, 145, 149–154,
161, 164, 167–172, 176, 179–239;
development patterns 23, 27–53, 186,
199, 211, concentration 40, 58, 60, 67,
75, 129, 199, decentralisation 41, 45,
205, 211; equity 3, 65–75; opportunities
52–60, 65–72, 84–85, 98, 130, 141,
145, 148–150, 158, 164, 167, 176,
209, 230, 233, 237, 239, 241–245;
planning 46–56, 59–78, 81–87, 93, 95,

98, 101–107, 118, 128, 130–135, 141,
145, 149–154, 161, 164, 167–172, 176,
179–239
Stern Report 7, 36, 49
strategy 7, 15, 92–110, 115–128, 130–149,
180–204, 233–238; place-based/
territorial 15, 48, 93, 105–107, 110,
115, 128, 180–183, 189–204, 210,
214–218, 239–244; sector 15, 34, 73,
82, 85–86, 92–93, 119–124, 130–135,
144–149, 157, 170, 218, 233–238
structures xi, 4, 9–17, 32–33, 66, 74–77,
79–84, 88, 103–105, 108–132,
174–185, 197, 215, 225–231; macro
32; space–time 32; urban 41
sustainability viii–xi, 1–3, 12–17, 28–33,
37–38, 56–68, 72–87, 98, 104,
108–110, 119, 122–123, 126–127,
132–134, 141, 143, 161–175, 176–
178, 180, 185–187, 197, 212, 214–216,
225–231, 233–249; environmental 180,
185–187, 187, 233–238; indicators
37–38, 44, 54–56, 67–71, 73, 76, 123,
131–134, 160–179, 188, multi-criteria
assessment 165–167, sustainability
threshold analysis 166–169, transport
carbon efficiency 164, transport
economic efficiency 162–163, transport
resource efficiency 164
sustainable ix–x, 1–23, 30–38, 44–78, 80, 89,
95–107, 108–135, 136–137, 144, 146,
150–152, 158, 160–166, 173–174,
178, 182, 185–189, 192, 218–231,
232–234, 239–249; city-region futures
13, 23, 38, 82, 239–240; development
9, 14, 34, 65, 72–77, 79, 104, 108, 126,
160–162, 166–167, 185, 188, 218,
ecological sustainable development 185;
people-mover 30
Sweden 7, 10, 13, 25, 44, 81, 85, 103, 142,
174, 176–178, 183, 185–198, 215,
226–230, 236, 238, 247; Deregulation
Act 1989 188; Malmö 186–189,
191–198, City Tunnel 191–192, clean
vehicles 196–198, Environmental
Programme 2003–2008 191, Traffic
Environment Programme 2005–2010
191–193, Ministry of Environment
187–188, National Resources Act
1987 187, Planning and Building Act
1987 186–187; Skåne 186, 194, 198;
Stockholm 189–190, road cordon toll
190; Swedish Environmental Protection
Agency 187

taxes 10–11, 29, 34, 81, 97–99, 103, 128,
　　137–138, 152–155, 179, 184, 186,
　　189–190, 201, 210–214, 227–228,
　　236; carbon-based 31, 47, 95, 190, 236;
　　distance-based 31, 201, 236; fuel 10–11,
　　29, 97, 138, 152, 189; revenue-neutral,
　　155; vehicle 11, 97, 138, 152, 155, 184,
　　189, 213, 236
technology 10, 13, 17, 20–25, 44, 56, 85–86,
　　138, 142–145, 152–155, 158, 163,
　　170–172, 180, 203, 210–214, 221–
　　227, 235; clean engine 138, 142, 152,
　　180; technological regime 25, 28–29
theory 19, 39, 79, 99, 134; classical location
　　19
tools ix–x, 2–4, 15, 48–49, 71–72, 75–77,
　　79–82, 89, 95–105, 108, 123, 128–133,
　　159–167, 174–179, 191, 202, 228, 235,
　　245–247; analytical 18; appraisal 4, 71,
　　123, 132–133, 235; financial/fiscal 135,
　　174, 202, 228, 233, 245, legal 96–98,
　　103, 135, 174, 228, 233–234, 245–247;
　　strategic 4, 77, 95–101, 235; strategic
　　impact assessment tool 48, 73–76, 68,
　　123, 137, 140, 166, 235
traffic viii, 5, 11, 19–25, 34, 40, 46, 48, 50–52,
　　60–65, 71, 86, 92, 94, 113, 117–125,
　　133–134, 138, 140, 145, 148–159,
　　161–175, 180–183, 189, 191–195,
　　201, 207, 212, 214–215, 217–223, 228,
　　237, 243; calming 86, 138, 156–159,
　　215, 228; management 86, 117, 121,
　　123, 145, 154–157, 221
transport: accidents 4, 29, 49, 51, 77, 147,
　　157, 164, 176, 201, 213, 222, 234;
　　air 4, 21–22, 30, 35, 44, 81, 94, 152,
　　155, 171; CO_2 charges 30, 81, 94, 152,
　　155, 171; congestion 19–20, 24, 29,
　　33, 41, 45, 51–52, 59–60, 66, 71, 90,
　　104, 121–124, 128, 130, 145–147,
　　152–157, 170–173, 190, 197, 201, 209,
　　217–223, 237, 243, London congestion
　　charge 219–220, Stockholm congestion
　　charge, 190; connectivity 19, 30, 33, 35,
　　43, 45, 50–77, 83, 106, 149, 170, 191,
　　235, 239, 245; demand ix, 8, 20–28,
　　29–38, 44–48, 59, 61, 65, 71, 97, 105,
　　119, 129, 134, 153–154, 17, 193, 201,
　　218, 232, 235, 246–247; environmental
　　impacts (air pollution) 3–6, 9, 48, 69,
　　77, 137, 163, 234, 246–247; freight
　　19–23, 32–36, 39, 44, 51, 57, 79, 86,
　　105, 122, 137–146, 155, 158, 161, 164,
　　170–173, 196, 201, 209, 214, 236,

242, distribution system 146, 209, inland
　　waterways 21, 34, just-in-time planning
　　19, 141; fuel (clean fuels) 5–9, 13, 16,
　　27–30, 34–36, 44–51, 75, 77, 94, 97,
　　123, 127, 134–143, 152, 157–159, 162,
　　170–173, 189–193, 196–197, 204,
　　213, 220–227, 234–236, 242, 247,
　　bioethanol 143, biofuel 8, 10, 13, 35–36,
　　44, 97, 138, 141, 143, 157, 226–227,
　　compressed natural gas 10, electric 13,
　　44, 138, 142, 204, fossil 9, 12, 143,
　　152, 170, 189, hydrogen fuel cells 10,
　　13, 44, 97, 138, 143, 173, 189, 197,
　　non-renewable 2, 34–35, 58, 75, 79, 95,
　　renewable 141–142, 152, 189; flows
　　19, 25, 39, 48, 60, 117–118, 122, 138,
　　153, 165, 222, 229, geography of flows
　　19; impact 2–11, 12, 14, 15, 23, 28–31,
　　37–38, 41–42, 48, 64–77, 81, 87, 110,
　　123, 132–137, 154, 161–167, 171–
　　176, 180, 188, 219, 234–235, 239, 243,
　　246–249, assessment 15, 48, 96, 123,
　　133, 137, 140, on children 64, 74, 95,
　　147, 151, 157, 195, socio-spatial 65–75;
　　infrastructure viii–x, 1–9, 1–16, 18–20,
　　25, 28–40, 43–49, 58, 61–66, 69, 72,
　　77, 82, 84, 86, 88–94, 96–96, 99, 103,
　　105–106, 108–112, 114, 118–122,
　　133, 136–138, 141, 144, 151, 155, 158,
　　161–162, 165, 168, 176, 182, 186–187,
　　192, 195–196, 198–202, 207–210,
　　212–213, 216–220, 225–228, 235;
　　instruments 17, 38, 81–103, 108, 118,
　　133, 135, 136–175, 176–179, 195, 201,
　　215, 228, 233–249; models viii, 2, 13,
　　15, 47, 49–110, 117–118, 122–123,
　　133, 177, 181, 232; network 1, 5,
　　11–13, 19, 27, 29–39, 42–43, 50–61,
　　64–65, 84–90, 93, 100, 117–118, 122,
　　140, 145, 161, 170, 200–204, 207–209,
　　212–214, 224, cycle network/route 146–
　　147, 151, 157, 191, 193, high distance
　　intensity 13, management 201, rail
　　network 11, 34, 43, 145, 203–209, road
　　network 11–13, 29–31, 43, 58, 64, 80,
　　148, 201, 212–214, 222–223, strategic
　　transport network 13, 84, 90, 137, 232,
　　Trans European Transport Network
　　33–34, 118, 140, 201; officers 14–15,
　　122–123; passenger 20–22, 34, 36,
　　51, 93, 140, 175, 177, 182, 193, 203;
　　plan 53–54, 104, 137, 182, 189, 201,
　　217, 223; public 11, 13, 19–20, 26–30,
　　33, 37, 40, 50–78, 83–84, 90–91, 94,

96, 99, 104, 112–115, 138–139, 149,
154, 168, 171, 173, 189, 193–197, 199,
202–208, 218, 226, 228, 236–237,
240–242, 244, 247–248; road 6, 8, 10,
12, 20–21, 60, 177, 222; system 1–4, 9,
12–13, 18–19, 23, 25, 29–31, 35–40,
44, 46, 48, 50–52, 60, 67, 69–70, 88,
91, 93, 95, 99–101, 103–105, 113, 124,
129–130, 134, 135, 138, 140–141,
144, 146, 149, 151–152, 157, 163, 170,
173, 182, 189–191, 193, 197, 214,
218–219, 238–239, 241; sustainable ix,
2, 4, 12, 14–15, 18, 30–31, 34–35, 37,
49, 75–76, 82, 85, 87–88, 95, 102–105,
108–135, 151, 162, 167, 174, 182, 189,
192, 227, 239, 244; technology 10, 13,
17, 24–25, 44, 56, 85, 138, 143–145,
152–155, 158, 163, 170–172, 180, 203,
210, 212, 214, 221–226, 235, hybrid
cars 8, 196; trips 22, 26–28, 41–43, 50,
59–60, 65, 68, 84, 146–147, 155, 163,
167, 184, 194–195, 207, 209, 214, 222,
224, 240, 242, non–work 27–28, 42,
59–60, 164, trip chaining 26, 50, 60,62,
trip frequency 43, work 27–28, 41–42,
59; urban 20, 35, 37–40, 44, 51, 85–87,
128, 152
Transport for London 93, 218–224
transport plan 53–54, 104, 137, 182, 189,
201, 217, 223; City of York 146–149;
United Kingdom Ten Year Transport Plan
2000 53
travel ix, 2–16, 18–33, 35–78, 82, 84–87,
90, 93, 97, 104–105, 108–109, 111,
114–115, 117, 121–127, 129–130,
132–134, 136–139, 142, 144, 147,
149–153, 155–159, 161–164, 167–
170, 173, 176, 182–184, 192–197, 201,
203, 218–220, 222, 224, 227, 229–230,
232, 235–237, 239–240, 243–244,
246–248; behaviour 2–3, 8, 11, 18, 20,
23, 25–26, 32, 40–43, 45–6, 48–49,
58, 61, 65–66, 71–72, 114, 121, 132,
142, 149–150, 167, 183, 201–219,
229, 235, 239, 243, 246, demographic
factors 23, 26, financial policies 10–11,
29–31, 34, 47, 81, 95, 97–98, 103, 110,
128, 137–138, 152–155, 179, 184, 186,
189–190, 201, 210–214, 227–228,
236, institutional issues 10, 23, 32–47,
79–107, 153, patterns 108, 142, 152,
243, socio-economic factors 13, 43, 48,

60–64, 177, 230, spatial development
patterns 23, 27–28, technological factors
23–25 global shrinkage 24 internal
combustion engine 23, 85 reinforced
concrete 23, transport policies 23,
28–31, 33, 49, 72, 92, 102–105, 114–
119, 161–172; business 31, 109, 161;
choices 11, 16, 18–20, 151, 163, 239,
individual 11; demand ix, 8, 18, 25–33,
38, 40, 45–48, 59, 65, 71, 105, 109,
119, 129, 153, 170, 201, 218, 224, 232,
237, 241, 246–247, derived demand
61, induced demand 25, 29, 153; diary
196; mode 26–30, 58, 74–75, 117, 130,
141, 197, 229; time 19, 24–26, 31, 39,
53–54, 62, 69–71, 76, 79, 161–162,
222, 237, 247, travel time budgets 25,
travel time savings 29–31, 62, 69, 71,
79, 161–162, 222, 237, 247, travel time
surveys 25; travel to work 39, 43, 59–62,
93, 122, 218, 227

United Kingdom 6–7, 92, 177–178, 230;
Independent Planning Commission 217;
London 53, 60, 63, 93, 129, 145, 148,
150–156, 218–225, 237, road cordon
toll 60, 154, 218–222, Greater London
Authority 218–227, Mayor's Climate
Change Action Plan 223, Mayor's
Transport Strategy 2004 223, Regulated
Bus Market 219, 222, Transport for
London 93, 218–223 Transport 2025
Transport Vision for a Growing World
City 223; Renewable Transport Fuel
Obligation 143; Ten Year Transport Plan
53; Yorkshire and Humberside 11
United Nations viii, 5, 9, 15, 65, 72, 80;
Commission on Environment and
Development 1992 15, 80; Conference
on Environment and Development 1987
viii, 9, 65; Convention on Climate Change
viii, 5; Intergovernmental Panel on Climate
Change viii, 5, 9; World Summit on
Sustainable Development 72
urban intensification 84
urbanisation viii, xi, 27
Urban Task Force 84

welfare 1, 8, 15, 28, 53, 66, 69, 94–95,
160–161, 178–182, 186–189; human 1,
15, 28, 69, 161, 188–189, 248
World Health Organisation 63